James Callanan currently teaches at the Uni
University of Newcastle and has also worked as a visiting lecturer at
Sunderland University. He is a specialist in Cold War and modern
American history and has done extensive research into the workings
of the US Intelligence Community, particularly the CIA.

INTERNATIONAL LIBRARY OF TWENTIETH CENTURY HISTORY

Series ISBN: 978-1-84885-227-3

See www.ibtauris.com/ILTWH for a full list of titles

COVERT ACTION IN THE COLD WAR

US Policy, Intelligence and CIA Operations

JAMES CALLANAN

BLOOMSBURY ACADEMIC
LONDON • NEW YORK • OXFORD • NEW DELHI • SYDNEY

BLOOMSBURY ACADEMIC
Bloomsbury Publishing Plc
50 Bedford Square, London, WC1B 3DP, UK
1385 Broadway, New York, NY 10018, USA

BLOOMSBURY, BLOOMSBURY ACADEMIC and the Diana
logo are trademarks of Bloomsbury Publishing Plc

First published in Great Britain 2010 by I.B.Tauris & Co. Ltd
Paperback first published by Bloomsbury Academic 2020

ISBN: HB: 978-1-8451-1882-2
PB: 978-1-3501-7083-4
ePDF: 978-0-8577-1166-3
eBook: 978-0-7556-3008-0

Series: International Library of Twentieth Century History, volume 21

To find out more about our authors and books visit
www.bloomsbury.com and sign up for our newsletters.

To the pioneers of America's cold war intelligence community, whose exploits made this book possible.

CONTENTS

CHARTS AND TABLES

ABBREVIATIONS

ACP	Albanian Communist Party
ADDP	Assistant Deputy Director of Plans
ADPC	Assistant Director of Policy Coordination
AEC	Atomic Energy Commission
AFL	American Federation of Labor
AID	Agency for International Development
AIOC	Anglo-Iranian Oil Company
Aramco	Arabian American Oil Company
CAT	Civil Air Transport
CCF	Congress of Cultural Freedom
CEF	Cuban Expeditionary Force
CENTO	Central Treaty Organisation
CFR	Council on Foreign Relations
CGIL	*Confederazione Generale Italiana del Lavoro*
CIA	Central Intelligence Agency
CIC	Counter Intelligence Corps of the Army
CIG	Central Intelligence Group
CIO	Congress of Industrial Organisations
CTV	Confederation of Venezuelan Workers
DC	Christian Democratic Party (Italy)
DCI	Director of Central Intelligence
DDA	Deputy Directorate for Administration
	Deputy Director of Administration
DDCI	Deputy Director of Central Intelligence
DDI	Deputy Directorate for Intelligence
	Deputy Director of Intelligence
DDP	Deputy Directorate for Plans
DDS&T	Deputy Directorate for Science and Technology
	Deputy Director of Science and Technology

DP	Displaced Person
DPD	Development Projects Division
DSB	Department of State Bulletin
ECA	Economic Cooperation Administration
EDES	Greek Democratic League
ELINT	electronic intelligence
ERP	European recovery Program or Marshall Plan
FBI	Federal Bureau of Investigation
FEC G-2	Far East Command Intelligence Directorate (United States Army)
FRD	*Frente Revolucionario Democratico* (Cuban exile movement)
FRUS	Papers Relating to the Foreign Relations of the United States
FTUC	Free Trade Union Committee
GOP	Grand Old Party (Republican Party)
GRU	Soviet Military Intelligence
HUAC	House Committee on Un-Amerian Activities
HUMINT	intelligence derived from human sources
IALC	Italian-American Labor Council
IBRD	International Bank of Reconstruction and Development
ICBM	intercontinental ballistic missile
ILGWU	International Ladies Garment Workers Union
INR	State Department Bureau of Intelligence and Research
IOD	CIA's International Organisations Division
IRBM	intermediate-range ballistic missile
IRCA	International Railways of Central America
IRD	MI6's Information Research Department
JCS	Joint Chiefs of Staff
KGB	Soviet Committee of State Security (internal security/foreign intelligence)
KKE	Greek Communist Party
KLO	Korean Labour Organisation
L-G	Far East Command Liaison Group (United States Army)
MGB	Soviet Ministry of State Security (predecessor to KGB)
MIT	Massachusetts Institute of Technology
MI5	British Security Service
MI6/SIS	British Secret Intelligence Service
M-26-7	26th of July Movement (Cuba)
NATO	North Atlantic Treaty Organisation
NCR	National Cash Register
NIA	National Intelligence Authority
NIE	National Intelligence Estimate
NIPE	National Intelligence Programs Evaluation

NKVD	People's Commissariat for Internal Affairs (predecessor to KGB)
NSA	National Security Agency
NSAM	National Security Action Memorandum
NSC	National Security Council
NSCID	National Security Council Intelligence Directive
NTS	National Labour Alliance (Russia)
OAS	Organisation of American States
OCB	Operations Coordinating Board
OCI	Overseas Consultants Incorporated
ONE	Office of National Estimates
OPC	Office of Policy Coordination
ORE	Office of Research and Evaluation
OSIA	Order Sons of Italy in America
OSO	Office of Special Operations
OSS	Office of Strategic Services
OUN	Organisation of Ukrainian Nationalists
PAR	Party of Revolutionary Action (Guatemala)
PBCFIA	President's Board of Consultants on Foreign Intelligence Activities
PBFIA	President's Foreign Intelligence Advisory Board
PCF	French Communist Party
PCI	Italian Communist Party
PERMESTA	Charter of Inclusive Struggle (Indonesia)
PGT	Guatemalan Communist Party
PKI	Indonesian Communist Party
PLA	People's Liberation Army (China)
PLI	Italian Liberal Party
PPS	Policy Planning Staff
PRC	People's Republic of China
PSB	Psychological Strategy Board
PSI	Italian Socialist Party
PSIUP	Italian Socialist Party of Proletarian Unity
PSLI	Italian Socialist Labour Party (Social Democrats)
PSP	Cuban Communist Party
RFE	Radio Free Europe
SAC	United States Air Force, Strategic Air Command
SANACC	State-Army-Navy Coordinating Committee
SEATO	Southeast Asia Treaty Organisation
SIGINT	signals intelligence
SOE	British Special Operations Executive
SPG	Special Procedures Group
SSU	Strategic Services Unit

SWNCC	State-War-Navy Coordinating Committee
UFCO	United Fruit Company
UN	United Nations
UNRRA	United Nations Relief and Rehabilitation Administration
USIA	United States Information Agency
WEI	Western Enterprises Incorporated
WEU	Western European Union
WiN	Freedom and Independence Movement (Poland)
X2	Counterintelligence Branch (OSS)

ACKNOWLEDGEMENTS

In bringing this book to fruition, I owe a debt of gratitude to a number of people and I am glad to have the opportunity to thank them publicly for their support. Howell Harris helped immeasurably, providing me with sound, friendly and expert guidance. Scott Lucas and Philip Williamson offered welcome advice and encouragement; the History Department at Durham University proved very supportive throughout; and Anthony Badger and Christopher Andrew were helpful during my research trips to Cambridge University. As all historians are well aware, successful research is heavily dependent on the input of high calibre archivists, and in this respect I would like to express my gratitude to the staff at the Truman, Eisenhower and Kennedy Libraries and their colleagues at the National Archives and Records Administration in Washington D.C. Last but not least, I have my family to thank, most especially my mother, Margaret, my uncle, Leslie Wood, my nephew Michael Curry – who ensured that any computer-related problems I encountered did not seriously hamper my efforts – and my late father, Michael, who was an early influence in cultivating my interest in history and politics.

INTRODUCTION

On 4 May 1948 the American State Department's Policy Planning Staff (PPS) declared "it would seem that the time is now fully ripe for the creation of a political warfare operations directorate within the Government".[1] The United States had in fact engaged in limited though resolute action of the kind suggested for several months prior to this point in support of the economic measures introduced by the Truman administration to help rebuild a war-torn Western Europe. The PPS recommendation was, nevertheless, a clarion call for Washington to mount a full-scale clandestine crusade that was spearheaded by the Central Intelligence Agency (CIA) and targeted primarily, though not exclusively, on the communist world in general and on the interests of the Soviet Union in particular. Though it was to continue for forty years, this secret war proved to be at its most fluid, risk-laden and tumultuous during the period that spanned the onset of the Cold War through to the Vietnam War. It is to these formative and uncertain years that this book addresses itself, telling the story of how, in its efforts to advance American foreign and defence policy, the CIA forged a covert action mission of eclectic and global proportions: one that spared little or no expense, and one that met with at least as many failures and tragedies as it did successes.

The United States' Senate Select Committee on Intelligence Activities defined covert action as "any clandestine operation or activity designed to influence foreign governments, organisations, persons, or events in support of American foreign policy".[2] This provides only a very broad outline, however, of the activities undertaken by the CIA's operations directorate, the mission of which is more accurately described as having encompassed four basic, often interconnecting categories: (1) propaganda and psychological warfare; (2) political operations such as supporting democratic parties and labour unions in friendly countries; (3) economic operations; and (4) paramilitary action, which includes counterinsurgency and assassination programmes.[3]

The demand for the agency to perform such functions first manifested itself in late 1947, when the Special Procedures Group (SPG) was assembled hurriedly within the CIA to counter the political challenge posed by the Italian communist-socialist Popular Front in the run-up to that country's elections in April 1948.

Though the SPG's campaign proved successful, responsibility for American covert action was subsequently placed under the control of an entirely new and anomalous instrumentality – the Office of Policy Coordination (OPC).[4] Established on 1 September 1948 and attached to the CIA for only the distribution of "quarters and rations", the OPC functioned as an autonomous entity. It drew on the personnel and support of the wider Washington bureaucracy in the execution of its mission, and its director, Frank G. Wisner, was a State Department appointee.[5]

Escalating superpower tensions and the Korean War provided the impetus for an enormous growth in the OPC's budget and resources over the next three years.[6] Continual conflict between Wisner's organisation and the CIA's intelligence gathering component, the Office of Special Operations (OSO), however, led the OPC to be integrated fully into the agency and merged with the OSO. This process was completed in August 1952 with the creation of the Deputy Directorate for Plans (DDP), which remained responsible for espionage, counterintelligence, and covert action throughout the Eisenhower and Kennedy presidencies.[7]

The rationale and justification for OPC/DDP covert action was defined clearly. The Soviet Union was seen as an expansionist power with designs on global domination, and Washington assumed the right to intervene with whatever measures were necessary to contain the threat and protect American strategic, political, or economic interests whenever and wherever they were deemed to be in jeopardy. The Cold War was, moreover, as much about perceptions as reality. In this context, it was imperative for the United States to not only secure and retain the upper hand against the Soviet Union, but also to be *seen* to do so and in many instances covert action provided the most appropriate means for the achievement of this goal.

Clandestine operations were, moreover, justified by Washington on the grounds that the Soviet Union had developed, refined, and continued to deploy the most effective political and covert warfare capacity in history.[8] It was therefore incumbent on the United States to fight fire with fire. This atmosphere was conducive to the expansion of covert action, which was essentially a political instrument of containment: a 'third' or 'silent' option that went beyond traditional diplomacy but fell short of precipitating war and the nuclear conflagration such an outcome implied.[9] The DDP's mission thus evolved into a multifaceted, widely dispersed one, which reached an all-time high in terms of the volume of operations undertaken during the mid 1960s, when the agency was called upon to mount a major clandestine action campaign in support of the overall war effort in Vietnam.

The emergence of the CIA as a key instrument of government led Sherman Kent, the head of the agency's Board of National Estimates, to maintain in 1955 that, though intelligence had evolved into "an exciting and highly skilled profession" and more importantly a discipline, it lacked a literature. While this remained the case, he added, the method, vocabulary, body of doctrine, and fundamental theory that governed and informed the CIA's increasingly diverse mission ran the risk of never reaching full maturity.[10] Kent's concerns were addressed originally to the intelligence professionals who were privy to the pages of the CIA's internal journal, *Studies in Intelligence*. Over the past thirty years, however, a great deal of information that was once the preserve of the intelligence community has entered the public domain, and has enabled those outside of that exclusive world to attempt to respond to Kent's call.

While in the sphere of intelligence collection and evaluation his challenge has largely been met, the "rigorous definition of terms" that he deemed to be essential if the significance of the CIA's accomplishments and its failures were to be properly measured has been less than comprehensive in the field of covert operations.[11] The received wisdom in this respect is best exemplified by Roy Godson. In characterising CIA covert action as a "double-edged sword" aimed at meeting the two goals of "containing the spread of Communism in the non-Communist world" and of "weakening Communist regimes on their own terrain", Godson identifies a two-way division of the OPC/DDP's mission between defensive and offensive operations.[12]

Instructive as this treatment is, it falls short of meeting Kent's criteria. In serving Washington's policy objectives, the CIA engaged in not two but three basic types of clandestine operation, each of which called on the agency to utilise the full roster of resources and techniques at its disposal. The first of these was *defensive covert action*, which was aimed at countering communist efforts to attack or undermine governments and societies that were allied to the United States. The bolstering of anticommunist political parties in Western Europe from the late 1940s onwards is an example of this type of action, as is the paramilitary and psychological warfare campaign through which the agency helped to defeat a communist insurgency in the Philippines between 1950 and 1954.

The converse and second mode of operation was *offensive covert action*. This was focused on destabilising, and in the more extreme cases removing, communist regimes that lay within, or, in the case of Cuba, were allied to, the Sino-Soviet bloc. That such measures first came into force between 1948 and 1956, calls into question the claim made by President Harry S. Truman after he had left office, that in first establishing the CIA he did not envisage it as engaging in operations such as that which was mounted against Fidel Castro at the Bay of Pigs.[13] Indeed, NSC 68, the top secret reappraisal of American foreign and defence policy issued by the Truman administration in April 1950, called specifically for the covert subversion of communist regimes.[14] This directive came into force on the eve of the Korean War. Thus, the resulting clandestine offensives mounted in Eastern Europe, Korea and China were, given that the Truman administration believed that it faced a Soviet-controlled communist monolith, effectively sanctioned under wartime conditions. OPC offensive operations had, however, been authorised by Washington prior to this point: against the Ukraine, the Baltic States, and Russia's Eastern European satellites, notably Albania, during the late 1940s, and they continued to be deployed throughout the 'captive nations' until the Hungarian uprising of 1956.[15] Offensive covert action was, however, used most extensively by the Kennedy administration against revolutionary Cuba and later as a complement to the wider war effort in Vietnam.

The third category of operation is best described as *preventive covert action*. Aimed at impeding and where possible neutralising the potential for Moscow to extend its control to developing countries that were aligned with neither superpower, enterprises of this kind came to prominence as a consequence of three basic factors. Prime among these was the geographical expansion of the Cold War from the Far East to the third world, which resulted from Stalin's death in March 1953 and the succession of a new Russian leadership that sought to advance Soviet influence in the developing world after the termination of hostilities in Korea.

If the need for the United States to respond to this challenge brought preventive covert action to the fore, then so too did Dwight D. Eisenhower's accession to the presidency. Though Truman had been prepared to authorise offensive measures against existing communist regimes, he wavered when it came to sanctioning action against democratically-elected governments. He did, it is true, approve Operation PBFORTUNE, a project aimed at unseating Jacobo Arbenz Guzmán's regime in Guatemala during 1952, but caved in quickly to pressure from his Secretary of State Dean Acheson and cancelled the enterprise before it got past its planning stages.[16] Eisenhower was, by contrast, less cautious in his calculation of risk and less concerned about ethical implications than his predecessor had been when authorising covert action, as Operation TPAJAX, which brought about the removal of the Iranian Prime Minister, Muhammad Musaddiq from power in August 1953, illustrates.[17] There was, as well, the point that Eisenhower's long and unique military career caused him to be well disposed towards the frequent deployment of the DDP.[18]

What none of the literature dealing with the agency stresses, however, is the extent to which wider strategic imperatives were key to Eisenhower's management of clandestine operations. John Lewis Gaddis has pointed out that Eisenhower's foreign and defence policy, the New Look, centred on the United States making asymmetrical responses. This, in brief, meant that Washington would respond to aggression emanating from what continued to be portrayed as a Soviet-controlled monolith, by applying western strengths against communist weaknesses, to the extent of changing the nature and shifting the location of any given cold war confrontation.[19] Thus, rather than countering an attack by the Red Army on Turkey with conventional military means on Turkish soil, for example, the United States would, at least in theory, respond by launching a nuclear attack on the Baku oil fields: the reasoning being that while the Soviet Union enjoyed an advantage over the United States in terms of land-based conventional military strength, America's airpower and nuclear capabilities were vastly superior to their Russian counterparts.

When looked at in the context of the asymmetry that was central to the New Look, Eisenhower's deployment of covert action takes on an entirely new complexion. The Iran coup, for example, was launched at a time when the Soviets were preoccupied suppressing riots in the Russian sector of Berlin and East Germany, and while a power struggle ensued in the Kremlin following Stalin's death. Likewise, Operation PBSUCCESS, through which the CIA brought about the removal of a Guatemalan government that was led by Arbenz and depicted by Eisenhower as Marxist, took place at the same time as the 1954 Geneva Conference on Indochina. Looked at from an asymmetrical perspective, then, PBSUCCESS was a counterattack, which drew attention away from the fact that the West had suffered a major ideological setback with the defeat of the French at Dien Bien Phu, the partition of Indochina, and the creation of a communist regime in North Vietnam.

The third major catalyst to influence the rise to prominence of preventive operations and indeed covert action generally between 1953 and 1961 related to organisational changes inside of the CIA itself. In essence, Eisenhower had a better resourced and more efficiently organised agency at his disposal than had Truman, for it was not until 1953 that the CIA "achieved the basic structure and scale which it retained for the next twenty years".[20] The appointment of Allen W. Dulles as Director of Central Intelligence (DCI) during the same year, moreover, brought the CIA under the leadership of a man who was a more vociferous advocate of clandestine operations than any of his predecessors had been.

The first civilian DCI, Dulles sought to utilise covert action in a manner that would bring fast, relatively cheap, and desirable outcomes to pressing foreign policy issues and so establish a strong reputation for the CIA within the Washington bureaucracy. In pursuit of this approach, Dulles refocused the DDP's efforts away from offensive operations against the Soviet bloc, which had proved largely fruitless, and towards preventive ventures in the third world, where he and his colleagues believed that successes could be more easily achieved. As the brother of Eisenhower's Secretary of State, John Foster Dulles, moreover, the DCI had unprecedented access to a president who, as has been mentioned, was already convinced of the efficacy of covert action. Taken together, these factors enabled Allen Dulles to short-circuit authorisation procedures, which in turn helped to create an internal dynamic inside of the DDP for the development of clandestine action programmes.[21]

The proliferation of covert operations that resulted secured fast, dramatic 'victories' for the agency in Iran in 1953 and Guatemala in 1954, and proved instrumental in establishing the Eisenhower years as the 'golden age' of operations. The downside was that such 'successes', provided only temporary solutions to complex problems that had a habit of rebounding on the United States over the longer term, as was the case with the rise of Ayatollah Ruholla Khomeini twenty-five years after the ouster of Musaddiq. Enterprises such as TPAJAX and PBSUCCESS also forewarned future targets of the agency of the potential for similar action to be attempted in their countries.[22] Thus, when the DDP deployed the Guatemala model in Indonesia during 1958, and again in Cuba at the Bay of Pigs in 1961, the results were entirely negative.

*   *   *

If the three-way distinction that separated the basic types of CIA covert action has not been fully explored in existing studies, then neither has the tendency for the agency to anticipate government policy and initiate operations ahead of being given official sanction for such moves. This is not to say that the CIA acted routinely as a rogue elephant.[23] There were, however, several instances in which it second-guessed Washington's medium to longer-term intentions and requirements and acted accordingly, especially in Western Europe, where American intelligence operatives such as James Jesus Angleton were prescient in recognising the scale of the challenge posed by communism and worked continuously to counter the threat between 1945 and 1947.[24] Such moves enhanced the agency's capacity to engage in larger-scale defensive covert action when Washington gave official approval for its deployment ahead of the Italian elections of April 1948.

A similar anticipatory tendency held true in respect of offensive operations. The SPG drew up plans to penetrate the Eastern bloc utilising psychological warfare techniques and radio propaganda before Washington created the OPC and gave official blessing for the United States to go on to the offensive behind the Iron Curtain.[25] The agency was also ahead of the game in the case of preventive covert action, which came to prominence between 1953 and 1961, but which was deployed in Syria during 1949, when the OPC is said to have participated in two coups d'etat to remove leftist governments from power, and again in July 1952, when the DDP assisted in the ouster of King Farouk of Egypt:[26] before the shift in focus of the Cold War to the third world and the accession of Eisenhower to the presidency.

Of additional and significant impact on the evolution of covert action during this period were domestic political developments. Particularly catalytic in this respect was Senator Joseph McCarthy's anticommunist crusade of the early 1950s. Demagogic red baiting of the kind favoured by the Wisconsin senator, in essence, precluded Truman from seeking a negotiated settlement with Beijing to end the hostilities in Korea. Such moves would, in effect, have invited charges of treachery and further damaged a Democratic Party that was already on the defensive as a result of McCarthy's efforts. The Korean conflict consequently became something of a stalemate by mid 1951, with the protagonists confronting each other on or around the thirty-eighth parallel. Under such conditions, CIA covert action offered a possible means of breaking the deadlock to the advantage of the United States without the adoption of a policy of full-scale rollback, which Truman regarded as carrying unacceptable risks since it greatly increased the prospect of a third world war. Washington thus provided for a huge increase in the OPC's mission from mid 1951 onwards significantly bolstering its resources and expanding its operational latitude.[27]

The McCarthyite witch-hunt also influenced Eisenhower's utilisation of the CIA. The Guatemala coup was, for instance, conveniently timed, since it coincided with the president's deployment of what Fred I. Greenstein describes as "hidden hand" tactics to expose serious defects in McCarthy's character.[28] Operation PBSUCCESS demonstrated to political insiders, the press, and the informed public that while the Wisconsin senator was busy making bogus and groundless claims against the United States Army, Eisenhower was focused on the real job of combating communism. This in turn assisted the president in his drive to seriously undermine the senator and thereby unite the Republican Party in advance of the 1954 congressional elections.

Kennedy too was alert to domestic considerations when authorising covert action. The strident anti-Castro rhetoric that became a feature of Kennedy's 1960 election campaign was a major factor in influencing him to approve the Bay of Pigs operation. The president was in fact never entirely convinced of the feasibility of this venture, though it should be stressed that he was not aware of how fundamentally flawed it actually was. To have cancelled the enterprise, however, would have attracted Republican charges of back-pedalling and hypocrisy after Kennedy's hawkish campaign pronouncements, and this consideration went a significant way towards influencing him to authorise Bay of Pigs operation.

The failure of the Bay of Pigs venture – code-named JMARC – was a defining moment in the CIA's history and debate still continues over whether this debacle was the fault of the agency or its political masters.[29] The key point, however, is that neither the White House nor the CIA learned from the mistakes of JMARC. Consequently, Kennedy continued to deploy covert action in the hope of removing the Castro regime from power, when the only feasible options open to the United States president were to either accept the existence of a communist state ninety miles from the American mainland, or mount a full-scale military invasion of Cuba to eradicate the threat. More than any other target of the CIA's attentions, then, it was Cuba that best defined the limits of what could and, more pertinently, what could not be achieved through the use of clandestine action.

*   *   *

As much as this book centres on CIA covert operations, it is also an exploration of the broader policy objectives they were designed to serve, for it is only through a full understanding of policy that the arcane environment in which the agency plied its trade can be properly comprehended. The United States never adopted a static position in the cut and thrust of the early Cold War, however. American policy evolved according to real and perceived changes in the nature of the communist threat. Consequently, the years 1945 to 1963 saw significant revisions in foreign and defence policy, and this held true within as well as between administrations.

Truman's conception of what was required to counter the Soviet Union, its allies, and its proxies stands as a case in point. His position changed fundamentally in response to the unexpected Russian entry into the nuclear club in 1949 and the 'loss' of China during the same year. The result was that the period 1950 to 1953 bore witness to a more robust and militarist, not to mention expensive, adaption of containment than had held sway during the first four years of Truman's presidency. Increased emphasis on the deployment of coercion in Washington's dealings with Moscow had been anticipated during the Berlin blockade and spelt out in NSC 20/4, the directive that outlined the need for a clandestine offensive against the Soviet bloc.[30] The point is, however, that during Truman's second term, covert action was envisaged as pursuing more expansive ends than those that had applied during his first term.

With regard to the book's format, then, Truman's tenure covers four chapters. The first of these examines his early cold war policy, and the factors that led him to first establish the CIA and subsequently authorise it to engage in covert operations. The necessary context is thus provided for the case study that follows in chapter 2: the Italian campaign of 1947 to 1948, which was the CIA's first official covert operation. Chapter 3 looks at the imperatives that led Washington to adopt a more offensively-oriented form of containment and create the OPC to carry the battle behind the Iron and Bamboo Curtains. The stage is thereby set for an assessment of Operation BGFIEND, which features in chapter 4. Sanctioned in 1949, this enterprise was directed against Enver Hoxha's communist regime in Albania, and was the most clear-cut example of American deployment of rollback in the Eastern bloc.

The revisions in foreign and defence policy that were implemented by Eisenhower, coupled with the operational trends and developments that took place within the CIA during his tenure – including assessments of the agency's modus operandi in Eastern Europe, Tibet and the Middle East – are explored in chapter 5. This paves the way for three case studies, which feature in chapter 6 and stand as seminal examples of Washington's use of preventive covert action during the Eisenhower period: the removal of Musaddiq in 1953, the first democratically-elected leader to be overthrown by the agency; the ouster of President Arbenz of Guatemala in 1954, the high-water-mark for the DDP and the model for its subsequent large-scale projects; and the failed effort to depose Indonesian premier Achmed Sukarno in 1958, the implicit warnings of which signalled the potential for failure in Cuba three years later.

Kennedy's policy position and the institutional changes that he rang in at the CIA are examined in chapter 7, while more specific scrutiny of his deployment of covert action is viewed in chapter 8. The anti-Castro campaigns mounted between 1961 and 1963, notably Operations JMARC and MONGOOSE, feature prominently in this chapter, but space is also given over to parallel enterprises that were mounted by the DDP in the Dominican Republic, Ecuador, Britsh Guiana and Venezuela during the same period with the overarching aim of countering the Cuban challenge in the wider Western Hemisphere.

Other operations are examined as needs demand. The assassination of the Congo's Patrice Lumumba is, for example, analysed in order to demonstrate the difficulties of mounting covert operations during presidential interregnums. The defensive and offensive projects conducted by the agency in Korea between 1950 and 1953, and in Indochina during the early years of the Vietnam War are, on the other hand, looked at in the context of how clandestine action was designed to mesh with wider war aims.

*   *   *

Disillusionment with the conduct of the Vietnam War was the primary catalyst for several former CIA officers to abandon their oath of silence in the 1970s and publish accounts of the agency's covert operations.[31] Along with earlier works, notably *The Invisible Government*, published in 1964, and the controversial *Ramparts* disclosures of 1966 and 1967, these apostatical works made meaningful though limited public scrutiny of the CIA's activities possible for the first time.[32] It was, however, the congressional investigations of the agency conducted during the mid 1970s – the Church and Pike Reports – that opened the sluice gates, and over the past thirty years a flood of books and articles have turned the study of the CIA and the American intelligence community as a whole into a cottage industry.[33]

The agency itself has, over the past two decades, assisted in this process and displayed a greater openness in relation to what it is prepared to declassify from its vaults, and so too has the State Department.[34] There has, moreover, been a concomitant increase in the availability of CIA-related manuscript depositions at other archives in the United States – notably the various presidential libraries and the National Archives in Washington D.C. For sure, there is much that remains to be uncovered. However, these sources, along with the printed primary and secondary material that is relevant to the subject, have been instrumental in the construction of as comprehensive a depiction as time and resources have allowed of how the CIA's covert action mission served wider policy aims. It is a picture that departs from the received wisdom; one that neither defends nor condemns the agency or its political masters; and one which confirms that Nicolò Machiavelli's observation that "many more princes have lost their lives and their states through conspiracies than through open warfare" was as true during the Cold War as it was when it was first offered over four hundred years earlier.

1

THE ARRIVAL OF AN IMPERFECT PEACE AND THE RISE OF THE SILENT OPTION

In 1945 the United States faced a task that Dean Acheson later characterised as being marginally less formidable than that posed in Genesis.[1] In brief, the challenge before America was to transform a war-torn chaotic Europe into a bastion of democracy, free trade, and private enterprise, the interests of which would correspond closely to those of the United States. Achievement of the American vision of a new world order was, however, hampered by the social and economic dislocation that six years of war had wrought, and opposed with increasing intensity by a deeply suspicious Soviet Union. It was, in effect, this rapid deterioration in Soviet-American relations that took place during the two-year period that followed World War II which led the United States to take the first steps towards adopting covert action as a tool of foreign policy, and place responsibility for such measures with the Central Intelligence Agency. The political action and psychological warfare campaigns that the CIA and its predecessor, the Central Intelligence Group (CIG), conducted in Western Europe between 1946 and 1948 are therefore best understood in the context of the broader policy and strategy that they were designed to serve.

The Truman Inheritance and the Onset of Cold War

On 12 April 1945, Harry S. Truman found himself catapulted into the office of president of the United States following the death of Franklin D. Roosevelt. Though unbriefed in the intricacies of foreign and defence policy, the new chief executive faced the unenviable task of overseeing American interests through a succession of events that would have tested the ingenuity and foresight of the most experienced of political leaders: the culmination of the most far-reaching and bloody war in history, and the onset of the atomic age; the menacing spectre of the Red Army firmly entrenched across much of Eastern Europe; and the establishment of the United Nations Organisation. All of these issues presented themselves in imposing succession. Greatness had, to be sure, been thrust upon Truman in as conclusive a manner as was humanly possible. The new president, nevertheless, recognised that he had inherited, rather than been elected to, his position at the head of government and was therefore obligated to continue with his predecessor's policies.[2]

Any hopes that Truman might have entertained of fulfilling Roosevelt's aim of extending Soviet-American wartime cooperation over into peacetime were quickly dashed, however, for the bonds that held the grand alliance together loosened as quickly as German resistance collapsed: so much so that even Roosevelt, who had long resisted taking what he regarded as an overly firm stance vis-à-vis the USSR, was beginning to advocate the adoption of a 'tougher' Anglo-American approach towards the Soviets than had "heretofore appeared advantageous to the war effort".[3] The president's remarks, made a mere six days before his death, indicated that he was moving towards endorsing an approach that had long been advocated by a preponderance of State Department Soviet experts, notably the American Ambassador to Moscow, W. Averell Harriman: that economic aid be deployed as a lever to influence Stalin to take action that was compatible with American interests.[4]

What Truman's succession to the presidency did was to accelerate this trend towards toughness, a development that arose largely out of Roosevelt's propensity to act as his own Secretary of State and confer little with Truman during his short period as vice president.[5] The consequence was that when Truman took over the presidential reins he had little choice other than to consult with State Department experts of the Harriman stamp, who were thus afforded the perfect opportunity to educate the unbriefed Truman as to their own perceptions of Soviet intentions. Indications that the "firm but friendly *quid pro quo*", which Roosevelt had held back on implementing, would be attempted by the new president were in evidence a mere eleven days after he took office, when he berated Soviet Foreign Minister Vyacheslav Molotov over Moscow's failure to deliver on what Washington believed to be pledges made by Stalin at the Yalta Conference: that Moscow would permit the countries of Eastern Europe to shape their own political destinies.[6]

It would, however, be wrong to say that the United States had already abandoned any hope of securing a viable working relationship with the Soviet Union at this early stage. Indeed, Truman was regarded as having overstepped what even the sternest critics of the USSR saw as prudent in his clash with Molotov.[7] After all, the war was not yet over and Russian support was still regarded by Washington as crucial, most particularly for securing the earliest possible end to hostilities in the Far East. As such, the United States adopted a mainly concessionary approach in its dealings with the Soviet Union during the final stages of World War II and in fact American efforts to seek accommodation with Stalin continued to dominate policy through to the end of 1945.

There were some conspicuous, albeit brief, departures. The successful testing of the atomic bomb, for instance, led an emboldened Truman to toughen his negotiating tactics at the Potsdam Conference in July 1945, and his Secretary of State James Byrnes made a failed attempt to deploy atomic diplomacy at the first Council of Foreign Ministers' meeting held in London during the following September. The consistently truculent position adopted by the Russian leadership at Potsdam, London, and the follow-on Moscow Council of Foreign Ministers' Conference in December 1945, made it clear, however, that neither the American atomic monopoly nor the lever of economic aid would serve as effective means for influencing Soviet behaviour.[8] Put simply, the principal contention between the two emerging superpowers could not be reconciled. American promotion of the principle of self-determination was incompatible with the Soviet Union's insistence that a security buffer zone be established along its western borders.[9] Rather than attempting to settle its differences with the Russian leadership through negotiation and compromise, the Truman administration now looked on the USSR as a potential enemy with vital interests that endangered the political and economic aims of the United States and its allies.[10]

In respect of Russian capabilities and intentions, the American political establishment was, at this crucial time, beset by a sense of uncertainty that was best summed up by James V. Forrestal in a letter written to journalist Walter Lippmann during January 1946. With regard to its relations with the Soviet Union, the Secretary of the Navy asked, was the United States "dealing with a nation or a religion"?[11] If Forrestal tended towards believing the latter, then his suspicions were reinforced by two major expositions on the nature of the Soviet state which together established the criteria through which the Truman administration was to interpret Russian behaviour – the American chargé d'affaires to Moscow, George Kennan's "Long Telegram" of February 1946, and the Clifford-Elsey Report, which was prepared on the president's orders and presented its findings in September 1946.[12]

These two analyses were at variance on several levels, with Kennan depicting the Russian leadership as being driven primarily by a traditional sense of insecurity, and Clifford-Elsey identifying ideology as the key determinant of Soviet motives and actions. Nevertheless, common to both appraisals were the assumptions that the Soviet Union was an opportunistic power and that the United States could neither afford nor should allow any further Russian territorial or political advances.[13] If proof was needed of the validity of these assessments then Americans needed to look no further than Stalin's intimidation of Iran and Turkey during late 1945 and 1946: developments which were seen by many in the administration as being analogous with the Munich crisis of 1938.[14] Consequently, the year 1946 saw the United States take significant steps towards meeting the Soviet threat. Russian pressure, whether of a military or political kind, was, and would continue to be, countered in a manner that was sufficient to deter but not to provoke. The USSR would, in short, be *contained* for as long as was necessary.[15]

*   *   *

The cornerstone of Washington's efforts to strike a balance of power, preserve the global equilibrium to America's advantage, and pave the way for the establishment of a multilateral capitalist free trading system was the drive to rehabilitate the economies of Western Europe.[16] Not only was this regarded as an end in itself, it was also seen by American policymakers as a *means* of containing communism: a reflection of the Truman administration's adoption of 'strongpoint defence'. This concept proceeded from the premise that the United States would select the most effective weapons in its containment arsenal and concentrate them on defending areas that were deemed to be of vital, as opposed to peripheral, importance to its national interests. Western Europe, with its good lines of communication, substantial natural resources and military-industrial capacity thus became the principal theatre of containment, with the economic instrument, in the shape of Secretray of State George Marshall's $13 billion European Recovery Program (ERP or Marshall Plan) and the interim aid packages that preceded it, being the primary means through which this would be achieved.[17]

Central to American efforts to restore Western Europe as a fortress of capitalism and democracy was the protection of the vital natural resources of the Middle East. Such considerations informed Washington's deployment of diplomatic pressure to force the Kremlin to pull out of Iran in the spring of 1946 and were implicit in the March 1947 Truman Doctrine speech. American calculations had it that withdrawal from the Eastern Mediterranean by a financially-threadbare United Kingdom would amount to an open invitation for the Soviet Union to step into the resultant vacuum and establish a strong presence in the region. This would, in turn, hold out the potential for Stalin to cut essential oil supplies at a time when Western Europe was suffering acute coal shortages. Denied essential Middle Eastern resources, a politically unstable Europe could, it was feared, go communist.[18]

If economic rehabilitation, followed by political stability, were the basic order of priorities in Washington's drive to rehabilitate Western Europe, then an American military buildup was regarded as an unattractive, if not unavailable, option.[19] Defence budgets fell victim to Truman's implementation of conservative fiscal policies between 1946 and 1949, and a Republican-dominated Congress simul-taneously used its power of the purse to accentuate this downward spiralling of defence spending.[20] Such moves were reinforced by the belief that America's mobilisation base would be enough to deter a Soviet Union which, at least in terms of naval and airpower, was anyhow ill-prepared militarily to fight and win a war against the West.[21] The United States, furthermore, held a nuclear monopoly at this time and was in the throws of establishing what military planners referred to as a 'strategic frontier': a comprehensive overseas base system located in countries on or close to the periphery of the Soviet Union. From here American airpower could be projected rapidly against the USSR or, alternatively, be deployed to counter any Soviet advance on the Middle East, should war come. American reasoning was, therefore, that Stalin had no plans for war and that economic and political imperatives should take precedence in determining containment policy.[22]

A further determinant of Washington's response to the burgeoning Soviet challenge was the encroachment of domestic concerns on to foreign policy. During the first two years of his tenure, Truman's management of America's economic transition from a wartime to a peacetime footing left much to be desired and his public approval ratings declined accordingly, opening the way for the Republicans to gain control of Congress in November 1946. For the president, then, reestablishing his credentials as a decisive leader and building bridges with Capitol Hill became priorities, and the Truman Doctrine, by expanding and making public his conception of America's international responsibilitites, served both ends.[23]

The president's portrayal in the speech of the problems confronting Greece as being symbolic of an ideological confrontation between totalitarianism and democracy was a clever ploy. Playing on wartime memories, it equated naziism with communism, enabled Truman to project himself as making a stand for the cause of freedom, and mobilised public opinion in a manner that prepared the way for the ERP. Congressional Republicans were meanwhile trapped into choosing between budget cuts and fighting communism, which left them with little room for manoeuvre. Failure to vote for aid to Greece and Turkey would have left the GOP open to criticisms of endangering the free world in favour of its own narrow aims. In supporting the Truman Doctrine, however, the Republican leadership made common cause with its Democratic counterpart and could subsequently offer little in the way of a distinctive foreign policy position during the 1948 election.[24]

The downside for the president was that the Truman Doctrine and the Marshall Plan alienated those in his own party who advocated conciliation with the Soviet Union and ultimately drove this faction to stand on an independent, Progressive Party ticket, under the leadership of former Vice President, Henry Wallace, in 1948. This spelt potential electoral disaster for Truman, since he faced an additional defection by Dixiecrats who opposed his liberal civil rights policy.[25] However, a succession of developments on the international stage, in the form of the Czechoslovak coup of February 1948, the war scare of the following month, and the onset of the Berlin blockade in June that year came to Truman's rescue. These events diminished Wallace's credibility and laid bare the extent to which he was out of step with the American public.[26] Truman was, furthermore, able to enhance his presidential status through his management of these crises without attracting criticism from his Republican opponent, Thomas E. Dewey, an internationalist who supported the president's containment measures.[27]

Crucial to Truman's broader calculations, however, was the point that it would take time for initiatives such as the ERP to have a discernable impact and for his core foreign policy objectives to pay full dividends. Meanwhile, there was an immediate need for containment to be *seen* to be working effectively against a communist threat that was gauged by the United States to be primarily political in nature. In this respect the covert operations conducted by the CIA in Western

Europe played an essential role in the overall implementation of American foreign policy. Though the agency varied its tactics according to the circumstances it encountered in any given country, its fundamental task remained the same: to counter Soviet-inspired subversion and political advances, and act as a necessary complement to the economic and military instruments of containment that Washington sought to deploy. Such a mission was something of a quantum leap from the role that America's political elite had initially envisaged a central intelligence organisation as performing in 1945.

The Birth of the CIA and the Emergence of its Covert Action Mission, 1945–1948

The period from the end of World War II through to the Berlin blockade saw the Truman administration initiate a unique series of advances in the concept of central intelligence. In the space of only three years the CIA was first founded then expanded from performing a limited coordination and evaluation function under its earliest manifestation – the Central Intelligence Group – to engaging in a diverse range of activities that included independent intelligence production, clandestine collection, and covert action.[28] Up to this point the agency's ability to conduct covert operations was confined, however, to the use of a limited psychological warfare capacity aimed at thwarting the political threat posed by indigenous Communist Parties in Western Europe.[29] The implementation of a more comprehensive programme of clandestine action was constrained by uncertainty in the Departments of State and Defense as to where control and responsibility for such a measure should reside: a debate that was resolved with the creation of the Office of Policy Coordination in 1948.[30]

The CIA was, of course, neither the only nor the most prominent component of the United States intelligence community. It operated alongside the FBI and the intelligence agencies of the Army, Navy, and State Department in an atmosphere that was noted for its competitive edge rather than its cooperative spirit. The role of "first among equals" in America's intelligence war with the Soviet Union was consequently one that the CIA succeeded to gradually rather than adopted immediately.[31] It was, moreover, a process that was not completed until 1953. The years 1945 to 1948 were, nonetheless, of great importance in the evolution of the agency's structure, size, and mission, and three determinants were primarily responsible for dictating its course: (1) institutional conflicts; (2) the personalities and influence of the respective Directors of Central Intelligence; and (3) the consistent redefinition of American organisational and informational needs that accompanied the Truman administration's increasing preoccupation with the Soviet/communist threat.[32]

*   *   *

The notion that the United States should maintain an independent and centralised intelligence organisation in peacetime originated primarily out of Washington's determination to avoid the mistakes of the past, most specifically the surprise attack on Pearl Harbor in 1941. Although Truman dissolved the Office of Strategic Servises (OSS) – the wartime predecessor of the CIA – in September 1945, his decision was in no way informed by a desire for discontinuity. Rather, it was driven by a determination to create a more efficient intelligence apparatus than the one that had sufficed in wartime, which had generally been confused and characterised by endemic feuding between the key intelligence providers.[33]

The most vocal champion of a central intelligence agency during this early period was OSS Director, General William Donovan, who from 1944 began campaigning for what boiled down to a continuation of his own organisation after hostilities had ended. The 'Donovan Plan' failed to pass muster with Truman, however. Dissatisfied with the intelligence handled by the OSS during the war, the president regarded Donovan as a shameless self-publicist who was doing little other than "making speeches and propagandising his own great achievements".[34] Not only this, but Truman saw it as essential that he tread cautiously in the sphere of intelligence. Conservative elements in the American press had, even before war's end, begun to circulate a number of articles that highlighted the dangers posed by an "American Gestapo". Alarmist though they were, these concerns struck a chord with the president and gave added impetus to his already pronounced determination not to found anything resembling a secret police that could one day be brought to bear against the American people.[35]

The establishment of a centralised body charged with the task of coordinating and evaluating the United States intelligence effort and rectifying the problem of departmental duplication, nevertheless, remained a crucial element in Truman's plans to unify and streamline the military. The final months of 1945 therefore witnessed a long series of disputes between the State, War, and Navy Departments and the FBI over who a new "national intelligence structure" would answer to, and how it would fit within the context of a unified Department of Defense. These debates were resolved on 22 January 1946 with the creation of the Central Intelligence Group. Corresponding, albeit in diluted form, to the recommendations of the Eberstadt Report, which was commissioned by Navy Secretary James Forrestal, the policies and procedures governing the CIG called for a civilian centralised intelligence structure answerable to a national intelligence authority that was to advise the president.[36]

The coming of the CIG coincided with the rapid deterioration in Soviet-American relations that occurred during the early months of 1946, and given the fact that "Washington knew virtually nothing about the USSR" at this stage, the group stood to be of great advantage, at least theoretically, to the Truman administration.[37] This applied in a domestic as well as foreign policy context, for by making balanced appraisals of the available information on the Soviet Union, the CIG could, if allowed to operate as intended, provide Truman with a ready instrument for countering the self-serving estimates of the military. The problem for the CIG was that it was trapped in a position of perpetual compromise in terms of its evaluation function. Jealously guarding their intelligence and advisory prerogatives, the Departments of State, War, and the Navy failed to relinquish either the quantity or quality of information necessary to make the evaluation process work. The CIG did not, however, possess the leverage to rectify this problem, for the same institutions that hampered its mission were also responsible for allocating its funds and personnel.[38]

The first DCI, Admiral Sidney W. Souers, did little to remedy these drawbacks. He was essentially a caretaker who avoided conflict with the departmental intelligence components and worked to the limited brief of establishing the bureaucratic legitimacy of the CIG until a more permanent replacement could be found.[39] His successor, Lieutenant General Hoyt S. Vandenberg, adopted a wholly more ambitious and at times confrontational approach. Assuming control in June 1946, Vandenberg served only eleven months as DCI, leaving in May 1947 to head the newly independent United States Air Force. He nevertheless made an enormous impact during his brief tenure as DCI and has subsequently earned the reputation of having been something of a visionary. Vandenberg's objective was, in brief, a preemptive one that posed a fundamental challenge to the departmental intelligence components: to transform the CIG from a small non-statutory body with limited influence, finite resources, and an uncertain future into an independent, self-sufficient intelligence organisation. The functional parameters of the projected central intelligence agency would thereby be in place, so Vandenberg calculated, in advance of such an institution being legally enshrined in the impending national security legislation.[40]

Commanding considerable influence both on Capitol Hill – where his uncle was the senior Republican Senator, Arthur Vandenberg – and in the Executive, the DCI: (1) gained authority for the CIG to carry out independent research and analysis; (2) persuaded Truman that the group required greater bureaucratic independence if it was to serve the White House more effectively; (3) won increases in the CIG's budget and personnel; and (4) as a result of such increases, established the Office of Research and Estimates (ORE) in August 1946 to improve interagency coordination. The most far-reaching measure to be introduced during Vandenberg's tenure was, however, his incorporation the Strategic Service Unit (SSU) – the clandestine collection component of the OSS – into the CIG.[41]

In terms of clandestine collection, Truman's disbandment of the OSS amounted essentially to a dispersal of resources. The Secret Intelligence and Counterintelligence Branches of Donovan's organisation were merged to become the SSU and placed under the command of Brigadier General John Magruder and the control of the War Department.[42] To all intents and purposes this was a holding operation that saw the nucleus and assets of the espionage and counterespionage capabilities established by the OSS in wartime retained in readiness for their transfer to the "Central Intelligence Agency as soon as it [was] organised".[43]

Meanwhile, Magruder and his successor Lieutenant Colonel William W. Quinn lobbied for an SSU-CIG merger from the moment that the latter organisation was founded, a process that was brought to fruition in October 1946 when the SSU was renamed the Office of Special Operations (OSO) and fully integrated into the Central Intelligence Group.[44]

The CIG's acquisition of the SSU has been likened to "a mouse eating an elephant". A much larger concern than Vandenberg's, Quinn's organisation "incorporated dozens of overseas stations and its own procedures and files running back to its wartime OSS origins".[45] The SSU was, moreover, financially well-heeled, with a budget of unvouchered leftover OSS cash funds amounting to some \$8 million, which Quinn allocated to his station chiefs on a pro-rata basis. Vandenberg thus inherited a well-oiled clandestine collection component that had been working "against the operations of foreign intelligence services and secret organisations" from the moment of its inception.[46]

Though sources dealing with the specifics of the SSU's activities are limited, a broad picture of its mission is discernible. Even before the end of World War II, James Murphy, the head of X-2, the counterintelligence branch of the OSS, had identified the need to combat the threat posed by Soviet intelligence agents in the West. The SSU subsequently began to work against Marxist groups, particularly Western Europe's Communist Parties, if not before then certainly immediately after the defeat of the Axis powers.[47]

The exact scope of these operations is not clear. Certainly, in respect of covert action, the executive order that disbanded the OSS specified that operations of this nature be terminated in peacetime.[48] Ian Sayer and Douglas Botting's exhaustive study of the Counterintelligence Corps of the Army (CIC), however, provides evidence that the SSU took advantage of its transfer to the War Department to circumvent this ruling. The CIC, in effect, provided a convenient cover and source of practical assistance, even to the extent of creating dummy CIC detachments behind which newly-created clandestine agencies, namely the SSU, were able to hide in the furtherance of their *sub rosa* activities: operations that in practice often involved a blurring of distinctions between espionage, counterespionage, and small-scale psychological warfare ventures.[49]

A January 1946 review of the SSU's activities and resources supports these arguments, pointing out that although the unit's clandestine action branches had been liquidated, "selected personnel [had] been integrated into the Secret Intelligence Branch", which was operating in Western Europe, the Near East, North Africa, and the Far East under military control.[50] Such moves were, moreover, in keeping with the received wisdom at the highest levels of the War Department. The first record of a ranking administration official suggesting that the United States engage in covert action of any kind is Secretary of War, Robert P. Patterson's proposal of March 1946, that consideration be given to the development of a psychological warfare capacity, the guidelines for which were drawn up by the State-War-Navy Coordinating Committee (SWNCC) in little over a year.[51]

That the CIG/CIA engaged in some form of covert action before the authorisation of NSC 4/A on 14 December 1947, which gave official sanction for the agency to conduct psychological warfare operations for the first time, is in fact a matter of public record. Following Patterson's psychological warfare proposal, the CIG began working towards the establishment of such a capacity. In June 1946, Souers reported to Truman on the progress of these first tentative steps into the field of postwar covert action and by February 1947, Hoyt Vandenberg was informing the president that "the clandestine operations of the CIG are being successfully established in most of the critical areas outside the United States and are proceeding satisfactorily".[52]

This correspondence fell short of making specific mention of what these ventures entailed and where they were targeted. However, research conducted by Eduard Mark has gone some way towards filling the gaps, revealing the CIG's earliest efforts in the field of covert action to have been mounted in Romania during the summer and autumn of 1946.[53] Details of this enterprise are incomplete, but it is said to have been aimed at complementing a Pentagon war plan that was to be activated in response to a Soviet invasion of Turkey – which was seen by Washington as a possibility for much of 1946. American military planners calculated that, in the event of a Russian move on European Turkey, Romania would serve as a key point of communication and supply for the Red Army and that preparatory measures therefore needed to be implemented to optimise the impact of an American countermove. Success in such an endeavour would, it was assumed, assist Turkish efforts to endure a Russian onslaught and allow enough time for United States airpower based in the Cairo-Suez region to attack and destroy Soviet industry and oil production in the Caucuses.[54]

It was with these considerations in mind that the SSU/OSO made contact with Romania's National Peasant Party (NPP), the organisation that had proven most effective in opposing pro-Soviet puppet rule in Bucharest. Beginning in July 1946 and continuing until October of that year, the SSU/OSO drew on existing anticommunist dissent in Romania and attempted to organise it in readiness for deployment against the USSR should war come. Moves were made to establish an American-financed, NPP-led partisan army based on the World War II French resistance model. Prominent anticommunists were flown out of Romania with the aim of founding an effective exile organisation, and contact was made with the Romanian royalists who mounted the coup d'état that freed their country from pro-Nazi dictatorship in August 1944.[55] Any hopes that the OSO's machinations would yield similarly successful results were quickly dashed, however. Russian intelligence and its Romanian counterpart had infiltrated the NPP, and by November 1946 the operation had been thwarted, forcing its American organisers to flee Romania and watch on impotently while the proxies that the OSO had recruited for the venture were subjected to a public show trial.[56]

Whether or not the Romanian campaign was a unique instance of Vandenberg being ordered to engage in covert action to serve wider policy goals is a matter of conjecture. Certainly, the CIG had, by August 1946, launched a programme to collect information on the underground movements that were active the Eastern bloc.[57] There were, moreover, specific challenges to be met, for throughout much of 1946 the SSU/OSO reported on a campaign mounted by Soviet intelligence to trigger separatist sentiment among Turkey's ethnic minorities.[58] The CIG is not on record as having implemented covert measures to counter such Russian moves, however, and any interventionist inclinations that Vandenberg might have had would have been tempered by the fact that his organisation did not have official authorisation to engage in covert action in peacetime. It was, after all, wartime imperatives that led to the sanctioning of the Romanian campaign and if similar preparatory enterprises were launched in Turkey or elsewhere then specific detail of them has yet to materialise. What is clear is that by April 1947, Vandenberg was testifying secretly before the Senate Armed Services Committee on the "necessity of clandestine operations", the objective being to have official authority granted for covert action ahead of the National Security Act – which in this instance was not given.[59]

Passed in July 1947, the National Security legislation altered the name and elevated the status of the CIG. It was henceforth known as the Central Intelligence Agency, an independent department responsible to the president through the newly created National Security Council (NSC). What remained at issue, however, was whether or not covert action now fell within the agency's remit, for the new legislation permitted the CIA to engage in an unspecified range of "functions and duties related to intelligence affecting national security".[60] This was deliberately vague language that was open to very broad interpretation. To Vandenberg, it was a 'catch all' clause: a euphemistic phrase that reserved the right for the agency to engage in covert operations if so directed.[61] His successor, Admiral Roscoe H. Hillenkoetter, who served as DCI between May 1947 and October 1950, was less sure. He expressed considerable doubt as to whether the CIA could or indeed should embark on such a course, believing that clandestine action was a military function that belonged in an organisation responsible to the Joint Chiefs of Staff (JCS).[62]

The fact remained, however, that one third of the CIA's personnel were former OSS officers, who had gained invaluable experience fighting against the Axis powers.[63] Indeed, some operatives had already brought their experience to bear – during the failed Romania campaign – in anticipation of another war, this time against the USSR. Not only this, but the OSS leadership had never been averse to blurring the lines between operational objectives. As Thomas Troy's internal study of the organisation demonstrates, Donovan had used analytical intelligence as a cover for secret operations.[64] Moreover, during the period of flux that characterised the end of World War II through to the beginnings of the Cold War the capacity for OSS-initiated ventures to evolve from serving one objective to working towards quite different ends became more, rather than less, pronounced. Peter Clemens provides a case in point with his study of Operation Cardinal, an OSS mission that was dispatched to Mukden, Manchuria in August 1945 to protect allied prisoners of war. Having achieved its primary aim, the Cardinal team altered its focus to gathering intelligence on the Soviet position in Manchuria and the strength the Chinese communist forces in the region, all of which resulted in the OSS men being forced to leave Mukden in October 1945.[65] Despite the bureaucratic issues that fuelled Hillenkoetter's doubts, then, operatives on the ground had, since the end of the Second World War, been afforded a good deal of latitude regarding the scope of the enterprises they were tasked with. Individuals of the calibre of Harry Rositzke in Germany, James Angleton in Italy, and Alfred Ulmer in Austria were therefore in strong positions to develop and implement covert projects quickly and efficiently. Indeed, this had been the case from before the OSO came into being.[66]

Hillenkoetter was also uncertain of whether clandestine operations could be conducted without the consent and advice of Congress, but it was a concern that proved to be unwarranted for several reasons. Firstly, from the time that the CIG came into being, the Truman administration had specified the activities that it and its successor organisation were permitted to perform through the authorisation of National Intelligence Authority (NIA) directives. NIA directives and the National Security Council Intelligence Directives (NSCIDs) that superseded them were, along with executive orders, the principal means through which the CIA's operational parameters were determined: a so called "secret charter" that was for the most part devised away from congressional scrutiny.[67]

Equally significant is the point that the Executive and the Legislature were driven by quite distinct priorities in establishing the CIA. For Congress, determination never to repeat the Pearl Harbor debacle loomed large. The primary focus was therefore fixed on intelligence collection, and Capitol Hill was far from reticent in calling DCIs and their senior colleagues to account when the agency's predictive competence was believed to have fallen short of expectations, notably when it failed to foretell Moscow's acquisition of the atomic bomb in 1949. The White House, on the other hand, saw the Soviet threat as taking precedence over all other issues and placed increasing emphasis on the primacy of covert action. Nevertheless, between 1946 and 1950 and indeed long afterwards, Capitol Hill was fully supportive of covert operations generally and approved giving nearly two thirds of the agency's budget and manpower over to what were euphemistically described as 'Cold War activities'.[68] All other considerations aside, such ventures represented a relatively inexpensive means of furthering foreign policy objectives at a time when the Legislature was as keen as the Executive was to keep spending down.

Recent research has, however, called into question the *Church Report*'s depiction of the Armed Services and Appropriations Committees, which assumed jurisdiction over the CIA, as adopting "relatively inactive" stances with regard to the oversight of covert operations. Rather than adhering to the 'need to know' principle espoused by Leverett Saltonstall and choosing not to delve too deeply into clandestine action programmes, senior congressional leaders were quite thorough in probing these activities.[69] For its part, the CIA ensured that its budget was "laid out in minute detail" for the Legislature to examine in full, but in an era when "the Cold War was ominous" Capitol Hill gave the fledgling organisation considerable room for manoeuvre.[70] Even if this had not been the case, the CIA was already in possession of a system of unvouchered funds for its clandestine collection mission, which ensured that Hillenkoetter did not need to approach Congress for separate appropriations.[71]

The chronology of events that took place between the passage of the National Security Act and the authorisation of NSC 4/A began in August 1947. At this juncture, Donovan urged Forrestal to utilise psychological warfare tactics to counter communist-instigated political disruption, most specifically in France. The former OSS chief added the veiled warning that a privately financed anticommunist campaign was in the offing which, Donovan was sure, Forrestal would regard as unwise to let pass beyond Washington's control.[72]

From Donovan's point of view, a successful approach to Forrestal less than a month before his appointment to the newly created and highly influential position of Secretary of Defense, presented an opportunity for the former OSS chief to build bridges with the administration. Forrestal had, after all, played a key role in ensuring that Souers was appointed as the first DCI.[73] Raising the spectre of independent, unfettered and potentially counterproductive anticommunist initiatives, moreover, provided a means of levering the United States government into action. Donovan would have been well aware of this, since less than two years beforehand the designs of an ex-OSS Deputy Director and Thomas Watson, the head of IBM, to launch a private intelligence company and offer its services to the government, had been neutralised with the creation of the National Intelligence Authority.[74] At this stage, then, Donovan may well have envisaged himself as securing, with Forrestal's help, the top post in a new covert operational branch of the CIA, should the administration have been prompted to establish such a body.

There were, however, more tangible reasons than the mere force of Donovan's arguments for the conversion of Forrestal to the need for more direct and extensive covert action, which reportedly took place between August and October 1947. As Secretary of Defense, Forrestal had a unique and newly-found insight into the limits of military power, especially when it was ranged against a political foe. A more appropriate instrument needed to be developed speedily and employed to counter the unprecedented onslaught of political disruption initiated by the communists following Moscow's establishment of the Communist Information Bureau (Cominform) in 1947. From an American standpoint, the most effective countermeasure against these efforts to undermine the Marshall Plan was to upgrade and intensify the small-scale CIA operations that were already in place in Western Europe.[75]

The central and most hotly debated issue during the closing months of 1947, however, hinged on who would control, and take responsibility for, the American covert action programme.[76] The question of control was less contentious than that of responsibility. Propaganda of all kinds was seen by both the SWNCC and the Joint Chiefs of Staff as falling within the jurisdiction of the State Department, and George Marshall himself was well disposed towards providing policy guidance for covert operations. The Secretary of State was unwilling to accept *responsibility* for such activities, however, on grounds that their exposure would discredit the State Department itself and, more importantly, would compromise the recently articulated European Recovery Program. He therefore insisted that Truman reverse a decision taken in early November 1947 that authorised psychological warfare to be directed by State.[77]

In essence, then, the CIA took operational responsibility for the United States' covert action programme as a consequence of Marshall's fear of exposure. The considerable degree of flexibility that the agency had been afforded through the passage of the National Security Act made it the organisation best placed to house such a capacity, at least for the time being. There was, as well, an urgent need for Washington to act, in the shape of leftist political disruption in France and the potential for a communist-dominated alliance gaining power through electoral means in Italy. It was to counter the latter prospect that official sanction was given for the CIA to conduct psychological warfare operations with the authorisation of NSC 4/A.[78]

How much authority this directive gave for the agency to engage in covert action was a contentious issue. The CIA's General Counsel Lawrence R. Houston advised an already doubtful Hillenkoetter that neither NSC 4/A nor the National Security Act constituted congressional authorisation for the agency to spend money to influence a foreign election result.[79] Valid as these arguments might have been, however, they made little impression on Truman and were swept aside in the face of the political threat posed to American interests by communism in Western Europe. A CIA covert operation was to be deployed and Italy was to be the agency's stamping ground. Recourse to such action, moreover, was regarded as being so urgent that the NSC is reported never to have met as a group to ponder the merits or demerits of the case.[80]

2

ITALY 1947–1948:
SECURING A EUROPEAN
STRONGPOINT

The period 1947 to 1948 saw the Truman administration playing for increasingly high stakes in an Italy that had become a microcosm of the wider Cold War conflict. Ideological and strategic imperatives dictated that the United States must retain Italy within the western sphere, but the principal challenge to this objective was of a *political* kind, resting as it did with the Popular Front or People's Bloc – an alliance of the Communist Party and Socialist Party of Proletarian Unity (PCI and PSIUP).[1] In response, the Truman administration utilised political instruments to combat the threat, and in the process gave official authorisation for the CIA to conduct a full-scale covert operation for the first time.

The agency's Italian campaign was to stand out as a model of how psychological warfare, when integrated with more overt American programmes, could be deployed to great effect. From Washington's perspective, Italy's centre-right Christian Democratic Party (DC) had to prevail in the country's national elections of April 1948. A victory at the ballot box for the radical-left would have severely undermined wider American efforts to reshape Western Europe in a democratic mould and in Truman's estimation would have raised the potential for "the iron curtain to [advance as far as] Bordeaux, Calais, Antwerp, and The Hague".[2] The fears that the president articulated exaggerated the threat posed by the Popular Front and overestimated the intentions not to mention the capabilities of the Soviet Union. Nevertheless, his concerns reflected the mood of the times and were highlighted in greater detail at the Anglo-American "Pentagon Talks" during October and November of 1947.

Here allied military planners took cognisance of the fact that Italy's position in the Mediterranean meant that the country was of enormous strategic value, for it dominated the Near East and flanked the Balkans. Consequently, the security of the entire region would be greatly endangered if the People's Bloc was to win power and allow the Russians to take control. Equally crucial was the offensive imperative, for Italy was of key value as a forward base for eastward air strikes should war come.[3] It was with these geopolitical concerns in mind that covert action emerged in late 1947 and 1948 as "a logical and at the time commendable extension of the policy of containment":[4] one that was deployed to make certain that Italy was retained and secured as a European strongpoint.

The Italian Political Landscape 1945–1947:
A Case of Continuous Polarisation

Historian Piero Barucci characterised the years from April 1945 to May 1947 as an "heroic period" in Italian history:[5] a short interval when real opportunities presented themselves for the reconstruction of a country that had become bitterly accustomed to two decades of ramshackle, corrupt Fascist dictatorship, and five years of war.[6] These opportunities went largely unrealised, however, and the political development of Italy in the aftermath of World War II was a story of steady polarisation, fuelled by short-sighted economic policies which benefited the rich *quatro partito*, alienated the poor, and led to an increase in support for the parties of the far-left – notably the Communists.

The postwar reconstruction of Italy was, even at the most optimistic of estimates, a formidable task that depended on: (1) the economic reconstruction of the country through the restoration of production and the stabilisation of the internal monetary situation; (2) the promotion of social stability, most especially through the rectification of the longstanding disequilibrium between the relatively advanced north, and the rural and politically-backward south; and (3) the establishment of a parliamentary democracy.[7] By any measure, the realisation of these closely interconnected objectives could only occur after elections for a constitutional assembly and the resolution of the institutional question, which was rectified in June 1946 when a majority of the electorate rejected the monarchy and voted for Italy to become a republic.

In terms of government, Italy had, from the final months of the war, been led by a disparate and unstable coalition of resistance groupings that had been appointed by the allies, and inherent instability continued to pervade Italian political life after the Constitutional Assembly elections.[8] In reflecting the electoral balance, the government formed by Christian Democrat leader Alcide De Gasperi in July 1946 included Communists and Socialists in several of its ministries. This was despite the fact that the Popular Front was vehemently opposed to, if not all of the DC's policies then certainly those that it introduced to tackle the country's economic problems.[9]

During the course of 1946, De Gasperi appointed two successive Treasury Ministers, Epicarmo Corbino and Luigi Einaudi, neither of whom proved able to cure unemployment or prevent the country from drifting into recession.[10] The political repercussions of these failures were far-reaching, for the cumulative hardships they brought caused growing numbers of alienated workers to identify ever more closely with the Communist Party. In response, the PCI used its position in government and, more importantly, its dominant role in the *Confederazione Generale Italiana del Lavoro* (CGIL) – a broadly-based labour movement which was established in 1944 – to fight for measures directed at creating a positive reputation for the Communists as defenders of working class interests.[11] The upshot was that PCI membership mushroomed from a reputed 500 thousand in 1944 to 1.8 million in 1947, and this growth was reflected in the municipal elections of November 1946, which resulted in a considerable fall in support for the DC, and led to an intensification of calls from the right for the expulsion of the Popular Front from government. [12]

De Gasperi chose to delay following such a course, however, and his decision was informed primarily by the general strategy being pursued by the PCI.[13] Neither the Communist leadership nor its Socialist counterpart saw a revolutionary situation as existing in Italy. The decision to act jointly through the Popular Front resulted largely from a shared perception that it was division on the left that had allowed Mussolini to take power, and therefore had more to do with the lessons of the past than with plans for the future. Italian Communist leader Palmiro Togliatti was a gradualist in his political approach and he took an essentially moderate stance on most of the questions that confronted him.[14] Most significantly, Togliatti and Socialist leader Pietro Nenni accepted Christian Democrat demands that the Constitutional Assembly have the limited function of drafting a new constitution – completed in January 1948 – rather than act as a parliament with full legislative powers, which was what the PCI and PSIUP had initially argued for.[15] The left thus acquiesced to allowing De Gasperi to rule by decree and he himself believed the People's Bloc to be less threatening inside government than outside of it, at least for the time being.

That the Italian premier would need to expel the left from his coalition was, nonetheless, widely regarded as an article of faith. What was more at issue was the timing of such a move. The defection of Giuseppe Saragat's rightward leaning Socialists from the PSIUP camp in January 1947, for example, came as a welcome development for the Christian Democrats (the PSIUP henceforth became the Socialist Party or PSI). It was not enough, however, to persuade DeGasperi to move against the Popular Front, for to have acted before the settlement of an Allied-Italian peace treaty, which was set to be concluded in February 1947, would have been an open invitation for the Soviet Union to impose stringent terms on Italy.[16] The DC leader, moreover, needed to be confident of securing the necessary input of American economic aid and political commitment to enable him to cope with the inevitable backlash that the expulsion of the left would bring.

Consequently, it was not until after the Truman Doctrine speech and the State Department's announcement of American intentions to investigate "the needs for the immediate and longer run stabilisation of the Italian economy" that De Gasperi saw conditions as being ripe.[17] He therefore expelled the Communists and Socialists in May 1947: a case of fortunate timing, for in acting a month before Marshall's Harvard speech, which articulated Washington's intentions to initiate the European Recovery Program, the Italian premier limited the potential for the left to label him as an American puppet.[18]

The termination of PCI participation in government thwarted Togliatti's ambitions but it was even more significant for the debilitating effects it had on Soviet designs. Stalin's broader European objectives were, in brief, governed by an overriding desire to secure the Soviet Union's position in the East and minimise threats from the West. The presence of the Italian Communist Party cooperating in a coalition of national unity and displaying moderation greatly assisted these objectives, for it encouraged the perception that Western Europe had nothing to fear from the left.[19] Innocence by association of this kind in turn heightened the prospect of a speedy and complete American disengagement from Europe, the fulfilment of which stood at the head of Stalin's wish list. [20]

Conditions changed fundamentally after May and especially June 1947, however, for the announcement of the Marshall Plan brought about a Europe-wide ideological division, and the PCI henceforth had to take a stance that would complement a more belligerent Soviet line. The same criteria would have applied even if the May expulsion had not occurred, for Communist parties outside of the Russian sphere became stigmatised by the United States and the western allies to whom Marshall had pledged support through the ERP.[21] The corollary was that the continuation of the PCI in government would simply have been incompatible with Italian receipt of American aid after this point.

With the Communists deploying their power over the CGIL to call political strikes throughout the autumn and winter of 1947, in defiance of the De Gasperi government, Italy had become a theatre of superpower conflict. The fault lines dividing Italian society now widened to the point at which some in the Truman administration feared the possibility of insurrection. Though privately De Gasperi did not share these fears, he certainly exploited them, hoping that such a ploy would attract more American aid.[22] Thus, the United States, which had already played a significant role in Italian affairs over the previous two years, raised its profile and prepared to make a still more active contribution.

Truman's Policy in Italy, 1946 to late 1947

The rise of the Italian left was a cause of growing concern for the United States. The Truman administration deduced from Togliatti's duplicity in taking a moderate line as Minister of Justice while simultaneously resorting to inflammatory rhetoric to organise political strikes, that the PCI was something of a fifth column. Industrial action of this kind, American policymakers feared, pointed the way towards a revolution that could detach Italy from the western sphere.[23] Washington understood, moreover, that the surest way to diminish the appeal of Popular Front was to ameliorate Italy's difficult economic conditions through the input of American aid. However, the scale of economic assistance necessary to remedy Italy's plight was not forthcoming up to spring 1947, largely because a fiscally conservative Congress tied Truman's hands.[24]

A major revision in the American position took place after April 1947, when Marshall returned from the Council of Foreign Ministers Conference in Moscow having failed to reach any agreement with the Soviet Union on the question of Germany. This was a defining moment in postwar history, for it was at this point that American plans for integrating German economic recovery with that of Western Europe as a whole were set in motion. Washington subsequently became convinced, however, that the Cold War's focus had shifted from Germany to Italy, and the Truman administration viewed developments in Italy during the critical autumn months of 1947 within a wider Cold War context.[25] Most significantly, the campaign of strikes and social agitation engineered by the People's Bloc throughout this period lent resonance to an analysis prepared by George Kennan's newly-created Policy Planning Staff, which forecast resort to civil war by the PCI as one in a series of possible Soviet-orchestrated moves to derail the ERP.[26]

Interpreting Togliatti's actions as assiduously following a Kremlin-prescribed strategy, Truman approved the first directive to be issued by the National Security Council, NSC 1/1, on 24 November 1947. Though it was subjected to two revisions, NSC 1/1 provided the basic analyses and guidelines on which Washington's overall programme for countering the far-left in Italy was based. Advocating American deployment of all practicable means possible to shore up De Gasperi, the Truman administration directed that overt measures such as "an effective U.S. information program", be used in conjunction with the injection of "unvouchered funds" into the anticommunist effort and the deployment of a clandestine information/disinformation campaign.[27] It was to meet with this requirement that the president authorised NSC 4/A.

What must be understood, however, is that covert action played a relatively limited role in securing De Gasperi's electoral victory in 1948. It was not, for instance, until the approval of NSC 1/3 in March 1948 – much of which remains classified – that explicit authorisation for covert funding of the Christian Democrats and the other centrist parties was granted. The CIA's psychological warfare and political funding programme can therefore only be placed in proper context by first examining the larger overt strategy it was designed to complement.[28]

Overt and Activist: Anticommunist Campaigning American Style

The overt campaign pursued by the United States in the run-up to the Italian elections hinged on the achievement of two basic objectives. The first was focused on optimising the strength and appeal of the democratic anticommunist parties and convincing the Italian electorate that the choice it faced in April 1948 was an ideological one in which the only option was to vote in a way that secured the country's future within the western bloc. Closely mirroring this aim was the second element of the American programme. This was directed at alerting the Italian populace to the dangers of voting for the far-left, and at sowing discord both between the Soviet Union and the PCI-PSI alliance and also within the People's Bloc itself. Crucial to the overall American strategy was the portrayal of the United States as patron, friend and guarantor of Italian democracy, and the Truman administration was dextrous in the application of all means at its disposal to ensure that its message struck home to maximum effect.

The most visibly deployed instrument in Washington's containment arsenal during the Italian campaign was economic aid. On 17 December 1947 Truman signed an interim aid package which, in essence, was a short-term palliative aimed at injecting essential raw materials and foodstuffs into the Italian economy, thereby diminishing the incentive for the man in the street to vote Communist.[29] The economic instrument did not operate in isolation, however. It was complemented by a calculated raising of the American military profile at opportune times.[30] Consequently, when the American troop presence that had been in place in Italy since World War II was finally withdrawn from the country on 14 December 1947, the United States mounted air and naval manoeuvres in the Adriatic and the Mediterranean, and backed up the action with a State Department announcement voicing Washington's determination not to allow Italian democracy to be overthrown by force. The objective was to influence Stalin into placing constraints on PCI action, and the fact that political violence and disruption in Italy waned considerably after this point suggests that this tactic achieved its desired effect.[31]

An additional plank in the American strategy, and one that is said by CIA operative F. Mark Wyatt to have been implemented at De Gasperi's insistence, saw Washington work to fuse the most significant non-communist forces in Italy into a coalescent alliance. Thus, in November 1947 the United States exerted pressure on the Italian Republican Party, the Liberals and Saragat's Social Democrats (PSLI) to join the Christian Democrat-led coalition. The inclusion of these moderate and secular groupings in a government dominated by the essentially clerical DC freed De Gasperi from the need to rely on neofascist parties.[32] This was of great benefit to the Italian premier, for it permitted him to construct a campaign platform that portrayed the political future of Italy as resting on a straight choice between freedom and totalitarianism. Such an approach would simply not have been credible if De Gasperi had needed to rely on the support of the far right.

If De Gasperi and his American allies presented the options that were open to Italians in a predominantly secular, political light, then the Catholic church provided a religious dimension to the issue. From September 1947 Vatican spokesmen played on the consciences of religiously inclined Italians whose political sympathies tended towards the Popular Front, by stating that it was impossible to belong to the Communist Party and remain a member of the church. Italians had to choose between atheism and Christianity. Given the traditions of the country, this was a powerful message that carried damaging consequences for the prospects of the radical-left. The Vatican's tactics were, moreover, closely coordinated with those of the United States. When, for instance, a minority among the Catholic clergy dissented from the church's political line, the Vatican, at American instigation, prevented these priests from making their support for the PCI-PSI public, thereby keeping this element of the overall anticommunist strategy airtight.[33]

Creating division within the Socialist Party itself and between the PSI and PCI was a further American objective. The assumption was that the establishment of the Cominform placed Togliatti in an untenable position, for it caused fissures in the ranks of the Socialists and diminished the potential for future collaboration between the two parties. The American line, then, was not to do anything that intruded on private grief.[34] The December 1947 decision of the PSI and PCI to fight the election as a single entity, however, signalled that this approach had backfired and despite the efforts of the United States, the Christian Democrats and the Vatican, the far-left was gaining considerable ground during January and February 1948 by playing on the country's economic difficulties and arguing that Italy was in danger of becoming an American satellite state. Indeed, the United States Ambassador to Rome, James C. Dunn, maintained that Togliatti and Nenni were refraining from revolution because they expected to win a political triumph in April, and the victory of the left in local government elections at Pescara on 17 February was widely interpreted as a precursor to the national vote.[35]

A complete reversal of De Gasperi's fortunes took place on the very day that the Pescara result was announced, however, for it was at this point that a crisis began in Czechoslovakia which prepared the way for a communist coup in that country seven days later.[36] Though on the surface the Czech coup intensified the Cold War, it afforded Truman the ideal opportunity to increase domestic support for the Marshall Plan and signal exactly where the demarcation lines between the American and Soviet spheres of influence in Europe lay.[37] This had a profound effect on the situation in Italy.

The revision of American strategy outlined in NSC 1/2, which was issued on 20 February 1948, presented the United States as facing two very unwelcome prospects in Italy. On the one hand, the People's Bloc could win power by popular suffrage. This was the worst-case scenario since it would mark the first real extension of Soviet territorial control since 1945, and it would be done by legal procedure. On the other hand, De Gasperi could win the election but face insurrection and possibly civil war. This was actually seen by Kennan as preferable to a bloodless Communist electoral victory.[38]

Truman's room for manoeuvre was, however, greatly increased after the Czech coup. He could now claim that Italy was succumbing to the same type of subversion that had delivered Czechoslovakia into Soviet hands, and thereby justify American military intervention to bolster De Gasperi. Should Stalin have been intent on supporting the PCI to the full then he would have needed to contemplate war, which was simply not worth the risk.

With the authorisation of NSC 1/3 on 8 March 1948 the Truman administration intensified and augmented its overall strategy in Italy.[39] From this juncture the United States began to make diplomatic moves in close collaboration with Britain and France to demonstrate that it was the western powers and not the Soviet Union which acted in Italy's best interests. Two joint statements issued by the allies in March 1948 were illustrative of this tactic. The first pledged the eventual return of Trieste to Italy and the second urged Italian membership of the United Nations.[40] Both of these proposals put the Soviet Union in a difficult position. Russian support for the return of Trieste to Italy would upset the Yugoslavs, but by opposing the Italian claim shortly before the election, Stalin would severely damage Togliatti's chances of success. Equally perplexing was the issue of United Nations membership. The Russians had consistently refused to contemplate Italian admission to the UN without simultaneous consideration being given to other former enemy states, notably Bulgaria and Romania. In the final analysis the balance of Soviet interests weighed in favour of opposing Italian and allied wishes on both counts. In the process Stalin enhanced, albeit reluctantly, the prospects of De Gasperi, whose campaign was already gathering near unstoppable momentum as a result of the Czech coup.[41]

As the election drew closer the United States continued to utilise both incentives and inducements in order to persuade Italians to follow an anticommunist line. A second interim aid package was passed swiftly by Congress as a visible display of American good faith. At the same time, Marshall went so far as to announce that the United States would cut off ERP funds to Italy in the event of a Communist victory.[42]

To complete the overall assault on the hearts and minds of the Italian public, the Truman administration made full use of the Italy lobby and Italian-Americans generally. Amongst the array of initiatives launched from this quarter was the dispatch of gifts and letters from the United States to Italy. Here the emphasis was placed on the close personal links between the two countries, the threat posed by communism generally, and the perilous consequences that would accompany a victory by the Popular Front.[43]

That Italian-Americans participated in this campaign with unprecedented zeal is nowhere disputed. What is more interesting is why Washington was able to mobilise these people in such significant numbers. In this respect, Stephano Lucani offers some interesting insights, suggesting that, for many, involvement in the anticommunist crusade provided a means of regaining social respectability. Italian-Americans, Lucani argues, had a recent history of association with extremist politics. In 1941, for example, Italian-American Peter Cachiane became the first Communist to be elected to the New York City Council, holding the seat until his death in 1947 and during the same year East Harlem's radical American Labor Party Representative, Vito Marcantonio, refused to vote for United States aid to Greece and Turkey. The taint from the right was even more pronounced, for while a number of prominent Italian-Americans, notably labour officials such as Luigi

Antonini, had always been critics of fascism, many others had been outspoken admirers of Mussolini. Consequently, when Italy entered the war against the United States questions of loyalty were raised and these doubts lingered even after the war was over.[44]

The anticommunist campaign of 1947 and 1948, therefore, provided the ideal opportunity for Italian-Americans to reestablish their *bona fides* with their adopted country and it is notable that organisations such as the Order Sons of Italy in America, and the Order Italian Sons and Daughters of America, both of which were vociferous in their support of De Gasperi and condemnation of Togliatti, had also looked favourably on Mussolini during the 1920s and 1930s. Keen to distance themselves, both from domestic leftists of the Marcantonio stamp and all-too-recent associations with fascism, then, Italian-Americans were only too ready to respond positively to Generoso Pope's New York based *Il Progresso Italo-Americano*, which spearheaded the letter writing campaign, and to other Italian language newspapers that followed suit.[45]

Alarmist as Washington's propaganda offensive in Italy was, it struck "with the force of lightning".[46] No shades of grey were evident in the western media campaign, the Christian Democrats' electoral platform, or the pronouncements of Pope Pius XII. The choice was between freedom and totalitarianism, between atheism and Christianity; and the Czech coup stood as a clear reminder of where Italian loyalties should be directed in what had essentially become a referendum on communism.[47]

The Christian Democrats emerged from the election of 18–19 April 1948 with 48.5 per cent of the vote and an absolute majority in parliament (see appendix 1). Open and extensive intervention by the United States had played a pivotal role in bringing this about. What was not apparent at the time, however, was that De Gasperi's cause had also been advanced by a covert counterpart that paralleled the outward support that Washington provided.[48]

The Methodology of Defensive Covert Intervention: The Italian Model

The CIA's Italian campaign was initiated with the authorisation of NSC 4/A.[49] It was mounted with little time to spare and it demonstrated the efficacy of the 'silent option' in what was now the Cold War. What contributed significantly to the programme's success was that James Jesus Angleton, who was head of all SSU/OSO operations in Italy from December 1945 to November 1947, and who before that served as X-2's chieftain in the country, had been working consistently against the PCI and its allies for well over two years prior to the DC's victory. Together with his principal assistant, Raymond Rocca, Angleton achieved an intricate understanding of, and influence over, Italian political life.[50] In the process he established the necessary channels of intervention through which the CIA was able to act quickly and effectively in support of De Gasperi in 1948.

To understand the James Angleton of the 1945 to 1948 period is to put aside the depiction of him in Tom Mangold's biography: the portrayal of Angleton as the ideologically-driven CIA counterintelligence supremo from the 1950s to the early 1970s who, in reaction to the discovery of the Philby betrayal, raised unfounded suspicions about Soviet penetration of the agency which damaged its confidence and standing, and led ultimately to his own dismissal.[51] Described by William Quinn as "the finest counterespionage officer the United States has ever produced", Angleton was awarded the Legion of Merit for his service in the OSS during World War II.[52] As the war against Hitler was ending, however, Angleton targeted his attentions on new enemies, most specifically Italy's "nascent Communist networks". Despite the enormous global-political changes that were occurring at the time it was, in effect, a case of business as usual for the X-2 chief and his colleagues.[53]

Italy's security forces were reorganised under the partial supervision of the OSS after 1944 and were mandated to put their organisational resources at the disposal of the allied occupation forces until 1946.[54] While close intelligence liaison existed between the United States and Italy before and indeed long after this point, the latter country's five intelligence services developed their own political and professional agendas, and Angleton saw it as being in American interests to monitor their activities. In the pursuit of this objective he cultivated an informant inside of Italian Naval Intelligence code-named SAILOR, who revealed details of meetings between the Italian and Soviet intelligence services and, in the autumn of 1945, turned over files detailing his meetings with a Russian operative in Istanbul. The prospect of an American penetration of Soviet intelligence was thus enhanced.[55]

The SSU/OSO Rome station utilised penetration tactics such as this in conjunction with official liaison arrangements. During early 1945, for instance, Angleton received a series of reports from the Italian Servio Informazio Segreta (SIS), which centred on the dangerous potential for a communist insurgency in Italy. The following year Italian Naval Intelligence's cryptographic service provided him with a partial reconstruction of a Yugoslav cipher. The SSU/OSO's ability to decode messages sent by the Russians to their field agents in Italy and elsewhere in the Mediterranean was consequently increased. More generally, Italy's intelligence services had long experience of working against their Soviet counterparts and shared information with the CIG/CIA on cases going back long before the war. Taken together, these activities and arrangements proved instrumental in enabling the OSO to piece together a composite picture of the far-left in Italy and the threat that it posed.[56]

Angleton, then, "knew his parish extremely well". He was, moreover, reported to have been prepared to go beyond his brief and act on the information he received long before official sanction was granted for the CIA to conduct covert psychological warfare. He is alleged, for example, to have filled the coffers of the Rome *Daily American*, a pro-De Gasperi English language newspaper founded in

1946.[57] Entertaining few scruples, he also sought to recruit ex-fascists such as Lieutenant Colonel Antonio Pignatelli and his wife Maria to the anticommunist cause. The Pignatellis had been double agents during the war, betraying OSS operations to the Axis powers. They were arrested but no proceedings were brought against them, largely because Antonio Pignatelli had organised a political intelligence network in southern Italy, which Angleton sought to revamp as an SSU asset and use against the communist underground.[58]

The recruitment of ex-fascists and Nazis by the CIA became commonplace once responsibility for covert action had passed to the control of the OPC and will be discussed at greater length in the next chapter. With regard to early operations in Italy, however, Pignatelli appears not to have been the only former enemy that the CIG/CIA toyed with using. The *Washington Post* reported in January 1947 that Lieutenant General Renzo Montagna, former chief of the Fascist Republican Police and once named as Mussolini's successor, had been permitted to "escape quietly" from allied custody by "a senior intelligence officer" and was then helped by "influential friends to establish a new identity".[59] While no record exists of high-level former enemies of this kind playing any role in American efforts to counter the People's Bloc, the labyrinthine system of contacts that had been set up during the war by the OSS provided the CIG/CIA with wide ranging sources of support from which to draw.

The most notable precedent of wartime cooperation to be continued after the cessation of hostilities was the near-symbiotic relationship that existed between elements of America's intelligence community and the country's two major labour organisations – the American Federation of Labor (AFL) and the Congress of Industrial Organizations (CIO). The OSS, for instance, provided the necessary channels for the AFL to fund its Europe-wide antifascist network, which in turn benefited the allied war effort.[60] Even before hostilities had ended, however, the AFL was giving unambiguous expression to the view that the Soviet Union had already displaced Nazi Germany as democracy's primary adversary. To counter the perceived Russian threat, the AFL transferred control of its European contacts, the preponderance of whom were anticommunists as well as antifascists, to a new body – the Free Trade Union Committee (FTUC). Under the direction of Jay Lovestone, one-time leader of the United States Communist Party and convert to the anti-Stalinist cause since the 1930s, the FTUC sought to combat the spread of communism and ensure that ideological kinsmen of the AFL in the European union movement were installed in positions of prominence in the postwar order.[61]

In taking such an approach, the AFL differed fundamentally from the American government's early postwar policy of promoting unity among the wartime allies. Yet there is some evidence of OSS-AFL cooperation being carried over to peacetime. For example, Serafino Romualdi, who was at the same time a representative of the International Ladies Garment Workers Union (ILGWU) and an OSS major, channelled AFL financial contributions into Italy until autumn 1945. The objective was to "strengthen the Socialist forces at the expense of the

Communists". Though Luigi Antonini, the founder of the Italian American Labor Council (IALC), demanded that such activities be conducted openly, Romualdi maintained that union funding of this kind was a clandestine operation, which, if exposed, would herald unwelcome political repercussions for the United States government.[62] Regardless of Washington's outward displays of support for Italy's united front governments during the final stages of the war and the immediate postwar period, then, American policymakers were eager to fracture the Popular Front and worked covertly, making full use of the labour unions in the hoped-for achievement of this goal.

Despite the absence of specific detail, a number of indicators suggest that the American intelligence services continued to collaborate closely with the FTUC in Italy between late 1945 and early 1947. To begin with, the State Department dispatched labour attachés to America's major European embassies from early 1945 onwards, and upgraded the programme to correspond to developments in the Cold War. The selection of these labour attachés was carefully vetted by Lovestone and his colleague Irving Brown, the AFL's full-time representative in Europe, to ensure that candidates with an understanding of the FTUC's operating criteria were appointed.[63] The point is that Lovestone and Brown applied semi-conspiratorial tactics in their management of the FTUC. They also enjoyed a close and enduring relationship with fellow practitioner of the covert arts, James Angleton, and more generally with an American intelligence community that has been characterised as being more "fantastical and Byzantine" than any of its rivals.[64]

The interests of the Truman administration stood to be advanced by continued cooperation between the AFL, the State Department, and the CIG/CIA. Assistant Secretary of State for Economic Affairs William Clayton maintained from as early as March 1946 that the United States should forward "political loans" to buoy up its allies in Italy. Great discretion and secrecy would have been essential in the pursuit of such a course, however, not least because the then Commerce Secretary and former Vice President Henry Wallace was vocal in his objections to administration efforts to influence foreign elections.[65] Under these circumstances Lovestone and Brown stood as ideal conduits through which American objectives could be achieved quietly. Certainly, Brown was working closely with the United States' Rome embassy in conveying funds to Italy's anticommunist forces from early 1946, when the Truman administration and the AFL first began to converge in their policies towards the Soviet Union and communism generally. The initial objective was to split the PCI-PSIUP alliance. After this tactic had failed and the Popular Front pact was renewed in October 1946, a two-pronged strategy was deployed aimed at fracturing the Socialist Party itself and simultaneously strengthening the position of the Christian Democrats.[66]

Equally significant to the modus operandi of the CIA and its predecessor organisations were the close ties that they built and maintained with the Italian business community. Arrangements of this nature in fact dated back to the pre-war and wartime periods. For example, James Angleton's father, Hugh, was the owner of the Italian franchise of National Cash Register (NCR) and had been president of the Italian Chamber of Commerce before the war. He had, moreover, established an unofficial American espionage network between 1939 and 1941, using the factories that NCR had dotted around Europe as listening posts and drawing on well-placed contacts in Italian business and in the country's Masonic Order, which had been banned but was still functioning in secret, for information. Recruited to the OSS during the war, Hugh returned to Italy when hostilities ended to build on his few remaining assets.[67]

The principal difficulty that confronted Italian business interests during the immediate postwar years was that their efforts to rebuild were impaired by what the CIG/CIA labelled the 'friendly firms arrangement'. What this amounted to was a leftist extortion racket that was designed to fill the coffers of the PCI and its allies, most notably the CGIL, while simultaneously stifling De Gasperi's efforts to put Italy on a more stable economic footing. The problem was especially acute in the north, where, under the threat of financially crippling strikes, major industrial concerns such as Fiat, Olivetti, and Montecattini were intimidated into paying large sums of money over to the CGIL leader Giuseppe De Devittorio. There was, however, a further debilitating dimension to the 'friendly firms arrangement', in that Italian companies were forced to pay vastly inflated prices for goods and resources that they imported from the Eastern bloc. The excess was then given by the Soviets to the PCI and other Italian communist concerns.[68]

From Washington's standpoint, the neutralisation of the 'friendly firms arrangement' was seen as crucial if the power of the People's Bloc was to be broken, and threats to withhold or withdraw economic aid were used to dissuade large Italian corporations from "playing the Communist game". For instance, congresswoman and would-be American Ambassador to Italy, Clare Boothe Luce threatened to "knock off every cent you get if you don't have your workers join a free labour union", and coercion of this kind proved effective in diminishing the flow of capital into the Popular Front's coffers.[69] Combating leftist extortion and shoring up Italian business were also crucial CIA objectives and Angleton worked with the AFL, CIO, and the non-communist Italian labour unions to help secure these aims.[70] Also advantageous in this drive to lend backbone to Italy's large corporations were the close connections that Angleton's father, maintained with the country's business fraternity, which was predominantly anticommunist and provided the OSO station chief with contacts and resources over and above those that were provided by the United States government.[71]

If maintaining expeditious liaison between private enterprise and the SSU/OSO proved crucial to Angleton's campaign to prevent the delicate political equilibrium in Italy from collapsing into revolution, it performed an additional and fundamental task. In short, it placed him at a perfect vantage point to ensure that any propensity for the Italian and/or American business communities to engage in independent anticommunist action did not rebound negatively on the United States. A particularly acute requirement, this was brought to Truman's attention within a week of the Italian elections. Hillenkoetter warned of increasing "incidents involving the clandestine transport of munitions" by "irresponsible privately-owned U.S. aircraft and U.S. unscheduled airlines" to areas of "extreme political sensitivity such as Northern Italy". These activities could have only "unfavorable effects on U.S. national security", the implication being that Washington needed to act to terminate these operations forthwith.[72]

Amongst the varied range of organisations and institutions that rallied to the anticommunist cause in early postwar Italy and allied themselves with the CIG/CIA, none proved to be more significant than the Vatican. Angleton is reported to have liaised on a weekly basis during 1947 with Monsignor Giovanni Battista Montini, the future Pope Paul VI, in an arrangement that saw the agency furnish Catholic Action, a large tightly managed propaganda organisation under Vatican control, with money and supplies. In return, Montini provided the OSO with information and contacts.[73] The question of whether these funds and resources came directly from the United States or were diverted from Angleton's Italian and American business contacts is a matter of speculation. A picture does, however, emerge of the OSO coordinating, or at least attempting to coordinate, the activities of all of the major anticommunist elements at work in Italy, the overriding objective being to diminish the strength and appeal of the far-left, while simultaneously pulling on the reins when independent anticommunist action became overzealous.

*   *   *

During the week following the authorisation of NSC 4/A, the CIA created the Special Procedures Group to "intervene in the Italian parliamentary elections in order to prevent the Italian Communist Party from gaining a role in the Italian government".[74] Though he had returned to Washington in November 1947 to assist in the OSO's creation of a Soviet Division, Angleton was placed in charge of the Italian operation and liaised closely with Rocca throughout the campaign.[75] The fact that the SPG was established within, as opposed to outside of, the OSO proved advantageous, for the logistics of the Italian campaign demanded very close interplay between intelligence-gathering and covert action. Some secret intelligence operatives, it is true, feared involvement in the programme might jeopardise their existing sources and so distanced themselves from Angleton's activities. The success of the operation suggests, however, that the SPG was not hindered by the type of intense rivalry that later plagued the relationship between the OSO and the OPC, and led to the eventual merger of the two components under General Walter Bedell Smith's directorship in August 1952.[76]

With a reported $10 million at its disposal, the SPG mounted what was essentially a two-pronged plan, the first element of which involved the acquisition then laundering of funds through suitable conduits to the DC, PSLI, the Republicans, the Liberals, and a number of CIA-controlled front organisations. In the initial stages of the campaign this posed a problem, for the SPG had to find the necessary capital and set the mechanics of the process in motion without arousing the suspicions of government agencies, notably the Bureau of the Budget. Failure in this task would have compromised the all-important principle of plausible deniability and might have given rise to searching questions being asked in Congress and elsewhere.[77]

The solution came with the selection of the Economic Stabilisation Fund as the source of finance. An anti-inflationary instrument established in part from confiscated Axis assets, the Economic Stabilisation Fund suited the CIA's purposes in two major ways. Firstly, it was operated and controlled under the discretionary authority of the Secretary of the Treasury John W. Snyder, who was permitted to spend its funds without reporting the details to Congress. Though Snyder was not a member of the NSC, he was a Truman confidante, which meant that knowledge of the operation remained confined to a small number of policymakers and officials. More importantly, the Economic Stabilisation Fund functioned ostensibly to ameliorate swings in the value of the American dollar and other foreign currencies. It thus operated in the world of international finance, which by nature was, and indeed is, a very secretive environment. Here, money laundering of the type engaged in by the CIA could be carried out discreetly with only a very minimal risk of detection.

The actual system operated by the CIA began with $10 million in cash being withdrawn from the Economic Stabilisation Fund. Following this, the money was laundered through individual bank accounts, the owners of which donated the funds to a number of front organisations that either purchased Italian lira or transferred the money directly to CIA-controlled assets in Italy.[78] Much of the SPG's Italian operation remains classified, but the identities of the actors involved in the laundering process are to an extent discernible through educated guesswork.

In March 1948, the State Department listed a number of American multinationals that could be of assistance in obtaining contributions for the anticommunist cause in Italy and act as private channels for the transfer of money. Amongst these companies was National Cash Register. Also involved was IBM, the director of which was Thomas Watson who, it will be recalled, had sought to establish a private intelligence organisation between late 1945 and early 1946. Even without any associations with the United States intelligence community, these companies along with others named, such as Standard Oil, General Electric, and Great Lakes Carbon, had large vested interests in Italy and were therefore prime candidates for collaboration with the CIA.[79] The same held true in the case of Amadeo Pietro Giannini, the Italian-American boss of the Transamerica Corporation, who is said to have put assets that included some two hundred small banks at the disposal of the agency to help secure De Gasperi's victory.[80]

Indeed, the American business community had, like the country's labour unions, viewed the Soviet Union as representing a threat to be countered from the end of World War II. Several major private concerns, notably the Ford and Rockefeller Foundations, had, accordingly, devised clandestine action plans and recruited personnel from the fields of economics, commerce, academia and advertising, many of whom had served in the OSS, to conduct the very type of democracy-propping exercise that was now called for in Italy. These moves were not, however, made in isolation. A degree of coordination with the Truman administration was maintained through the Council on Foreign Relations (CFR), a well-heeled and highly influential association, located on Park Avenue and composed of the power elite from both inside and outside of government.[81] The CFR served as the principal forum through which ever closer interaction between public and private sector activities in the field of covert action was to take place throughout 1947, and several of its most prominent members, including Forrestal, Donovan, Allen Dulles, and Frank Wisner played key roles in securing private finance for the Italian operation.[82]

Additional light is shed on the SPG's laundering techniques in top-secret correspondence between the American embassy in Italy and the State Department from 24 February 1948. The document details how funds were being transferred through Lovestone to a contact in Switzerland, then on to leading PSLI politician Giuseppe Faravelli in Rome.[83] The revival of the PSLI was in fact a State Department priority, for American policymakers believed that the PCI, by associating itself with the social and economic reforms required by the peasants and workers, had won the loyalty of the working class. The only instrument available for undercutting this loyalty, so American logic had it, was the PSLI.[84] Thus came the need for a large infusion of funds into Luigi Saragat's party, which since its inception had been largely ineffective.

With so much money being relayed to so many sources, the CIA introduced a complicated procedure to make certain that its programme remained legal as well as secret. To cover the transactions involved in the laundering process, the individuals concerned were advised to place a three letter/number code on their income tax forms alongside their claimed "charitable deduction" and to keep the amount out of their income tax liability calculations. Three basic considerations justified this procedure: (1) it enabled the individuals who assisted the CIA to do so without violating American tax laws; (2) it gave the CIA an internal audit procedure whereby the agency could check on the flow of money as it passed through the laundering process; and (3) by using many individuals to make contributions to a variety of front organisations, the CIA connection was almost impossible to detect.[85]

*   *   *

The second major strand of the Italian covert action programme saw the Truman administration and the CIA adopt the philosophy of Thomas Pendergast and transplant the tactics of the American political machines to Italy. The delivery of votes was paramount and, to borrow a Pendergast quote, "efficient organisation in every little ward and precinct" determined the election, as did the hands-on approach taken by Truman himself, particularly his demand that Agriculture

Secretary Clinton Anderson "get more wheat" delivered to assist De Gasperi's electoral fortunes.[86] By bringing such factors into play, the SPG's campaign set a precedent. Indeed, future DCI William Colby cited his experience in the New York City Democratic Party as being of benefit when he served as the CIA's chief of special operations in Italy between 1953 and 1958.[87]

The SPG's game plan proceeded from the premise that providing blanket support for the Christian Democrats, and for the PSLI wherever it stood, would constitute a misuse of resources. Thus, on the basis of what CIA intelligence reports gauged to be the respective strengths and weaknesses of the DC and the Popular Front, Angleton and Rocca targeted those seats most likely to give control of the government to De Gasperi. This approach was to bear fruit in all but two of the two hundred seats selected, and it depended on the successful application of a number of propaganda techniques.[88]

All of the constituencies selected for SPG attention were subjected to campaigns of black propaganda. Unattributable pamphlets were widely distributed highlighting the brutality of the Red Army in Eastern Europe. The ominous picture of communism generally was reinforced by alarmist stories planted in local and national newspapers.[89] While such techniques may, as Colby has argued, have been of limited value during the 1950s, the close proximity of the Czech coup to the Italian election meant that black propaganda of this kind could be utilised to more effect than might otherwise have been the case.[90] In short, a great deal of mileage was to be had from projecting the Czech scenario to Italy.

While creating a general anticommunist tone for the campaign, Angleton and Rocca also tailored their strategy to cater for the specific conditions in each of the targeted constituencies, in order to mobilise the necessary volume of votes at grass roots level. Here, profiles were assembled on all of the prospective PCI-PSI candidates in the two hundred selected seats, after which the SPG printed derogatory literature on the personal and sex lives, past misdemeanours and idiosyncrasies of these Communists and Socialists.[91] The aim was, in brief, to diminish the voter appeal of the far-left.

Of course, this was negative anticommunism that also sought, through the use of forged documents and letters purporting to come from the PCI, to accentuate rifts within and between the Communist and Socialist Parties: rifts that had anyway become more pronounced since Yugoslavia was ejected from the Cominform.[92] However, such activities were not, in the estimation of one future operative, the most effective means of countering the People's Bloc. Colby maintains that during his tenure more positive measures, principally the shoring up of party organisation to ensure that the DC, PSLI, Liberal, and Republican memberships were well armed with arguments to debate with their PCI-PSI counterparts, had more impact than black propaganda.[93] Indeed, these elements were very much in evidence in 1948, and proved, in the assessment of James Dunn, to be highly effective during the final run up to the election. American dollars and Vatican-supplied political workers, the ambassador reported, were matching and surpassing the Communists and Socialists in grass roots organisation.[94] The close and longstanding working relationship between Angleton and Montini, it would seem, was paying high political dividends.

Taken as a whole, then, the SPG propaganda machine helped to build a perception of the duplicitous antidemocratic nature of communism generally, and the unsavoury tendencies and opportunist dispositions of particular PCI and PSI candidates. A further aspect of this element of the CIA's covert campaign was that it lent weight to what might best be described as the semi-overt propaganda that the United States also deployed. For example, a mysterious and short-lived organisation known as the Committee to Aid Democracy in Italy advanced half a million picture postcards to Italy with graphic portrayals of the country's fate should it fall into communist hands.[95] Grey propaganda of this kind, whatever its source might have been, could be integrated with, and complemented by, both overt American initiatives, such as the letter writing campaign, and the disinformation distributed by the CIA.

While the SPG allegedly paid under-the-counter bonuses to voting officials, there is no definite evidence of vote rigging. [96] In a sense, the Czech coup had already built up sufficient fear in the Italian public by the time that the provisions of NSC 1/2 and NSC 1/3, which authorised the intensification of Angleton's programme and the wider American effort, were taking effect. Indeed, Dunn articulated this very point in March 1948.[97] Looked at in this context, actual vote rigging was not worth the risk.

There were, as well, more subtle and airtight ways of maximising anticommunist support, for Italy's dual citizenship laws permitted thousands of Italian-Americans to vote in the election. In essence, the Truman administration and the CIA transplanted New Deal Coalition *votes* as well as New Deal Coalition *methods* to Italy in order to help assure a Christian Democrat victory. The individuals who volunteered their votes to save the motherland of course sacrificed their American citizenship under the 1940 Neutrality Act. They were, however, rewarded with a reinstatement of United States citizenship in 1951.[98] This tactic mirrored Justice Department warnings that Italians who joined the PCI would be denied emigration to the United States, and was one more strand in a campaign designed to secure a vital European strongpoint within the western sphere.[99]

The Soviet Viewpoint

The extent of the Soviet Union's financial and political commitment to the PCI during the 1948 election is the subject of some contention. Ivan Lombardo, whose Socialist Unity Party was a partner in the De Gasperi coalition, claimed that the American campaign was "relatively minor compared to the tremendous propaganda machinery of the Communists and their allies [who were] supported and evidently financed by the Russians".[100] Christopher Andrew's study is more balanced, maintaining that Russian involvement was "equally active" to that of the

United States. This, however, flies in the face of Miles Copeland's adage that "in an election in such-and-such a country, the KGB (NKVD in 1948) backs a candidate, the CIA backs a candidate, and the CIA candidate wins", primarily because the United States had far greater resources at its disposal.[101]

Some of the methods used by the People's Bloc were tinged with more than a hint of desperation. PCI workers, for instance, travelled incognito to the Abruzzi Mountains and told illiterate anticommunists that the way to prevent the Popular Front from winning power was to mark a cross against the portrait of Garibaldi: blatantly misleading advice given that the People's Bloc was using the famous Italian patriot as its symbol for the elections.[102]

On a more substantive level, documentary evidence and verifiable figures that would help to quantify the respective commitments of the United States and the Soviet Union are elusive and potentially misleading. Mark Wyatt's claims on this count provide an interesting case in point. He maintains that the agency and Italian intelligence estimated the PCI, Devittorio and other communist interests as having received upwards of $8 million a month in black bag money during the crucial period of November 1947 through to April 1948, and that this came directly out of Villa Abomelek, the Soviet compound in Rome.[103] These are enormous figures by late 1940s standards, but even if they were proven to be accurate, which they have not been, they do not necessarily provide a satisfactory estimate of Russian support for the Popular Front. If these funds came in part or entirely from the 'friendly firms arrangement' then the role played by Moscow was to a greater or lesser degree one of conduit rather than financier, the key benefactors of the People's Bloc being the large Italian corporations. A measure of caution needs to applied to an assessment of this kind, however, because Italian business interests had already begun to resist leftist extortion by the time of the 'crucial period'. If, on the other hand, the money dispersed from Villa Abomelek was provided in addition to the monies procured through the 'friendly firms arrangement' then the Soviet Union's financial stake in the 1948 elections was considerable and certainly greater than that of the United States, if the $10 million allocated to the CIA is taken as the benchmark.

The only published evidence of how much was spent during the 1948 campaign came in a survey carried out by the Italian Bureau of the United Press. Contrasting sharply from Wyatt's figures, this study estimated the anticommunist parties as having spent seven and a half times as much as the Communists and Socialists. Indeed, the Christian Democrats alone were calculated to have spent four times that of their leftist political adversaries.[104] The accuracy of these figures is certainly open to question. The greater part of the Italian press, after all, opposed the far-left, and the figures may have been fabricated in an attempt to cause disillusionment among PCI supporters at the Soviet Union's lack of interest.

What lends more weight to the proposition that whether on a political or financial level, Russian support for the People's Bloc was dwarfed by the comprehensive backup provided by the United States to the Christian Democrats and their coalition partners, is the Soviet Union's actions. When reports first reached Moscow that the DC was receiving substantial injections of capital to bolster its electoral prospects, the Soviet leadership was sceptical. The suspicion was that Russian field personnel, in collusion with the PCI, were raising the stakes fictitiously in order to get more money out of Moscow. A senior Russian intelligence official was consequently dispatched to Italy to scrutinise these claims. His considered appraisal of the situation, however, amounted to a complete misinterpretation that stood as testament to the effectiveness of the SPG's campaign. The Soviet official mistakenly deduced that, though secret funds *already in excess* of $10 million had been made available to De Gasperi, the source of finance was the Vatican and not the United States. The Soviet leadership subsequently concluded that they were too far behind the church in the spending race to make any difference to Togliatti's fortunes, and henceforth provided only token support.[105] In this instance, Stalin's famous Potsdam quote had rebounded. The pope, so the Russians believed, had more divisions at his disposal than the Soviet leader did.

Further evidence of Soviet apprehension about becoming overly committed in Italy and provoking an aggressive western backlash was apparent in Stalin's handling of the UN membership and Trieste issues. The Russian stance in both cases gave the impression that Stalin: (1) regarded the situation in Italy as being too volatile for comfort: (2) feared the ramifications of Anglo-American military intervention in the event of a Popular Front victory; and (3) sacrificed the Italian Communist Party as a result. Indeed Stalin's quashing of French Communist Party plans to instigate an insurrection to bring down the Fourth Republic in 1947, and his rebuke of Bulgaria and Yugoslavia during February 1948 for supporting the Greek Communist Party (KKE) in the civil war that was taking place in that country, might just as easily have been applied to the situation in Italy. Under no circumstances was the Russian dictator prepared to allow the Soviet Union to become embroiled in a conflict, whether it be political or military, that might lead to war with the United States, "the most powerful state in the world".[106]

Conclusion

The success of the Italian campaign helped to convince America's political elite of the value of psychological warfare as a tool of containment. A well-coordinated adjunct of the main thrust of United States foreign policy, the SPG's operation played a key role in filling the breach and forestalling an extension of communist power in a strategically crucial country while the Marshall Plan was being implemented and taking effect.[107] What must be stressed, however, is that Washington regarded the problems of Italy in a wider regional, rather than a purely national, context. From the Truman administration's perspective, the challenge posed by the People's Bloc was: (1) twinned with Communist-Socialist efforts to undermine democracy in France; (2) linked with the KKE insurgency in Greece;

and (3) part of a much larger threat that was planned and coordinated by Moscow and aimed at bringing the entire Mediterranean region under Soviet control.[108] In accordance with this analysis, the United States deployed political weaponry as an essential backup to economic aid in all three countries. Thus, while the Italian campaign was the first official covert operation authorised by Washington, it was not the only defensive clandestine action programme to be mounted by the United States in the 1947 to 1948 period.

The CIA launched a propaganda and funding campaign in France during 1947 which, being aimed at bolstering the parties of the centre and undermining the radical-left, closely approximated the Italian operation, though on a smaller scale.[109] A paper drafted in 1961 by the Kennedy administration, moreover, revealed covert American involvement in Greece from 1947. United States military advisors were sent to Greece from April of that year as part of the economic aid mission that followed in the aftermath of the Truman Doctrine speech. From December 1947, American personnel were secretly mandated to provide logistical and operational support and were sent into combat alongside Greek government forces in a mission that broadened rapidly to incorporate full-scale American-led counterinsurgency programmes. These developments were hidden from public and congressional scrutiny but came into force in early 1948.[110] The 1961 report does not make clear whether there was any CIA involvement in these ventures. Certainly, Greece was listed in a memorandum outlining the SSU's assets and resources as a country where "extensive semi-covert operations were taking place under military commanders". This review was dated January 1946.[111] It therefore long predated official American commitment to Constantine Tsaldaris's regime in Athens, but so too did the estimates of the Kennedy administration report, which examined United States involvement in Greece "for the critical years 1946 to 1948", and beyond up to the defeat of the KKE at Grammos in 1949.[112]

What is clear is that by mid 1948, Washington deemed a defensive covert action capacity, which incorporated paramilitary programmes as well as psychological warfare, to be necessary for the protection of the interests of the United States. American policymakers had, furthermore, by this time accepted Kennan's argument that Washington dispense with any pretence that it was acting out of "high-minded altruism" in the furtherance of foreign policy objectives.[113] Adopting the logic that the end of countering communism justified the means, the CIA and the military cavorted with some unsavoury bedfellows in the pursuit of clandestine objectives in 1947 and 1948.

The most obvious example was the recruitment of the Greek Democratic League (EDES), a right-wing territorial militia that had worked with German occupation forces during World War II.[114] In its successful effort to break the communist-engineered general strike in France in December 1947, the CIA is rumoured to have hired elements of the Corsican Mafia, some of whom had served as henchmen to the Nazis during the war.[115] In Italy, as has been discussed, the CIG/CIA reorganised, and drew on the resources of, the very security forces that had served Mussolini just a few short years before. In some instances the agency and its predecessor organisations allowed war criminals to either evade capture altogether, or to escape from allied custody almost as quickly as they were caught: all in the hope that these former enemies could be brought on board in the battle against the Popular Front. Not only was the stage set, then, for an expansion of covert action as De Gasperi celebrated his victory in April 1948. The trends that would become ever more pronounced in subsequent years were already beginning to take hold even before the onset of the Berlin blockade and the decision of the Truman administration to establish the OPC and go on to the offensive.[116]

3

ON TO THE OFFENSIVE

Throughout the second term of Truman's presidency containment remained the centrepiece of American foreign and defence policy, but the spread of the Cold War to Asia and the outbreak of hostilities in Korea led Washington to place ever greater emphasis on military instruments to counter the communist threat. This period saw control of CIA covert operations transferred from the SPG in June 1948 to the Office of Policy Coordination – an entirely new body which, though it was housed in the agency for administrative purposes, functioned ostensibly as an independent entity with wide operational parameters and little in the way of oversight provisions governing what it could and what it could not do.[1]

It was during the short lifetime of the OPC, 1948 to 1952, that covert action was established as a permanent and well-resourced tool of statecraft, and this arose largely as a consequence of the very different policy requirements of the Executive. The State Department, for example, tended to encourage political action and propaganda activities to reinforce its diplomatic objectives. The Defense Department, on the other hand, requested paramilitary activities in support of the Korean War effort. The result was that the OPC had to diversify as well as expand, and this in turn created an internal dynamic as operatives competed with one another in developing ever more ambitious projects.[2]

The expansion of the OPC's organisational and functional scope gathered pace through three escalatory stages which were brought about by: (1) the introduction of the 1949 Central Intelligence Act, which made provision for an increase in the CIA's manpower and funding, and exempted the agency from federal disclosure laws; (2) the authorisation of NSC 68 in April 1950, which stipulated the need for a non-military counteroffensive against the Soviet Union; and (3) the onset of the Korean War, which provided the impetus for the CIA to increase enormously its operational capacities. Statistics show clearly the extent of the OPC's growth. Its manpower mushroomed from a staff of 302 in 1949 to 2,812 in 1952, with an additional 3,142 overseas contract personnel. Its budgets multiplied in concert, from $4.7 million in 1949 to $82 million in 1952, and the number of stations out of which the OPC worked rose from seven to forty-seven over the same period.[3]

The OPC was equally significant in the sense that it conducted, with Washington's authorisation, offensive covert operations against the Sino-Soviet bloc as well as defensive projects in support of democracy in Western Europe and later in Asia.[4] This was a major departure, for though the SPG had launched at least one venture behind the Iron Curtain, it did so without official approval.[5] What should be stressed, however, is that the OPC's offensive operations were essentially harassment exercises. Only in the case of the Albania operation, which began as an Anglo-American enterprise, did Washington make any outright attempt to overthrow a communist regime within the Soviet orbit.[6] The assumptions on which the OPC was founded and its modus operandi, nonetheless, provide clear evidence that Truman's claim never to have had "any thought that the CIA would be injected into peacetime cloak and dagger operations" was at odds with the facts.[7] During the second half of his presidency, covert action evolved into a key weapon of foreign policy as the Cold War intensified and expanded into a global confrontation.

The Cold War, 1948–1953: A Geographical Expansion and a Proliferation of Means

By 1948 the Cold War had developed into a spheres of influence conflict centred on Europe, but it was a conflict between two very unequal adversaries. At this time the foreign policy designs of the Truman administration proceeded from the premise that the United States' nuclear monopoly coupled with its unrivalled military superiority in the air and on the sea, and its mobilisation base guaranteed that the balance of power was weighted heavily in Washington's favour and would remain so over the medium term. American policymakers maintained that for a Soviet Union that was only beginning to recover from the devastating toll reaped by World War II, the risks entailed in a military adventure to extend Russian control beyond the Eastern European satellites were prohibitive.[8] Moscow would, for certain, probe western weaknesses and indeed it was a key imperative of the CIA's covert action mission to ensure that political conditions in Western Europe were such that the seeds of Soviet/communist-inspired dissent fell on stony ground. In terms of the big picture, however, Truman's calculations were clear: when Stalin's pursuit of Russian interests raised the potential for a clash with American power, he would temper his ambitions and settle for the best deal he could get for the Soviet Union.[9]

Such faith in the primacy of the United States over its 'superpower' adversary guided the Truman administration during the war scare of March 1948. The same basic logic held true, moreover, during the Berlin blockade. Beginning in June 1948, the nearly year-long crisis saw the Kremlin play at brinkmanship, but the Anglo-American airlift that was mounted to sustain the city carried a stark message for Stalin: either acknowledge the existence of a western enclave in Berlin or be prepared to go to war. So convinced was the American Ambassador to Moscow and future DCI, Walter Bedell Smith, that the Soviet Union would plump for the first option, that he announced his willingness to go and sit on the airfield at Wiesbaden, a centre of operations for the airlift, in full confidence that the Russians had no intention of starting a war.[10]

Significant as the Berlin blockade was in heightening Cold War tensions, it failed to influence Washington into making an extensive military commitment to the defence of Western Europe. Economic measures remained central to containment policy and in military terms the emphasis was focused on self-help. The provisions made by Britain and the Benelux countries through the Brussels Treaty of March 1948 and the subsequent creation of the Western European Union (WEU) were, however, considered by Pentagon planners to be too limited to provide for adequate defence against the Soviet Union. An expanded version of the alliance that incorporated the United States, Canada and a number of other strategically-vital countries and locations, including Greenland, Iceland, and the Azores – which since World war II had been key points in America's outer line of defence – was therefore brought into being with the establishment of the North Atlantic Treaty Organisation (NATO) in April 1949.[11]

It should, nevertheless, be emphasised that the founding of NATO was primarily a political move. It was conceived as a confidence booster aimed at raising the sense of security and psychological well-being in Western Europe, reinforcing the ERP, and preventing America's trans-Atlantic allies from succumbing to Russian pressure and adopting neutralism.[12] There was, additionally, a strong element of what Gaddis refers to as "double containment" involved in the establishment of NATO, in that it helped to allay European fears about the dangers posed by an independent West German state.[13]

The whole nature of the Cold War changed irrevocably, however, as an outcome of two events that took place in the latter months of 1949. Soviet acquisition of an atomic device in late August of that year brought about a proliferation of means and a fundamental alteration in the balance of forces to the detriment of the United States, and Mao Zedong's proclamation of the People's Republic of China (PRC) the following month resulted in the geographical expansion of the conflict to Asia. These factors, along with the intensification of domestic anticommunism within the United States that they spawned, were central catalysts in influencing Truman's decision to announce a crash programme to produce a thermonuclear weapon and in bringing about a root and branch revision of American strategic thinking as outlined in NSC 68.

NSC 68 was authorised in April 1950 with the purpose of prompting the bureaucracy and Congress into supporting a more robust version of containment than had hitherto applied. Portraying the Soviet Union as an ideologically-driven, expansionist state that aspired ultimately to world domination, the document stands as a landmark in American national security policy history, not to mention cold war rhetoric. Unlike Kennan's earlier conception of containment, NSC 68 made no distinction between those areas that were vital to American interests and those that were not. Perceptions were seen as all-important and a "defeat for free institutions anywhere" was deemed to be "a defeat everywhere" – the so-called zero-sum game calculation.[14] All that prevented cold war from erupting into hot war, according to NSC 68, was a lack of preparedness on the part of the Soviets to embark on such a course. The onus was consequently on the United States to mount a massive rearmament programme to meet any type of challenge posed by what was depicted as a Soviet-controlled global communist monolith.[15]

The budgetary implications of this were enormous and there is considerable doubt as to whether the scale of deficit financing necessary for the United States to meet with such an expansive national security commitment would have found such ready support in Congress without the trigger of the Korean War. The fact, nonetheless, remains that from mid 1950 onwards the Truman administration deployed neo-Keynesian policies in an attempt to provide for massive increases in defence expenditure while simultaneously seeking to maintain domestic living standards.[16]

The mushrooming of defence costs that took place between 1950 and 1953 bears out the extent to which NSC 68 departed from the strategic thinking that dominated containment policy from 1946 to 1949.[17] Truman's budget estimate for 1954 envisaged national security-related spending at $55.6 billion. Representing an enormous 70.7 per cent of total expenditure, and creating a projected budget deficit of $9.9 billion, this amounted to a fourfold hike in defence costs from the $13.5 billion allocated in 1950.[18] Behind such increases lay the assumption, outlined in NSC 68 and reinforced by North Korea's invasion of its southern neighbour, that vigilance and preparedness needed to be America's watchwords. Consequently, as well as embarking on a land war in Asia – a move which military planners had long sought to avoid – Washington also committed itself to the militarisation of NATO, which saw the bolstering of the American troop presence in Western Europe and the first moves being made towards the arming of the fledgling West German state, which had been established in May 1949.[19]

Two factors that arose as a result of the Korean War, of June 1950 to July 1953, warrant a brief mention here, not only because they are significant in themselves but also because they had some bearing on the development of covert action. Firstly, Korea demonstrated how narrow the line between containment and rollback was. General Douglas MacArthur's counteroffensive, which by October 1950 had reversed Kim Il Sung's initial successes and pushed his forces back towards the Chinese border, went beyond the UN's objective of restoring the thirty-eighth parallel as the dividing line between North and South Korea. Beijing's intervention in the Korean War during the following month, however, came as a warning to Truman that if he revised American war aims and sought to reunite Korea by force, then he risked raising the stakes to the point at which a third world war became possible. The drawbacks of following such a course far outweighed the benefits and the president opted for a reaffirmation of containment.[20]

The Korean War is, secondly, illustrative of the extent to which domestic issues, namely the four-year witch-hunt that Joseph McCarthy mounted to weed out alleged traitors in the Democratic Party and Executive Branch, could influence foreign policy.[21] Much as the Wisconsin senator's efforts heightened Truman's determination to bring regions such as Indochina under the containment umbrella in order to prevent any further American 'losses' in the Far East, they also limited the president's room for manoeuvre in his management of the Korean War. On the one hand, he had no wish to expand the conflict and risk the very dangerous repercussions that a policy of rollback implied. On the other hand, he could not negotiate with the Chinese for fear of the domestic backlash that would result from the McCarthyites and the China lobby they were closely allied to. The result was that by mid 1951 the Korean conflict had settled into a stalemate centred near to the thirty-eighth parallel, and for the remainder of Truman's tenure the GOP made political capital by persistently criticising the president for what Republicans argued was his inability to bring the war to a satisfactory conclusion.

The geopolitical environment of the 1948 to 1953 period, then, saw the United States extend its commitment to contain communism to global proportions and the CIA's covert action mission grew in tandem with these expanding policy requirements. Containment had, from its outset, been more than a defensive response to Soviet pressure on Western Europe. The policy had also been one of calculated and gradual coercion aimed at inducing Moscow to mend its ways over the longer-term.[22] The Berlin blockade led Washington to place greater stress on the coercive element of containment. One outcome of this change in emphasis was the creation of the OPC and the initiation of an offensive covert warfare mission that provided the means through which the Truman administration was to straddle of the line between containment and rollback. [23]

The Office of Policy Coordination

In the aftermath of the CIA's Italian campaign psychological warfare was catapulted into the ascendancy as a tool for advancing American foreign policy, and appetites were whetted in Washington for an expansion of covert action generally. The paradox was that while De Gasperi's victory had highlighted the SPG's operational competence, America's covert action mission was subsequently transferred to an entirely new entity – the OPC.[24] Several closely related factors dictated that this would be the case.

In the broadest Cold War context, America was, from 1948, neither at peace nor at war and though the communist threat was still deemed to be principally a political one, it was nevertheless growing more acute. In response, Kennan began to argue from the spring of that year for official sanction to be granted for the development of a clandestine action capability that went beyond psychological warfare to incorporate direct covert intervention against America's prospective enemies as and when occasion demanded it. What this proposal amounted to was a

State Department bid to wrest jurisdiction over covert action away from the CIA and to the Policy Planning Staff.[25]

For his part, Hillenkoetter resisted Kennan's plan but the DCI's efforts were compromised by what the State and Defense Departments regarded as the excessive caution that had characterised his use of the CIA's covert action mandate.[26] At the same time, the potential for the Italian operation to boost Hillenkoetter's prestige was cancelled out by doubts about the CIA's predictive efficiency. Most specifically, the agency's critics argued that it had failed to give advance warning of riots in Bogota that disrupted Marshall's visit to the Colombian capital in April 1948 for a conference of the Organisation of American States (OAS).[27]

These charges were in fact inaccurate. A congressional inquiry mounted immediately after the events in Bogota revealed that the CIA had alerted the State Department, first in January 1948 and again during the following March, to the danger of the conference being marred by leftist-orchestrated riots "aimed primarily at embarrassing officials of the U.S". Blame could thus be more adequately attached to the State Department for its failure to listen than to the CIA for its failure to predict accurately, but this was overlooked at the time. Consequently, doubts remained about Hillenkoetter's ability to ensure that properly evaluated information reached top-level policymakers in a timely enough fashion.[28] This damaged the DCI's standing generally and could only have hampered his efforts to fight the agency's corner in the bureaucratic turf war over the future of covert action.

Additional and still more basic factors also figured in the decision to remove clandestine operations from the OSO. In essence, the issue of how to reconcile the often-conflicting imperatives of control and responsibility lay at the heart of the problem, just as it had done when covert action was first authorised. Put simply, the CIA was considered to be too accountable to carry out the full range of operations envisaged by Kennan.[29] In theory at least, every venture that the agency proposed was subject to review by the NSC and could therefore rebound on the NSC if sanctioned then later compromised.

Indeed, Washington had a foretaste of these potential pitfalls a year before covert action had official approval, when the OSO's efforts to destabilise communist rule in Romania were uncovered during the autumn of 1946. Fortunately for the United States, this received little attention in the western media, but it provided Petru Groza's communist regime with a propaganda victory and justification to intensify the already hard-line policy it was pursuing against those it labelled as dissidents.[30] Whether or not the Romanian fiasco registered with any great impact in Washington is a matter of conjecture. What is certain is that in deciding to make covert action a more permanent and comprehensive instrument of foreign policy than had hitherto been the case, the NSC also adopted Kennan's proposal to appoint an instrumentality that was effectively outside of the normal oversight loop to carry out the mission.[31]

On 18 June 1948, the National Security Council established the Office of Special Projects – which was soon renamed the Office of Policy Coordination – and approved NSC 10/2 to supersede NSC 4/A and serve as the new organisation's founding charter.[32] Some five months later, the Truman administration authorised NSC 20/4 and thereby specified the OPC's overarching policy objectives. Reiterating longstanding American concerns that Eurasia be prevented from falling into the hands of a hostile power, NSC 20/4 stipulated that "all methods short of war" be utilised to impair and reduce the power and influence of the Soviet Union until it no longer constituted a threat to the United States, its allies or indeed the free world as a whole.[33] As such, the document articulated the core assumptions that were to be adopted by the authors of NSC 68.

The OPC itself was headed by Frank G. Wisner, a Wall Street lawyer who had served in the OSS in Egypt, Turkey, and most notably as station chief in Romania between September 1944 and late January 1945. He completed his wartime service working out of the OSS station in Wiesbaden, Germany in September 1945 and after a brief return to Wall Street took up the post of Deputy Under Secretary of State for Occupied Areas, which he held from the summer of 1947 until becoming Assistant Director of Policy Coordination (ADPC).[34]

What should be stressed about the OPC is that from its outset it was a bureaucratic anomaly. Wisner was appointed to head the organisation by the Secretary of State and the ADPC looked to the PPS and, when occasion demanded it, the Pentagon for policy guidance. The OPC was not, however, formally associated with either the State or Defense Departments. Conversely, Wisner's organisation was housed officially within the CIA, but only for the provision of "quarters and rations", and the DCI had next to no control over its activities, at least until 1950 when Walter Bedell Smith succeeded Hillenkoetter. In practice, the provisions governing the design and conduct of covert action were very loosely structured from mid to late 1948 onwards. The CIA was sidelined, while the OPC was afforded the widest possible latitude in the drive to achieve its now often-quoted defining mission of countering "the vicious covert activities of the USSR, its satellite states, and Communist groups". The principal condition governing the functioning of Wisner's organisation was that, should any of its ventures be uncovered, Washington could "plausibly disclaim any responsibility for them".[35]

The creation of the OPC was also significant in the sense that it was the outcome of a gradual meeting of minds that took place between the federal government and America's private sector in the sphere of foreign policy. As has already been mentioned, the Council on Foreign Relations served as the principal agent in this convergence of interests. It was, for instance, common practice for PPS reports to be communicated to the CFR.[36] Likewise, the CFR's president, Allen Dulles, a New York lawyer, former OSS station chief in Berne, Switzerland, and future DCI, sponsored covert activists such as Wisner, Tracy Barnes, John A.

Bross, and Cord Meyer for membership to its ranks. The council, then, played a key role in the recruitment of the OPC's hierarchy.[37]

The CFR, furthermore, served as the vehicle through which administration officials were kept informed of independent covert initiatives mounted by the Ford and Rockefeller Foundations, and they in turn assisted the Truman administration's own surreptitious efforts.[38] Particularly prominent in this respect was the Ford Foundation, which in spite of being formally opposed to aggressive cold war operations, allocated somewhere in the region of $500,000 for the resettlement of refugees and defectors, and was far from reticent when asked to serve as a financing conduit for Wisner's Free Europe Committees and other front organisations.[39]

The OPC's funding provisions themselves were as anomalous as those governing its oversight. Officially, its appropriations from Congress multiplied more than sixteen-fold between 1949 and 1952.[40] Significant as this growth was, however, it tells only part of the story, for the Economic Cooperation Administration (ECA), the organisation that managed the European Recovery Program, provided Wisner with an additional and secret budget. Under the conditions of the Marshall Plan, Western European signatories had to match each dollar received in American aid with an equal amount in local currency. Of this, 95 per cent was used for ERP projects. The remaining 5 per cent, termed counterpart funds and amounting to approximately $200 million per year, covered administrative and miscellaneous costs incurred by the American government, and a proportion of these monies was set aside for the OPC.[41]

Exactly how much Wisner siphoned off from this source is not clear. A 1949 memorandum from the OPC's Finance Division to the ADPC stated only that "certain portions" of the counterpart funds were allotted to the OPC.[42] The account of Richard M. Bissell, who at the time was the ECA's deputy assistant administrator and later headed the CIA's operations directorate, is equally pertinent and equally difficult to gauge. On the one hand, he maintains that a "modest amount" from these monies went to the OPC. On the other, he states that he would not have been surprised "to learn that the 5 percent counterpart funds were used for many OPC operations", which implies that Wisner had access to a considerable proportion of the yearly $200 million sum.[43] Leaving the absence of specific figures aside, interviews conducted by Evan Thomas with several former OPC operatives reveal that the organisation was awash with what was described as an unlimited supply of money. Counterpart funds were, furthermore, unvouchered and though guidelines were laid down for their use, Wisner's organisation was, in practice, bound by neither spending restrictions nor accounting procedures. OPC operatives could "write a project in brief and vague language, funding was easily obtainable".[44]

Though the OPC has featured prominently in several very good studies of the CIA, a definitive work on Wisner's organisation has yet to be written. The ADPC himself outlined his organisation's work as subdividing into the five "functional groups" of psychological warfare, political warfare, economic warfare, preventive direct action, and miscellaneous activities (for a more extensive *verbatim* breakdown see appendix 3).[45] However, detailed and comprehensive analysis of the OPC's mission, especially in the areas of commodity and fiscal covert operations and the establishment of front organisations, would require access to information relating to sources and methods. Welcome as it has been, the greater openness that has characterised the CIA's approach to declassification over recent years has not stretched to the point of breaking such a sacred intelligence taboo, nor, understandably, is it ever likely to. With such constraints in place, existing treatments on the OPC have tended to present a somewhat skewed picture, focusing on the organisation's psychological warfare, political action, paramilitary and cultural programmes, while paying scant attention to the crucial sphere of economic warfare.[46] While it is not possible to rectify this imbalance, for the reasons outlined above, it is nonetheless incumbent on any study of American covert action to point out that the imbalance exists and to provide as full an analysis of the OPC as sources will allow.

Looked at holistically, the OPC was essentially tasked with four closely-related overarching objectives: (1) to marshal as many active and potential anticommunist elements as possible; (2) to provide these organisations with financial and where necessary operational support, so bringing them under some degree of American control; (3) to deploy these groups and any other resources that were at the disposal of the United States on a speciality of function basis; and (4) to ensure that the overall covert effort against the Soviet Union and its satellites was well-oiled, coordinated, and struck in a manner that brought maximum benefit to American foreign policy objectives.[47] The OPC was, however, more than just a mobiliser, organiser, and financier of anti-Soviet discontent. The expertise and discretion of the Wall Street lawyers and Ivy League academics with whom Wisner so enthusiastically filled his ranks qualified the organisation eminently for a key dimension of its mission, namely the waging of economic warfare against the communist bloc.

Economic Warfare

According to Wisner, OPC economic warfare subdivided into two categories. Commodity operations incorporated what he described as clandestine preclusive buying, market manipulation, and black market projects, while currency speculation and counterfeiting fell under the rubric of fiscal operations.[48] As to what these activities fully entailed, the CIA has permitted very little to reach the public domain. An examination of wider American policy objectives in the economic sphere, however, helps to shed some light on these highly sensitive OPC ventures.

Richard Bissell described the OPC as functioning as a complementary instrumentality to the Marshall Plan and several factors support his contention. The lifetime of Wisner's organisation, 1948 to 1952, closely approximated that of the ERP; the ECA bolstered the OPC's budget secretly through the injection of counterpart funds; Wisner's organisation replicated the ERP's geographical divisions; ECA projects that overlapped into the sphere of grey or black propaganda were coordinated closely with the OPC; and the OPC's charter stipulated that the operations that it embarked on "pertaining to economic warfare be conducted under the guidance of the appropriate agencies and departments", namely the ECA, and the State and Commerce Departments.[49] There is, however, a key element missing from this picture of close interconnection. The introduction of the Marshall Plan was accompanied by a less visible, more offensively oriented complementary *policy*, which took the form of an American-led western embargo of strategic goods to the communist bloc.[50]

Taking account of the fact that World War II had left the Russian economy severely impaired, this policy sought to slow down the rate of recovery and growth of the Soviet Union's military-industrial capacity by preventing Moscow from procuring what were termed 'strategic commodities'. Utilising its various aid packages as political levers, Washington induced all of the Marshall Plan signatories, along with some fifty other countries worldwide, to join the embargo. The principal objectives of the policy were to ensure that the American nuclear monopoly endured for as long as possible and that the relative power of the United States vis-à-vis the Soviet Union was maintained. In light of these aims, Washington adopted a very broad interpretation of what constituted a strategic commodity. Anything that was deemed to provide Moscow with a 'net strategic advantage', most obviously nuclear materials and munitions, was proscribed, but so too were rubber, steel, and fertilisers – much to the chagrin of those among America's allies whose economic well-being was affected detrimentally by a contraction of trade with the Eastern bloc.[51]

The problem with such restrictive and widespread export controls was that they were difficult to enforce. Western businessmen, sometimes with the tacit agreement of their governments, exploited loopholes in the embargo or sought to circumvent it by smuggling goods to the Soviet bloc through clandestine channels set up by the Russians, most notably between East and West Germany.[52] Indeed, Moscow was quick to exploit the opportunities that the occupation of a significant proportion of its former enemy's territory offered, and East Germany was regarded by Stalin as being crucial, both to the revival of the USSR's war-ravaged economy and the Soviet atomic programme.[53]

Acquisition of all the materials necessary for the building of an atomic weapon posed a problem for the Russians. While some of the necessary resources could be got from the I.G. Farben plant at Bitterfeld and similar so-called Joint Stock Companies in the Russian zone, other materials had to be procured from the West, and the OPC and CIA countered such moves in two ways. The first was to make full use of their intelligence-collection capacity and act accordingly. Thus, when it was revealed that I. G. Farben needed high-grade steel, which was only available in the West and was on the export control list, Wisner and his colleagues were able to act pre-emptively and ensure that the embargo was enforced.[54]

The second means of countering Moscow's attempts to circumvent western export controls was the use of what Forrestal referred to as "the pre-emptive and preclusive buying of strategic commodities". This involved the United States purchasing and stockpiling commodities and resources that were vital to the maintenance and expansion of Soviet power. Demand would thus far exceed supply and Moscow would, at best, be prevented from purchasing these goods altogether or alternatively be forced to pay highly inflated prices for them on the black market, which would in turn place added stress on the Soviet economy.[55] Wisner's reference to clandestine preclusive buying, market manipulation, and black market operation, then, points to his organisation as having played a key role in the implementation of the embargo policy.[56]

Though East Germany was viewed as being a key location for economic warfare initiatives, Czechoslovakia, with its close geographical proximity to the West and its porous borders, was regarded as the most promising target for this type of venture.[57] With relatively easy passage both into and out of the country, the OPC/DDP was able to mount counterfeiting operations that were designed to destabilise the Czechoslovak economy and complement wider covert action objectives aimed at increasing dissent and weakening the Russian hold over this important satellite.[58] The mechanics of at least the economic dimension of this campaign are, however, are a matter of speculation. They were, in essence, a category of covert operation that Richard Bissell appropriately characterised as "truly secret".[59]

What can be said with greater certainty is that some OPC/DDP economic warfare projects, most specifically the creation of front companies, were in part designed with longer-term objectives in mind. The convergence of three major benefits enjoyed by the OPC – an abundance of unvouchered funds, expertise in the fields of wholesale banking and economics, and wide operational latitude – enabled Wisner to establish private companies and banks that, while providing cover behind which the OPC conducted its multifarious mission, also functioned on a *bona fide* basis. In some instances, these corporate structures generated income quite separate from either the OPC's official budget or the monies it received through the counterpart fund arrangement.[60] These 'proprietories', furthermore, provided the CIA with independent sources of financing long after the OPC had been fully merged into the agency and the counterpart fund arrangement had ended following the demise of the Marshall Plan.

The history of Civil Air Transport (CAT) stands as a seminal example of "the entrepreneurial drive of OPC personnel in designing projects that paid for themselves while aiding the national security effort".[61] CAT began operating in 1946 as a private concern owned by Major General Claire Chennault and Whiting Willauer. It flew missions in support of the Nationalist Chinese and was purchased by the OPC in what were effectively instalments during 1949 and 1950 for a total of $950,000. For over twenty years CAT, and Air America as it became known after the reorganisation of the CIA's Far Eastern air arm in 1959, provided air support under commercial cover for the CIA and other American government agencies in the Far East. The employer of over 11,000 personnel, the airline ran an enormous maintenance facility in Taiwan, and turned over $30 million in net profits to the Treasury Department when it was liquidated in 1973.[62]

European Theatre Operations

If the OPC's own ventures benefited greatly from its access to an abundance of resources, then so too did the operations that the organisation mounted in conjunction with America's western allies. This was evident in the close links that the OPC forged with the British Secret Intelligence Service (SIS or MI6).[63] Anglo-American cooperation in the field of special operations had wartime precedents, which had seen the British security forces provide training and operational support for the OSS.[64] The OPC-SIS partnership was, however, founded on the fact that, though MI6 had experience in the field of covert action that far exceeded that of its American counterpart, Whitehall lacked the financial muscle to put this expertise to full use. A key role of the OPC, at least during the early stages of its existence, was therefore to act as banker and ensure that British-originated ideas had a chance to come to fruition.[65]

For Wisner, the benefits of collaboration with SIS were twofold. Exposure to British techniques put the OPC on a steep learning curve, which provided it with the know-how to take full control of projects that began as Anglo-American affairs, such as the Albanian and Iranian operations.[66] Being custodians of a still extensive though declining empire, the British also tended to control strategically useful locations for the mounting of covert operations, as the use of Malta as a training base and jump-off point for the Albanian operation demonstrates.[67]

The resources-for-expertise basis on which the OPC-SIS relationship functioned in its formative period was equally prominent during the early western attempts to support anti-Soviet partisan movements in the Baltic States. In 1949, MI6 devised a plan to use the Royal Navy's Baltic fisheries patrol as cover to infiltrate agents into Latvia, Lithuania, and Estonia by boat. The drawback was that, while the British were in an opportune position to mount such a venture, since their occupation zone in Germany included the Baltic coast, budgetary constraints prevented SIS from acting.[68] Once again, the OPC stepped in with the necessary finance. A three-way division of labour and responsibility subsequently developed, whereby Wisner provided the funds and MI6 refitted the E-Boats that were used for the mission, and planned and directed the project.[69] The third contingent in the partnership was a former Wehrmacht intelligence unit, which, under the command of General Reinhard Gehlen, had been preserved intact by the American Army at the end of the war.[70] Deployed by the OPC to spy on and conduct operations against the Soviet Union, the Gehlen organisation recruited the crews for the Anglo-American boat operations, drawing from one-time German motor torpedo flotilla personnel who had served in the Baltic during the war.[71]

The sea-borne enterprises in the Baltic were but a few of the many collaborative ventures that the OPC mounted using erstwhile enemies. During his time as Deputy Under Secretary of State for Occupied Areas, Wisner and his State Department colleagues at the PPS began to examine the potential for utilising the 700,000 refugees who had fled Eastern Europe in the face of the Red Army's advance in 1944 and 1945. Temporarily settled in the Displaced Persons (DP) camps that dotted western Germany in the early postwar years, these émigrés were predominantly anticommunist. They therefore provided a vast pool from which Wisner sought to draw in order to: (1) acquire information about the Soviet Union; (2) establish various front organisations, for instance student and farmers' groups, in an effort to mirror and in turn counter the tactics used by the Kremlin; and (3) recruit agents, guerrilla groups, and private armies to be deployed in the event of war, either to confront the Red Army directly or to function as stay-behind units.[72] A key element in the OPC's overall mission, this programme came into force under the code-name of Operation Bloodstone as soon as Wisner's organisation became functional.

The DPs earmarked for recruitment by the OPC varied widely in cultural background, ethnicity, and political persuasion, ranging from social democrats and anti-Stalinist Marxists on the left to monarchists of an authoritarian stamp on the right. Also included in this broad band of anti-Soviet discontent, however, were ex-allies of the Third Reich.[73] Indeed, American efforts to reconstitute *some* of the resources that the Nazis had established to counter the Russians during World War II were crucial to Operation Bloodstone, and for being the co-author and instigator of this strategy, Wisner has attracted the indignation of critics such as Christopher Simpson and John Loftus.[74]

Viewed from an entirely objective standpoint, however, the ADPC was not in a position to allow moral ambiguities to take precedence over the practicalities of launching a wide-ranging covert action programme. The OPC, it should be noted, began life in September 1948 with a staff of ten and under pressure from the Pentagon to become fully operational as quickly as possible.[75] In such circumstances, Wisner had to exploit whatever viable resources and expertise were available, including former German diplomats and military personnel with first-hand experience of fighting the Russians. To a greater or lesser extent, any German who had served, or non-German who had collaborated with, Hitler was tainted by naziism. What the OPC did was balance the degree to which the individuals it sought to recruit were tainted against the advantages their recruitment would bring in countering a Soviet Union which Wisner regarded as being as malevolent as the Nazis had been. The application of this axiom meant that few ex-Nazis had chequered enough pasts to be precluded from working for the OPC.[76] Indeed, the 1949 Central Intelligence Act permitted émigrés who were of use to the OPC, but who might not meet with American immigration requirements, to enter the United States at the rate of one hundred per year.[77]

The case of Gustav Hilger is instructive of the choices faced by the OPC. A one-time career diplomat, Hilger specialised in the recruitment of collaborators to fight alongside the Germans on the eastern front during the war. He had also been Foreign Office liaison to the SS and in this capacity had been party to the imprisonment and murder of Gypsies and Jews in Eastern Europe and Italy. For the OPC, however, the pluses outweighed the minuses and Hilger was employed to help organise underground émigré forces to be deployed in Eastern Europe and the Ukraine.[78] There was, moreover, the additional point that Washington knew little about its communist adversaries. The know-how of Hilger and other ex-Nazis and collaborators, such as Baron Otto von Bolschwing, the SS envoy to Romania, and Nikolai N. Poppe, an anti-Stalinist quisling and expert on Soviet South and Central Asia, could therefore be brought to bear in the analysis of Moscow's policy aims and of captured Russian records.[79]

Similar, though much more extensive, ambiguities characterised the OPC's relationship with the Gehlen organisation. The former *Fremde Heere Ost* (Foreign Armies East) intelligence division was widely believed to harbour ex-Nazis and this, it was feared, opened the way for some of Gehlen's colleagues to be compromised, which in turn provided a viable means through which the Soviet intelligence services could uncover the actvities of their western counterparts. There was, moreover, the danger that public exposure of the close connections that agencies of the United States maintained with these former Nazis would hand a huge propaganda victory to the USSR. Indeed, these concerns were raised quite frequently within CIG and CIA circles.[80]

However, the perceived advantages of working with the Gehlen Organisation overrode ethical considerations and concerns about security. In return for being granted a continuing role in the field of intelligence after the war had ended, Gehlen turned over to his American captors the extensive espionage network that he had built up during the hostilities. With access to the German general's files and control of the agents in his employ who had remained behind Russian lines when the Red Army advanced westward, the OPC and OSO inherited a substantial foundation on which they believed they could build. Gauged to be equally advantageous was Gehlen's reconstitution of the *Fremde Heere Ost* technical staff, which acted on behalf of the OPC, vetting, training, and evaluating recruits for inclusion in the underground paramilitary irredentist forces envisaged in Operation Bloodstone.[81]

*   *   *

All of the major studies of the OPC underline the futility of the offensive operations it conducted against the Soviet bloc, and viewed purely at face value, this certainly was the case.[82] Stalin was, for sure, a determined and ruthless adversary. His intelligence and security apparatus maintained tight control over all of the USSR's satellites and brought its long experience to bear in dealing with 'the nationalities problem'.[83] Deportations were commonplace in the Baltic States, Moldavia, and the Western Ukraine as part of the Russian drive to take away the foundations of support on which guerrilla movements relied.[84] Another tactic saw the Soviet intelligence services create 'false-flag' units, which posed as partisan militias and committed atrocities aimed at turning local populations against the very groups that were fighting for the freedom of these 'captive peoples'.[85]

The result was that the Eastern European partisan movements, such as the Forest Brothers in Lithuania and the Organisation of Ukrainian Nationalists (OUN), both of which had been strong in the immediate aftermath of World War II, had been either neutralised or seen their strength reduced significantly by 1949. The agent teams that the OPC and the other western intelligence agencies parachuted, or infiltrated by boat, into the denied areas thus arrived too late to make any meaningful impact.[86]

Equally debilitating was the fact that many of the operations that the OPC conducted, either on its own initiative or in conjunction with the SIS and/or the Gehlen organisation, were thoroughly penetrated by Soviet intelligence. At the highest level, Wisner and his colleagues were betrayed by Harold Adrian Russell (Kim) Philby, the MI6 liaison officer in Washington between 1949 and 1951. For its part, the Gehlen Organisation proved to be as vulnerable to Russian penetration as the more wary among America's intelligence professionals had warned, the most high profile case being that of Heinz Felfe. A senior Gehlen official who made the logical progression to the Bundesnachrichetndienst (BND) – the Federal German Intelligence Service – when it was founded in 1956, Felfe had served in the SS and was blackmailed by the NKVD/KGB into working as a double agent under threat of disclosure to the denazification court.[87] Further down the chain of command, Soviet intelligence had riddled the DP camps with spies, some of whom passed CIC and Gehlen organisation vetting procedures and were recruited by the OPC, only to compromise the operations in which they were involved.[88]

There was, as well, a tendency on the part of the OPC, and indeed MI6, to allow their determination to weaken the Soviet empire to run ahead of caution. The most conspicuous example of this trait, and of the dexterity that the Kremlin's security forces showed in exploiting such western weaknesses, came with the Anglo-American effort to support the Freedom and Independence Movement (WiN) in Poland. Beginning in 1950, this fiasco saw Russian military intelligence trick the OPC and SIS into revising their belief that anticommunist resistance in Poland had been wiped out by 1947, which was true, and supporting WiN.[89] For nearly two years WiN was supplied with money, radio transmitters, and ammunition from the western intelligence services until, in December 1951, Polish Radio broadcast details of the bogus nature of the organisation. Moscow was, in the process, presented with a huge propaganda triumph.[90]

Focusing on the failures of Wisner's organisation in Eastern Europe, however, detracts from the crucial point that the OPC's mission in this region was largely a preparatory one. The fundamental purpose of forging contacts with the resistance movements inside the communist bloc was to create the capability to attack the Red Army behind its own lines in the event of a Soviet invasion of Western Europe. The agent teams infiltrated behind the Iron Curtain had orders to contact and assist resistance groups but not to fight alongside the partisans with whom they made contact except in the event of war.[91] The fact that war did not break out makes it difficult to determine accurately how successful this strategy really was.

Wisner's organisation did, in fact, make some significant breakthroughs in Eastern Europe, as the OPC/DDP's funding and support for the Investigating Committee of Free Jurists demonstrates. Formed in 1948, this group of East German lawyers scored a number of victories in countering legal violations by the country's communist regime and its Soviet backers. The Free Jurists' Committee was, furthermore, held in high regard by the OPC for its potential as a 'force multiplier': an organisation that was widely acknowledged as an independent source of guidance for ordinary East Germans, and one that could provide enough detailed information on the East German and Soviet security structures to enable the OPC to 'turn' high-level communist officials and so advance Operation ENGROSS – a CIA defector programme that spanned the entire Soviet bloc.[92] The Free Jurist project ran into difficulties, however, as a consequence of decisions made by the OPC/DDP during 1952 and 1953 to involve the organisation in paramilitary activities. Diverted from its stated purpose, the Jurists' Committee became as vulnerable to attack from the Russian and East German security forces as other, less effective CIA-sponsored groups, such as the Kampfgruppe Gegen Unmenschlichkeit (Fighting Group Against Inhumanity).[93]

There were, then, limits on how much could be gained from covert action offensives and they tended to run into trouble when their objectives overshot their original parameters. Indeed, it was considerations of this kind that led the DDP to become more cautious in its approach to the 'captive nations' from 1953 onwards. From this juncture, greater emphasis came to be placed on the 'molecular theory', whereby paramilitary activities were watered down and stress was placed on the cultivation of more politically-oriented organisations, such as the Russian Narodnoy-Trudovoy Soyus (NTS). An initially hard-line group, NTS revised its strategy during the early fifties, using graffiti and other basic propaganda methods to goad the Soviet authorities and so act as a catalyst for the promotion of ever widening dissent which, the OPC/DDP hoped, would gradually gather momentum and ultimately bring down the Soviet edifice from within.[94]

Turning the 'molecular theory' into practice offered additional benefits, moreover, because it dovetailed with Wisner's overarching propaganda offensive. Envisaged as serving medium to long-term aims, this programme saw the OPC use high-level balloons to airdrop millions of leaflets behind the Iron Curtain and deploy radio broadcasting, firstly into Eastern Europe under the aegis of Radio Free Europe (RFE) from 1951, and later to the Soviet Union itself through Radio Liberty from 1953. Known collectively as 'the Mighty Wurlitzer', Wisner's radio networks were technically under the 'private' ownership of the National Committee for a Free Europe, but they received an estimated $30 to $35 million yearly from the CIA over the next two decades.[95]

*   *   *

RFE and similar radio-centred enterprises proved to be the most effective of all America's propaganda tools throughout the time that the OPC/DDP was active and indeed long afterwards. The Cold War was, however, fought at many different levels and Wisner's organisation also achieved tangible advances through a programme of clandestine cultural patronage that sought to promote and manipulate artists, composers, intellectuals, and writers on Western Europe's non-communist left in a broadly based, long-term effort to counter communist ideas.[96]

As was the case with many other covert enterprises initiated during this period, the OPC's cultural campaign was coordinated closely with that of its British counterpart, MI6's Information Research Department (IRD), and between 1950 and 1951 an International Organisations Division (IOD) was created within the CIA, under the control of Thomas Braden, to upgrade the cultural offensive in accordance with the requirements of NSC 68.[97] Pivotal to the OPC/IOD's plans was the Congress of Cultural Freedom (CCF), which served as the key organiser and conduit for a vast array of CIA-supported cultural projects, including: (1) the founding of *Der Monat*, *Preuves*, *Encounter* and some twenty other pro-western magazines; (2) the staging of art exhibitions and concerts; (3) the publication of over a thousand books, including Boris Pasternach's *Doctor Zhivago*; and (4) the production of several films, notably an animated version of George Orwell's celebrated novel, *Animal Farm*.[98] To ensure that a veneer of independence was maintained and that these cultural initiatives were fronted by credible sponsors, the OPC once again made full use of the public-private nexus, drawing on the support of the Ford, Rockefeller and Carnegie Foundations and establishing shell companies and organisations such as the Farfield Foundation, which, from 1952, served as the principal source through which CIA finance was funnelled to the CCF.[99]

Recent studies of the CIA's cultural mission are in broad agreement that many of those who received OPC largesse were aware of the connection, but the degree of control that Wisner and his colleagues were able to exercise remains a contentious issue. Frances Stonor Saunders depicts the agency as having exerted enough influence to persuade, and occasionally coerce, its front organisations to adopt positions that were in keeping with Washington's interests. Hugh Wilford, on the other hand, maintains that the OPC's cultural clients exercised considerable independence and that Wisner's capacity to call the tune was far more tenuous than Saunders suggests. [100]

What stands out as crucial to understanding the OPC/DDP's relationship with, and control over, its cultural beneficiaries, however, is the point that the CIA deliberately avoided supporting organisations and individuals who were publicly recognised as being overtly pro-American. Preferable candidates were, as has been mentioned, those on the centre-left, such as the British Fabians, who were opposed to Soviet totalitarianism and communism, but also had track records of criticising the United States when such criticisms were seen as justified. If the CIA objective was, in essence, the suasion of the ideologically uncommitted through the use of such credible, independent-minded actors who, on the surface, were unconnected with the American government, then the agency's efforts were best served if it *did not* exercise too much control. Indeed it did not need to exercise much control, since the aims and values of these organisations were, in the majority of cases, attuned to those adhered to by the CIA itself.

There were, nevertheless, exceptions and the most contentious and stupefying of these was the issue of McCarthyism. A sizeable proportion of those who were beneficiaries of the CCF were deeply disturbed by the Wisconsin senator, labelling his activities as 'know-nothingism'. The very nature of the cultural offensive ensured, however, that public criticisms of McCarthy were largely the preserve of high profile luminaries, such as the mathematician and philosopher Bertrand Russell, who were far less beholden to the CIA and/or MI6 than most CCF-affiliated commentators and artists.[101] As Wisner pointed out in a 1952 memorandum, the cultural committees were put together "for the purpose of providing cover and backstopping for the European effort", and much as the CIA's hierarchy despised McCarthy, it was seen as prudent to maintain a low profile. To have done otherwise would have risked sending "McCarthy's bloodhounds sniffing around the Agency's Non-Communist Left programme".[102]

Consequently, general coverage of the Wisconsin senator's activities tended to be rather muted, with *Encounter* and similar magazines playing what Saunders describes as the 'lesser evil' card, as advocated by Peregrine Worsthorne: the American God had its failings, not least among which was the rise of McCarthyism, but the communist God had, on close examination, turned out to be a devil.[103] Worsthorne has responded to Saunders's criticisms, describing her as having adopted a wrong-headed and at times censorious stance. CIA intervention in the cultural field, he argues, was necessary and justified given the gravity of the Soviet threat and the often insidious methods adopted by the USSR to justify its hold on Eastern Europe and spread its ideology around the world.[104] Valid as these points are, they do not alter the fact that, in their approach to McCarthyism, the CCF and many of its affiliates too often applied a double standard: they reneged on their stated aim of exposing infringements on artistic, intellectual and political freedom of expression when such curtailments applied to domestic anticommunism in the United States. For its part, the CIA continued unabated with its cultural projects until the entire enterprise was exposed in a series of articles that were published during the 1960s and culminated in the *Ramparts* revelations of 1967.[105]

The OPC/DDP, then, played a largely unseen but, at times, influential role in the economic, political and cultural life of Europe during the early Cold War years, drawing on the support of a diverse range of associates and conduits in the process. Europe was not, however, the only arena in which Wisner and his colleagues plied their arcane trade, for the OPC/DDP also became increasingly proactive in determining outcomes in the Far East between 1949 and 1953.

The Far Eastern Dimension

Though OPC offensive covert action anticipated NSC 68, the authorisation of this directive and the outbreak of the Korean War provided the impetus for the enormous growth of Wisner's organisation that was to take place over the next two years.[106] Most significantly, Pyong Yang's attack on its southern neighbour led the State Department and the JCS to call on the OPC to initiate paramilitary and psychological warfare operations against North Korea and China. Wisner was, as a result, afforded the opportunity to override the objections of General Douglas MacArthur, the commander of American forces in the Far East, who had previously forbidden the CIA or anything connected with it from operating in his theatre.[107]

What should be stressed, however, is that the capacity of the OPC/DDP to carry out its mission in East Asia continued to be impeded by the military.[108] Ignoring Washington's stipulation that responsibility for covert action was the sole preserve of the CIA, MacArthur ordered his Far East Command Intelligence Directorate (FEC-G2) to build a covert warfare capability from scratch and engage in a wide range of clandestine operations in support of the UN war effort.[109] CIA unconventional warfare programmes thus came second in volume, magnitude and complexity to those conducted by the FEC, and relations between the two organisations were fractious throughout the war.[110]

Nevertheless, OPC functional parameters grew at an unprecedented rate, particularly after the front in Korea stabilised in mid 1951 and the authorisation of NSC 10/5 – which superseded NSC 10/2 – provided for a widening of CIA clandestine activities.[111] Expansion in the Far East, moreover, had a knock-on effect, for it led other regional divisions in the agency's operations directorate to press for comparable increases, and the widespread western perception that Korea was a decoy for a more significant communist offensive elsewhere ensured that these arguments did not fall on deaf ears. The fact that Congress was willing to authorise $100 million for stay-behind units in the event of war breaking out in Europe is evidence of this.[112] Indeed, the *Church Report* estimated that by 1952 there were approximately forty different covert action projects under development in Central Europe alone.[113]

Statistics aside, the OPC's track record in the Far East closely resembled the European pattern. Defensive covert action programmes generally proved successful, as the counterinsurgency campaign mounted under the direction of Edward G. Lansdale – an Air Force colonel contracted to the CIA's operations directorate – against the Hukbalahap guerrillas (Huks) in the Philippines between 1950 and 1954, demonstrates.[114] Conditions in the Philippines were, however, more favourable than in many of the host countries in which the agency operated, not least because it had been a colony of the United States until 1946.[115] Moreover, though many of the Huks were communists, the uprising itself derived from the inequitable distribution of land on the Luzon Plain, from where the bulk of the guerrillas came. The problem was therefore far more parochial than the Manila government's depiction of it as a Soviet-orchestrated, ideologically-driven insurgency – and the CIA well understood this.[116]

Consequently, Lansdale's task was primarily a political one: to cut back Huk strength by fostering agrarian and democratic reform, thereby diminishing the grievances on which the insurgents thrived, while simultaneously using military means to bring about a slow ebbing away of Huk strength. This policy required the use of psychological warfare, political action, and paramilitary stratagems for its fulfilment, and it had succeeded in breaking the back of the insurgency by 1954.[117]

If defensive covert action proved instrumental in defeating a localised communist-dominated challenge in the Philippines, then the offensive operations mounted by the OPC in Asia proved to be ill-conceived and, save for a few endeavours launched in direct support of the Korean War effort, served only to frustrate American designs. Domestic and foreign policy considerations dictated that "Truman had to do something about the Red Chinese but not something so draconian that it would drag the United States into a world war", and covert action seemed to provide "a measured response" in light of these imperatives. Under the direction of Desmond Fitzgerald, OPC/DDP objectives in the Far East were therefore threefold: (1) to support the American effort on the Korean peninsula itself; (2) to organise incursions onto the Chinese mainland in the hope that such moves would divert People's Liberation Army (PLA) divisions away from the Korean theatre; and (3) to test the extent of Beijing's control over its outer provinces.[118]

The corollary was that much of the OPC/DDP's East Asia programme was diversionary in nature, the aim being to identify and recruit existing anticommunist strength, often through the CIA front company Western Enterprises Incorporated (WEI), and deploy these guerrilla forces around the periphery of Red China. In line with these prescriptions, a force of Chiang Kai-shek loyalists in the employ of WEI launched a series of boat incursions against the southeast coast of China from some fifty or so nationalist-controlled offshore islands between 1951 and 1954.[119] Much further to the West of the PRC, Beijing's resolve was again tested in a campaign that saw CAT pilots supplying the Turkic speaking Hui horsemen of the Tsinghai region west of Lake Kokonar, in a conflict that spanned the Korean War, continued until the mid 1950s, and was fought in an area larger than Japan.[120] Similar diversionary objectives applied in Fitzgerald's deployment of a Nationalist Chinese force of several thousand men, which, under General Li Mi, escaped to Burma in 1949 and mounted a series of incursions into Yunan province on China's southern flank between 1950 and 1954.[121]

Other operations mounted during the same period were conceived as having a direct bearing on the Korean theatre itself. Notable among these was a major and potentially decisive CIA offensive that involved the infiltration of over a thousand Nationalist Chinese agents into North Korea and Manchuria. Code-named Operation TROPIC, this venture was, again, heavily dependent on CAT air support and aimed at building guerrilla networks from scratch, mobilising existing resistance to Mao Zedong in China, and complementing the UN effort in Korea.[122]

Though some of these operations achieved limited degrees of success, notably the boat sorties on the South China coast, their impact was negligible and, overall, the OPC/DDP's offensives in the Far East failed to pass muster. Several factors are crucial in explaining this, but at core the assumptions that informed the design of enterprises such as Operation TROPIC were entirely inaccurate: that Mao's grip on power was weaker than was actually the case and that resistance to his rule was greater than proved to be true. For example, Fitzgerald believed, at least in the initial stages of the China campaigns, that American support would serve as the touch-paper for half a million anticommunist guerrillas on the Chinese mainland – a so-called "Third Force" – to rise up against Beijing. The OSO assured him that no such force existed, but he carried on regardless. The second major drawback was that the OPC campaigns on mainland China were as thoroughly penetrated as those mounted in Eastern Europe. As such, Mao was forewarned and forearmed.[123]

Whether resistance on the scale that Fitzgerald originally anticipated would have surfaced in the event of a third world war involving the PRC is, as with the case of the underground movements of Eastern Europe, a matter of conjecture. What can be said with certainty is that the spread of the Cold War to the Far East, like the advent of the OPC, served as a key dynamic in the evolution of the CIA in general and its covert action mission in particular between 1948 and 1953. There is, however, a third and vital element to be taken into account in gauging the agency's development during this formative period: the personality and professional status of General Walter Bedell Smith, who succeeded Hillenkoetter in October 1950 and served as DCI until February 1953.[124]

The Bedell Smith Reforms

The events leading up to Bedell Smith becoming DCI began in July 1949, when Truman opted to reorganise the CIA according to the recommendations of the Dulles-Jackson-Corea report – as NSC 50 – and appoint a new DCI to ring in the changes.[125] However, it took a year of deliberations, a presidential order and an appeal to duty on the part of Truman himself before an initially reluctant Smith was finally prompted into accepting the appointment. Limited as his knowledge of the intelligence community was, the general's high rank, organisational prowess, and right-wing anticommunist credentials – which had sharpened during his period as ambassador to Moscow between 1946 and 1949 – made him an ideal choice to head up the agency at this juncture.[126] Logic had it that, with McCarthyism on the rise, a DCI who was widely known to hold hard-line views would provide a buffer for protecting the allegedly liberal CIA in the event of a challenge from the Wisconsin senator. McCarthy had indicated that after scrutinising the State Department he would focus his attention on the CIA, and his efforts were fuelled by J. Edgar Hoover who, after the FBI's loss of jurisdiction over intelligence activities in Latin America to the CIA in 1947, engaged in what was essentially interdepartmental rivalry behind an anticommunist veil.[127]

On becoming DCI, Smith found "the kind of vacuum he liked to fill", and set about satisfying what he described as the nation's need for "an effective *intelligence* organisation".[128] Indeed, he was to consistently express concerns throughout his tenure that the agency's growing preoccupation with covert action was diverting attention away from what he saw as its principal mission of intelligence collection.[129] The continuing war in Korea, however, made certain that the DCI's efforts to limit the CIA's covert operational commitments were frustrated.

From the moment that he took control, Smith recognised that the anomalous relationship that existed between the CIA and its covert action branch should be terminated. An arrangement that found the DCI with no management authority over the OPC, in spite of the fact that its budget and personnel were allocated through the agency, was as unacceptable to Smith as it had been to his predecessor. The new DCI succeeded where Hillenkoetter had failed, however, and in October 1950 representatives of State, Defense, and the JCS formally accepted that the DCI would henceforth assume control of the OPC.[130] Another hitherto intractable problem that demanded Smith's immediate attention was bureaucratic in-fighting between the State Department, the military services and the CIA. This was in fact hampering the entire American covert warfare effort and to counter it Smith once again drew on his rank and forceful temperament to persuade the NSC to establish the Psychological Strategy Board (PSB) in April 1951.[131]

Conceived as "a command post [rather] than an information center", the PSB was an autonomous organisation. Its director, Gordon Gray and his successor C.D. Jackson were independent appointees selected by the president, and the organisation itself was tasked with providing a centralised planning apparatus that would ensure the activities of all the departments involved in America's political warfare campaign were coordinated and conformed to overarching policy objectives.[132] This was never achieved, for throughout the PSB's existence, from 1951 to 1953, both Gray and Jackson were impeded by a State Department that was determined to maintain exclusive control over all aspects of foreign policy.[133] The Psychological Strategy Board strengthened Smith's position, however, because it provided some measure of guidance as to what was and what was not permissible in the field of covert action. Most significantly, it served as an instrument for either sanctioning or vetoing newly proposed operations, or for abandoning less-than-fruitful existing ventures through what were termed murder boards.[134]

Despite the existence of such provisions, the DCI remained cautious about testing the limits of his authority. Fearing that the more audacious covert action plans that came to him for approval would, if exposed, seriously jeopardise his own and the country's standing, Smith sought Truman's advice as to how to proceed. No such reticence was displayed in the president's response, however, for he held to the view that a broad scope of clandestine activity was fully justified, given the nature of the communist challenge, and granted Smith a blanket pardon to allay any further apprehensions he might have in carrying out his duty.[135] The president's willingness to take such an unprecedented step demonstrated that he held Smith in high regard. Truman had, after all, "personally selected Smith to be DCI, had personally overcome Smith's reluctance to accept that office, and probably felt a corresponding personal obligation to Smith for having done so".[136]

It was, however, the general's professional aptitude that stood out as the most crucial consideration in commending him to the White House. Immediately on becoming DCI, Smith initiated a fundamental restructuring of the CIA's intelligence mission that led to the creation of the Deputy Directorate for Intelligence (DDI) in January 1952. This was essentially one in a triumvirate of components which also included the Deputy Directorate for Administration (DDA), through which Smith sought to tighten up the internal management of the agency (see appendix 4).

The third pillar on which the revised CIA rested was the Deputy Directorate for Plans. Born partly out of a desire on Smith's part to streamline the agency's operations mission, the creation of the DDP owed more to his determination to resolve the persisting friction that had impeded relations between the OSO and the OPC from the time that the latter group was formed.[137] In brief, resentment over salary differentials and an unwillingness to cooperate in areas where OSO and OPC interests overlapped ensured that a permanent gulf remained between the professionals of intelligence collection on the one hand, and the elitist "Park Avenue cowboys" recruited by Wisner from the Ivy League on the other.[138] A solution that met with approval in the higher echelons of the agency was Allen Dulles's proposal for the merger of the two groups. For his part, Bedell Smith entertained hopes of shedding the mission of covert subversion altogether and he therefore resisted the merger plan throughout much of 1951. The appointment of Dulles, an influential enthusiast of covert action, to Deputy Director of Central Intelligence (DDCI) in late August 1951, however, signalled the general's realisation that such hopes could not be fulfilled and from this point a transitional period of "benign co-ordination" began which paved the way to the establishment of the DDP in August 1952.[139]

The extent to which the covert action mission had come to dominate the CIA by this time was readily apparent in the personnel changes that came about with the birth of the DDP. Wisner became Deputy Director of Plans, which meant that two of the three top positions in the agency were filled by strong proponents of covert action. Though Richard Helms, from the OSO, was appointed as Wisner's second in command, to strike a balance at senior level, it was the operatives who had hitherto answered exclusively to the OPC that were to benefit most from the merger, and tension continued between the agency's two formerly independent operational components.[140]

Conclusion

The 1948 to 1953 period saw the largest and most comprehensive expansion of CIA covert action in the agency's history. Against a backdrop of intensifying international turmoil, and under the control of as anomalous an organisation as Washington has ever created, CIA clandestine operations became a key means through which the United States sought to undermine its communist adversaries. In the sphere of defensive covert action, the agency built on the precedent it had set during the Italian elections, mounting successful projects throughout Western Europe and chalking up its first major victory in Asia, with the defeat of Hukbalahap insurgency in the Philippines. Equally significant was the authorisation of offensive covert action, which quickly became a favoured weapon of engagement for a Truman administration that sought to contain communism effectively while simultaneously adopting as coercive an approach as was possible in the struggle against the USSR, the PRC and their allies.

In rising to the challenge of penetrating the Iron and Bamboo Curtains, the OPC met with few documented victories, but to dismiss its efforts altogether is to overlook the fact that much of what it attempted was done in preparation for a third world war that thankfully never happened. Indeed, there was a strong preparatory dimension to the entire OPC project, for its mushrooming manpower and burgeoning budgets enabled Wisner to create a worldwide network of CIA-owned banks, private businesses, and front organisations that proved indispensable to the successful prosecution of agency projects for the next thirty years. In respect of its operational parameters, the OPC was permitted enormous scope, but encountered severe setbacks in carrying out its mission in the 'denied areas'. Nowhere was this more pronounced than in the four year offensive that Wisner and his colleagues mounted against communist Albania.

4

OPC INTERVENTION IN ALBANIA: AN EXPERIMENT IN OFFENSIVE COVERT ACTION

Between 1949 and 1953, the OPC/DDP conducted a covert operation, initially in partnership with MI6 but from 1952 as an exclusively American enterprise, to bring about the downfall of the Soviet-controlled communist regime, which, under Enver Hoxha, had ruled Albania since the end of World War II. Code-named BGFIEND and envisaged as "a clinical experiment to see whether larger rollback operations would be feasible elsewhere", the Albanian project was *the* archetypal offensive covert action campaign, in that it marked the first and only western attempt to unseat a communist regime that lay within the Soviet orbit.[1] That the venture was also an unqualified failure that "proceeded resolutely from one disaster to another", is nowhere contested.[2] What remains open to question is why this should have been the case.

Most treatments of BGFIEND attribute varying degrees of blame for the debacle to Kim Philby, who as MI6 liaison officer in Washington played an instrumental role in coordinating and managing the British dimension of the operation. Philby was, of course, a Soviet agent who, by his own admission, betrayed the venture until he was uncovered by the CIA in mid 1951.[3] His treachery goes only part of the way towards explaining the failure, however, for BGFIEND was also retarded by: (1) the tendency of the western intelligence agencies to overestimate their own abilities and underestimate their enemies; (2) the ill-advised decision to select an Axis-tainted group to front the operation's political wing; and (3) the OPC's and MI6's failure to maintain tight enough security in their recruitment of Albanian exiles from the DP camps, where leaks were commonplace and Soviet spies were known to be active. Not only did these flaws compromise the Albania campaign, they were a replication of the wider drawbacks that rendered CIA offensive covert action ineffective in the Soviet bloc generally during the 1948 to 1956 period. BGFIEND was, then, unique for what it sought to achieve but at the same time typical in that it was impaired by similar drawbacks to those that hampered CIA offensive operations elsewhere in Eastern Europe.

Above all other considerations, however, the Albania campaign proved that clandestine paramilitary methods were not, in themselves, enough to secure the overthrow of even the weakest of Soviet satellites.

Albania and the Balkans: The View from Washington

The Truman administration's decision to make the Hoxha regime a target of the OPC was influenced by both offensive and defensive considerations. The most backward of the Kremlin's satellites, Albania was separated geographically from the Soviet bloc following Tito's expulsion from the Cominform in 1948. Washington reasoned that this opened the way for the possible rollback of a country that, prior to Moscow's rift with Belgrade, had been regarded as "little more than a Yugoslav republic".[4] Cut off from its allies, Albania was also diplomatically isolated. It was neither a signatory to the Balkan Peace Treaties, which meant that it was still technically at war with Greece, nor was it a member of the United Nations. Indeed, Tirana was in conflict with the UN following Albania's refusal, in April 1949, to comply with an International Court of Justice ruling requiring it to pay compensation to the United Kingdom for illegally mining the Corfu Straits and damaging two British destroyers in the process.[5]

Russian concerns vis-à-vis the Hoxha regime were a mirror of American ambitions. If only for reasons of prestige, Moscow could not afford to allow a further satellite defection. Weak though Albania was, moreover, it was of considerable strategic value to the Soviet Union: for flanking operations against the Yugoslavs; for supplying the Italian communists; and, before Stalin withdrew his support from the communist insurgency in Greece, as a base for the KKE.[6] The Kremlin had, in addition, began with the construction of a submarine base on the island of Saseno at the entrance of Valona Bay by 1948, and this was seen by the United States as posing a major long-term threat to western interests in the Adriatic and the Mediterranean.[7]

Acutely aware of the extent to which the Hoxha regime was vulnerable to a western or Yugoslav takeover, Moscow enforced a control over Albania that was regarded by Washington as being "the most open and direct of any in the Soviet orbit".[8] Russian advisors organised and held key positions in Hoxha's military and security forces, while the Albanian Communist Party (ACP) was routinely purged of potential dissidents, and "all members of the government [were kept] under continual surveillance".[9] Comprehensive as these measures were, they created conditions that the OPC could exploit, for they induced fear and resentment of the Soviet Union rather than loyalty to it. This was pointed out in a State Department paper, which estimated that opposition to Hoxha and his Soviet patrons was so pronounced that it "included almost everyone not directly involved in the regime".[10]

Washington's belief that Albania represented the most viable target for rolling back Soviet power was given further impetus in October 1949, the month that the first OPC/MI6-directed infiltration of the country was launched, when Hillenkoetter reported that the Kremlin was reconsidering its position towards the Hoxha regime as part of a major revision of Moscow's overall Balkan strategy. The Soviet Foreign Office feared that continuing Albanian support for the KKE might lead to an international crisis "which the U.S.S.R. is now unwilling to face". Russia's aim was, rather, to "ease tensions among Athens, Belgrade, and Tirana", and in line with this policy the Soviet Foreign Office was recommending "a withdrawal from the Adriatic to Bulgaria".[11]

Taken together with the fact that Hoxha's country was already unique amongst the Soviet bloc nations, in that Moscow had never signed a Mutual Security Pact with Albania nor admitted it into the Cominform, these developments invited outside intervention.[12] Geopolitical realities dictated, moreover, that it was safer for the United States and its allies to attempt to dislodge Albania from the Soviet orbit than any of the other Eastern European satellites, simply because it was not part of Moscow's defensive buffer zone.[13] Thus, while its removal would damage Russian prestige, it would make little difference to the security of the Soviet Union itself.

Wider regional considerations also informed the decision to move against Albania. American plans for Southeastern Europe and the Balkans hinged on bringing Italy, Yugoslavia, and Greece together "in a common front against the Soviet bloc".[14] The establishment of an anti-Cominform bulwark of this kind was not only envisaged as strengthening containment, it also opened the way for the United States to mount offensive covert moves against the underbelly of Moscow's Eastern European defence perimeter. As John C. Campbell, who served as the State Department's Assistant Chief of Division for Southeast European Affairs during the late 1940s and early 1950s, maintained, the United States ran operations that focused on "trying to stir up opposition and [giving] support to potential opposition" in Bulgaria, Hungary, and "elsewhere" in the region, as well as in Albania, during this period.[15]

Detail on these ventures is sparse, but Campbell describes them as being aimed at "causing trouble for" rather than rolling back the enemy.[16] What can be said is that such enterprises approximated the objectives that American allies were pursuing or would like to have seen pursued. "A Pan-Danubian Federation" consisting of the former countries of the Austro-Hungarian empire was, for example, the Vatican's prescription for combating communism in the Balkans. How much the church actually did to create such an organisation is a matter of speculation, but certainly the CIC took account of the plan, and the OPC is alleged to have recruited Vatican-backed Croatian Ustase veterans, who fought with the Germans during the war, to take part in Operation Bloodstone.[17]

The Yugoslavs also had an interest in sowing discord within the borders of their Russian-dominated neighbours. During 1948 and 1949, Moscow conducted a "war of nerves" with Belgrade, positioning between five and nine divisions around the Yugoslav periphery. Tito responded by sponsoring guerrilla action in Albania and especially Bulgaria, as well as exploiting tensions between 'nationalist' and 'internationalist' communists that first came to light in the Soviet bloc when Belgrade was expelled from the Cominform.[18]

The deployment of OPC covert action against Hoxha was seen as complementing these initiatives as well as serving American policy in the Balkans. BGFIEND would, if successful, rid Yugoslavia of a troublesome adversary without forcing Belgrade to take overt action and run the risk of coming into direct conflict with Moscow. Tito had, in fact, attempted to engineer a coup against the Tirana government between 1948 and 1949, only to see his plans thwarted when Koci Xoxe, the pro-Yugoslav Albanian Interior Minister who Belgrade favoured as Hoxha's successor, was purged in June 1949. After this point, Tito's options were limited, which made him more amenable to working in concert with the United States.[19] Indeed, Albanian writers have alleged that, as was the case with the Greeks and the Italians, the Yugoslavs actively supported BGFIEND.[20] Though the evidence is far from conclusive on this count, such cooperation would have been consistent with the rapprochement that took place between Washington and Belgrade at this time. It would, furthermore, have served as a *quid pro quo*, given that the OPC arranged for the secret dispatch of five shiploads of American arms to Yugoslavia, thereby strengthening Tito's position without providing Stalin with the justification to march on Belgrade.[21]

The principal assumption informing the Truman administration's decision to seek Hoxha's ouster was, however, that success in such an endeavour would, following on from the Yugoslav schism, further undermine the image of Soviet omnipotence in Eastern Europe. The most desirable outcome envisaged by Washington as resulting from the successful execution of BGFIEND was the immediate entry of a democratic, independent Albania into the western fold, with a communist Albania closely allied to Yugoslavia as the next best option.[22] The crucial point is that, either way, Russian influence in Tirana would have been eradicated and this was viewed as serving as a catalyst for bringing about further fissures in the Soviet bloc.

At the same time, an Albania free from Russian control was not without its problems. Prime among these was the fact that both Yugoslavia and Greece coveted large areas of Hoxha's territory. This ran against western interests since it opened the way for the possible partition of Albania and a heightening of tensions between Athens and Belgrade, which Moscow could exploit. The United States believed, however, that incentives and inducements could be applied by the western powers to ensure that, if the need arose, Yugoslavia and Greece could be made to respect the territorial integrity of Albania.[23] Cold War imperatives took precedence over the intricacies of Balkan politics, then, as the United States, in partnership with Great Britain, sought to bring about Hoxha's overthrow.

BGFIEND: Organisation and Preparations

Operation BGFIEND began as a British enterprise. Sanctioned by Whitehall in February 1949, it was aimed at displacing Hoxha with the exiled Albanian King Zog, thereby enhancing Britain's position as a political force in the Eastern Mediterranean. What stood between London and the fulfilment of these aims was money, or more accurately the lack of it. It was with these considerations in mind that MI6 and the British Foreign Office lobbied CIA and State Department officials to secure American financial backing for the project. Recognising that the Albania proposals presented an opportunity to both deliver a blow against Moscow and learn from an SIS that was renowned for its expertise in the field of covert action, the OPC persuaded its political masters to second the British plan in April 1949, which from this point became a joint MI6-OPC venture.[24]

An Anglo-American Special Policy Committee consisting of the OPC's Frank Lindsay, Robert Joyce of the PPS, Earl Jellicoe of the British Foreign Office, and the SIS liaison officer in Washington, Kim Philby, was subsequently appointed to manage the enterprise from the American capital.[25] James McCargar served as the OPC's senior coordinator for the project, but the picture becomes unclear as far as who played what role further down the chain of command, at least on the American side. The confusion arises largely as a consequence of Wisner's deployment of the New York law firm model in his management of early OPC operations, whereby several people were appointed to the same project in order to foster competition and originality, and thus achieve optimum results. Effective as this might have been in the practice of law, it did not, according to McCargar, transfer well to the field of covert action.[26]

For BGFIEND to have any prospect of success, it needed to have the appearance of being an indigenous affair, and this presented the project's managers with a basic question that would pose recurring difficulties for the CIA in mounting covert operations throughout the 1950s and early 1960s: the problem of who the OPC and MI6 should select to front the operation and replace the targeted regime should it be overthrown. In this respect, a large and various array of candidates presented themselves. The OSS had identified 55 different groups as being active in Albania under some hundred different leaders at the end of World War II. It was, therefore, only after much political manoeuvring, that the rightward-leaning Balli Kombëtar (National Front) was chosen to front the operation's political wing. The National Committee for a Free Albania was, however, far from a perfect construct for Anglo-American requirements, not least because the majority of Balli Kombëtar's leaders were tainted as a result of their involvement in the administration of Albania while it was under Axis control.[27] Indeed, the French intelligence services, which were mounting their own operations against Hoxha as part of the so-called MINOS project and were generally supportive of Anglo-American objectives in Albania, refused to take part in the launch of the Free Albania Committee because they regarded it as an "unrepresentative fabrication".[28]

In terms of operational dichotomy, BGFIEND – or Operation Valuable as it was tagged by its British contingent – envisaged MI6 as mounting boat incursions along Albania's southern coast and overland missions from Greece. For its part, the OPC was to operate in northern and central Albania, its favoured means of infiltration being through parachute drops from planes flown by British-contracted Polish pilots.[29] The overall enterprise was projected as becoming operational in November 1949, and in preparation the OPC and MI6 recruited thirty Albanians from the DP camps. Labelled 'pixies' by the British Special Operations Executive (SOE) and American OSS veterans who trained them, these would-be insurgents were readied for action at Fort Bin Jema, a formerly disused castle near the town of Mdina on the British-controlled island of Malta. Additional logistical support was provided through an American base at Whelus Field in Libya. Finally, an OPC-SIS monitoring station was established at a rented villa in Corfu and a private schooner, the *Stormie Seas*, was chartered to put the insurgents ashore for the first operation, which was launched a month ahead of schedule.[30]

Robin Winks suggests that in giving BGFIEND the final go-ahead, Wisner and his OPC and SIS colleagues were possessed of a naïveté that led them to allow enthusiasm to override caution.[31] While there is some substance to this argument, it is not wholly accurate. As Evan Thomas, drawing from the CIA's in-house histories, maintains, Wisner was "not completely unrealistic about the chances of success" in seeking to roll back Russian power anywhere in Eastern Europe. Records at the Truman Library reveal, furthermore, that the CIA knew that the Soviet hold on Albania was tight and that the prospects for a successful covert operation were at best limited, despite the fact that there was considerable opposition to the Hoxha regime in the country. The point is that the OPC saw itself as being under an obligation to probe behind the Iron Curtain, and Albania presented the most promising target for driving a wedge in the Soviet bloc.[32]

Where the judgement of BGFIEND's planners was seriously flawed was in their failure to recognise the fact that little in the way of a sense of national identity existed in Albania. The country was essentially a collection of tribes. In some respects this had worked to Anglo-American advantage. The SOE and OSS had been able to secure the support of the northern Catholic tribes during World War II.[33] Moreover, considerable resistance to the Hoxha regime emanated from this region, as is evident from the fact that Tito was able to initiate an insurrection with the help of the northern Hoti and Shala tribes in 1948.[34] Dissent from this quarter was, however, partial and Hoxha was reportedly able to keep at least some of the tribes happy by offering bribes of daily supplies of alcohol. This lack of patriotism greatly diminished the prospect of mobilising nationwide support for the exile movement and opposition to Hoxha, both of which were necessary if BGFIEND was to succeed.[35] That the OPC and MI6 were not sufficiently well informed of conditions on the ground in Albania is also evident from the tactics that they used. Some of the insurgents that were infiltrated into the country were, for example, given anticommunist propaganda leaflets to distribute, but such moves were of questionable value since 80 per cent of the Albanian populace was illiterate. Wisner's launch of the short-lived Radio Free Albania proved equally futile, given that the country had little in the way of electricity and very few radio sets or batteries.[36]

Targeted on a tightly controlled Soviet satellite and compromised by a traitor at the heart of MI6, then, BGFIEND was also doomed to failure by ill-conceived planning and the primitive nature of the host country. However, it took four years before these and other drawbacks inherent in the plan registered fully. If any serious doubts were raised about the viability of BGFIEND as the OPC embarked on the venture in 1949, then Wisner certainly did not allow them to puncture his optimism.

BGFIEND: The Action Phases: From the Karaburun Mission to the Purges of 1954

The first of the covert operations to be mounted against communist Albania began on 3 October 1949, when two groups of insurgents were infiltrated from the *Stormie Seas* onto the Karaburun peninsula.[37] The specific aims of this venture remain unclear, but the fact that it marked the initial move against Hoxha, and that the target area was the hub of Soviet maritime activity in the Adriatic, point to its having been conceived primarily as an exploratory, intelligence-gathering mission. If this was the case then the operation was not the failure that it is depicted as having been in some treatments of the Albania campaign. A CIA intelligence estimate from December 1949, which detailed recent Russian naval developments in "the rocky Karaburun peninsula and Saseno Island, which guards the entrance to Valona harbor", supports this argument. Evan Thomas's contention that "useful information" was procured as a result of the operation likewise challenges earlier arguments that characterise the project as having "accomplished nothing".[38]

At the same time, the Karaburun landings could in no way be interpreted as having been an unqualified success. To begin with, as an almost exclusively British enterprise it was extremely vulnerable to betrayal by Philby, and indeed Albanian security forces scoured the region in anticipation of the landings. The Hoxha regime, nevertheless, enjoyed only limited success in its efforts to intercept MI6's 'pixies'. Estimates vary as to how many men took part in the Karaburun mission. Thomas's figures of 20 insurgents being landed, with a loss rate of 20 per cent are at odds with other studies, which number nine infiltrators as having been dispatched. Of these, four are said to have evaded Hoxha's security cordon to distribute propaganda leaflets in the town of Nivica before escaping to safety; three were killed; one was captured; and one disappeared.[39] Whichever account is accurate, the key point is that all imply that the information relayed to Tirana was general rather than specific. This in turn raises doubts about the extent to which Philby compromised the operation, if he compromised it at all, given that, as co-commander of the project he would have had unfettered access to the logistical details of the mission.

Certainly, the capacity for OPC-MI6 plans to fall into enemy hands was considerable without any treachery on the part of Philby. The Albanian community in Rome, from where the recruits for the Karaburun landings came, was full of leaks and sprinkled with Soviet agents. The insurgents had, furthermore, been permitted to socialise freely in Mdina and the surrounding Maltese towns prior to the operation. The possibility therefore existed for BGFIEND to have been betrayed through two sources quite separate from Philby, which goes some of the way towards explaining why the MI6 liaison officer succeeded in betraying the Albania campaign for as long as he did: put simply, suspicion fell elsewhere.[40]

Leaving aside the issue of treachery, the first mission suffered enough in the way of logistical drawbacks to ensure a negative outcome. To begin with, the operation was marred by a shortage of radio transmitters and this was compounded by the failure of the OPC and MI6 to provide the insurgents with training in the use of Morse code. Radio communication was therefore maintained over open channels and so was not difficult to break, and the rudimentary codes that were used by the 'pixies' made interception even easier.[41] Not only this, but the OPC *knew* that BGFIEND was compromised, because Angleton, who as an OSO officer was not informed officially of its existence, discovered the details of the operation from one of his Italian contacts and told McCargar.[42] The clear implication, therefore, was that if Angleton knew, then Hoxha might know too. This information was, however, relayed after the *Stormie Seas* had set sail. The OPC and MI6 were thus unable to act quickly enough to cancel the Karaburun mission, the outcome of which left the SIS discouraged but Wisner, who regarded 20 per cent losses as acceptable, determined to continue.[43]

The aftermath of the Karaburun operation brought several changes in the organisation of BGFIEND. Firstly, the OPC began to play a more prominent role from this point onwards, in a trend that was to continue until, by 1952, the Albanian operation was almost entirely an American project. Karaburun, moreover, alerted its Anglo-American architects to the need for greater security. Thus, training for the 250 émigrés who, under the name of Company 4000, were recruited for the subsequent stages of BGFIEND, was conducted at a base near Heidelberg in Germany, where precautions against leakage were much tighter than had been the case in Mdina.[44] These organisational revisions were accompanied by a major personnel change when, in April 1950, McCargar was replaced as OPC coordinator, in a move that came about more as a consequence of his dissatisfaction with political rather than paramilitary developments in the Albania programme.[45]

Though Balli Kombëtar had never been an entirely satisfactory entity for serving Anglo-American requirements, it did at least have the merit of being led by "the distinguished writer, scholar, and former diplomat" Midhat Frasheri, who, despite having been a wartime collaborator, was deemed to be of an acceptable enough pedigree to lead the Albanian National Committee.[46] Problems arose, however, when Frasheri died suddenly in the Lexington Hotel in New York City on the very day that the *Stormie Seas* was dispatching 'pixies' onto the Karaburun peninsula. Whether the Albanian politician's untimely demise was the result of foul play or natural causes is still unclear. The coroner opted for the latter, but Frasheri was at risk from Hoxha's agents, who, so Frasheri claimed, were active amongst the Albanian community in the United States, and from rivals within the émigré movement itself, some of whom were in New York City at that time for the very reason of discussing the organisation of the National Committee.[47]

What caused McCargar's exit was the selection of Hasan Dosti as Frasheri's replacement. Dosti was Albania's Minister of Justice during the Axis occupation of the country and was severely tainted, as were the individuals he sought to promote within the National Committee. For McCargar, the appointment of fascist stooges of this calibre took away any appeal that BGFIEND's political wing might have had, and without the existence of a feasible political alternative to Hoxha the Albanian operation was, regardless of the effectiveness or ineffectiveness of its paramilitary element, severely impaired.[48] The onset of the Korean War, however, heightened Washington's determination to wrest another satellite from Moscow's control and Albania remained the most viable target. Operations were thus intensified over the following year under the command of McCargar's successor, Gratian Yatsevich, an American Army colonel who had extensive experience of working in the Balkans, most recently in Bulgaria.[49]

Despite the personnel changes and an increase in resources allocated to BGFIEND/Valuable, the campaign continued to falter. Two British overland infiltrations mounted in June and September 1950 resulted in failure, partly through lack of cooperation on the part of the Greek authorities. Equally fruitless were MI6's boat incursions launched in November of that year, which were aimed at making contact with Gani Kryeziu, an anticommunist northern tribal chieftain, but which likewise resulted in the death or capture of most of the Company 4000 volunteers who took part in the venture.[50]

It was at around this time that an American airborne campaign that focused on Albania began to kick into full gear, but the results of these efforts conformed to the same pattern that characterised the British operations. For example, an OPC propaganda programme that was initiated during the late summer of 1950 and depended on the dropping of leaflets from high altitude balloons proved to be of little avail, not least because several of the drops were misdirected and landed in Bulgaria, Yugoslavia and the sea rather that on the intended target areas.[51] One failure stacked on top of another when, in November 1950, a contingent of nine Company 4000 volunteers, who, astonishingly, had not been given any parachute training, were dropped into Albania only to be intercepted on entry to the country.[52]

Amateurish though they were, these enterprises preceded a period that saw the OPC and MI6 making uncharacteristic headway. In January 1951, Wisner and his colleagues mounted a coordinated air-sea operation that succeeded in infiltrating forty-three Company 4000 guerrillas into northern Albania, from where they were able to mobilise the support of the local Catholic tribes. Only after a gun battle that continued for several days were Hoxha's security forces able to suppress the insurrection and subsequent incursions that took place during the following month again attracted a considerable measure of local support. By May 1951, however, Hoxha was using the most brutal methods of suppression to ensure that any potential for Albania to erupt into outright rebellion was quickly neutralised, and the OPC's problems were compounded by the fact that, though security at its training base in Heidelberg had been tightened, it was not airtight enough to prevent leaks. Anglo-American missions launched during mid to late 1951 and 1952 thus corresponded to a familiar picture that saw many of the insurgents caught by Hoxha's secret police, if not on entry into Albania then shortly afterwards.[53]

The most commonly cited explanation for this compromising of BGFIEND is treachery. Philby himself claimed to have betrayed the Albanian campaign and several studies have followed suit in making the MI6 liaison officer central to the failure of the venture.[54] Yet, as Robin Winks points out, this is not wholly convincing when details of two airborne incursions on the Martanesh plain to the east of Tirana, are subjected to scrutiny. The first of these flights was aborted after the Polish pilots could not locate the drop zone. During a second attempt mounted the following week, the pilots again failed to find the drop zone, but nine émigrés jumped anyhow, with their supplies falling on a village rather than the designated site. Hoxha's forces intercepted seven of the parachutists, while two others escaped. Such success could not, however, have come about through Tirana having access to pinpoint information, simply because the insurgents did not land where they were supposed to.[55]

Indeed, the poor execution of the Martanesh operations might, ironically, have been responsible for them having been given away. The postponement of the first mission gave the Albanian authorities forewarning of at least the potential for a second attempt. More significantly, the fact that supplies were mistakenly dropped on a village during the second mission was, in itself, enough to have alerted Hoxha's security forces to the presence of insurgents in the area.[56] There was, then, some substance to Philby's claim that the OPC's failure to take proper measure of conditions in Albania, its mismanagement of BGFIEND generally, and its disregard for the lives of the 'pixies' it recruited were as responsible for the debacle as the MI6 officer's treachery.[57]

In spite of the failures that littered the 1950 to mid 1951 period, the following two years saw a redoubling of efforts on the part of the OPC to unseat Hoxha. It was during this time that Wisner temporarily established Radio Free Albania, and an increase in resources allocated to BGFIEND resulted in the infiltration of some sixty exiles into the country by land, sea, and air during late 1951 and 1952. Almost all of these insurgents were either captured or killed, leaving Alfred C. Ulmer, who

Wisner appointed as CIA station chief in Athens in 1951, to maintain later that "we realised after a while that we were dropping [the Company 4000 recruits] into a controlled situation".[58] This, of course, begs two obvious questions, the first being who or what was responsible for such a systematic uncovering of the venture?

To be sure, some of the blame again rests firmly on the shoulders of Philby. By July 1951, however, the CIA had investigated the background and activities of the MI6 liaison officer and had substantiated suspicions that he was a Soviet agent to a sufficient degree to persuade Bedell Smith to declare him *persona non grata* and send him back to London.[59] The betrayals that took place beyond this point, therefore, would have to have come from another spy or spies within the organisation of BGFIEND. Certainly, CIA suspicions that the enterprise was penetrated did not end with the uncovering of Philby. Yatsevich and Angleton are said to have picked out some "lower level plotters" from the Free Albania Committee who were identified as security risks, but whether the operation was compromised by a higher-level source other than Philby remains a matter of conjecture.[60]

Hoxha's success rate in countering western efforts to engineer his downfall during the middle to latter stages of BGFIEND might also be attributable to developments within Albania itself. In February 1951, which marked a point when internal dissent in Albania was particularly pronounced, a bomb exploded at or near the Soviet embassy in Tirana, killing or injuring a number of Russian diplomats and military personnel. Hoxha used this as a pretext to introduce an emergency decree that laid down even more draconian measures than had already been implemented.[61] Not only did this tighten further the Tirana regime's hold on power, it also presented Hoxha with an additional means of penetrating Anglo-American plans, for he could blackmail exiles who were involved in BGFIEND into betraying the programme by threatening relatives who were resident in Albania.

A second and equally perplexing question to arise from the study of BGFIEND is why, in the face of such unremitting failure, did the OPC/DDP continue with the enterprise for so long? Elusive as the answers to this might be while so much of the Albania campaign remains classified, evidence drawn from interviews conducted by Burton Hersh, Evan Thomas, and others with those involved in the operation suggests that part of the explanation boils down to human nature. The abandonment of a project that had consumed an enormous investment of time, effort, and resources, as well as having cost hundreds, or if Chapman Pincher's figures are accurate, perhaps a thousand lives, was extremely difficult to contemplate.[62] Like the gambler who overestimates his luck and stays too long at the roulette table, hoping in vain to make good on his losses, Wisner was driven by a negative dynamic, whereby the longer the Albania campaign went on, the harder it was to terminate.

Also decisive to the OPC/DDP's reluctance to abort was the point that BGFIEND spanned the full duration of the Korean War. In this sense, covert paramilitary action in Albania was a constant thorn in Moscow's side.[63] Company

4000 émigrés killed on the Martanesh plain were, like American soldiers killed on the 38th Parallel, casualties of a wider conflict that the western powers were engaged in with what they perceived to be a Soviet-controlled monolith. To have conceded defeat in Albania would have taken pressure off the Kremlin at a crucial time, and the OPC/DDP was not in the business of making life easier for the Russians, however many Albanian lives such a move would have saved. The uncovering of Philby went much of the way towards explaining the failure of the Albania campaign during its first two years, moreover, which could only have caused Wisner to view the prospects for BGFIEND in a more optimistic light from mid 1951 onwards. Indeed, misplaced optimism was a fundamental element in the final defeat of the four-year effort to unseat Hoxha.

By 1952, the Albania campaign had, by default, become an exclusively American enterprise. Indigenous input now came from the monarchists, the Balli Kombëtar contingent having lost its enthusiasm and extricated itself from the project, just as MI6 had done.[64] Between late 1952 and early 1953, however, radio messages emanating from DDP/royalist assets in the target country told of growing unrest and dissent among Hoxha's military and police, to the extent that, by spring 1953, Albanian security forces were said to be on the brink of rebellion.[65] Accompanied by requests for money, weapons, radio transmitters, and human expertise, these reports raised the expectations of Yatsevich and Wisner, though not of the DDP's radio operators or counterintelligence experts, who noticed that the fist – the distinguishing key pattern adopted by the telegraph operator in Albania who was believed to be sending the messages – was wrong. These fears were proven to be woefully accurate when, in a ruse that recalled the Polish WiN deception, royalist insurgents who were infiltrated into Albania in response to the radio appeals were arrested by waiting security forces. The most determined, persistent, but at the same time futile offensive covert operation that the CIA mounted during its early years thus ended with Tirana hosting a string of very public show trials staged in the early months of 1954.[66]

Conclusion: Deceptions, Legacies, and Lessons

BGFIEND raises as many questions as it offers answers. From the perspective of how offensive covert action was envisaged as advancing American policy, both towards Albania and in the context of Washington's wider Balkan and cold war designs, the objectives were clear. The displacement of a rigidly-doctrinaire, Russian-controlled junta in Tirana by a pro-western, or failing that a Yugoslav-aligned regime, would: (1) deliver a blow to Soviet prestige and encourage repeat performances behind the Iron Curtain; (2) enhance Tito's position vis-à-vis Stalin; and (3) remove a strategic threat to western interests in the Adriatic.

On a tactical level, however, the Albania campaign was deeply flawed from the time of its inception through to its demise. The lack of a viable political alternative to Hoxha; poor management on the part of the OPC/DDP and MI6; and the failure of these same parties to fully appreciate the gravity of the task that confronted them in attempting to unseat a regime that was so closely supported by the highly professional Soviet security forces and so willing to resort to terror as was Hoxha's: all of these factors have led recent studies of the Albania operation to conclude that it would have ended in failure without any help from Philby.[67] More than forty years after his time as the OPC's psychological warfare head, Joseph Bryan confessed that he had never disabused himself "of the feeling that we were a bunch of amateurs", and nowhere was this more pronounced than with BGFIEND. Indeed, Bryan was referring to the Albanian venture when he offered this observation.[68]

Lord Bethell, the author of what is still the most comprehensive study of the Anglo-American programme to remove Hoxha, asked in a later work why the project was allowed to continue after Philby's exposure in July 1951, and some effort has been made here to address this issue.[69] There is, however, a more pressing question to arise from the Philby case, namely why was he appointed to such a sensitive position as MI6 liaison to Washington at all? His past was, after all, replete with inconsistencies that raised doubts about his character and his loyalties.[70]

To expand, in December 1939, Walter Krivitsky, a senior Soviet intelligence officer in The Hague, defected and revealed to American State Department officials that "a British journalist who had gone to Spain during the Spanish Civil War" – a description that fitted Philby – was in the employ of the NKVD. The information was forwarded to London, remained on Secret Service files, and was augmented in autumn 1945 by yet more incriminating claims that resulted from the defections of Igor Gouzenko and Konstantin Volkov, both of whom pointed to a prominent MI6 counterintelligence officer as being Moscow's man.[71] Indeed, Philby's management, or more accurately mismanagement, of the Volkov affair, which in effect bought time for Soviet intelligence to orchestrate the 'disappearance' of its defector, raised further doubts among some British Security Service (MI5) officials and with Angleton about Philby's loyalty.[72] These were, in fact, just some of the time bombs that ticked away down the corridors of Philby's murky past and had mounted up prior to his move to Washington in 1949.[73] If such information did not prove he was a spy, then it certainly should have been taken into account before selecting him for such a sensitive posting.

By the autumn of 1950, however, Wisner had deduced that OPC-MI6 offensive operations in the Soviet bloc were being compromised by a high-level traitor and the prime suspect was Philby.[74] Exactly what action was consequently taken is unclear, but it seems credible to assume that it was on the strength of these fears that the then head of CIA counterintelligence, William K. Harvey, initiated the investigation that led to Philby's uncovering. Whether Wisner or any of his colleagues harboured any suspicions in respect of Philby prior to this point is open to debate. The CIA is alleged to have reports on the MI6 officer in its "Black Files" – a collection of supersensitive files containing information that could severely embarrass the American government – which reveal that Harvey regarded Philby as suspect in 1949 when he first came to Washington.[75] That these documents have never reached the public domain makes this claim impossible to verify. What is notable, however, is that some of those who were involved in BGFIEND gave the MI6 liaison officer a wide berth even before he came under official investigation. Carmel Offie, the OPC official responsible for Albanian Liberation Committee staffing requirements, for instance, was so suspicious that Philby might be a spy that he, Offie, made a point *never* to appear in public with the MI6 officer.[76]

One theory that was apparently leaked from Angleton to William Corson is that at some time during the late 1940s, the CIA discovered through its connections with Israeli Intelligence (Mossad), that Guy Burgess, Donald Maclean and Philby were Soviet agents. Rather than expose them immediately, however, the agency is said to have opted to use them to spread disinformation.[77] According to Major General Edwin L. Sibert, who joined the CIA as an assistant director with zone responsibility for strategic deception, Philby was used in an elaborate and highly secret ruse. Mounted "at the time of the Korean war", this project was aimed at convincing Stalin that the American Strategic Air Command (SAC) had the capability to carry out its mission effectively in the event of war breaking out between the superpowers.[78]

The so-called Trojan Plan envisaged the SAC as dropping 425 atomic bombs on 90 targets in cities across the Soviet Union. This was to be executed in two phases as soon as hostilities began, with the aim of delivering a "single war-winning blow". Pentagon studies raised doubts about the feasibility of the plan, however, most particularly in its second phase, and it was assumed that the Kremlin had also been alerted to the SAC's inadequacies. A deception programme was thus deemed necessary, but CIA calculations had it that Stalin would neither read, nor be induced to take seriously, intelligence reports on the effectiveness of the SAC unless they came from a tried and tested source.[79]

That Philby had a history of supplying high-grade information to the Kremlin made him an ideal conduit. Moscow would, furthermore, have had little reason to become suspicious that a deception was in progress, for it was part of Philby's job to handle much of the Anglo-American dimension of Trojan.[80] The problem with this claim is in its corollary: that the CIA allowed Philby to compromise BGFIEND, other offensive operations behind the Iron Curtain, and the VENONA decrypts – through which the FBI had intercepted signals sent by Moscow to its agents in the United States between 1944 and 1945 – in order to give credibility to the information that he relayed about Trojan.[81] These were extremely high sacrifices to make. Could not Philby have been used as a conduit without being given access to such sensitive intelligence? Deterring Stalin from acting on any warlike designs that he may or may not have had by convincing him that the SAC was an extremely potent force capable of delivering a single war-winning blow, moreover, might well have been a priority for Washington. However, there was no guarantee that the Trojan deception would have any impact on the Soviet dictator, under which circumstances the CIA would have handed over vital intelligence for nothing.

Leaving aside further speculation on the Trojan plan and its possible impact on the Albania campaign, the picture of BGFIEND is an incomplete one, and appears destined to remain so while British and American authorities continue to refuse access to official documents that fully explain what Lord Bethell describes as "this mad escapade".[82] The CIA, MI6, and other western intelligence agencies assured, moreover, that any potential that existed for shedding light on the affair by examining it from Tirana's perspective was quickly extinguished, when they reputedly bought the more important cold war records from the former communist Eastern European security services during the early 1990s.[83]

Certainly, Philby was not the only source of leakage in the Albania campaign. Indeed, Frank Lindsay doubted that "the Kremlin wasted Philby on Albania", arguing that "the operation went down the drain because we couldn't maintain security in the DP camps and because the communist security apparatus was so damn strong".[84]

While the view that the MI6 liaison officer played no role in betraying BGFIEND is questionable, given the weight of evidence to the contrary, the aftermath of the Albania operation did see the CIA launch a hunt for Soviet agents, other than Philby, who might have compromised the project.[85] This search for spies, coupled with an interconnected desire to emulate and improve on communist brainwashing techniques, was instrumental in triggering one of BGFIEND's most fascinating legacies: the redoubling of the agency's mind-control programmes, which were begun by the OSS, revamped during the late 1940s, and gained new-found impetus when they were grouped collectively under the umbrella of Project MKULTRA from 1953 onwards. At least some of these mind-control experiments came under the direction of Sheffield Edwards, who headed the CIA's Office of Security, which was tasked with protecting agency personnel and facilities from penetration, but overall control of the venture was the responsibility of Dr. Sidney Gottlieb. The head of the CIA's Technical Services Staff, Gottlieb reported directly to Wisner and Helms and worked closely with Edwards's department and the Army Chemical Corps' research and bacterial warfare centre at Fort Detrick in Maryland.[86]

MKULTRA programmes found the CIA experimenting in the fields of applied science and technology, psychosurgery, psychoanalytic and psychokinetic methods, drug-induced behavioural manipulation, and electric shock treatment, all of which were aimed at enhancing the agency's ability to penetrate the Iron and Bamboo Curtains, and preventing Soviet penetration of the CIA's own operations. At their most extreme, these hoped-for advances in the field of mind-control were conducted to improve the CIA's capacity to perform assassination.[87]

The OPC had in fact created a unit in 1949, labelled PB-7, to handle 'wet affairs' – namely kidnappings and murders of traitors and other undesirables – but it is said not to have been very effective. When, for example, CIA operative E. Howard

Hunt uncovered and sought the elimination of an Albanian monarchist who was believed to have betrayed BGFIEND, Colonel Boris Pash, the Russian émigré who headed PB-7, did nothing.[88] With the advent of MKULTRA-related enterprises such as Project Artichoke, however, the CIA investigated assassination in a more clinical manner, in this instance seeking to assess the hypothetical problem of whether or not individuals of particular ethnic descent could be transformed involuntarily into programmable assassins "under the influence of Artichoke", namely through the use of drugs and/or hypnosis.[89] Such activities may have been macabre and unethical, not to mention impractical, but they demonstrate how political murder became accepted as a necessary and, by the early 1960s, routinely-deployed tool for advancing American interests in the Cold War.[90] This trend can be traced back to the searching questions that were asked within the CIA in the wake of BGFIEND and the failure of other offensive covert operations launched by the agency during the same period.

The Albania campaign was, finally, significant for what it taught. The operation was, like similar western enterprises mounted concurrently against the Soviet bloc, "overly ambitious [and] too big to be really secure".[91] Yet, despite the recognition by some in the CIA hierarchy that big is not always best, and the fact that the failure of BGFIEND came as a "searing defeat" that governed "much of the suspicion around the real security problems of the Agency" for literally years, the CIA went on repeating this basic mistake throughout the 1950s and early 1960s.[92] More fundamentally, the Albania debacle demonstrated the enormous difficulties involved in mounting offensive operations against Soviet-backed communist regimes. Thus, while BGFIEND came as a blow to agency prestige, it also provided confirmation of the wisdom of the CIA leadership's decision to look to fresh pastures on which to flex the DDP's muscles during the Eisenhower presidency.

ERRING ON THE SIDE OF ACTIVISM: EISENHOWER AND THE ERA OF PREVENTIVE COVERT WARFARE

With the coming of the Eisenhower administration, the CIA's covert action mission was elevated to a position of unprecedented prominence as a tool of American foreign and defence policy. Geographically, the Cold War was widely perceived to have expanded from the Far East to the third world from 1953 onwards, and this was accompanied by a corresponding shift in the means by which the conflict was fought, from military to political.[1] These conditions required Eisenhower to fight his corner in a quiet but ruthless manner, with the aim of creating the inescapable impression that the United States had the upper hand in the Cold War and was maintaining its position more categorically, but at less cost, than ever before. In the sense that it was, at least in theory, silent and relatively inexpensive, covert action was the perfect instrument for meeting Eisenhower's needs. Essentially, it "held out the promise of frustrating Soviet ambitions without provoking conflict", at a time when the United States was placing outward emphasis on the doctrine of massive retaliation.[2]

In accordance with the objectives of its political masters, the CIA intensified its propaganda effort against the Sino-Soviet bloc, notably through RFE and Radio Liberty, which was entirely in keeping with Eisenhower's conception of achieving rollback by peaceful means. Political and paramilitary offensives to weaken the Kremlin's hold over Eastern Europe likewise continued, in spite of the fact that containment remained central to American foreign and defence policy throughout the fifties, hinging as it did on preventing any extension of communist power beyond the Iron and Bamboo Curtains.[3]

Indeed, the agency regarded the death of Stalin as presenting an opportunity to be exploited to the maximum. His succession by a Soviet leadership that sought to allow greater autonomy within its satellite states and rehabilitate leading Eastern European nationalist-communists who had been purged during the late 1940s, was seen by the CIA as presenting an opportunity for triggering the type of implosion that Kennan had forecast for the Eastern bloc. Only after the Russian invasion of

Hungary in 1956 did the message fully register that anticommunist underground organisations, whether agency-sponsored or purely indigenous, were impotent against a hegemonic adversary armed with thermonuclear weapons and possessed of the political will to use raw military power to maintain its grip.[4] In the face of such realities, the DDP largely abandoned its offensive paramilitary operations against the 'denied areas', restricting its activities to probing and where possible undermining communist control in isolated, outlying regions, such as Tibet.[5] At the same time, emphasis continued to be focused on the agency's defensive programmes in Western Europe and other areas that were lodged firmly in the American camp.

The Eisenhower years saw CIA covert action take on an extra dimension, however, in that the Cold War climate of the 1950s placed a premium on the agency's capacity to conduct what might be most accurately described as preventive covert action: the removal of third world leaders whose nonaligned stances left their countries vulnerable to communist takeover, and the subsequent replacement of those leaders with strongly pro-western successors who could be relied upon to pursue policies that were compatible with American interests, if not always with the interests of the populations that they represented. Enterprises of this nature had been deployed sparingly during Truman's tenure – in Syria and Egypt during 1949 and 1952 respectively – but the coming of the Eisenhower administration saw the DDP go into overdrive with its use of preventive covert action, mounting operations that spanned the globe, from Iran to Guatemala, Indonesia to the Congo, and ultimately to Cuba and the Caribbean.[6]

The individuals singled out for attention were, furthermore, not exclusively leftist rulers who were feared to be leading their countries too far to the left. The roll-call of targets also included reactionaries such as the Dominican Republic's Rafael Trujillo, whose repressive authoritarian regime was seen by Washington as holding out the danger of triggering a copycat revolution of the kind that saw Fidel Castro depose Cuba's rightist dictator Fulgencio Batista in 1959. Commenting on the wider policy dilemmas faced by Eisenhower during his two terms in the White House, H. W. Brands lauded the president for recognising the risks of "erring on the side of activism", and wisely accepting "a minor setback rather than hazard a major disaster".[7] When confronted with developments in the third world that he judged to be running contrary to American interests, however, Eisenhower was far less circumspect.[8] Indeed, in his deployment of covert action he demonstrated an appetite for the proactive that, with the possible exception of Ronald Reagan, went unmatched throughout the entire Cold War period.

Ike's White House

Dwight D. Eisenhower was, in many respects, a fortunate president. Having won the 1952 election on a wave of extrapartisan faith in his presumed ability to secure a speedy and honourable resolution to the Korean War, Eisenhower subsequently found that his accession to the presidency coincided with a fundamental change in the climate of the Cold War itself.[9] In the two months that followed the former general's inauguration, Stalin died and Georgi M. Malenkov, chairman of the Soviet Union's ruling Council of Ministers, announced the willingness of the new collective Russian leadership to resolve all outstanding differences between the superpowers "peacefully and by mutual agreement".[10] For the American president, however, conciliatory gestures were not enough. If Eisenhower were to be persuaded that the Kremlin's 'peace offensive' was more than a mere tactical change designed to achieve the same long-term objectives as those held by Stalin, then Moscow would have to match its rhetoric with action.[11]

Amongst the ongoing Cold War developments that presented themselves as possible indicators of Russian sincerity, none proved more persuasive than the pressure Moscow brought to bear on Beijing and Pyong Yang to agree the armistice of July 1953 that ended the Korean War.[12] It nevertheless took a further two years before Eisenhower was prepared to meet with his Soviet counterparts – at the Geneva Summit of July 1955.

Delay of this kind led Eisenhower's critics to accuse him of failing to seize moment, but very pragmatic imperatives informed his caution.[13] To begin with, a complex power struggle engulfed the Kremlin in the two years following Stalin's death and it served the interests of clarity for Washington to hold back from entering into top-level dialogue until it knew exactly whom it would be dealing with. The prospect of a summit thus increased considerably once Nikita S. Khrushchev emerged supreme in 1955.[14] Domestic considerations also prefigured in Eisenhower's calculations. Though McCarthyism proved to be a useful, if crude, tool for advancing Republican fortunes up to and during the 1952 presidential election, the GOP victory did nothing to curb the Wisconsin senator. The McCarthyite challenge was eventually neutralised by Eisenhower through the use of what Fred I. Greenstein describes as 'hidden hand' tactics, but these measures required time to take effect.[15] It did not, therefore, make sense for the president to participate in the first summit since Potsdam until after McCarthy's censure in December 1954, especially in view of the fact that he and his right-wing allies among the Republican Old Guard were demanding that Washington repudiate the Yalta agreements.[16]

There was, as well, the point that the United States could not gain optimum benefit from a summit unless it was able to negotiate from a position of strength. Eisenhower therefore preferred to wait until after a short-term settlement of the Indochina conflict had been reached at the 1954 Geneva Conference, which, while not entirely to America's advantage, had the merit of temporarily preventing the communist Vietminh forces from making any further advances.[17]

The presidential brakes were similarly deployed to ensure that direct talks with the Russians followed, rather than preceded, the successful American effort to overcome French objections to the integration of West Germany into NATO, which took place in May 1955 and led Moscow to respond by creating the Warsaw

Pact. The long-term division of Germany was thereby recognised as a *fait accompli* by both superpowers. If this made conditions particularly ripe for summitry, then so too did the signing of the Austrian State Treaty during the same month, which established that country's neutrality and marked the first instance of a Red Army withdrawal since 1945.[18] What the Geneva Summit amounted to when it finally did take place, then, was superpower confirmation and acceptance of the Cold War divide in Europe.[19] Eisenhower was, nevertheless, committed to the containment of communism throughout his presidential tenure and he sought to achieve this aim through the deployment of the so-called New Look policy that he introduced in 1953.

The New Look: Asymmetry in Practice

The most fundamental departure in foreign and defence policy made by Eisenhower on becoming president was his determination to implement more cost-effective management of American national security requirements than his predecessor had achieved. Unlike Truman, the new president did not see the United States as facing a point of maximum danger – identified in NSC 68 as occurring in 1954. Rather, he viewed the Cold War as a prolonged struggle requiring prudent economic management as well as effective political leadership, in order that America might preserve and enhance its global security without having recourse to degenerate into a garrison state – a danger which Eisenhower saw as jeopardising the very freedom for which his country stood if economic constraints were not imposed on the military. Thus, in April 1953, he proposed a $5.2 billion cut in Truman's national security budget and set a course for implementing the first phase of what would become known as the New Look.[20]

Several treatments of the New Look present it as having rested, if not exclusively, then in large measure, on the capacity of America's nuclear potential to deter communist aggression.[21] Certainly, Eisenhower placed great faith in his country's nuclear primacy, the assumption being that the United States was duty-bound to maintain its global preeminence and that such weaponry provided the only affordable means through which this could be guaranteed. He was, moreover, afforded greater flexibility in considering the tactical as well as strategic worth of nuclear weapons than Truman and the architects of NSC 68 had been, simply because the variety and range of America's nuclear arsenal had grown enormously by the time he, Eisenhower, took office and continued to grow during his tenure.[22] Dependence on the deterrent value of atomic and more particularly thermonuclear weapons, however, was only one among several elements of national security policy deployed by the United States between 1953 and 1961.

In January 1954, Eisenhower's Secretary of State John Foster Dulles talked of the need for the West to be able to respond to communist aggression "at places and with means of its own choosing".[23] Often interpreted as an allusion to massive retaliation, this actually signalled something much wider: the adoption of asymmetrical defence as Eisenhower's guiding maxim in the sphere of defence policy. The New Look would, in short, provide for a wide range of possible responses to *any* given challenge. Communist aggression would be met, to use John Lewis Gaddis's phrase, "in ways calculated to apply one's own strengths against the other side's weaknesses, even if this meant shifting the nature and location of the confrontation". The United States would thereby retain the initiative at a sustainable cost. This contrasted sharply with the symmetry of NSC 68, which assumed the atomic bomb to be a weapon of last resort, and envisaged America as responding in kind, both in manner and location, to its adversaries, even if this meant stationing large armies at great expense in regions such as Korea, which had formerly been of only peripheral value.[24]

The outcome of a reassessment of American national security requirements that was requisitioned by Eisenhower and tagged Operation Solarium, the New Look comprised five basic elements: (1) the extension of the system of alliances which was initiated by Truman and was based on the use of indigenous ground forces backed up by American air and naval power; (2) nuclear weapons; (3) psychological warfare; (4) covert action; and (5) negotiations. Each of these components were intended, both individually and collectively, to maximise American defence and foreign policy options following the authorisation of the New Look, as outlined in NSC 162/2 in October 1953.[25]

An examination of global political events between 1953 and 1956, moreover, indicates that Eisenhower was not slow to convert theory into practice. Regardless of whether or not Washington's use of the threat of massive retaliation was actually responsible for intimidating Mao and Kim Il Sung into suing for peace, brinkmanship was nonetheless deployed as part of the American effort to bring about the Korean armistice. The deterrent strategy was also used during the crisis over Quemoy and Matsu between late 1954 and early 1955, while the founding of the South East Asia Treaty Organisation (SEATO) in 1954 and the establishment of the Baghdad Pact in 1955 were examples of the alliance system at work.[26] Although it took place before the New Look received official approval, the overthrow of Iranian leader Muhammad Musaddiq in August 1953 supplies proof, as does the Guatemala coup of June 1954, that the closely interconnected components of psychological warfare and covert action were very much in use. Finally, the 'Atoms for Peace' and 'Open Skies' negotiating proposals might also be viewed in the context of asymmetry in practice, since each resulted in Eisenhower winning valuable propaganda victories.

There were inherent weaknesses in the New Look, the most obvious of which relate to the use of brinkmanship. Within ten months of American acquisition of thermonuclear weaponry in November 1952, the USSR successfully tested its own hydrogen bomb and worked tirelessly to develop the delivery systems to enable the Kremlin to respond in kind if threatened with massive retaliation. These developments were viewed in the 1957 Gaither Report as making the United States increasingly vulnerable to thermonuclear attack, and therefore less likely to deploy brinkmanship.[27] Massive retaliation was, furthermore, subject to the law of diminishing returns: the more often it was used, the less credible it would become. Relaince on pacts also carried drawbacks, in that they could be exploited by friends as well as foes to incite the United States into intervening in areas that would otherwise not have been crucial to American interests – this was not, of course, unique to the Eisenhower administration, but the risk was greater simply because more reliance was now placed on pacts than had previously been the case. For their part, covert action and psychological warfare projects carried the risk of having a negative impact on the integrity and credibility of the United States, should such operations be unmasked.

Eisenhower nonetheless continued to utilise each of the key elements of the New Look throughout his presidency. Massive retaliation was again threatened during the second Quemoy and Matsu crisis in 1958.[28] The Baghdad Pact was reconstituted as the Central Treaty Organisation (CENTO) after Iraq left the alliance in 1959, thereby reaffirming American determination to enforce containment along the northern tier, and Eisenhower continued to use negotiations to enhance global stability and secure propaganda victories against the Russians. His decision to take the initiative on the test ban issue in 1958 and halt nuclear tests in the atmosphere stands as a case in point.[29] Finally, presidential resort to the many and varied forms of covert action was always evident, and this extended well beyond efforts to instigate quickly executed coups d'état.

Eisenhower's predilection for asymmetry goes some way towards explaining why, during his tenure, such strong emphasis was placed on the two camps view of an American-led free world being confronted by a Soviet-controlled global communist challenge. Much as Washington was aware that intra-communist rifts existed and were pregnant with possibilities for the West to exploit, it served Eisenhower's purposes to stick publicly with his overtly doctrinaire appraisal of international communism as monolithic.[30] Aimed partly at inducing a heightened spirit of independence in Mao's China and indeed elsewhere in the communist world, the crude, ideologically-based global dichotomy that Eisenhower and Foster Dulles were so eager to promote was absolutely essential to the asymmetry of the New Look. It would not, for instance, have been feasible for Washington to caution Beijing against action in Indochina by warning that such moves might have repercussions elsewhere; to maintain that a Russian attack on Turkey would not necessarily be countered on Turkish soil;[31] or to depict the Iran and Guatemala coups as victories against international communism, unless the 'free world' was pitted against a monolith – or was portrayed as such.

*   *   *

A major criticism of the Eisenhower administration generally and Foster Dulles in particular is that their adoption of this oversimplified and patently false bipolar worldview impaired their ability to distinguish between neutralism and communism.[32] While there is an element of truth to this portrayal, it is far from precise and therefore in need of some refinement.

The key to understanding the stance taken by Eisenhower and Dulles towards neutralism is that they regarded it as fluid rather than static, and the principal determinant influencing whether they supported or opposed it was the direction in which they believed it to be leading. Thus, the onset of neutralism in Eastern Europe was viewed by Washington in a positive light. For Dulles, Yugoslavia's detachment from the Soviet orbit set a welcome precedent, because it was accomplished peacefully and it opened the way for other communist states to follow suit, thereby signalling the potential for the break-up of "the Soviet empire without war".[33] Still more significant to Eisenhower's and Dulles's conception of utilising neutralism as a trigger for rollback by peaceful means was the signing of the Austrian State Treaty in 1955. Whereas Yugoslav nonalignment, in retaining Marxist governance, was seen as spawning only a contagion for *independence* from Soviet rule, Austrian neutrality was regarded as fuelling aspirations for *freedom* behind the Iron Curtain.[34]

The validity of these appraisals became evident when first Poland then Hungary sought to loosen their bonds with Moscow after Khrushchev's repudiation of Stalin at the Twentieth Congress of the Soviet Communist Party in February 1956. The drawback in the Eisenhower administration's analysis of 'separate paths to socialism' as leading westwards, with the Yugoslav and Austrian models pointing the way, was in its naïve belief that the process could be achieved peacefully. De-Stalinization and peaceful coexistence aside, Khrushchev had no intention of dismantling voluntarily the security buffer zone that the Russians established in 1945, as is evidenced with his crushing of the Hungarian uprising.

It is for their approach to neutralism in the third world, however, that Eisenhower and Foster Dulles have drawn most fire. In brief, post-revisionists maintain that the president and his Secretary of State viewed third world nationalism "through the distorting lens" of the Cold War and "simplified complicated local and regional developments, confusing nationalism with communism" and wedding the United States to "inherently unstable and unrepresentative regimes".[35] This picture has considerable credibility but again is in need of some qualification.

The term 'third world' is so broad as to defy adequate definition, but the one goal common to the nations categorised under this unsatisfactory rubric was that they all sought to achieve social, economic, and political advancement as rapidly as possible. In this respect, the Soviet Union enjoyed a decided advantage over the western powers, because the Bolshevik model of accelerated development offered an attractive precedent for third world countries to follow. The impingement of cold war issues on the developing world became more pronounced from 1953 onwards, for while Stalin had held back from supporting non-communist movements outside of the Soviet bloc, his successors proved to be far more flexible. The core assumption informing Malenkov and Khrushchev was that third world neutralism "contained an inherently anti-western bias, given the legacy of colonialism", and could serve as a way-station for the spread of communism proper.[36]

In terms of American policy towards the third world, Washington's fears were an echo of Moscow's ambitions, the overriding American anxiety being that nonalignment in developing regions was following a decidedly leftward trend. More particularly, Eisenhower and Foster Dulles were driven by a determination to prevent the creation of political vacuums. Failure to do so would enable local Marxists to subvert newly emerging nations that were not educated to the dangers posed by international communism and thereby provide an opening wedge for more direct Soviet penetration in areas of vital strategic and economic importance to the United States.[37]

These considerations became crucial in a Cold War that, after the cessation of hostilities in Korea, was primarily a political conflict, in which perceptions were of vital importance. Any form of communist advance was deemed to be a blow to the United States and its allies, not only in material terms, but also for the psychological impact it would have on the western powers and the uncommitted: and for the Soviets the same zero-sum game logic applied in reverse. It was against this background that CIA covert action as a whole, and preventive operations in particular, came to play such a prominent role during the 1950s.

The CIA 1953–1961: Fully Grown and Coming of Age

Eisenhower's accession to the presidency brought with it a unique set of factors, which converged to allow the CIA to attain a prominence and respect that had hitherto evaded it and which it has since failed to recapture. Crucial among these was the fact that the DCI, Allen Dulles, was the Secretary of State's brother and that both men quickly won and continued to enjoy the trust of the president. Such close personal ties enabled formal procedures between the NSC, the CIA, and the State Department to be bypassed easily.[38]

First-hand experience, both in commanding the western allies in Europe during World War II and NATO forces afterwards, had provided Eisenhower with an appreciation of the value of effective intelligence collection and clandestine operations. The development of covert action programmes, furthermore, served as an inexpensive alternative to the use of conventional military force and was a necessary component of the New Look. Eisenhower was, however, also fortunate that by the time of his inauguration the CIA had multiplied sixfold since 1947 and acquired the basic scale and structure that it was to retain for the next two decades.[39] It was therefore an effective organ of government, ready for immediate deployment under the supervision of a president who favoured 'hidden hand' strategies and a DCI who proved to be the most proactive in the agency's history.

Allen Dulles's enormous enthusiasm for covert action is stressed in all of the primary and secondary works on the CIA. His reputation as "the quintessential case officer" originated during his days as OSS chief in Berne, Switzerland during World War II. Though he returned to work for the New York law firm of Sullivan and Cromwell in 1945, Dulles maintained close contact with the CIG/CIA and was proactive in the fight against communism from the earliest days of the Cold War, notably through his efforts as the chairman of the Council on Foreign Relations. Indeed, Dulles's activism was so conspicuous that Soviet agents assumed that his legal business for Sullivan and Cromwell was a cover.[40]

Moscow was not, however, alone in viewing the would-be DCI's activities, whether as a private citizen or a leading official of the CIA, with trepidation. Having observed what he regarded as Dulles's over eagerness to resort the covert, where restraint or another more appropriate form of action could be better employed, Bedell Smith harboured serious reservations about his deputy. Consequently, when Eisenhower took office and proposed to move Smith to the post of Under Secretary of State, the outgoing DCI urged the president to think carefully before handing the management of the agency over to Dulles, who was seen by many as the natural successor to the job. From Eisenhower's standpoint, however, the respective positioning of Foster Dulles and his brother as Secretary of the State and DCI offered clear advantages and Allen Dulles was thus appointed to run the CIA on 26 February 1953.[41]

At the outset of his directorship, Allen Dulles understood that the CIA was still a relatively new and insecure organisation which "had to prove itself and gain the respect of its elders", namely the State Department and the military.[42] The agency needed to produce demonstrable successes in order to enhance its reputation, and it needed to do this quickly if only for considerations pertinent to Dulles: (1) he was the first civilian DCI; (2) he did not enjoy the prestige and status of his predecessor; and (3) he was eager to place his own stamp on the new administration. The most productive course of action was therefore to prioritise the agency's covert action mission.

Several factors guided Dulles's reasoning. The CIA was alone in its ability to deploy political, economic, paramilitary, and psychological warfare programmes, and the post-Korean War global environment lent itself to the promotion of these unique clandestine functions.[43] The political requirements of Eisenhower and Foster Dulles were matched by the professional inclinations of the Secretary of State's brother. Allen Dulles's experience, interests, and expertise lay in the operational aspects of intelligence, and he found the use of covert action easy to justify. In the fight against communism, the DCI later wrote, the United States "should not shy away from mobilising [its] efforts and assets and applying them vigorously".[44]

The degree of vigour that the DDP was able to muster during the Eisenhower years was, however, influenced by international developments and tempered by changes in the nuclear balance. Washington's readiness to deploy offensive covert operations against the communist bloc had long been conditional on America's possession of sufficient military power to deter Moscow from taking aggressive action in response to such activities. The feasibility of pursuing a clandestine warfare campaign against the Soviet bloc, then, was called increasingly into question following Russian acquisition of thermonuclear weapons. Consequently, from 1953 onwards ever greater emphasis was placed on the need for the United States to adopt a more conciliatory approach in its dealings with the USSR and by 1956 a succession of internal reviews had led the Eisenhower administration to stop its offensives behind the Iron Curtain. The United States would henceforth opt for an 'evolutionary strategy', which was aimed at encouraging the 'captive peoples' to work to change the communist system from within.[45] The Eisenhower White House and the CIA, nevertheless, learned some bitter lessons before arriving at these conclusions.

Communist Bloc Operations 1953–1956:
The Limits of Offensive Covert Warfare

The abandonment of offensive covert operations in Eastern Europe and the Soviet Republics was proposed from as early as 1952 by some of the very people whose responsibility it was to carry out such ventures. In the autumn of that year, the CIA's outgoing Director of Operations for Eastern Europe, Frank Lindsay, produced an internal memorandum on the effectiveness of covert action in the region that had been under his charge. The report was requisitioned by Allen Dulles and though it has subsequently been 'lost' from the CIA's files, Lindsay himself has made it clear that his conclusions were uncompromisingly negative. The overall assessment was that Wisner's efforts to penetrate the Soviet bloc had proved entirely futile and constituted a grave misuse of agency resources, not to mention a tragic waste of human life.[46] Though Dulles disputed Lindsay's findings, Bedell Smith's murder boards had, by 1952, weeded out an estimated one third of the operations that the DDP mounted behind the Iron Curtain.[47] However, what Wisner described as the "thoroughgoing re-examination of [the] means and methods" deployed by the OPC/DDP over the previous four to five years did not amount to a rejection of offensive covert warfare.[48] On the contrary, the death of Stalin and the cessation of hostilities in Korea gave renewed momentum to such operations.

With no single Russian leader emerging supreme in the year and a half that followed Stalin's demise, conditions were seen by Washington as being ripe for the implementation of Operation CANCELLATION, a CIA effort to incite fissures in the Politburo following Stalin's death.[49] This was especially true during 1953, when the inclusion of such avowed adversaries as Lavrenty Beria, Vyacheslav Molotov, and Nikita Khrushchev in the collective Kremlin leadership meant that the Politburo was, anyhow, consumed in a fractious power struggle that culminated with the arrest of Beria in June 1953 and his execution six months later.[50] That all of the Russian leadership contenders advocated reforms which included the easing of travel restrictions throughout the Soviet Union and Eastern Europe also proved advantageous for American interests, because it enabled the CIA to practice what Harry Rositzke terms 'legal' methods of penetration.[51]

However, the most explicit indications that a changed Cold War environment would create new opportunities for the CIA to exploit came in June 1953, when anticommunist riots erupted in East Berlin and spread throughout the GDR.[52] These events have been the subject of conjecture and prime among the issues contested is the role played by the DDP in fuelling the protests. At the time, Allen Dulles assured the NSC that "the US had nothing whatsoever to do with inciting these riots", but evidence uncovered by W. Scott Lucas exposes the disingenuousness of this statement.[53] Lucas has shown that a concerted American psychological warfare effort, which began in 1950 and was spearheaded by Radio in the American Sector (RIAS), proved significant in fuelling discontent in East Germany and that this enterprise climaxed with the 1953 riots.[54] The DDP was, it is true, caught off guard by the protests but what surprised the officers at the CIA's Berlin Operations Base (BOB) and officialdom in Washington was not that East Berlin had become the focus of anti-Soviet discontent. Rather, it was the intensity of the protests and the speed at which they spread.[55]

Given that the uprising *had* gathered unforeseen momentum, Dulles, Wisner and Eisenhower had next to decide on how to respond. Here again, the received wisdom is in need of revision in light of recently published research and memoirs. Common to almost all versions of the riots is the claim that the CIA station chief in Berlin's western sector, Henry Heckscher, sought permission from Washington to smuggle firearms into the Soviet zone, only to be overruled by Wisner and John Bross. The injection of such weaponry would, the DDP and his Eastern European Division chief are alleged to have argued, be tantamount to murder in the face of Red Army might.[56]

However, former CIA officer David Murphy, who worked out of BOB at the time of the riots, maintains that this exchange never took place and that the very tenets on which it is based are inaccurate. To begin with, no record of the cables exists, but even if correspondence of this kind did take place, Heckscher could not have initiated it. He had, according to Murphy and his former colleagues, been transferred from Berlin to another posting before June 1953, to be replaced by William Harvey as station chief. Not only this, but requests of the kind that Heckscher is alleged to have made would have undermined the authority of the CIA's Chief of Mission in Germany, General Lucian B. Truscott and would, in Murphy's assessment, have resulted in the dismissal of the cable's sender. Murphy's account does, nevertheless, depict the Berlin uprising as having caused "a great deal of hand-wringing within the CIA" after Wisner passed on Washington's decision that the agency should restrict its activities to propaganda tactics and "do nothing to incite East Germans to further action which will jeopardise their lives".[57]

The Berlin riots provide a seminal example of how cold war realities defined the limits of offensive covert action. Eisenhower might initially have inclined towards arming the East German protesters and have toyed with authorising direct American military intervention should the uprising have become more widespread. However, he retreated quickly from such proactive, risk-laden considerations.[58] Despite the great rhetorical emphasis that the president, and more especially Foster Dulles, had placed on liberating the 'captive peoples', the new administration's freedom of action was bound by similar parameters to those that constrained its predecessor. Put simply, the United States lacked the military capacity to build on the CIA's offensives in East Germany and wrest the satellite from Moscow's orbit.

If the East German uprising clarified that rollback could come only through peaceful means, then what is less clear is the extent to which the message hit home in American government circles. Undaunted by the sense of impotency that the Berlin riots laid bare, the CIA subsequently redoubled its efforts in the 'captive nations', drawing on the Eisenhower administration's plan to organise a military force composed of Eastern European exiles and tagged the Volunteer Freedom Corps (VFC).[59] Authorised in May 1953 as NSC 143/2, this initiative met with opposition from nervous Western European allies and from the JCS, who were resistant to the idea of allocating resources to "undisciplined elements in the DP camps", at a time when Washington was cutting back on defence spending.[60] Nevertheless, NSC 158, which was approved during the following month and outlined American objectives and actions to exploit unrest in Russia's satellite states, called for the implementation of the VFC proposal.[61]

Much as Eisenhower found pretexts to delay carrying out NSC 143/2, Allen Dulles adapted the VFC concept to serve CIA designs, recruiting and training Hungarian, Polish, Czechoslovak, and Romanian paramilitary forces at a base near Munich for a large-scale operation that functioned under the code-name of Red Cap.[62] Arms caches were smuggled into the denied areas and buried in preparation for a move by these forces should conditions become ripe for their deployment. In an attempt to ensure that conditions *would* become ripe, the agency mounted a complementary, political action programme aimed at the identification and recruitment of prominent nationalist-communists who might spearhead anti-Soviet dissent within their respective countries.[63]

What distinguished these moves from earlier OPC/DDP Eastern bloc operations was that they were not mounted with the primary objective of preparing for war, as had been the case between 1948 and 1952. Rather, Wisner and his colleagues now sought to exploit the widespread thirst for independence and freedom that they anticipated as arising in Eastern Europe as a result of the more conciliatory approach to foreign affairs that had been adopted by the Kremlin following Stalin's death.[64] Exactly what final outcome the CIA leadership envisaged as resulting from these moves is difficult to discern. Allen Dulles is said by Robert Amory to have seen "little profit in encouraging the evolution of semiautonomous – but still Communist societies". Richard Bissell reinforces this view, maintaining that what he and the DCI saw as really desirable were "takeovers we planned, with political outcomes we could control".[65]

What calls these claims into question is the fact that neither draws any distinction between short-term and longer-range objectives. The Eisenhower administration, it will be recalled, regarded Yugoslav-style independence and Austrian-style neutrality as staging posts on the road from Soviet communism to western democracy. Bearing this in mind, there *was* profit to be had from "encouraging the evolution of semiautonomous – but still Communist societies", since such societies pointed the way to the ultimate objective of rollback by peaceful means. Not only this, but Allen Dulles's strategy following Khrushchev's February 1956 speech to the Soviet Communist Party, in which he repudiated Stalinism, also casts doubts on Amory's and Bissell's views.

Delivered in closed session, the half-day long speech was, of course, extremely significant. It confirmed Khrushchev's position as undisputed Soviet leader and its relentless and detailed content laid bare many of the excesses and inefficiencies of Stalinism.[66] For the CIA, then, procuring a transcript of the speech was of paramount importance, since its possible consequences needed to be gauged as quickly as possible so the agency could initiate plans to take advantage of the situation. Within two months, the DDP had produced two authentic copies of the speech.[67] The actions taken by Allen Dulles at this point, however, raise questions about the extent to which he believed the agency could or should control events within Eastern Europe.

Following the CIA's acquisition of Khrushchev's much-coveted transcript, a debate took place as to how its contents might best be utilised. From the analytical wing of the agency came Ray Cline's argument that the speech should be released in full for the world to scrutinise. It was, after all, the most comprehensive indictment of Soviet totalitarianism ever to emerge from behind the Iron Curtain, and it had been delivered by no less a person than the leader of the USSR himself.[68] Wisner and Angleton, on the other hand, had more complex and integrated plans for exploiting the speech, which depended on releasing it piecemeal to specific Eastern European countries, with the aim of controlling the nature and magnitude of dissent in each of the captive nations. These DDP projections made provision for RFE and Radio Liberty lacing the revelations with disinformation. Finally, simultaneous moves to upgrade the Red Cap programme would be set in motion to ensure that CIA-trained paramilitaries could be injected into their homelands if and when such forces could have a viable and positive impact on the course of events.[69]

At the core of the debate over the use of Khrushchev's speech, then, was the issue of control, with Wisner and Angleton pressing for the CIA to maintain the optimum degree of control and Cline arguing for events to be left to take their own course. Allen Dulles came down in favour of Cline, however, which flies in the face of Bissell's claim that the DCI favoured takeovers that the agency planned and political outcomes that it could control.[70]

As it was, the two major expressions of national disaffection and insurrection that followed Khrushchev's speech, in Poland and Hungary, resulted from indigenous conditions rather than anything that the CIA initiated. Poland was spared from a full-scale Red Army invasion: Hungary was not. As was the case with the Berlin riots the CIA rejected claims that RFE played a role in inciting the Hungarian uprising, but these denials do not stand up to scrutiny.[71]

Along with Czechoslovakia, Hungary had, since 1953, been the target of the agency's VETO and FOCUS programmes, which utilised radio propaganda; the injection of counterfeit currency into the host countries; and balloon drops of leaflets that demanded local autonomy, market reforms, and the de-nationalisation of key industries.[72] The DDP propaganda campaign in Hungary was, moreover, stepped up after Khrushchev's denunciation of Stalin and intensified further in the wake of the concessions that Wladislaw Gomulka wrested from Moscow during the so-called Polish October. RFE essentially "cross-reported" events in Poland and Hungary during the critical period of October and November 1956. It also picked up low-powered radio signals that emanated from dissidents inside of Hungary and broadcast these insurrectionary pleas over the 'Mighty Wurlitzer' to ensure that they reached every corner of the country and the wider Eastern bloc.[73]

CIA claims that its radio outlet limited its activities to "straight news reporting" and offered no "tactical advice" were, therefore, barely credible.[74] One RFE broadcast, for instance, implied that Congress might approve armed American military intervention in Hungary if the resistance continued until after the United States presidential election of 1956.[75] If this was aimed at maintaining the momentum of the uprising, then other statements suggested that the CIA was eager to see it spread beyond Hungary. RFE's assertion that "eight days of victorious revolution have turned Hungary into a free land [and] neither Khrushchev nor the whole of the Soviet army [can] oppress this liberty", stands as a case in point.[76] Rather than triggering copycat rebellions, inflammatory language such as this could only have goaded the Kremlin and increased the prospect of the full-scale Russian invasion that was to crush the Hungarian revolution.

Significant as the measures deployed by the CIA during the uprising were, they fell short of Wisner's call for all means at America's disposal, including overt military power, to be deployed in support of Imre Nagy and his countrymen.[77] The DDP's urgings went unheeded essentially because Eisenhower lacked the political will to provide active assistance to Hungary. All other considerations aside, the country was land-locked, as the president pointed out, and he rejected categorically the proposition that recently-negotiated Austrian neutrality be violated to enable American troops to go into Hungary and thereby risk starting World War III.[78] There were, as well, factors of timing and justification to be considered: how could the United States move against the Russians in response to their repression of Hungary, while during the same period America's foremost allies, Britain and France, were making common cause with Israel and mounting a similarly unwarranted act of aggression at Suez?[79]

Specialisation

The Hungarian uprising demonstrated clearly that if the CIA was to make good on Allen Dulles's plan to specialise in the field of covert action and achieve visible operational successes without incurring unacceptable risks, then it would need to shift its focus away from the European theatre. What should, however, be stressed is that such reasoning only lent weight to a trend that had been very much in evidence since 1953. The *Church Report* listed the CIA's regional priorities in the 1950s as being: (1) Europe; (2) the Far East; and (3) Latin America. This was, however, a very broad and generalised overview.[80] For sure, Europe attracted a great deal of attention from the agency, but from 1956 onwards clandestine operations mounted in this vital continent were concentrated on political containment in Western Europe, and were predominantly defensive in nature.

In terms of offensive covert action outside of Europe, new ventures were launched in locations where communist control was deemed to be tentative and local resistance strong. Most notable among these ventures was the CIA's STCIRCUS programme, which began in 1956 and exploited deeply felt Tibetan antipathy towards Red China, which had been growing since Beijing laid claim to Tibet in 1949 and seized the capital, Lhasa, in 1951. An extensive and enduring enterprise, STCIRCUS found the CIA providing guerrilla training for the most promising of its Tibetan recruits at Camp Hale, an isolated base in Colorado. Crucial to the campaign was the agency's provision of arms, munitions and other supplies to encampments in northern Nepal, from where Khamba warriors and other Tibetan exiles, led by the Camp Hale graduates, launched raids and spying missions into their home country between the mid 1950s and the early 1960s.

These operations met with some successes, notably the capture, in 1961, of a large stash of Chinese military documents, which highlighted the failures of Mao's 'Great Leap Forward'. The CIA, likewise, figured in the flight of the Dalai Lama from Lhasa in 1959.[81] However, the mounting of an operation on the scale of STCIRCUS was fraught with problems, not least among which was the fact that measures short of war proved insufficient in the face of a determined foe such as Mao proved to be. Indeed, it was the eruption of popular dissent into open rebellion and the PLA's crushing of that uprising that caused the Dalai Lama to flee. Moreover, Beijing's construction of a highway on which troops and supplies could be transported quickly from the Chinese province of Sinkiang to Tibet rendered the agency's prospects of loosening, let alone rolling back, the PRC's control of Tibet all but null and void.

Also significant in impairing STCIRCUS was the fact that its fortunes were very much dependent on wider political and domestic factors. Looming largest in this respect was an Indo-American relationship that proved variable over the near twenty years that STCIRCUS continued. Thus, when disputes arose between Delhi and Washington, the Indian authorities applied pressure on Nepal to constrain the activities of the CIA-supplied Tibetan exiles on its territory. When, on the other hand, relations warmed, for instance during and after the 1962 Indo-Chinese border conflict, the result was a coming together of American and Indian interests, and the STCIRCUS Task Force benefited accordingly. In the sphere of domestic politics, the Tibetan cause attracted a good deal of sympathy in the United States, but this was tempered by the efforts of the China lobby, which, at the insistence of Chiang Kai-shek – who in this case was at one with Mao – contested the legitimacy of Tibetan independence. Where greater cooperation could have been expected was within the CIA itself, but STCIRCUS fell victim to disputes between the agency's Near East and Far East Divisions.

Despite these drawbacks, the programme endured. What it could not endure, however, was a radical change in Sino-American relations, and the Nixon administration's adoption of détente during the late 1960s and early 1970s sounded the death knell for a programme that began under Eisenhower's watch and continued for the best part of two decades.[82]

*   *   *

Of all the tools in the agency's covert arsenal, the one that gained most currency in the international climate of the fifties, however, was its capacity to act pre-emptively to stop communism taking hold in the third world. Preventive operations were in fact deployed before Eisenhower's tenure. The OPC is thought to have had some input in two coups d'etat that were mounted successfully during 1949 by conservatives in Syria against leftward-leaning nationalist governments.[83] However, the changed global environment that took hold from 1953 onwards led Eisenhower to place much greater urgency on the need to act preventively than Truman had been prepared to do. From the CIA's perspective, this trend was not driven purely by the requirement to achieve tangible successes in order to impress its political masters and counter its bureaucratic rivals. It was also fuelled by a sense of political conviction on the part of the individuals responsible for carrying out the DDP's mission in the developing world.

In the eyes of many CIA operatives, the agency's interventions in the third world amounted to well-intentioned assistance. Indeed, Allen Dulles put this view across very clearly himself, arguing that Moscow was utilising an "orchestra of subversion" to bring the unwitting backwaters of the developing world into the Soviet Union's ideological sphere. Therefore, in the genuine belief that it was morally obligated to foster global freedom and democracy, the CIA saw itself as being perfectly justified in resorting to any means necessary to counter such underhand and duplicitous Russian tactics.[84] Heavy on cold war rhetoric, Dulles's worldview was notable for its identification of a Soviet-directed communist menace as central to all of the serious challenges that confronted the United States and its allies in the developing world, yet this did not always, indeed did not often, conform to reality.

The Middle East stands as a case in point. [85] The most pronounced opposition to western interests in this region during the 1950s came from nonaligned pan-Arab nationalism, as personified by Gamal Abdul Nasser: and Nasser himself came to be very familiar with the machinations of the CIA, both as a client and as a target.[86] After receiving an unspecified and still debated degree of agency support in his ouster of King Farouk of Egypt in July 1952, Nasser, along with Muhammad Naguib and the Revolutionary Command Council of Free Officers that they led, were initially viewed by the agency as assets.[87] Distrustful of the British as Nasser was, his programme for the rapid development of Egyptian industry and agriculture was largely welcomed by Washington. Consequently, the Eisenhower administration gave an initially positive, if cautious, response when Nasser sought finance to help fund the construction of a dam on the Nile, which was seen as essential in order to provide hydro-electric power to meet Egypt's anticipated needs – a prudent move, given that it was feared a rejection by the United States might lead Nasser to seek the alternative of Soviet aid.[88]

What sent Egyptian-American relations into sharp decline was the increasingly nonaligned stance that Nasser adopted during 1955 and 1956. Cairo's purchase of arms from Czechoslovakia in 1955, its repudiation of the Baghdad Pact in 1956, and its recognition of the PRC during the same year eroded Washington's confidence in Nasser and caused Eisenhower to withhold funding for the Aswan Dam, which in turn proved crucial in triggering the Suez crisis.[89] More to the point, these developments also transformed Nasser, and other prominent figures in the Middle East who shared his pan-Arab views, into targets for the CIA's attentions.

As discussed previously, the OPC/DDP was active in the Arabian Peninsula and the wider Middle East prior to Washington's fall-out with Nasser – especially in a politically unstable Syria, where a succession of military coups saw leftward-leaning nationalists and conservatives displace each other no less than three times in 1949 alone.[90] However, more substantive CIA covert action was implemented with Project OMEGA, an overarching region-wide campaign, authorized in 1956 and designed to strangle Nasserite pan-Arabism in its infancy, on the grounds that it was a Trojan horse for a Soviet political advance on the Middle East.[91]

The resultant initiatives met with varying degrees of success. DDP support helped ensure that the Jordanian and Saudi Arabian monarchies held firm in the face of two attempted coups – in 1957 and 1960 respectively – and proved significant in maintaining the pro-western, Lebanese president, Camille Chamoun in power until 1958, when Washington invoked the Eisenhower Doctrine and sent in the marines to secure Chamoun's position.[92] Otherwise, the agency's efforts proved ill-fated. Its strategy to bring about regime change a Syria, through the Anglo-American Operation STRAGGLE, was interrupted by the Suez crisis and thwarted by Syrian counterintelligence in late October 1956. Plans were once again set in motion in 1957, with the exclusively American Operation WAPPEN, but the agency's hand was quickly exposed and WAPPEN served only to accelerate Syria's decision to join with Egypt and Yemen, to establish the short-lived United Arab Republic (UAR) in 1958.[93]

American efforts in Egypt itself proved to be similarly discouraging. Washington and London had not always been at one on the subject of Nasser but, in spite of the rupture in Anglo-American relations that resulted from Suez, the two powers reached a meeting of minds with the authorisation of Operation SIPONY in 1957. A joint DDP-MI6 plan to secure Egyptian army support and thereby topple Nasser in a palace coup, SIPONY failed to achieve its intended objective.[94] The same held true in Iraq, where the CIA was unable to prevent Colonel Abdul-Rauf al-Qassim, an authoritarian who attached himself to the ideas expounded by Nasser, from sweeping into power in a bloody coup that saw the murder of Iraq's ruling family and the country's president, Nuri as Said.[95]

What stands out about the CIA's interventions in nearly all of these countries is that, in American calculations, they were justified on grounds that a hidden Russian hand was directing events and creating the conditions that forced the agency to act. This was palpably not the case. However much the Eisenhower administration convinced itself that Egypt might fall under Moscow's control or that Syria was tantamount to a Soviet satellite, neither Nasser nor his neighbouring allies were communist stooges.[96] The Egyptian leader's paramount objective was to establish a nonaligned Arab bloc and he sought to play East off against West, most notably in negotiating funding for the Aswan Dam, in order to get the best possible deal for his country and secure his own position as the undisputed leader of the Arab world.[97] For Nasser, Israel and Britain were the principal enemies and not the Russians, who he regarded as having demonstrated "no signs of hostility" towards Egypt.[98]

*   *   *

Though much of what the CIA sought to achieve through its covert operations in Egypt and Syria came to nothing, the same cold war ethos and mindset that provided justification for their authorisation and execution also informed the agency's more successful interventions of this period: notably the campaigns mounted in Iran and Guatemala, both of which stand as pivotal events in CIA history. Quick and relatively bloodless affairs, these ventures were instrumental in causing policymakers in Washington and agency officials alike to acquire a sense of confidence in the CIA's capacity to produce operational successes in the furtherance of foreign policy. As a result of these and other less publicised 'victories', the DDP continued to be viewed as a "directorate apart" and to predominate in terms of financial resources and personnel within the agency throughout the 1950s.[99]

In specialising in covert action, however, the CIA's managers demonstrated an accompanying disinclination to develop the agency's intelligence-gathering, coordinating, and estimating functions. Indeed, Allen Dulles's neglect of the DDI has subsequently been seen as having amounted to a lost opportunity.[100] Yet in pursuing such a course, the DCI was in a sense merely recognising the difficult realities of attempting to interact with other agencies in an expanding and diversifying intelligence community.

The CIA was established to coordinate, streamline, and make more efficient, the entire American intelligence effort. However, from the time of its inception the agency consistently failed in this mission. Despite Bedell Smith's reorganisation of the CIA's collection and evaluation procedures, the most pressing problem endured. The Defense Department's intelligence components continued to guard their own information jealously and excluded the DDI from military analyses.[101] Allen Dulles identified the essence of the CIA's difficulties in this respect when he later reflected that "it is in the nature of people and institutions that any upstart is going to be somewhat frowned upon and its intrusions resented at first by the more well established and traditional institutions".[102] This problem was particularly acute during the 1950s, moreover, when all branches of the military were making determined attempts to defend their ground against post-Korean War cutbacks.[103]

There was, as well, the additional consideration that *none* of America's intelligence agencies had been successful in securing reliable information on the Soviet Union, which rendered the task of assessing Russian capabilities and intentions accurately all but impossible. The agency was therefore well advised to shift the primary focus of its activities away from prediction, regardless of whether or not the military and State Department intelligence components were prepared to cooperate. Also to be taken into account is the point that the CIA was established very hurriedly. It consequently did not have time to build up long-term undercover networks and so had to rely on information passed on from the intelligence agencies of America's allies. Unfortunately, all of the prime sources of support were to a greater or lesser extent compromised. Thus, the CIA was as suspicious of ex-Nazis in the Gehlen organisation as it was of Zionists in Mossad, and the defections of Burgess and Maclean, along with the uncovering of Philby, left the British SIS tainted.[104]

The agency's efforts in the sphere of traditional espionage and prediction during the 1950s were thus disappointing. The whole world had, as Allen Dulles pointed out, become an arena for conflict and it was impossible to foretell where the next danger would develop.[105] Senior policymakers did not, anyway, read the National Intelligence Estimates (NIEs) that the DDI circulated, which could only have accentuated the sense of futility surrounding the whole exercise.[106]

Equally influential on the CIA's disinclination to prioritise the collection and evaluation of intelligence by traditional methods was the trend towards specialisation in the intelligence community generally, as exemplified by the National Security Agency (NSA). Founded by secret presidential signature on 4 November 1952, the NSA was established in an effort to meet the recommendations of the Brownell Committee, which during the previous June had stipulated the need for the United States to improve its capacity to produce SIGINT (intelligence derived from the interception and analysis of signals). Well aware of the invaluable role played by the Anglo-American MAGIC and ULTRA decrypting offensives in the defeat of the Axis powers during World War II, and of VENONA in the fight against communism, Eisenhower poured enormous resources into the NSA during his two terms as president. Consequently, the new agency very quickly became the forerunner in the research and development of computer technology, and it soon outgrew the CIA in terms of both budget and personnel.[107]

Eisenhower's commitment to the NSA was not misplaced. Advances in SIGINT technology produced results that literally revolutionised America's intelligence-collection and evaluation capacity. The new agency enabled the United States to monitor the first Russian Intermediate Range Ballistic Missile (IRBM) launches, and it also detected gaps in the Soviet air defence system that left a large section of northern Siberia without radar cover. There was, however, a downside to this discovery in that it paved the way for possibly the most audacious and risk-laden spying mission of the entire Cold War – Project Homerun.[108]

Carried out over a seven week period during the spring of 1956, Homerun deployed some fifty American Air Force bombers, which were temporarily stationed in Greenland and flew a succession of espionage missions in groups of eight to ten aircraft over 3,500 miles of the northern USSR from Murmansk to the Kola Peninsula. Extremely dangerous and potentially provocative in itself, what made Homerun doubly menacing was that its flight path followed a direct line over the North Pole: the shortest route for an American air attack on the Soviet Union. Given that Russian radar operators could not have known – if they ever became aware of the incursions – what the purpose of the American bombers was, then these overflights risked triggering a third world war.[109] Bearing Homerun in mind, then, it was fortuitous that Washington was soon able to utilise safer, though still risky, methods of aerial reconnaissance in its information-gathering offensive against the USSR – with the advent of the U-2 spy plane.

The U-2 Spy Plane

The fact that Eisenhower placed a premium on information provided by a civilian agency, the NSA, to enlighten him on the military-industrial potential of the prospective enemy and at the same time enable him to scrutinise, and where necessary refute, the claims of the American military, pointed the direction in which the CIA's intelligence mission would evolve. To preserve and enhance its position at the cutting edge of the information-gathering offensive against the USSR, the agency again sought to specialise, just as it did in the sphere of covert action. The opportunity arrived when Eisenhower authorised the Aquatone Project on 9 December 1954, thereby ordering the CIA to develop the U-2 spy plane.[110]

Built in greatest secrecy by the agency and the Lockheed Aircraft Corporation with the assistance of the Polaroid and Hycon photographic companies, the U-2 was essentially a glider fitted with a jet engine and armed with innovative camera technology. It could fly over great distances at such high altitudes that it remained beyond the reach of Russian anti-aircraft facilities and impervious to attacks from Soviet fighters.[111] As with SIGINT, wartime experience had confirmed Eisenhower as an enthusiast of aerial photoreconnaissance, and the president was similarly determined to keep the U-2 programme out of the hands of the military. In this respect, Eisenhower was particularly suspicious of permitting the Air Force – which he believed had deliberately orchestrated a 'bomber gap' controversy in order to pry funds out of Congress – to assume sole control over the collection and evaluation of the highly sensitive intelligence on the Soviet Union that the spy plane was likely to produce.[112] Thus, despite the attempts of General Curtis LeMay to first kill off the U-2 programme at birth, then, having failed in this effort, bring the enterprise under the exclusive control of the Strategic Air Command, the Aquatone Project proceeded apace with the CIA and the Air Force proving effective partners.[113]

Agency participation in the U-2 enterprise had essentially four elements. Firstly, the programme was placed under the direction of Richard Bissell, who was charged with streamlining the whole process, maintaining maximum secrecy, and ensuring that it did not become entangled in the bureaucracy of the Defense Department. Consistent with the role of paymaster that the OPC/DDP had frequently played in operations since the late forties, the CIA was, secondly, "the procurement organisation" for Aquatone, funding the project through its Contingency Reserve, which was appropriated and voted on by Congress.[114] Thirdly, and in compliance with Eisenhower's stipulation that "no U.S. military aircraft [be permitted] to penetrate Soviet airspace" (an oddly contradictory demand, given that Eisenhower is said to have personally authorised Project Homerun), the agency provided civilian cover for the pilots and ground staff recruited from the ranks of the Air Force to carry out the mission. Finally, the CIA supplied the photointerpreters who, under Arthur Lundahl, analysed the material that the U-2s brought back.[115]

The U-2 made its first operational flight in July 1956 and over the next four years spy planes carried out approximately two hundred missions, filming the Soviet Union's most secret industrial and military installations. Providing unprecedented amounts of data on Soviet nuclear weapons and ballistic missile test programmes, Aquatone enabled the CIA to assert itself as a pioneer in the field of advanced technological intelligence collection.[116] Indeed, until the shooting down of Francis Gary Powers's spy plane over Soviet airspace in May 1960, the agency was in effect providing Eisenhower with a clandestine alternative to his Open Skies proposals, and thereby directly advancing American foreign policy objectives.[117]

A further dimension of the U-2 project was that it enabled the CIA to work in partnership with the NSA to supply the best intelligence possible on any given issue. For example, U-2s on occasion carried NSA payloads that recorded emissions from Soviet radar, microwave and ground communications. During the Suez crisis, NSA reports of vast increases in diplomatic traffic between Tel Aviv and Paris, combined with U-2 photographic evidence revealing a rapid increase in Anglo-French military activity in the Mediterranean, gave Eisenhower a clear indication of the likely direction of events. Through specialisation, then, the CIA took its place alongside the NSA at the technological frontier of intelligence work.

Unlike the FBI, which could only assist the NSA's activities through low level "black jobs", such as penetrating foreign embassies to obtain information on ciphers and install listening devices, the CIA was able to complement the new agency on an equal footing.[118]

Although Aquatone was ostensibly an intelligence-gathering operation, there was a psychological warfare dimension to it. The fact that American spy planes could "overfly [the Soviet Union] with impunity and [Moscow] couldn't do a goddamn thing about it" exposed the technical superiority that the United States enjoyed over its superpower rival. The U-2 thus gave Washington a psychological as well as material advantage in the Cold War and was in itself "a good deterrent".[119] In this respect there were parallels between Aquatone and Operation Gold. Here the CIA and SIS constructed a 1,476-foot tunnel from West to East Berlin and for nearly a year – from the spring of 1955 to 1956 – tapped into a 350-line phone cable that connected the Russian sector of the city with military bases all over Eastern Europe. The enterprise was compromised by the British double-agent George Blake, and its uncovering by Soviet security forces was initially regarded as a major western setback. There was, however, a more positive element to Operation Gold's exposure, in that it revealed American ingenuity was being effectively applied in the fight against communism, and thereby served as an enormous morale booster for West Germans in general and West Berliners in particular.[120] If, then, Eisenhower was not rolling back communism, he certainly was placing sufficient emphasis on the coercive element of containment to maintain unremitting pressure on the USSR and its allies.

Conclusion: The Trend Towards Preventive Operations – Continuity and Change

The Eisenhower administration has frequently been characterised as having overused covert action in its efforts to assert American power around the globe, and as having departed from earlier precedents in doing so. While concurring with the logic of the Truman administration, that 'friendly' governments should be supported, Eisenhower, it is argued, did not share his predecessor's resistance to removing what Allen Dulles described as communist 'stooges'.[121] This is not entirely true. As has been shown, there were instances of clandestine operations being mounted against non-aligned third world leaders, particularly in the Middle East, during Truman's tenure. What the coming of the new Republican administration did was to bring about an acceleration of this trend, which consequently bred an overzealous reliance on surreptitious methods to solve difficult foreign policy issues.

Proposals for covert action could, of course, be subjected to high-level scrutiny. Bedell Smith had, after all, created the Psychological Strategy Board for this very purpose, and Eisenhower revised the guidance procedures for clandestine operations twice during his presidency, replacing the PSB with the Operations

Coordinating Board (OCB) in September 1953, and providing for additional oversight through the establishment of the Special Group or 5412 Committee in December 1954.[122] Much as these various acronyms might have implied presidential determination to observe control procedures with increasing stringency, the Executive lacked the political will to provide firm policy guidance during Eisenhower's tenure. For its part, the Legislature has been shown by David Barrett to have been far more frequent and thorough in calling Allen Dulles and his colleagues to account than was previously believed. However, the CIA's track record in the sphere of covert action during the Dulles years suggests the DCI's claim that Congress showed "little hesitation" in supporting and financing the agency's work has more than a ring of truth to it. In essence, then, favourable attitudes towards the DDP prevailed across the full spectrum of government. Thus, when efforts were made to secure firm oversight procedures, notably by Senator Mike Mansfield, they were frustrated by both the Executive and in Congress.[123]

The proliferation of CIA covert action projects during the 1950s was also attributable to capricious administrative procedures in the agency as a whole and especially within the DDP. Allen Dulles earned renown as a sympathetic manager of the CIA, who stood firm against McCarthy, warning of severe repercussions against any employee who cooperated with the senator in his efforts to investigate the agency. The DCI was not, however, an advocate of strong internal management. On the contrary, he and his senior colleagues in the operations directorate viewed the imposition of strict lines of authority as being counterproductive to the functional dynamics of a covert action mission that, by this time, had reached its pinnacle. Clear evidence of this emerged with the CIA's ouster of the governments of Iran and Guatemala in 1953 and 1954 respectively.[124]

6

A TALE OF THREE CAMPAIGNS: LANDMARKS IN THE HEYDAY OF COVERT ACTION

Eisenhower's period as president signalled the high-water mark for the deployment of clandestine operations by the United States, and the three campaigns featured in this chapter stand out both as prominent events in themselves and signposts in the evolution of covert action during this era. While the coming of the new administration saw little change in the CIA's modus operandi in Western Europe, Eisenhower took a more aggressive approach in his application of covert action in the third world. Here, his propensity for the deployment of preventive operations quickly asserted itself, and the first venture of this nature to be authorised during his tenure was Operation TPAJAX, the CIA-engineered coup that resulted in the removal of the Iranian Prime Minister, Muhammad Musaddiq, from power in August 1953.

The Iran coup signalled a significant departure and set an important precedent, and is thus the first case study to be included in this chapter.[1] CIA preventive covert action had been sanctioned to depose governing regimes before, but Musaddiq was the first democratically-elected leader to be removed through such methods. What must, nevertheless, be stressed is that TPAJAX was designed to serve long-term American policy. The replacement of Musaddiq by a less nationalistic, more western-friendly Iranian leader who, at least in American perceptions, was less vulnerable to a communist takeover, was seen by Eisenhower as essential if the United States was to: (1) safeguard supplies of Persian oil to the West; (2) secure Iran as a country of vital strategic importance for containing communism; and (3) advance American plans to transform Iran into a modern westernised state.

Initiating a coup d'état was far from the most enlightened way to serve these objectives, in that replacing Musaddiq with a dictator, however temporary the arrangement was originally planned to be, was hardly the best way to foster democracy. Moreover, Eisenhower took little account of the negative long-term effects on American-Iranian relations that the coup would have. There was, as well, the point that the policy itself was fatally flawed. Modernisation on a western model did not rest easily with the traditional cultural, social and religious structures in Iran. This, combined with the absence of democracy after 1953, served only to widen the gap between the political elite and the masses of the country, who remained impoverished and turned ultimately, not to the communists but to the religious right for succour. Nevertheless, misguided as they were, successive American administrations did have long-term policy objectives to serve in Iran and the sanctioning of the 1953 coup was at the time seen as assisting these aims.

In the case of the Guatemala coup, code-named PBSUCCESS, Eisenhower's primary objective was to remove an overtly leftist government, which implemented policies that, in American calculations, opened the way for the establishment of "a Soviet beachhead in the Western Hemisphere".[2] Deeper research into the ouster of Guatemalan President, Jacobo Arbenz Guzmán in June 1954, however, suggests that it was driven by more multifarious motives than at first seems apparent. In brief, PBSUCCESS served as a ready expedient. It drew attention away from the French withdrawal from Indochina while simultaneously acting as a catalyst for Foster Dulles's achievement of anticommunist hemispheric solidarity in the Americas. Arbenz's downfall, furthermore, illustrated to informed opinion in the United States that Eisenhower was able to pursue a hard line against what was represented as international communism without resorting to war, which in turn assisted the president in his plan to neutralise Senator Joseph McCarthy's influence on the GOP.

A similar mindset governed the decisions to sanction TPAJAX and PBSUCCESS. Richard Immerman's argument that Arbenz's downfall resulted from the Cold War ethos, which exaggerated Washington's perception of communist infiltration in Guatemala, could just as easily be applied to the ouster of Musaddiq.[3] Not only this, but the fact that TPAJAX succeeded had a huge impact on the administration's decision to sanction PBSUCCESS.

The Guatemala coup said much about Eisenhower's style of leadership, in the sense that he blurred the distinction between policy and strategy during the venture and in the process acted more in the manner of a general than a president, in order to achieve a number of widely dispersed but intricately connected short-term goals. The irony was that in acting to neutralise communism where its influence was limited, the Eisenhower administration inadvertently helped to create the conditions that would enable the Soviet Union to extend its influence to Cuba and subsequently the Americas by the dawn of the next decade.

PBSUCCESS was additionally significant for the nature of its execution. Unlike the covert action programmes in Western Europe or indeed Iran, there were no existing intelligence networks in place in Guatemala immediately prior to the preparations for the coup. Those contacts that the CIA had put in place previously were wiped out in a botched mutiny against Arbenz in March 1953.[4] The agency thus created something from nothing in establishing an entirely new covert action infrastructure, and despite having to muster the necessary resources very hastily the

CIA scored what was interpreted at the time as an unqualified success. This heightened the administration's future preparedness to utilise covert action as a golden bullet to resolve pressing foreign policy issues elsewhere. The Guatemala campaign was thus the model for the failed attempt to depose the Indonesian premier Achmed Sukarno in 1958, the final case study to be featured here, and the Bay of Pigs fiasco of 1961. Both of these operations were embarrassing debacles for the United States. They sprang, however, from an overconfidence and lack of foresight that can be traced back to June 1953, when Eisenhower sanctioned Operation TPAJAX.[5]

America, Britain and Iran: Shifting Policy Positions

Long-range planning for the advancement of United States interests in Iran began in 1945, when a seven year, $656 million economic development plan was devised at the request of the Iranian Shah, Muhammad Reza Pahlavi, by Overseas Consultants Incorporated (OCI), a private consortium with close links to government circles in Washington.[6] Approved by the Iranian parliament (the Majlis) in February 1949, the OCI plan and concurrent American government initiatives sought to provide the necessary aid and expertise to help transform a hitherto backward Iran into a modern, economically vibrant, and socially cohesive democracy.[7] The problem for the United States was that its modernisation plans quickly became undermined by an Anglo-Iranian dispute that centred on the future of Persian oil.[8]

The questions of who should control Iran's oil reserves and where political power in the country should be concentrated had long been at issue. From the early 1900s the Anglo-Iranian Oil Company (AIOC) maintained a near monopoly over Persia's oil, and this was accompanied by what most Iranians regarded as unwarranted interference in their country's internal affairs by a British government that owned fifty per cent of AIOC's stock. Ending the British stranglehold, as such, became the focus of escalating Iranian discontent and this came to a head in the spring of 1951 when a broadly based National Front coalition, headed by Musaddiq, won power and passed a nationalisation bill aimed at expropriating the AIOC's assets. The United Kingdom responded by closing down its Abadan oil refinery and initiating a worldwide boycott of Iranian oil from July 1951. A crisis that was to continue for two years thereby began.[9]

In response to these developments, the United States sought a compromise aimed at persuading Musaddiq to accept an agreement that approximated the fifty-fifty profit sharing arrangement that American oil companies had struck with Saudi Arabia, while simultaneously placating the British and, where necessary, deterring any designs at direct intervention emanating from that quarter.[10] At the core of American policy was a determination on Truman's part to prevent the Anglo-Iranian dispute from triggering a wider conflict at a time when international tensions were already high as a result of the Korean War. Washington feared that direct British military intervention would present the Russians with a pretext to occupy Iranian Azerbaijan and support a seizure of power by the Tudeh – the Iranian Communist Party.[11]

By December 1952 the British embargo was fuelling widespread economic discontent for the Tudeh to exploit and an increasingly alarmed Secretary of State Dean Acheson consequently revised Washington's policy position, seeking to persuade both sides to submit their differences to the International Court of Justice. Aimed at finally settling the crisis, this initiative proved acceptable to the British, who agreed to lift the blockade on Iranian oil exports while the court deliberated. For Musaddiq, however, the Acheson proposals and the generous aid package that Washington offered with it as an incentive to secure Iranian acquiescence, proved unacceptable.[12] In effect, then, the United States had exhausted the possibilities for reaching a negotiated settlement by January 1953. Few of the treatments that deal specifically with the Iran coup acknowledge this point, but it is nevertheless important because it narrowed the avenues left open to Washington and thus increased the prospect of a covert operation being launched regardless of who succeeded Truman as president.

Eisenhower had become well versed in the nuances of the Iranian oil crisis while Supreme Allied Commander in Europe, and he received official briefings on how the dispute was developing during the 1952 election campaign and while president-elect.[13] Consequently, when Musaddiq wrote to the new president outlining the heightened danger of a Tudeh takeover if increased American aid was not forthcoming, the Iranian leader paved the way to his own ouster.[14] Equally significant in sowing the seeds of Musaddiq's political demise was the revision of broader American policy that was brought about by Nasser's rejection of Foster Dulles's plan for an Egypt-centred Middle Eastern defence organisation. Still committed to regional collective security, the Secretary of State moved to establish an alliance system along the northern tier, incorporating Iraq, Pakistan, and Turkey.[15] The inclusion of a strong and stable Iran was pivotal to Dulles's projections but this was not achievable whilst Musaddiq remained in power. The implication was therefore that Iran would have to be 'saved' from itself, if only for the sake of western strategic interests in the Middle East.[16]

The fact that Eisenhower was anticipated as favouring intervention in Iran where his predecessor had opted for restraint is evident from the advice proffered by the head of the CIA's Near East and Africa (NEA) Division and would-be project chief of TPAJAX, Kermit 'Kim' Roosevelt, to SIS officials late in 1952. British intelligence should wait, Roosevelt suggested, until the new Republican administration was installed before proposing the launch of an Anglo-American covert operation to remove Musaddiq from power.[17] Roosevelt's assessment was, moreover, quickly confirmed when, in March 1953, Foster Dulles and the United States Ambassador to Iran, Loy Henderson gauged the risks involved in replacing the Iranian premier with General Fazlullah Zahedi as being acceptable.[18] Despite his history as a one-time Nazi sympathiser and his possession of almost no military assets, Zahedi's readiness to acquiesce to Washington's wishes made him the preferred candidate to replace Musaddiq in a campaign that would serve not only the interests of the United States government but also those the American oil industry.[19]

Oil Multinationals and Economic Warfare

United States policy in Iran and the Middle East generally was dictated by a complex combination of mutually reinforcing geopolitical, strategic, and economic considerations. American petroleum companies served their country's foreign policy objectives from 1948, when Standard of California, Exxon (Esso), Texaco, and Mobil formed the Arabian American Oil Company (Aramco) in order to exploit Saudi Arabia's as yet untapped oil reserves. Aramco gave the United States a foothold in a region that had previously been dominated by European powers and, more importantly, Saudi Arabian oil production, while providing Aramco with enormous profits, also helped fuel the ERP and provide energy supplies for NATO.

Further public private sector collaboration followed in 1950 when the Truman administration permitted the Aramco companies to share their profits with the Saudi Arabian government on a fifty-fifty basis and deduct the payment to Riyadh as a business expense when calculating their American income taxes. The quite separate and ostensibly conflicting policy objectives of affording Israel overt American support, while providing Saudi Arabia with a subsidy that bound it more closely to the United States could thereby be achieved.[20] Aramco's fifty-fifty deal with Saudi Arabia, and similar arrangements negotiated by American companies with Kuwait in December 1951 and Iraq in February 1952, moreover, stood as blueprints for what Iranian nationalists could reasonably expect to gain from the AIOC.[21] Much as this accentuated the Anglo-Persian dispute, it also served United States ambitions in Iran.

American designs on breaking the British monopoly over Iranian oil were apparent from as early as 1943, when James Byrnes argued that the United States should press for a one third share of Persia's oil reserves as compensation for American contributions to the war effort. Though Franklin Roosevelt vetoed this proposal, American ambitions in relation to Iran continued into the postwar period.[22] The British-initiated international boycott of Iranian oil, of course, had the full backing of the American oil companies. It was not, after all, in the interests of any multinational to allow Musaddiq to succeed in expropriating AIOC's assets unilaterally and thereby set an example for other third world leaders who might wish to follow suit. The closure of Abadan, moreover, presented an opportunity for American petroleum firms to increase production in Saudi Arabia, Iraq and Kuwait to cover the shortfall.[23] This does not, however, alter the fact that American companies sought a share of the lucrative Iranian industry. Indeed, Truman's Assistant Secretary of State George McGhee was forced to go to considerable lengths during 1951 and 1952 to prevent American oil companies from exploiting AIOC's difficulties.[24]

For his part, Eisenhower proved to be even more concerned than Truman had been to ensure that the activities of the American petroleum multinationals should reinforce foreign policy. Referring to the oil industry in August 1953, the president stressed to his Attorney General that the enforcement of antitrust legislation introduced by Truman "may be deemed secondary to the national security interest".[25] Eisenhower well understood that Iranian nationalism was providing a lever through which to prise open AIOC's hold on Persian oil reserves, as was implicit in a letter sent by the president to Prime Minister Churchill in early May 1953.[26] In return for deposing Musaddiq, the United States sought to exact a cost. American oil companies were to be given 40 per cent of the Iranian oil industry, with AIOC retaining only 40 per cent of its former monopoly, and a further 14 per cent being allocated to Royal Dutch Shell and 6 per cent to Compagnie Française de Pétroles. The United States government thereby rewarded the American multinationals for their restraint over the previous two years.[27]

A multinational in turn rewarded Kim Roosevelt, not only for executing the coup successfully, but also for conducting a three-year campaign of economic warfare in the Middle East, which was launched after Overseas Consultants became concerned that the crisis in Iran was nullifying their Seven Year Plan and turned to the OPC to break the deadlock. In the execution of this programme, Roosevelt played a central role in negotiating the fifty-fifty deal with the Saudis that proved such a crucial factor in undermining the British position in Iran and triggering off the string of events that led to the autorisation of TPAJAX.[28] For his efforts, Roosevelt was named vice president of the Gulf Oil Corporation in 1960.[29]

TPAJAX: A Covert Action Precedent

Kim Roosevelt, of course, wrote his own account of the Iran coup and if only for the reason that he commanded Operation TPAJAX, it remains a valuable a source. However, *Countercoup* raises as many doubts as it answers questions. Even the central contention of the book, that TPAJAX was sanctioned in order to prevent the very real threat of a takeover by the Russian-backed Tudeh Party, which Roosevelt presents as being in alliance with Musaddiq, fails to convince.[30]

To begin with, the Kremlin was far from unequivocal in its support the Tudeh, believing the overtly doctrinaire approach taken by the Iranian communists to be out of step in a country where *nationalist* credentials carried most weight.[31] Though the Tudeh operated with a modicum of freedom, moreover, it was declared illegal in 1949 and Musaddiq proved ready to clamp down on communist demonstrations whenever they were deemed to be threatening to political stability in Iran, most notably in July 1951.[32]

No tangible evidence has yet materialised to support the claim that either Roosevelt or any other American official possessed proof that the Soviet Union wished to see a communist takeover. However, the fact that the Russians withdrew from Iran under American pressure in 1946, when coupled with the Soviet leadership's efforts to build bridges with the West at the time of the coup itself, suggests that Moscow was as keen to see a Tudeh takeover in Iran as it had been to see the PCI prevail in the Italian elections of 1948. Put simply, a local communist victory carried potentially damaging ramifications for superpower relations, and in Russian calculations this was too high a cost for the Soviet Union to contemplate.

The true nature of Musaddiq's flirtation with the Tudeh, only comes to light when the internal dynamics of Iranian politics are taken into account. The National Front coalition was an extremely fractious organisation, which incorporated groups ranging from Ayatollah Abdul Qassim Kashani's Society of Muslim Warriors to the liberal and secular Iran Party. Musaddiq's close association with the liberal nationalists drew fire from Kashani, who broke with the National Front and from 1952 began cooperating quietly with the shah. Under these circumstances the Iranian premier forged a very tentative arrangement with the communists based on a mutual interest in survival, but he became ever more reliant on this relationship as pressure from his indigenous opponents, the British, and later the United States intensified.[33]

On 4 April 1953, the CIA's Iran station was allocated a budget of $1 million to undermine Musaddiq's government over a four-month period and thus pave the way for his removal. A Special Iran Task Force commanded by Roosevelt was established within the DDP to plan and oversee the campaign and official blessing for the coup-proper was subsequently granted on 25 June 1953.[34] What should, however, be borne in mind is that this was far from the first instance of CIA intervention in Iran's internal affairs. As Mark Gasiorowski has demonstrated, the OPC/DDP engaged in a wide range of clandestine activities in the country from 1948. Code-named BEDAMN, the earlier enterprise found the OPC working in conjunction with two Iranian brothers, tagged Nerren and Cilley, to: (1) undermine the Iranian communists through false flag attacks on mosques and key public figures; and (2) weaken Musaddiq's base of support by offering bribes to his rivals within the governing coalition.[35]

Beyond BEDAMN and in line with wider American war plans, the OPC/DDP also drew up contingencies for the creation of stay-behind units recruited from the Qashqua'i tribe. Essentially preparatory in nature, these measures were drafted at about the same time as the CIA's Middle Eastern economic warfare programme was implemented. Looked at collectively, however, the various initiatives discussed put the agency at a decided advantage once Eisenhower had authorised TPAJAX.[36]

The manipulation of Iran's Muslim clerics, for instance, proved important to the BEDAMN programme and crucial during a TPAJAX campaign that, at its most extreme, resorted to the "sham bombing" of an unnamed cleric's residence. In that it mobilised some of the mullahs into taking action against Musaddiq, this tactic was gauged by the CIA to have contributed to the "positive outcome" of TPAJAX.[37] The deployment of *agents provocateurs* was, likewise, a key component of both the BEDAMN programme and Operation TPAJAX, as Roosevelt's reliance on bogus crowds to heighten political tension illustrates.[38] Miles Copeland, who was dispatched to Iran by Roosevelt to make a logistical survey in preparation for the coup, sheds further light. Having arrived in Tehran, Copeland discovered that CIA operatives had already charted the routes that the demonstrating hordes would have to take, and pinpointed the targets that anyone organising a coup would need to seize. He was also introduced to the "Zirkaneh Giants", a group of weightlifters who were funded covertly by the CIA and would, at the appropriate time, be used to "direct and control the rent-a-mobs".[39]

Of additional advantage to Roosevelt was the fact that he inherited SIS networks, which were controlled by the Rashidian brothers, and had been active in Iran since 1951 as part of the overall British strategy to remove Musaddiq from power. MI6 had in fact conducted two failed covert operations in March and October 1952 with the specific purpose of deposing the Iranian leader and the second of these had resulted in Musaddiq breaking off diplomatic relations with the United Kingdom.[40] The closure of the British embassy created serious problems for SIS, for although its networks remained in place, there was no secure base from which to coordinate operations. This was essentially why the principal MI6 operative in Persia, Christopher M. Woodhouse, was so keen to secure CIA and the State Department support for an Anglo-American operation to remove Musaddiq.[41]

Roosevelt's Iran Task Force assistant Donald Wilber later claimed to have been the sole author of TPAJAX, but this is refuted in most accounts of the 1953 coup, which generally support British charges that the operation was a rewrite of earlier plans developed by SIS Chief Sir John Sinclair and his colleague George Young.[42] The most crucial point, however, is that in presenting his bosses in Washington with either a modified version of the British-proposed Operation Boot or a new plan devised by Wilber, Roosevelt was in a fortunate position. A new administration that was well disposed towards replacing Musaddiq surreptitiously had come to power and, though Whitehall footed some of the bill, the bulk of the input in terms of resources was to come from the United States.[43] SIS therefore had little other option than to place its assets at Roosevelt's disposal if TPAJAX was to succeed.

Having received official sanction to proceed with Operation TPAJAX, Roosevelt crossed secretly from Iraq into Iran on 19 July 1953. The first stage of the plan involved persuading the shah to exercise the royal prerogative and dismiss Musaddiq in favour of Zahedi. Roosevelt's reliance on firstly Princess Ashraf, the shah's sister, then Brigadier General H. Norman Schwartzkopf, a confidante of the shah's, to perform this task proved fruitless.[44] Only after the intercession of Eisenhower, who agreed to include a cryptic signal in a speech to which Roosevelt urged the shah to listen, was the support of the vacillating monarch secured.[45] The initial stage of the plan backfired, however, when Musaddiq, who had been alerted of the plot, arrested the military commander who delivered the royal decree appointing Zahedi as prime minister. Zahedi was consequently forced into hiding, and the shah left hurriedly with his queen for Rome.

Some debate surrounds what actually happened once the shah reached Rome, for he booked into the same hotel at which Allen Dulles was staying as part of his annual summer vacation. Peter Grose characterises this turn of events as a case of "unfortunate proximity" and maintains that although the monarch and the spymaster were both staying at the Rome Excelsior from 18 to 22 August, their paths never crossed.[46] This argument strains the bounds of credibility to breaking point, especially when taking into account John Prados's claim that a similar "coincidence" occurred only a few days previously when Princess Ashraf and Loy Henderson turned up at San Moritz and met Dulles on the Swiss leg of his holiday.[47] The DCI had a strong interest in ensuring that the shah kept his nerve and that the coup succeeded, if only for the fact that the CIA faced a challenge on the domestic front from McCarthy during the summer of 1953. Indeed, Grose acknowledges this and he also states that Dulles left San Moritz for Rome on 16 August with the intention of monitoring events in Iran.[48] The DCI's vacation was thus at best a working holiday and more likely a cover, all of which lends weight to the argument of David Wise and Thomas Ross, that the shah went to Rome to confer with Dulles.[49]

With the shah and Zahedi temporarily out of the picture, the BEDAMN and Rashidian networks were put on overtime, planting black propaganda in the Iranian media highlighting the dangers confronting the shah, and alleging that a communist-aligned Musaddiq was unable to govern effectively. Raising the tempo of the campaign, the CIA next engineered a bogus Tudeh demonstration that was unwittingly augmented by genuine communist supporters, all of which lent force to the perception that Iran was falling prey to a leftist takeover. This opened the way for Henderson to pressurise Musaddiq into crushing the demonstration on the grounds that the lives of United States citizens resident in Iran were in danger: an argument which would have carried little weight but for the fact that the Tudeh newspaper was calling for the expulsion of American "interventionists".[50] The Iranian leader thus did the ambassador's bidding and suppressed the communist crowds on 18 August, which is evidence in itself that even at this point Musaddiq was not a 'communist stooge'.[51]

The following day saw Roosevelt shift tactics and orchestrate a royalist demonstration, which focused its fire on the Iranian leader rather than the Tudeh. Having been fed radio propaganda, described by Roosevelt as "a pre-truth", which stated that the shah had dismissed Musaddiq and appointed Zahedi as premier, the rapidly growing crowd proceeded to lay siege to Musaddiq's Tehran home.[52] Here, a nine-hour battle ensued before Musaddiq loyalists finally capitulated to their royalist counterparts. Having first escaped, the Iranian premier himself surrendered to Zahedi on 20 August, thereby leaving the way open for the shah to return and continue ruling for a further twenty-six ignominious years.[53]

There are several parallels, at least on a superficial level, between the conditions that prevailed in Iran and in Guatemala prior to the respective CIA actions. Each country was headed by a democratically-elected premier who attempted to expropriate assets from a powerful multinational organisation and in each case reform programmes that were designed to achieve economic independence were interpreted by the United States, either by accident or intent, as being communistic. What, however, is most significant about the Iran coup is that it was a speedy affair executed with, in the estimation of the Eisenhower administration, minimum loss of life and maximum political impact.[54] It thereby set a precedent that would soon be followed in Guatemala.

Guatemala 1954: The Art of Killing Four Birds with One Stone

In 1944 Jorge Ubico Castaneda, the most recent in an unbroken line of dictatorial military strong men (*caudillos*) who had ruled Guatemala since it gained independence in 1821, was overthrown in a popular revolution. His successor and the country's first democratically-elected president was Juan José Arévalo, a university professor who led a coalition known as the Party of Revolutionary Action (PAR). Arévalo oversaw the ratification of a new constitution in 1945, and made significant advances towards democratising Guatemala.[55] Complementary legislation designed to diminish the archaic agrarian system, which had tied the country inextricably to external markets and thus bedevilled its progress during the *caudillo* period, however, set Arévalo on a collision course with an entrenched aristocracy, and more importantly a powerful foreign corporation – namely the United Fruit Company (UFCO).[56]

The largest employer in Guatemala and holder of three vast plantations (*finca*), United Fruit provides a classic example of the enclave organisation. The company monopolised Guatemala's telephone and telegraph facilities, controlled Puerto Barrios, the country's only major port, and owned almost every mile of railway track on Guatemalan soil through its subsidiary company, International Railways of Central America (IRCA). Such holdings allowed United Fruit to maintain exclusive control over Guatemalan banana production and export.[57]

Arevalo's implementation of the 1947 Labour Code, which sought to lay down guidelines for a more equitable relationship between management and workers, alarmed United Fruit. It was this measure that led the company to mount a propaganda campaign in the United States aimed at portraying Guatemala as moving dangerously to the left.[58] The controversy intensified when Arévalo's six year term ended and his Defence Minister, Jacobo Arbenz Guzmán, was elected president in November 1950. On coming to power, Arbenz set about introducing a comprehensive range of political and economic measures, the most far-reaching of which was the 1952 Agrarian Reform Bill. Providing for the expropriation and redistribution of some of the idle land held by the larger plantations, this legislation fuelled the fires of United Fruit's propaganda campaign, helping to persuade many in the United States, including the Eisenhower administration, that Guatemala was teetering on the brink of turning communist.[59]

As several writers have pointed out, the programmes introduced by Arévalo and Arbenz were less radical than those pursued in Britain by the Attlee government between 1945 and 1951, and would probably have been welcomed by the administrators of the Alliance for Progress.[60] The participation of communists in the political process in Guatemala was, moreover, proscribed in the 1945 constitution on grounds that they adhered to a doctrine of "foreign or international character". It must, nevertheless, be added that Arbenz legalised the Guatemalan Communist Party (PGT) in 1952 and quickly came to regard it as one of those organisations of "varying tendency" that aided his government. To eject the PGT from his ruling coalition, of which they were a small though important component, was seen by Arbenz as being "the equivalent to suicide for the democratic and revolutionary movement of Guatemala".[61] In essence, then, the Arbenz government developed policies that were distinct from, but at the same time supported by, the communists. As a result of these policies, Arbenz came under growing pressure from the United States, and as a consequence was forced to place ever-greater reliance on all of the elements that supported him, including the PGT.[62]

It was in light of these considerations, and CIA suspicions that Arbenz had been complicit in the assassination of his principal conservative rival, Francisco Javier Arana, prior to the 1950 election, that the agency proposed Operation PBFORTUNE.[63] Approved by the Truman administration in July 1952, this venture was initially seen as carrying acceptable risks. The potential for a superpower conflict arising through a CIA project backfiring in Latin America was, after all, far more remote than was the case in other contemporary trouble spots such as Iran. Nevertheless, on learning of PBFORTUNE during the following October, Acheson became concerned at the possible repercussions and convinced Truman to shelve the plan. Regardless of this setback, Joseph Caldwell (JC) King, who headed the DDP's Western Hemisphere Division, kept the operational machinery well oiled in the hope that Eisenhower would "breathe new life into the project".[64]

The trigger for a renewed agency initiative came in March 1953, after rightist Guatemalan rebels, acting on their own volition, made a failed attempt to overrun an Army barracks at Salámá in March 1953. Providing Arbenz with a pretext to clamp down on suspected subversives, the attack resulted in the CIA losing all of its assets in Guatemala. Equally debilitating was Salámá's impact on the State Department's handling of Arbenz. State's Latin America chieftain, Thomas C. Mann, had previously believed that Arbenz was an opportunist rather than an ideologue and that firm and sustained persuasion on the part of the United States would induce him into moderating his policies. The post-Salámá purge, however, eliminated organised opposition in Guatemala. Consequently, there was neither a viable alternative to Arbenz nor any element capable of weaning him away from his association with the communists.[65]

For Washington, then, a reversal of the process that Arévalo had set in motion, Arbenz had accelerated, and the PGT was exploiting, was imperative, but the options that were available for achieving this aim were as limited as they had been in the aftermath of Acheson's final attempt to solve the Iranian crisis in January 1953. Overt military intervention or economic sanctions would violate treaty commitments and alienate the Latin American republics, but continuing with the policy of firm persuasion, which had so far proven fruitless, would be tantamount to doing nothing. Eisenhower, moreover, held to the conviction that "finding creative responses to communist penetration of peripheral areas like Guatemala posed one of the critical tests of his ability as a leader". He therefore opted to deploy covert action to neutralise the clear and present danger that Arbenz was deemed to represent. There was, however, another dimension to PBSUCCESS that went well beyond the bounds of Guatemalan politics. The venture was to be a "prototype operation for testing means and methods for combating communism" in the third world generally.[66]

Expediency: The Principal Reason for a Coup D'État

When exploring the motives behind the decision to depose Arbenz, it is essential to take account of three related challenges faced by Eisenhower during the 1953 to 1954 period. On the international stage, another domino seemed poised to fall to what the United States perceived as a global communist offensive in Indochina, whilst at home the administration was engaged in conflict of a different kind, as it worked to undermine Joseph McCarthy's investigation of the Army. At the same time, Eisenhower and Foster Dulles were determined to transform the Monroe Doctrine into a Western Hemispheric anticommunist charter. Against the backdrop of such realities the Guatemala coup emerges as a perfect expedient. It stood as a demonstrable blow against communism, executed with impeccable timing to draw attention away from Indochina. Concurrently, it provided proof, by an indirect method and for the consumption of informed opinion in the United States and Latin America, that Eisenhower was not soft on communism. It therefore enhanced Eisenhower's standing, both with his foreign allies and in Congress, at a crucial juncture in his presidency.

During the spring and summer of 1954, the worsening French position in Indochina presented the American leadership with a situation that offered stark choices and had enormous ramifications. Sending twenty B-26 bombers to aid the French at Dien Bien Phu, Eisenhower was careful to make it clear to congressional leaders that Southeast Asia must not be allowed to fall, and he stressed at an NSC meeting that Dien Bien Phu might be a critical point at which the United States must make a stand. Invoking the domino theory, the president made his logic clear, pointing out that America and its allies were better off fighting in Indochina where a large French army was already engaged, than in Burma or Thailand.[67]

British support was not, however, forthcoming and as a consequence Dien Bien Phu fell on 7 May 1954. The United States thus contemplated the humiliating prospect of a French surrender at the Conference on Indochina, which was scheduled to begin the following day in Geneva. Of enormous symbolic significance, the conference was the first formal meeting between the leaderships of all of the major powers since Eisenhower had taken office, and for the West it was taking place under the worst of conditions. Communist forces were rolling back a western power and Anglo-American relations were strained over military assistance to the war-weary French, who themselves were showing increasing determination to reach a negotiated settlement. For their part, Eisenhower and Foster Dulles were anxious that the French should carry on fighting and would have preferred the talks to have broken down.[68] Thus, when the negotiations were suspended between 12 June and 14 July, the Americans were afforded a breathing space in which to reaffirm western solidarity, and diminish the impact of a potential French defeat and the establishment of a communist state in North Vietnam.

The problem for Washington was that its room for manoeuvre was restricted. Direct American military intervention, as Foster Dulles pointed out, lacked justification in international law and was subject to the constitutional constraint of requiring a congressional declaration of war, which Capitol Hill would have been extremely reluctant to grant. Even if these obstacles could have been overcome, a large military force could not have been assembled and dispatched in sufficient time to rescue the French position in Indochina, and anyway Eisenhower had long been convinced that victory was not achieveable there.[69] The alternative, and a more feasible course of action, was to make an asymmetrical response: to characterise Indochina as being symptomatic of a global communist challenge, which Washington did constantly in its rhetoric anyhow, and attack the monolith in a location where the risks were acceptable, and where victory was achievable and could be exploited to full symbolic effect, namely in Guatemala.

That Eisenhower viewed events in Guatemala and Indochina as parts of a wider communist threat is evident from a meeting that he conducted with legislative leaders in late April 1954. The president characterised both areas as critical and, referring to the overall international situation, added that American prestige would be seriously eroded if the communists were permitted to make any further incremental gains.[70] These were, of course, high policy considerations, but they filtered down to American military advisors, who, in seeking to educate the Guatemalan officer corps on the "facts of life", were more explicit: "it should be perfectly clear to [the Guatemalan officers targeted] that the Soviet Union is exploiting them only to create a diversion in the US backyard while Indochina is hot".[71]

The absence of any solid evidence to support the proposition that the crises in Indochina and Guatemala were interrelated and emanated from the same source did not deter Eisenhower from authorising covert action to counter Moscow's alleged diversionary tactics. The issue was essentially one of timing, and in this respect PBSUCCESS was remarkable if only for the determination of Allen Dulles to ensure that it remained on schedule. The DCI, for instance, removed J.C. King from active participation in the operation primarily because his methods were considered too cumbersome and he was regarded as impeding the progress of the venture. Added to this is the point that even after Arbenz had uncovered and published details of PBSUCCESS in January 1954, Dulles opted to carry on regardless.[72]

What calls the argument that Eisenhower timed the Guatemala coup to serve wider foreign and domestic policy requirements into question is Nicholas Cullather's contention that PBSUCCESS was scheduled originally to take place in mid May 1954, but problems with training caused it to be delayed until mid June. This claim does not, however, hold true when the core issue, namely the quality of the insurgents recruited for the operation, is subjected to scrutiny.

Central to the CIA's plans for deposing Arbenz was the creation of a small indigenous force, which would cross into Guatemala from Honduras and be depicted by agency propaganda as the spearhead for a much larger invasion. To meet with this requirement the CIA recruited a 480-man rebel army led by Carlos Castillo Armas, a disaffected Guatemalan military officer.[73] The capabilities of this force have been the subject of some debate. Frederick Marks contends that it was an effective well-equipped organisation commanded by an efficient officer.[74] This assessment is, however, completely at odds with declassified CIA records, and the account of William 'Rip' Robertson, the agency paramilitary specialist who attempted to train the would-be insurgents at a base in Florida and on plantations in Nicaragua. Here Castillo Armas and his recruits are depicted as a "tenth rate" band of semi- and total-illiterates led by a brave but inept man, whose limited military prowess was exceeded only by his inability to articulate anything resembling a coherent political philosophy.[75]

The point is that whichever of these accounts comes closest to the truth, both raise serious doubts about Cullather's claim that PBSUCCESS was delayed by a month because of problems with the training. If the CIA's and Robertson's assessments are correct then the agency gave itself a near-impossible task in attempting to train Castillo Armas's men to an acceptable standard between January 1954, when they were first recruited, and May of that year, when the operation was set to go ahead. If, on the other hand, Marks's account is accurate, then the CIA insurgents were, from the outset, competent enough to perform the task required of them, and so would have needed little in the way of training. What also raises questions about the delay is the fact that, despite the alleged ineptitude of Castillo Armas and his men, the CIA "graduated 37 saboteurs in March 1954 [and] 30 field officers by mid-April". It was not until mid May that the "handful of communications specialists", earmarked for training by the agency passed muster.[76] If, however, Washington had wanted to press ahead with the operation at this time, the CIA could have brought in radio experts from its own ranks or hired contract personnel, just as it did when recruiting pilots for PBSUCCESS's air arm.[77]

The only real deadline for the execution of the Guatemala coup was one imposed by nature: that it be carried out before Latin America's heavy summer rains, which were due in July.[78] That Eisenhower had determined that PBSUCCESS would be timed to serve wider policy requirements, moreover, is evident from a telephone conversation between the president and Bedell Smith in late April 1954. Here, a number of pressing foreign policy issues, most prominently Indochina were discussed, and both men concurred that Guatemala "is not a matter we want to make an explosion on right now". Rather, the administration chose to wait until the time was ripe for the ouster of Arbenz to have a strong impact not only in the Western Hemisphere but also on global events, and the optimum time to strike was during the suspension of negotiations on Indochina.[79]

On 15 June, a mere 72 hours after the temporary cessation of talks in Geneva, PBSUCCESS's invasion forces moved to their staging posts in preparation for the operation proper, which went ahead on schedule three days later.[80] In giving final approval for this deployment of covert action, the Eisenhower administration was implementing a strategy that conforms closely to Gaddis's theory on the New Look.[81] The United States, in effect, shifted the focus of the Cold War from Southeast Asia to Guatemala and by deposing Arbenz made an asymmetrical response aimed at countering the prospect of a global communist victory in Indochina.

It is also significant that Arbenz's downfall took place on 27 June and thereby coincided with the visit to Washington of Churchill and Anthony Eden, which had begun two days earlier and was widely seen as a reassertion of allied solidarity. In this sense the coup contribruted to a piece of symbolism that was vital to the West at this time. It helped to maximise the impression that the leaders of the free world again stood as one, and in consequence the counterattack against communism had already started. The fact that the Guatemalan problem was resolved whilst the British leaders were in Washington also helped to ease the strains that had occurred in the Atlantic Alliance over the American decision to stop and search any suspicious vessels bound for Arbenz's country.[82]

As it was, the July 1954 Geneva Accords signalled outright victory for none of the protagonists and France made, what was on balance, an honourable withdrawal from Indochina.[83] If PBSUCCESS assisted Eisenhower's efforts to combat, and draw attention away from, a communist advance in Indochina, however, the Guatemala coup was also seen as helping Washington in its drive to meet the Marxist challenge head-on in Latin America as a whole.

*   *   *

In developing an overarching policy towards Latin America, Eisenhower and Foster Dulles followed a resolute and dogmatic line. The administration believed that, in light of global developments, the democratically-oriented among the United States' southern neighbours were insufficiently appreciative of the dangers posed by communism. The priority, therefore, was to outlaw foreign ideologies in the American republics and achieve hemispheric solidarity through an extension of the Monroe Doctrine, thus securing the region from any form of Soviet-inspired infiltration.[84]

The administration was successful in gaining reluctant acquiescence from the Latin American democracies for this policy, along with the unyielding support of the region's dictatorships, in the form of the Caracas Declaration. This was an anticommunist proposal presented by Foster Dulles to the Tenth Inter-American Conference held in Caracas during March 1954. In brief, the declaration stated that communist control of any country in the Americas represented a threat to the whole region, and would warrant "appropriate action in accordance with existing treaties" – namely the 1947 Rio Pact, which provided for consultation between the Organisation of American States foreign ministers, to discuss appropriate countermeasures against any real or anticipated aggression.[85]

The existence of a supposedly communist government in Guatemala served Dulles's strategy at Caracas very well. It provided the means by which he was to attempt, albeit unsuccessfully, to draw attention away from his Latin American counterparts' most pressing requirement – a Marshall Plan for the region.[86] Instead, Dulles was able to deliver a rhetoric-littered diatribe focused directly on Guatemala, which in essence alleged that communism had already taken hold on the continent and that urgent action was essential to avert its spread.[87]

Though Guatemalan Foreign Minister Guillermo Toriello's reasoned response earned the respect of many delegates, it did not prevent Dulles's resolution from being passed with the approval of seventeen countries. Argentina and Mexico abstained, and only Guatemala opposed the resolution, which was, of course, convenient for the United States since such an action implied that there was some substance in Dulles's claims.[88] The passage of the Caracas resolution, however, handed Foster Dulles more than an ill-deserved propaganda victory. It also acted as a diplomatic cover, forming "a charter for the anti-Communist counterattack" that was to follow, as well as convincing Arbenz that the United States was preparing to act against him and that international opinion would not rescue him.[89]

*   *   *

While the projection of Arbenz as a communist proved useful to the United States' achievement of hemispheric solidarity in the Americas, the removal of the Guatemalan leader also helped to maximise Eisenhower's domestic standing and unify the Republican Party. For Eisenhower, the congressional elections of 1954 held the potential for the Republicans to improve on the narrow majorities won in 1952, but the vote also carried the danger that a disunited party might lose out heavily to the Democrats.[90] The Republican Party was divided on the issue of anticommunism, a weakness that the Democrats were not slow to exploit. Adlai Stevenson pointed out, for example, that the GOP was torn into two factions, one of which was aligned with Eisenhower, and the other with McCarthy.[91]

Determined to starve the Wisconsin senator of the oxygen of publicity on which he so clearly relied, Eisenhower used 'hidden hand' methods, releasing incriminating documents that neutralised McCathy's strength and invoking executive privilege to prevent administration employees from being subjected to congressional interrogation during McCarthy's investigation of the Army. The senator was consequently left with no alternative other than to appeal for witnesses to defy Eisenhower's injunction in these nationally-televised hearings, which proved decisive for the president and disastrous for the senator, and paved the way towards the latter's censure in December 1954.[92]

The issue of anticommunism was by definition one that overlapped into the sphere of foreign affairs, however, and in this respect the Guatemala coup was well timed to contribute to the undermining of McCarthy. Coming less than a fortnight after the Army-McCarthy hearings, Arbenz's overthrow helped Eisenhower to both isolate the Wisconsin senator and steal his thunder. Together with the passage of the 1954 Communist Control Act, PBSUCCESS demonstrated to Old Guard Republicans on Capitol Hill, who had hitherto been supportive of McCarthy, that the administration could pursue a hard line on communism without any input from the senator. This, in turn, meant that the GOP could unite behind Eisenhower before the 1954 congressional elections.

Preparation

Covert action against Guatemala was authorised by the NSC staff on 12 August 1953 and over the following month a general plan for the ouster of Arbenz was drawn up by J.C. King's Western Hemisphere Division. Submitted on 11 September, the project was approved by Allen Dulles on 9 December, and allocated a budget of $3 million. PBSUCCESS was, from its outset, "a governmentwide operation led by the CIA", and overt measures designed to complement the agency's clandestine offensive were crucial to the plan.[93] The State Department, for instance, conducted a campaign in the OAS to isolate Guatemala, which bore fruit with the Caracas Declaration. State also selected individuals who had experience of working with the CIA to represent the United States in those countries that were directly involved in the operation. Thus, Civil Air Transport's Whiting Willauer became Ambassador to Honduras, from where the invasion was to be launched, and Thomas Whelan was dispatched to Nicaragua, where the agency was to broadcast disinformation and train its rebel army.[94]

Prime among State's team of activist diplomats was John Peurifoy, who was appointed on Wisner's recommendation as Ambassador to Guatemala in October 1953. Peurifoy knew nothing of the country in which he was to be America's first minister and could not speak Spanish. What he did have, however, was the reputation of being "a most willing and able ally" of the CIA: credentials that had been established while he was Ambassador to Greece between 1950 and 1953.[95]

Equally important in the drive to exert maximum pressure on Arbenz was the input of the United States Navy and Air Force, which worked with State to enforce an arms embargo and initiated a series of overt measures, culminating in a sea blockade of Guatemala. Code-named HARDROCK BAKER, this came into force on 24 May 1954 following Arbenz's purchase of arms from Czechoslovakia and was designed to "create an atmosphere of fearful expectancy", and thereby enhance the effectiveness of covert action.[96] To close the circle still further, a group of New York City businessmen were assigned to put covert economic pressure on Guatemala, "creating shortages of vital imports, cutting export earnings", and adding further force to an overarching CIA campaign that utilised psychological warfare as its dominant tactic.[97]

Though the plan for PBSUCCESS was devised by the Western Hemisphere Division, the venture was organised and executed as an autonomous unit within the DDP.[98] Establishing a pattern that was to be repeated during the Bay of Pigs campaign, the DDI was completely sidelined. Wisner assumed overall control from CIA headquarters and Tracy Barnes served as liaison between Washington and the base at Opa Locka, Florida – code-named LINCOLN – from where the project's field commander Colonel Albert Haney managed the operation. E. Howard Hunt was appointed chief of political action and David Atlee Phillips was recruited to organise radio propaganda. Meanwhile, Richard Bissell, who had taken up the post of special assistant to the DCI in February 1954, served as a detached observer and troubleshooter.[99] Higher up the chain of command, Allen Dulles focused on "the broader strategic issues", conferring daily with his brother by phone.[100] For his part, Eisenhower continued with the practices established during TPAJAX, remaining aloof from events but receiving oral reports on the progress of the operation from Foster Dulles and more especially Bedell Smith (see appendix 5 for the PBSUCCESS organisation chart).[101]

The autonomous nature of PBSUCCESS was partly attributable to very practical considerations. Much as it was standard practice for the CIA to compartmentalise its operations in order to maximise secrecy, this requirement was compounded by the unprecedented magnitude of PBSUCCESS. Not only this, but the venture incorporated some highly sensitive elements, prime among which were the DDP's plans to assassinate Arbenz and some of his associates.[102]

The use of assassination in Guatemala was first contemplated during PBFORTUNE. It was revamped with the authorisation of PBSUCCESS, and was to have been carried out during the invasion by teams of specialists dubbed "K-groups". For leading CIA and State Department officials, however, the advantages of assassination were never clearly spelt out and the proposed murders were therefore never sanctioned.[103] What the agency did place a good deal of emphasis on was the *threat* of assassination. Projected victims were sent mourning cards, hangman's nooses, and similar macabre items in what was described as "a nerve war against individuals". Deployed primarily for their psychological worth, these tactics were designed to "scare not kill", and they tied in with the agency's political action or "K-Program", the principal purpose of which was to pressurise government officials and more especially the Guatemalan officer corps to defect.[104]

Gerald K. Haines's in-house history of these activities and Cullather's research suggests that assassination was a constituent part of the K-Program, though no definite connection is made in either work. As it was, these measures proved unsuccessful. Indeed, the only notable penetration during the PBSUCCESS venture resulted from the CIA's dispatch of its Berlin chief of station, Henry Heckscher, to Guatemala City in an attempt to 'turn' elements of the country's military. Amateurish and conspicuous as Heckscher's efforts are alleged to have been, he was successful in recruiting one spy on Arbenz's staff who proved useful.[105]

As has already been discussed, Castillo Armas's rebel army was central to agency planning. This small indigenous force was not, however, envisaged as posing a serious military threat. Rather, it was one of the several psychological weapons, which, it was hoped, would ignite an unstoppable momentum, thereby mobilising latent anti-Arbenz elements into action and forcing the Guatemalan leader to flee or be deposed.[106] For his part, Castillo Armas was selected then retained as 'Liberator' because there was no viable alternative to him, and he followed in the Zahedi tradition: he could be depended on to adhere to the wishes of the CIA.[107]

More crucial to the operation's success was airpower and radio propaganda, each of which was envisaged as essential to the creation of the right psychological climate prior to and during the invasion. Agency calculations followed from the premise that control of the skies would be easy to achieve, given the small and obsolescent nature of Arbenz's Air Force and that, while few Guatemalans owned radio sets, the target population "probably regarded radio as an authoritative source".[108] In line with these assumptions, a small air arm manned by contract pilots and personnel transferred from CAT was established at Puerto Cabezas in Nicaragua, while a mobile transmitter controlled by Phillips broadcast from Nicaragua and Honduras under the code-name of SHERWOOD. Beginning in May 1954 and assuming the name of the "Voice of Liberation", SHERWOOD transmitted disinformation that was portrayed as the work of dissidents broadcasting live from inside Guatemala and was intensified to coincide with the invasion.[109]

Before acting against the Guatemalan government, Washington required a pretext that would demonstrate that Arbenz was a communist and in league with Moscow. The necessary justification could not, however, be secured and CIA moves to manufacture evidence by planting an arms cache complete with Soviet markings on the Guatemalan coast had little impact.[110] Ironically, it was Arbenz's own actions that proved decisive in providing the United States with the excuse it needed. When the Guatemalan leader discovered, in January 1954, that the CIA was plotting his downfall, he reacted by procuring $4.86 million worth of arms from Czechoslovakia, which were shipped to Guatemala the following May aboard the Swedish freighter *Alfhem*. Much as the CIA was initially alarmed by this development, it was quickly realised that the arrival of the weapons in Guatemala on 15 May provided Washington with the evidence it needed to justify intervention against Arbenz.[111]

The Deed: Execution of the Guatemala Coup

As was the case during the preparatory stages of PBSUCCESS, psychological warfare was the primary tool of engagement during the period encompassing Castillo Armas's invasion through to Arbenz's resignation, with paramilitary tactics reinforcing the propaganda broadcast by SHERWOOD. The final outcome was, moreover, due less to the successful implementation of the operation than to poorly-evaluated decisions made by Arbenz at crucial points in the campaign, which allowed the agency to retain the initiative. If not entirely the author of his own defeat, the Guatemalan premier certainly demonstrated a lack of judgement that proved instrumental in bringing about his political demise.

Beginning on 18 June, the first phase of the invasion gave the CIA hierarchy little cause for optimism. Having divided into four contingents, Castillo Armas's insurgents advanced only six miles into Guatemala, making no effort to proceed to their assigned targets.[112] Performing only slightly better, the rebel air force dropped leaflets on Guatemala City and small explosives on Puerto Barrios, but these efforts aroused little panic or dissent and left three agency planes incapacitated in the process.[113]

Had it been left to Wisner then PBSUCCESS would have been aborted at this early stage, but Dulles and Bissell proved more determined. Believing the agency's reputation to be at stake, they secured an audience with Eisenhower and requested four additional planes.[114] The meeting provides an important insight into the president's management methods and mindset. On giving the go-ahead for the invasion, Eisenhower had adopted a stance that was more akin to a general than a politician, stating "when you commit the flag, you commit it to win".[115] While lobbying for the extra planes, Dulles assessed the prospects of victory at only 20 per cent. For Eisenhower, however, the Rubicon had been crossed. Defeat was not an option, and bolstering the CIA's chances of success was a more feasible course of action than the alternative of authorising overt military intervention and accepting the accompanying risks. The DCI therefore got his extra aircraft.[116]

Meanwhile, Arbenz delivered the first in a series of self-inflicted wounds that were to prove fatal for his presidency. A key piece of propaganda broadcast by Phillips's 'Voice of Liberation' was the claim that Arbenz planned to betray his Army and distribute weapons to communist and labour-led militia groups. Planting doubt in the minds of the Guatemalan officer corps, this disinformation led one

Air Force colonel to defect and denounce Arbenz on the rebel radio station. The Guatemalan leader's response, however, was one of overreaction. Fearing that further desertions would follow, he grounded his Air Force, thereby ceding control of the skies to the CIA.[117] For the next three days the rebel air force bombed Guatemala City with impunity, while Castillo Armas's troops fought an Army garrison based at Chiquimula. Neither action was decisive militarily, but they provided "vivid evidence of overt battle", which gave credibility to SHERWOOD's claims that a full-scale invasion was underway, and in turn had a powerful psychological impact on Arbenz and his people.[118]

It was, however, the Guatemalan leader's own lack of resolve under pressure, combined with growing dissent from within his military, that finally brought him down. Recognising the need to silence the 'Voice of Liberation', Arbenz ordered a power cut, which proved to be self-defeating because it caused a blackout and increased the sense of panic that the CIA was so eager to promote. He then did exactly what SHERWOOD had forecast and ordered the distribution of weapons to people's organisations, which was regarded as an unacceptable lurch to the left by the Guatemalan officer corps, who responded by demanding his resignation. Arbenz was therefore overthrown, not by the CIA, but by a military coup.[119] Eleven days and five juntas later, Castillo Armas assumed the presidency of Guatemala. The country thus played host to the return of the *caudillos*, and it remained under the heel of successive dictatorships long after Castillo Armas's assassination in July 1957.[120]

Subsequent examinations of Arbenz's ouster have concluded that the coup's immediate benefits did not compensate for the detrimental repercussions that PBSUCCESS had on the credibility of the United States in the third world, but this was not apparent to the few officials and observers who were familiar with the details at the time.[121] While taking preventive action in a country where American interests were deemed to be in jeopardy, the agency helped the administration to achieve two political objectives in the wider international arena and simultaneously improved Eisenhower's domestic standing. The Guatemala coup was, in short, the definitive example of the art of killing four birds with one stone. Not only this, but PBSUCCESS provided a model to be emulated on future subterranean cold war battlefields of Eisenhower's choosing, as became clear with the CIA's Indonesian campaign four years later.

Indonesia 1958: An Alarm from the Malay Archipelago

A point made by Roy Godson in relation to the theory of covert action is that it is utilised most effectively when an existing intelligence infrastructure is in place prior to the planning of any given operation.[122] Historical evidence supports this clearly. The ill-fated Operation BGFIEND was doomed to failure for the lack of adequate collection, analysis, and counterintelligence provisions, and covert action networks. On the positive side of the ledger, the CIA was able to draw on an existing infrastructure during the Italian operation, while in Iran, the BEDAMN and Rashidian networks proved crucial to the success of Operation TPAJAX.

In the case of the Guatemala campaign, however, the botched Saláma mutiny and the purge that followed in its wake ensured that the CIA had no substantial infrastructure in place prior to Eisenhower's decision to proceed with Arbenz's ouster. Yet PBSUCCESS lived up to its name and Washington subsequently assumed that the same hastily assembled model could be applied to advantage in other theatres. This was short-sighted, both at a strategic and tactical level, as became readily apparent with the sanctioning of Operation HAIK in September 1957, the objective of which was to depose the Indonesian premier, Achmed Sukarno.

Some indication that HAIK was afflicted by an absence of foresight, even in its planning stages, was evident in the selection of Al Ulmer as the operation's commander. That Ulmer was an experienced station chief was beyond doubt. He had, after all, managed the agency's Athens station very effectively, but he was not sufficiently familiar with the Far East to direct an operation of the magnitude that HAIK proved to be.[123] Adhering closely to the Guatemalan scenario, the Indonesian campaign divided into two phases. A psychological warfare programme was to be launched to create an atmosphere of political insecurity, after which an uprising by dissident elements of the Indonesian military supplemented with mercenaries and supported by CIA airpower would complete the coup.[124]

That such a plan was permitted to go ahead at all showed, to borrow from the damning post-mortem conducted by the President's Board of Consultants on Foreign Intelligence Activities (PBCFIA) in the aftermath of HAIK, "no proper estimate of the situation", for conditions in Indonesia bore little resemblance to those that had applied in Guatemala four years previously.[125] Guatemala is a small country both in terms of size and population and is located close to the United States. Indonesia, on the other hand, is the largest country in Southeast Asia. It stands ten thousand miles away from the mainland of the United States and its population is an ethnically diverse one that numbers over a hundred million people located in six major islands and thousands of minor ones.[126] The logistical problems of launching a covert operation in such a country were therefore immense.[127]

On a very superficial level, Indonesia corresponded to the familiar pattern of a third world leader expropriating the assets and resources of his country from a first world power or business concern – in this case rubber plantations, tin mines, and oil wells that had formerly been Dutch possessions were confiscated – but there the similarities between Indonesia and Guatemala ended. Unlike Arbenz, Sukarno was a political veteran who founded the Indonesian Nationalist Party during the 1920s and collaborated with the Japanese after their invasion of Indonesia in 1942, in the hope of preventing the country's Dutch colonial masters from returning. Following World War II and a revolution that ended Dutch rule in 1949, Sukarno became the country's president and he subsequently chose to pursue a policy of nonalignment in the Cold War.[128]

Given his past record, then, Sukarno was unlikely to bend under the type of psychological pressure that had proved instrumental in bringing down Arbenz. Not only this, but PBSUCCESS had forewarned third world leaders around the globe of the potential for the United States to resort to covert action if it perceived its interests as threatened. The world of 1958 was consequently a considerably less naïve place than it had been in 1954.

In many ways Washington had more justification for acting against Sukarno than it did against Arbenz or Musaddiq, not least because the Indonesian premier's political aspirations ran contrary to United States' plans for Southeast Asia and the Far East as a whole. Outlined in the Dodge Plan, American objectives for the promotion of economic growth and political stability in the Far East centred on the revival of Japan as the workshop of Asia. Essential to these prescriptions was a complementary, regional division of labour that envisaged the countries of Southeast Asia as: (1) specialising in the production of food and raw materials for export to Japan; (2) providing markets for any surplus in Japanese manufactured goods; and (3) serving as outlets for Tokyo's finance capital. In the sense that they implied continued economic dependency for the Asian rimlands and were centred on the revival of a still-distrusted Japan, these plans elicited little enthusiasm in the countries of Southeast Asia – regardless of their political complexion.

The challenge posed by Sukarno, however, was particularly pronounced. His advocacy of economic diversification and rapid industrialisation was viewed by the United States as having autarkic undertones, and was the very opposite to the primary commodity-producer status that Washington wished to see Indonesia adopt.[129] Not only this but he provided a very public platform, at the 1955 Bandung Conference, for communist China to make common cause with the nonaligned world, all of which made him a red flag to the Dulles bull. The victory of the revolutionary movement that Sukarno led, moreover, had produced an unstable political environment that was accentuated further by Indonesia's complex ethnic and religious mix and this continued to be the case following the country's first elections, which were held in 1955.[130] In respect of resources, Sukarno's country possessed plentiful supplies of vital commodities, which, from an American standpoint, would be better secured in the hands of a more western-friendly leader. Finally, Indonesia's geography made it a crucial strategic location, because it lies in a three thousand mile arc across the Malay Archipelago in the Indian and Pacific oceans, which meant that communication lines between Japan and Australia would be broken if Indonesia turned communist: and in this respect there were ominous signs.[131]

Although the Soviet Union recognised the Indonesian Republic in 1950, relations between the two countries remained distant until the Indonesian Communist Party (PKI) won six million votes in the 1955 elections and was invited to join Sukarno's ruling coalition. This move was designed primarily to strengthen the Indonesian leader's power base. However, to western observers it signalled a dramatic shift to the left, which became more pronounced after Sukarno returned from a visit to Moscow in September 1956, replaced his country's parliamentary system of government with a quasi-dictatorship tagged 'guided democracy', and invited Soviet President Kliment Voroshilov to make a goodwill tour of Indonesia in May 1957. What made Sukarno additionally dangerous was the fact that he had made his determination to wrest neighbouring West Irian from Dutch hands explicit, and this claim now had Soviet support.[132] The Indonesian premier was therefore a source of regional instability and a threat to the global interests of Holland, an important ally of the United States.

There were, then, good reasons for considering covert action against Sukarno and this held true before Joseph Smith, the CIA's operations officer in the Indonesian capital, Djakarta, was ordered by Wisner to find justification for such a move in 1957. Indeed, the Eisenhower administration had identified Indonesia as a country where "communist subversion [had] reached a stage in which military type action was immediately or potentially required", from as early as 1955, purely on the strategic merits of the case.[133] Approval was consequently granted for the agency to provide the Masjumi, Indonesia's principal Islamic party, with $1 million in what turned out to be a failed attempt to counter the appeal of the PKI during the national elections.[134] Nevertheless, the disruption of Voroshilov's visit by anti-Soviet demonstrations, whether they were instigated by the CIA, a genuine expression of indigenous concern about the introduction of guided democracy, or a combination of the two, could only have encouraged the view that Sukarno actually could be deposed.

The prospects for a successful coup were further enhanced by growing regional frictions within Indonesia. Though central government in the country was based in Djakarta, on the island of Java, where the bulk of the population was concentrated, Sukarno's control tended to be balanced and diffused by local power. The relative autonomy that military leaders based on islands outside of Java had long enjoyed was, however, set to be undermined as the consequence of a decision taken in 1956 by the head of the Indonesian Army, Major General Abdul Nasution, to rotate his regional commanders. Designed to curb the power of his subordinates and prevent them from engaging in long-established illegal trading practices, Nasution's order drove Sumatra's military leaders into open dissent and led the principal power broker in the central region of the island, Lieutenant Colonel Achmad Hussein, to pledge his support to any American effort that might be launched to remove Sukarno.[135]

If conditions were not, as yet, ripe for such an objective, then the resignation of Sukarno's vice president and former ally, Muhammad Hatta, in December 1956, and the spread of military dissent to the island of Celebes in 1957 prepared the ground for the authorisation of HAIK. Given the recent trend towards separatism, Washington reasoned that, should the operation's principal objective of deposing Sukarno prove unattainable, then a partial success might be secured: the secession of oil-rich Sumatra from the Indonesian whole, which would protect private Dutch and American interests and investments. It was thus with the blessing and support of the United States that, following the articulation of the 'Charter of Inclusive Struggle', the PERMESTA movement was formed in February 1958 by the breakaway military factions and the conservative Muslim groups they were allied to in Sumatra and Celebes.[136]

*   *   *

The issue of where responsibility lay for initiating Operation HAIK is a matter of some debate. Ray Cline, who as head of the CIA's Taiwan station was closely involved in the enterprise, claims that the agency took the initiative.[137] Yet the PBCFIA presented a very different picture, maintaining "in its active phases the operation was directed not by the DCI but the Secretary of State, who undertook *all* decisions down to and including even the tactical military decisions".[138] Significant as Foster Dulles's role was, this depiction overstates the extent to which he initiated and controlled events.

The genesis of the Indonesia project can in fact be traced back to an NSC meeting held on 1 August 1957, during which Eisenhower and his advisors gauged clandestine action against Sukarno to be a possible option and appointed an ad-hoc committee composed of appointees from State, Defense and the CIA to determine how it might best be deployed.[139] Following several weeks of deliberation, the committee recommended that the United States utilise "all feasible covert means", and to do so as a matter of urgency in order to halt the growing influence that the PKI was bringing to bear on Indonesian politics in general and Sukarno's governing coalition in particular. Approved by the NSC in late September 1957, the measures that were implemented as a consequence of these findings led to a redoubling of CIA action, which, as has already been pointed out, had previously been restricted to the funding of political parties and establishing contacts with would-be dissidents.[140] Thus, from January 1958 the DDP began arming its separatist allies in Sumatra and Celebes, augmenting their ranks with mercenaries, and securing the necessary resources to provide for a dissident air arm.[141]

These measures were not focused on bringing about the removal of Sukarno in one single blow, however. Rather, the aim was to provide the PERMESTA rebels with the requisite weaponry and logistical support to solidify their control over the existing island strongholds and, if necessary, extend the dissident challenge to Java. Allen Dulles calculated, wrongly as it turned out, that such moves would force Sukarno and Nasution to negotiate with the dissidents, and induce the Indonesian premier to not only desist from making common cause with the communists in his governing coalition, but also order his military to clamp down on the PKI and neutralise its power.[142]

If a complementary incentive was necessary to persuade Djakarta to do Washington's bidding, then the sweetener came in the form of an offer of American military equipment and training to the Indonesian armed forces. Alert to the fact that Nasution and most of his senior colleagues were anticommunists, the Eisenhower administration reasoned that the promise of this much-needed aid could be used to persuade the Indonesian military to play a more active political role in the country and thereby set the process in motion through which Sukarno could be marginalised and ultimately deposed. Whatever the positive long-range merits of these plans might have been, they were hamstrung by a more immediate problem: they required Nasution to enter into talks with the dissidents and refrain from using American-procured arms to suppress the rebellion. Under no circumstances was he willing to comply.[143]

The failure of Washington to co-opt the Indonesian military – an effective fighting force led by predominantly western-trained officers – was one in a number of drawbacks that left HAIK severely impaired.[144] Certainly the CIA's analysts saw little chance of the rebellion succeeding. DDI Robert Amory scrutinised the progress of the operation carefully and warned of impending failure, and these views were shared by the American Ambassador to Indonesia, John Allison, who argued persistently that the enterprise was too risky.[145] Yet the venture went ahead regardless and Allison was recalled from Djakarta and replaced by the less critical Howard P. Jones on 7 March 1958.[146]

In a retrospective assessment of Operation HAIK, Ray Cline drew a general lesson on the difficulties of covert action. The weakness of clandestine paramilitary action is, he argued, that the United States is faced with the stark choice of either abandoning a cause or converting to a policy of overt military intervention once the CIA connection is revealed prematurely and an operation becomes com-promised.[147] This is a very valid point, but it does not apply to the Indonesian campaign. Put simply, the objectives and demands of Operation HAIK went beyond what could be achieved through covert action.

From the outset of the campaign the United States followed a strategy that was tantamount to overt military intervention. Indeed, Foster Dulles searched for, but failed to find, a credible pretext to do exactly this.[148] A complex of training and support facilities, which included the provision of air and naval bases in the Philippines, was established across the entire Pacific region. American submarines were dispatched to guard the waters around Sumatra, and naval destroyers were anchored in Singapore, reflecting significant British involvement in the operation and the repair of the intelligence alliance between Washington and London that followed in the wake of Suez and functioned through a series of high-level Anglo-American Working Groups. Logistical and tactical air support for the Indonesia venture was provided by CAT, and U-2 planes monitored Sukarno's military installations.[149]

The sheer size of HAIK was in fact its main weakness. Maintaining secrecy during the smaller-scale Operation PBSUCCESS had proved impossible. In the case of HAIK, the Asia-wide recruitment of mercenaries left the campaign open to penetration by the numerous Chinese and Soviet agents who were active in the region. There was therefore considerable potential for Eisenhower's claim, that the

United States was assuming a position of careful neutrality and proper deportment, to be compromised once the PERMESTA insurrection had started.[150]

Operation HAIK began in earnest on 15 February 1958, when the PERMESTA dissidents proclaimed a new government. Unlike Arbenz, however, Sukarno was warned rather than intimidated by this course of events and he reacted quickly and effectively, ordering the Indonesian military to suppress the rebellion. Dissident radio stations were bombed out of existence, which meant an instrument that had proven vital in previous covert operations was taken out of the equation in the opening stages of the campaign. By early May, Sukarno's forces had invaded Sumatra, captured the key rebel strongholds of Padang and Bukittinggi, and brought most of the island back under government control.[151]

The PERMESTA forces on Celebes fared rather better, for it was here that HAIK's air arm was based. Between mid April and mid May, CIA planes flown by Filipino, Nationalist Chinese and American contract pilots, and Polish veterans from the agency's Eastern European campaigns, mounted a succession of sorties against Indonesian government positions on Celebes. These missions proved instrumental in enabling the rebels to make considerable gains, the most significant of which was the seizure of a strategically-significant Air Force base on the island. The tables were turned, however, when, on 15 May, Sukarno's Air Force launched a surprise attack that destroyed almost all of the CIA's aircraft as they stood on the ground. The element that had proven most crucial to the Indonesia campaign, just as it had done during PBSUCCESS, was thus neutralised and any hint of more active American intervention was stymied by a veiled threat from Sukarno to accept an offer from Beijing to supply extra air support and men to assist the Indonesian military.[152]

Operation HAIK had, in effect then, already failed by the time that CIA pilot Allen Lawrence Pope was forced to bail out of his B-26 to be captured by Indonesian government forces on 18 May. If Pope had obeyed orders and left all incriminating evidence of his links with the CIA at home, then the United States would not have been implicated in the PERMESTA rebellion. To ensure that he was not executed as a stateless combatant, however, Pope took the precaution of flying with documents on his person, which linked him to previous bombing raids. Eisenhower's initial claim that Pope was a soldier of fortune thus proved not only futile but also extremely embarrassing for the president, and Foster Dulles saw no alternative other than to "[pull] the plug" on the venture. CIA operatives on the ground in Indonesia balked at the Secretary of State's decision, so much so that the order to abort needed to be transmitted three times before the DDP finally complied, thus ending the agency's largest and most ambitious covert operation to date in failure. [153]

As much as Operation HAIK is instructive in defining the limits of covert action, it also provides a classic example of how failure to maintain plausible deniability could result in the United States being subjected to blackmail. On weighing up the advantages and disadvantages of making the Pope affair and the

CIA's involvement in Indonesia public, Sukarno opted for silence and extracted thirty-seven thousand tons of rice and $1 million worth of arms from the United States as the cost.[154]

Conclusion

A distinguishable outline of how covert action developed and expanded during the Eisenhower years can be traced clearly through the CIA's operations in Iran, Guatemala, and Indonesia. TPAJAX demonstrated that the new administration was prepared to act against a democratically-elected leader in circumstances that had led its predecessor to opt for caution. By future standards the Iranian venture was an exercise in minimalism: a small number of operatives conducted an inexpensive campaign that altered the balance of political forces sufficiently to remove Musaddiq from power.[155]

Following TPAJAX Eisenhower's appetite for clandestine action was whetted. The larger-scale Guatemala operation was consequently sanctioned with enthusiasm and its success proved instrumental in lighting the fuse for a comprehensive expansion of CIA activities. In terms of covert operations, however, there was the problem that the agency had already reached, and in fact gone beyond, the limits of what could feasibly be kept *covert* with PBSUCCESS. Indeed, to informed observers such as James B. Reston, a respected *New York Times* reporter who made explicit reference to Allen Dulles's involvement in the Guatemala uprising even as the events were unfolding, the American contribution to Arbenz's downfall was transparent:[156] so much so that PBSUCCESS might best be described as a semi-covert operation.

The Eisenhower administration as a whole and especially Foster Dulles did not take adequate account of this point in its future calculations of when and when not to utilise clandestine action. Thus, when the Guatemala blueprint was applied to the much larger and more ambitious Operation HAIK the result was failure. The principal lesson of the Indonesian debacle was clear: covert operations could not be deployed successfully in circumstances that required overt military action, nor could enterprises such as HAIK, which was to all intents and purposes a hybrid between the two. The Eisenhower administration was fortunate that it avoided the consequences of its failure to learn this lesson. President John F. Kennedy discovered this three years later when he picked up the tab, not only for his own lack of judgement but for the shortcomings of his predecessor, in the full public glare of the Bay of Pigs fiasco.

7

FLUCTUATING FORTUNES

The accession of John F. Kennedy to the American presidency brought with it a reaffirmation of the activist foreign policy pursued by Eisenhower. If, as William Corson suggests, the CIA hierarchy was at first uncertain about the new president's readiness to meet the rising costs of the U-2, the SR-71 and their follow-on satellite systems, then these doubts were unfounded.[1] Determined to assert American global predominance with increased vigour, Kennedy committed himself to supporting continued agency specialisation in the sphere of technological intelligence collection. His adoption of flexible response as the guiding maxim of United States defence policy, moreover, provided the impetus for an even more comprehensive application of the CIA's covert action arm than had been exercised under Eisenhower. As well as utilising its existing capacity to engage in political action, economic operations, psychological warfare, and propaganda activities, the agency came to incorporate an expansive range of paramilitary capabilities as part of its modus operandi, working closely with the Defense Department in the process. Such measures served as necessary complements to the wider American counterinsurgency and military programmes that were being deployed on an escalating scale, most notably in Indochina.[2]

Kennedy, however, encountered major problems in his relations with the CIA: difficulties that sprang primarily from the fact that the president knew too little about, and expected too much from, the agency and the intelligence community generally. This led an ill-informed chief executive to sanction an ill-conceived covert operation, code-named JMARC, against the Castro regime at the Bay of Pigs.[3] A very public failure, this enterprise damaged the prestige of the Kennedy administration and had serious repercussions for the CIA itself, in that it led the president to subject the agency's activities to comprehensive examination. The resulting Taylor Committee Inquiry recommended the most fundamental shake-up that the CIA had yet endured: a shake-up that saw primary responsibility for paramilitary covert action transferred from the agency to the Pentagon in autumn 1961, though it should be added that the Defense Department's operational role remained relatively limited through to 1963.[4]

A lack of presidential foresight in regard to clandestine action was apparent throughout Kennedy's tenure. Having failed once at the hands of Castro, the American president again authorised wide-ranging covert action programmes between late 1961 and 1963. Initiated from inside of the White House, these ventures were placed under the direct supervision of Robert Kennedy, who in effect took on the role of DDP during this period, at least as far as Cuban operations were concerned. Such measures did not, in fact, "embody a concept [that was] radically different from [what had already] been contemplated in the summer and fall of 1960", which had been the foundation for the Bay of Pigs invasion.[5] In terms of strategy deployed against Cuba, then, John Kennedy failed to communicate a distinct, feasible, and single-minded objective to the CIA or to the governmental bureaucracy as a whole. The campaign against Castro therefore "followed an uncertain trumpet".[6] In a more general strategic sense, Kennedy's failure to make a clear connection between means and ends led him to make an ever greater American commitment to the survival of South Vietnam, a legacy from which his successor, Lyndon B. Johnson, could not retreat. CIA fortunes thus fluctuated between 1961 and 1963 against a background of unrealistically high expectations on the part of the Executive.

JFK and the Doctrine of Flexible Response

Kennedy's election in November 1960 reflected a change of political mood in the United States. Eight years of Republican rule had, for sure, delivered stability and prosperity to many in America, but the picture of Eisenhower as a "comforting symbol of consensus" presiding over a contented nation was hardly a complete one. There had been three recessions during his tenure and the sharpest of these, between 1957 and 1958, had brought an unqualified backlash against the Republicans in the 1958 congressional and state elections. Public disillusionment was, moreover, heightened as a result of Eisenhower's tendency to give priority to foreign policy issues rather than domestic ones and this worked to the detriment of Richard Nixon's election prospects.[7] Nevertheless, Kennedy won by the narrowest of margins in 1960, with his ability to exploit the media and project an aura of freshness and vitality proving decisive in the defeat of the less-charismatic Nixon.[8]

Though Kennedy's fourteen-year record in Congress suggests that he was essentially an opportunist, one subject on which he did maintain consistency whilst in the Legislature was his aversion to colonialism.[9] He had, in addition, long believed that the apparent failure of the Eisenhower administration to distinguish between nonaligned third world nationalism and communism had proven self-defeating for the United States. Consequently, the arrival of the new administration brought with it a sharply contrasting foreign policy stance from what had previously applied, as a retrospective overview by Kennedy's Secretary of State, Dean Rusk, revealed: "We weren't really bothered by third world countries that refused to take sides in the Cold War". Any country that was "independent and secure" was deemed to be acting in the interests of the United States.[10]

Kennedy was convinced that in order to counter a communist movement that espoused spreading its doctrine to susceptible underdeveloped nations, the United States needed to establish a meaningful partnership with a highly diverse third world, specifically through the provision of political support and the injection of economic aid. Under such conditions each country would develop at its own pace and on its own terms, and consequently choose western democracy rather than Marxist-Leninism as its favoured form of government.[11] The new president did not, however, rule out intervention in nonaligned countries where there was a danger of communism taking hold.[12] There was, as well, a clearly pronounced threat, for Khrushchev had thrown down the gauntlet immediately prior to Kennedy taking office in a speech that hailed "the uprisings of the colonial peoples against their oppressors", promising Russian support for "anticolonialist forces" in these "wars of liberation".[13]

Coming as it did in the aftermath of the United States' severance of diplomatic relations with Cuba on 6 January 1961, Khrushchev's rhetoric may have been primarily designed to bolster Castro's resolve, but Kennedy responded in an equally unequivocal manner in his State of the Union Address in March that year. America was, in the president's view, faced with the task of convincing the Soviet Union and China "that aggression and subversion [would] not be profitable" routes through which to pursue their expansionist ends.[14] Here, Kennedy was, in effect, restating the same basic argument that had held sway during Truman's second term and throughout Eisenhower's entire tenure: that Washington must prevent communism from prevailing anywhere outside of the Soviet bloc and China. Failure to do so would create a perception across the globe that the United States was losing ground in the Cold War, and this in turn would constitute a victory for communism everywhere, despite the fact that the two major communist powers now had markedly different and conflicting agendas. It was with this zero-sum game logic in mind that Kennedy ordered a revision of Eisenhower's defence policy and strategy.[15]

From the point of view of the Kennedy administration the New Look was severely flawed on the grounds that it placed too much reliance on the doctrine of massive retaliation.[16] Eisenhower had, of course, incorporated a wide range of other instruments, including military alliances, covert action and psychological warfare, in order to contain communism and protect American interests, but these measures had been implemented with a keen eye on minimising costs, which, Kennedy maintained, had jeopardised the credibility of America's conventional forces. The risks were thereby maximised of the United States either not responding to small-scale aggression at all, or escalating such conflicts to a point where direct confrontation with the Soviet Union and resort to nuclear war beckoned. The consequences of this policy were, in Kennedy's view, both negative and foreboding: the communist world had been able to engage successfully in so-called 'brushfire wars', expanding its power and influence through low-level incremental advances, and Kennedy feared that if this trend continued to go unchecked it would lead ultimately to the Soviet Union and China each achieving their respective objectives through piecemeal aggression.[17]

To remedy the drawback of having to choose between "escalation or humiliation", the Kennedy administration opted to replace the New Look with a policy and strategy that drew on the idea of 'flexible response' as its theoretical base. In brief, this doctrine recommended that the United States provide and utilise a wide range of military and economic instruments in order to deter and counter all types of warfare, and convince all potential adversaries that recourse to any level of aggression would incur prohibitive costs. The nuclear threshold was, in short, to be raised in a defence strategy that reverted to the symmetry of NSC 68: communist aggression would be matched and bettered in the area where it threatened and with means that were both proportionate and adequate to counter the challenge.[18]

In accordance with meeting the requirements of flexible response, Kennedy and his successor Lyndon B. Johnson presided over a 150 per cent increase in America's strategic nuclear armoury and a concomitant 60 per cent expansion in the number of low-yield battlefield nuclear weapons. Huge hikes were also very much in evidence in the sphere of conventional military capabilities, with budgets and manpower expanded to meet a two-and-a-half war standard: one which provided the means for the Pentagon to fight two major wars – in Europe and Asia – and a minor war elsewhere.[19]

Flexible response was not without its critics. Some argued that the emphasis on conventional force was very expensive and implied a lack of faith in the nuclear deterrent, despite the president's adherence to the principle of 'assured destruction'. However, the string of crises that took place during Kennedy's tenure in locations as far removed as Berlin, Indochina, and Cuba only strengthened the case for a substantial conventional build-up to ensure that the United States fulfilled its global commitments. Indeed, the president credited the existence of usable conventional power as being instrumental in forcing the Soviet Union to remove its missiles from Cuba in 1962. In this case the two-and-a-half war standard provided ample proof that Washington could assemble a credible invasion force without compromising its military commitments elsewhere.[20]

If, however, the United States was to seize and maintain the upper hand in a Cold War in which Khrushchev had pledged support for 'anticolonialist' movements in the third world then something more than conventional military strength was required. To fulfil this need, Kennedy implemented an extensive range of socio-economic measures, altering the emphasis in foreign aid from military to economic programmes under the guidance of the Agency for International Development (AID) and creating the Peace Corps to foster greater understanding between the United States and the developing world.[21]

Of the Kennedy initiatives that applied to specific regions, the most notable was the Alliance for Progress, through which Washington agreed to provide $20 billion in economic aid to Latin America in return for the participating nations pledging to undertake economic and democratic reforms. Though the groundwork for these measures was laid with Eisenhower's albeit less ambitious Social Progress Trust Fund, the Alliance for Progress fitted comfortably, in theory if not in practice, with Kennedy's drive to immunise the third world against communism.[22] Along with the other measures highlighted, it amounted to counterinsurgency in a velvet glove and it leapt straight out of the pages of *The Ugly American*.[23]

Much as Kennedy intended to promote prosperity and democracy in the developing world through socio-economic measures, however, he well understood that they did not, of themselves, offer blanket insulation against the communist threat. Only through the essential complement of militarily-oriented counter-insurgency provisions could this realistically be achieved.[24] In keeping with these assumptions and imperatives, therefore, Kennedy authorised a $19 million budget augmentation to finance the training of an extra three thousand elite special forces in unconventional warfare techniques.[25] Commonly referred to as 'green berets', these troops were coached in the intricacies of jungle warfare at Fort Bragg and in the Canal Zone in Panama, from where they were dispatched to regions such as Indochina as part of a symmetrical American response to the communist challenge in the third world.

It was in combination with these counterinsurgency provisions, both military and non-military, that CIA covert action was most demonstrably deployed during Kennedy's tenure. This was evident from the president's preparedness to sanction a wide array of clandestine programmes that spanned from the campaigns mounted against Castro's Cuba, to the comprehensive range of initiatives that the agency conducted in support of the American war effort in Indochina. Even more so than during the Eisenhower presidency, the CIA functioned as the "cold war arm of the U.S. government", and it performed this role at a time when superpower tensions reached an all-time high. [26]

The Big Picture, 1961–1963: Escalating Superpower Tensions

In the broadest of terms, the years 1961 to 1963 brought an unprecedented intensification of the Cold War, and this came about primarily as the result of a power struggle within the Soviet hierarchy. In brief, Khrushchev sought to decrease military expenditure and promote a more consumer-oriented Soviet economy. He consequently drew the fire of hard-liners, who sought to expand the Kremlin's already deep commitment to the military and the large American arms build-up authorised by Kennedy did nothing to strengthen Khrushchev's hand. At the same time, the Soviet leader took comfort from what he saw as Kennedy's failure to act decisively during the Bay of Pigs operation. Khrushchev henceforth seized on any opportunity to exploit what he perceived to be the weaknesses of the American president in order to win bloodless Cold War victories. A climate of escalating tension thus took hold, firstly over the status of Berlin during July and

August of 1961, and secondly during the Cuban missile crisis of October 1962. Khrushchev's logic was that success in such endeavours would enhance the global standing of the USSR and would, crucially, silence his domestic rivals on grounds that Russian objectives would have been achieved without an expansion of the guns-not-butter economy that the Soviet leader so hoped to reform.[27]

Competition with the United States was not, however, the only consideration faced by Khrushchev. Over the 1950s, the relationship between the Soviet Union and China had deteriorated from one of cooperation in the final years of Stalin's rule, to distrust during the middle fifties, and outright suspicion at the end of the decade. By 1961 the Sino-Soviet split was emerging as a major factor in international politics, as each of the two leading communist powers laid exclusive claim to the title of champion of the world's leftist revolutionary movements.

Indeed, Khrushchev's pledge of support for the forces of revolution in their "wars of national liberation" was gauged by many to be geared primarily towards beating off the Chinese challenge in the contest for the affections of the third world, rather than throwing down the gauntlet to the United States.[28] Such motivations were also evident during the Bay of Pigs invasion, when the Russian leader announced "Cuba is not alone" and implied that the Soviet Union might make a retaliatory move, possibly in Berlin.[29] The underlying message in Khrushchev's rhetoric here was that the Soviet Union strongly advocated self-determination in the third world and was, furthermore, the *only* power with both the means and the will to counter the attempts of the United States and its allies to reverse this trend in world affairs.

Despite the emergence of China as a power in its own right with distinct interests and aims, however, the international stage continued to be dominated by the conflict between Washington and Moscow throughout the early 1960s. Indeed, the Kennedy administration remained convinced that the United States was confronted by a communist monolith, overlooking the ever-widening chasm in Sino-Soviet relations that was concurrently taking place.[30] American and Russian objectives and concerns mirrored one another during this period, as each superpower's desire to enhance its global standing was matched by a fear of losing face to the advantage of its principal adversary. The desires of Khrushchev and Kennedy to test each other's mettle served as additional and important variables in this heightening of the Cold War conflict. As each leader attempted to ascertain his counterpart's strengths and weaknesses so an atmosphere of tension was first created then compounded through a series of crises that have left many to characterise the 1961 to 1963 period as the most dangerous of the Cold War.[31]

For its part, the CIA played an instrumental role in each of the major crises that confronted the Kennedy administration. The ill-conceived Bay of Pigs operation saw the agency take action that proved detrimental to the interests of the United States and raised questions about the character of the president himself. In contrast, the CIA procured invaluable information from its highest placed penetration agent, Colonel Oleg Penkovsky, the deputy head of the foreign section of Soviet Military Intelligence (GRU), during the Berlin crisis, who confirmed that Khrushchev's belligerent statements on the city's status were "all bluff".[32] This strengthened Kennedy's hand during the dispute. It also paved the way to a resolution of the crisis that permitted the Soviet Union to seal off East Berlin, while the United States gave firm guarantees of its commitment to the security of the western sector – guarantees that were backed up by a largely symbolic bolstering of the American military presence in West Berlin. During the Cuban missile crisis, the CIA again provided vital information through U-2 overflights and HUMINT (intelligence derived from human sources), which helped Kennedy to finally prevail over Khrushchev in the battle of wills that had characterised the previous twenty-two months.[33] Wider international events, then, ensured that agency fortunes were on something of a rollercoaster during the Kennedy period. These years also brought important changes in the management and structuring of the CIA itself, which had an enormous bearing on how the agency developed and was deployed between 1961 and 1963.

The CIA, 1961–1963: Rollercoaster Years

It has been argued by one prominent intelligence specialist that "at the outset of the Kennedy administration, no compelling incentives existed to stimulate reform in the intelligence system".[34] This is not entirely accurate. Kennedy did, to an extent, pursue a strategy of continuity and reassurance towards the intelligence community as a whole. His announcement in November 1960 that Dulles and Hoover would be retained in their respective positions at the CIA and the FBI is evidence of this.[35] The new incumbent in the White House was, nevertheless, driven by a determination to instil what has been aptly described as a "muscular laissez faire" ethos into his administration. The design and execution of policy needed to acquire, Kennedy insisted, a sense of urgency and vigour, which he had criticised as having been lacking during the Eisenhower years.[36] Consequently, the new president: (1) downgraded the NSC, on the grounds that it was incompatible with the style of leadership he intended to pursue; (2) abolished, in February 1961, the Operations Coordinating Board, through which the NSC had carried out its responsibility to coordinate covert action projects; and (3) disestablished – also in February 1961 – the PBCFIA, which was created five years earlier to serve as a watchdog group, pointing out the potential risks associated with those covert operations that were under consideration.[37]

In a general sense, Kennedy's view of the NSC was accurate. It had, over the years, become a rather bloated instrumentality and Eisenhower had tended to bypass it when seeking solutions to crucial foreign policy issues. In relation to Eisenhower's management of the CIA, however, the NSC had been the fulcrum between policy and intelligence. A very necessary instrument of the invisible government, it had been organised by the president on a modified military staff concept to ensure that all points of view were considered in the decision-making process governing covert operations.[38] The PBCFIA had, in turn, functioned as an extra fail-safe device if and when its services were required.

Kennedy's decision to either ignore or to terminate the provisions through which his predecessor had exercised control over the CIA was an impetuous and ill-judged move. What little experience the new president did have of intelligence was restricted to a brief and undistinguished period with the Office of Naval Intelligence during World War II.[39] He was, to all intents and purposes, ignorant of the machinations of peacetime intelligence. Yet Kennedy did not hesitate to remove the safeguards that the vastly more experienced Eisenhower had felt it necessary to maintain. Moreover, this was done in one fell swoop within a month of Kennedy's accession to power, while he simultaneously decided to retain the 5412 Special Group: a clear indication of his desire to continue the practice, started by Eisenhower, of involving the White House closely in the management of the DDP's activities.[40]

Looked at from this perspective, impetus for change did exist from the outset of the Kennedy administration, and it was change that gave rise to the Bay of Pigs debacle. Indeed, the Taylor Commission made this point abundantly clear when it reported in June 1961: the Bay of Pigs disaster occurred at least in part, Taylor maintained, because Kennedy had destroyed the only institutional decision-making bodies – the OCB and the PBCFIA – that might have had sufficient weight to contradict the president.[41] In addition, Kennedy discovered to his regret that in removing these advisory structures he limited the potential scapegoats to the White House and the CIA in the event of an operation going wrong. The president, of course, shouldered the blame for JMARC, reflecting very eloquently that "victory has a thousand fathers and defeat is an orphan", but, as Rhodri Jeffreys-Jones has so shrewdly observed, "in adopting the orphan so conspicuously, Kennedy fuelled speculation about the real paternity of the Bay of Pigs fiasco".[42] The ultimate scapegoat was in fact the hierarchy of the CIA and not the president.

A major drawback in tracing the evolution of the CIA during the Kennedy period is that the Bay of Pigs venture and its immediate effects tend to overshadow the fact that concurrent developments and events also signalled the need for a revision of the way the agency was managed. To begin with, the approval procedures for covert action had, by the time Kennedy took office, become more lax than in the previous decade. During the 1950s responsibility within the agency for the sanctioning of clandestine action was restricted to the Deputy Director of Plans, his assistant, and the DCI himself. CIA covert operations had, however, proliferated to such an extent by 1960 that the delegation of approval authority became a bureaucratic necessity. Two or possibly three individuals could simply not make competent and efficient judgements on the multitude of ventures that were proposed. A graduated approval process therefore began to operate in the DDP from about 1960, whereby station chiefs and division chiefs were authorised to approve those projects that were deemed to be of low cost and risk. More sensitive proposals continued to be referred to the agency hierarchy.[43]

It was argued in the *Church Report* that the extent to which these procedural changes "affected the number and nature of projects [was] unclear".[44] Nevertheless, the very fact that operations were allowed to proliferate to such a scale that responsibility for their approval was dependent on more officials, and lower ranking ones at that, heightened the potential for an operation that ran contrary to American policy objectives to be sanctioned. Furthermore, the danger of a project that was not in the interests of medium to long-term American policy being authorised, even at the most senior level, was especially pronounced during periods of transition from one administration to another, when exact policy positions were not always easy to ascertain. The differing positions of Eisenhower and Kennedy towards the Congo stand as a case in point.

To Kill or not to Kill? Eisenhower, Kennedy and the Turbulent Congolese Ex-Prime Minister

Difficulties in the Congo began when the country gained its independence from Belgium on 30 June 1960. Brussels assumed that, regardless of the Congo's new status, it would continue to depend on Belgian political and economic know-how, for the local population was not sufficiently well-educated to take control of its own affairs. It was reasoned that this was the most satisfactory way for Belgium to maintain its near monopoly-control over the Congo's resources. If, however, the former colonial masters intended to pick the Congo's fruits without having responsibility for owning the orchard, then the plan backfired. In July 1960, elements of the Congolese army mutinied and in the process significant numbers of European settlers were killed, thus provoking Brussels to dispatch a regiment of paratroops to restore and maintain order. In response, the Congolese President, Joseph Kasavubu and his Prime Minister, Patrice Lumumba – the leading power-broker in the country – asked for and received a multinational force from the UN to assist peacefully in the eviction of the Belgians.[45]

Eisenhower's initial approach to the Congolese problem was focused on keeping the Soviet Union out of the dispute. It was the American president who advised Lumumba to seek UN assistance, reasoning that the deployment of a multinational force was the surest way to prevent Russian involvement. Events moved very rapidly, however, and while the UN force was in transit, the Belgians orchestrated the secession of the Congo's richest province, Katanga, under the leadership of Moise Tshombe.[46] Lumumba responded by requesting military aid from the United States to regain Katanga, and when this was not forthcoming he turned to the Kremlin, which airlifted a contingent of trucks and small arms. The situation deteriorated considerably in August 1960, when Lumumba joined Khrushchev in calling for the UN peace-keepers to leave.[47] This led Eisenhower to conclude that Lumumba was an irrational demagogue whose courtship with the Soviet Union would open the way for a communist takeover in the Congo, and provide a base from where Russian influence would spread throughout Africa.

Lumumba would have to be removed, and the 5412 Committee "did not rule out any particular kind of activity" which might contribute to this objective.[48] The Congolese prime minister was, in short, to be assassinated.

Records relating to the American assassination plot against Lumumba are sprinkled with bureaucratic euphemisms and are generally vague and ambiguous in their content. The concept of plausible deniability and the protection of the integrity of the president dictated that this should be the case.[49] What is, however, clear is that Allen Dulles cabled Lawrence Devlin, the CIA station chief in the Congolese capital, Leopoldville, on 26 August, requesting in the strongest of terms that Lumumba be removed as a matter of urgency.[50] Ten days later, Kasavubu dismissed Lumumba from his post. Whether this came about through American pressure or because Kasavubu opposed Lumumba's plan to terminate the UN presence is hard to tell, but certainly the Eisenhower administration continued to look on Lumumba as a serious threat. On 21 September, Dulles suggested at an NSC meeting that the former Congolese prime minister be "disposed of", and at about this time the DDP's Science Advisor and controller of the MKULTRA project, Dr. Sidney Gottlieb, was asked by Bissell to prepare a biological toxin that would kill Lumumba.[51]

Accounts differ on the subject of Lumumba's eventual murder. A State Department chronology of the Congo crisis implies that events ran ahead of the CIA's plans. General Joseph Mobutu seized power and kidnapped Lumumba, who had placed himself in the custody of the UN when the coup first took place. The former prime minister was then flown to Elisabethville in Katanga, where he was murdered within hours of his arrival.[52] John Prados offers a more insightful version of the circumstances surrounding and leading up to Lumumba's death. Here, the CIA is alleged to have provided the Mobutu camp with surveillance reports that proved instrumental in Lumumba's capture, a point that runs contrary to the Church Report's conclusion that the agency's plotting ultimately proved irrelevant in the final outcome of the Congolese crisis. There is, however, a good deal of evidence to support Prados's claim and indeed to expand on the line of argument he pursues.

The killing of Lumumba with biological poison was dependent on the CIA gaining access to such personal possessions as his toothbrush, or to his food. The record makes it clear that neither Devlin nor any other agency-controlled operative came close to achieving this objective.[53] It would, moreover, have been optimistic in the extreme for the CIA and the American government to have placed all their hopes on such a far-fetched plot. It was therefore in the interests of the United States to prepare an alternative plan, especially in light of the fact that the Congo boasted significant deposits of uranium and Lumumba remained a powerful force, whether inside or outside of government.[54]

Most of the CIA's major preventive covert operations had depended on the agency producing an indigenous leader, who would act as the focus for inciting popular feeling in the host country and would serve as a front for the agency's activities. If the same criteria had been applied to the Congo, then the CIA would have needed to find someone other than Tshombe to lead the takeover of the country. The United States, after all, supported UN policy, which was aimed at making every effort to ensure that the Congo remained a whole entity.[55] Not only was Tshombe in the pocket of the Belgians, he was also seeking to bring about the partition of the Congo, all of which precluded him from being selected as the candidate to lead a wholesale takeover of the country.[56] Mobutu, on the other hand, was a military man, who emerged from the shadows in a similar fashion to the way Zahedi and Castillo Armas had done.

It is significant that when Devlin, recognising that the murder of Lumumba would be a delicate and time-consuming enterprise, requested that a case officer be dispatched from Washington to Leopoldville to supervise the proceedings, Bissell sent Justin O'Donnell. O'Donnell was head of an operations unit in the DDP, but he was opposed to the practice of assassination in peacetime. Though he travelled to Leopoldville, O'Donnell made it clear that he would not take part in the poisoning of Lumumba: all of which begs the question why he, O'Donnell, was employed by the DDP in the first place and then sent on a mission that he regarded as unethical. O'Donnell was, however, prepared to ensure that Lumumba was delivered from the security of the UN into the hands of Mobutu.[57] This was tantamount to an act of murder anyhow, but it was also consistent with two orders that were cabled from Washington to Leopoldville in the space of one day in October 1960. The first was directed to the ambassador, his political staff, and the CIA, and it specified that the "immobilisation" of Lumumba was desirable but should be an exclusively Congolese effort. The second cable was delivered to Devlin and stipulated that it remained a matter of the "highest priority" that the CIA rid Eisenhower of a turbulent Congolese ex-prime minister.[58]

Taken together, all of these factors suggest that the DDP developed not one but two plans for the execution of its target in the Congo. When it became obvious that the poisoning of Lumumba with Gottlieb's biological toxin was impractical, the agency adopted a second plan. This was aimed at supporting Mobutu as the prime candidate to take over control of the Congo – which came about ultimately in 1965 – and making sure that he was provided with the opportunity to eliminate Lumumba in an act that has since been interpreted as the consequence of tribal rivalry.

The most important aspect of the Congolese operation, however, was that it culminated during a period when it was far from certain that the CIA was acting even in the short-term interests of American policy. Whether Lumumba was kidnapped or escaped from the UN remains a matter of conjecture.[59] A retrospective analysis suggests that it was not to his advantage to wilfully leave the safe haven of UN custody where he had, after all, *placed himself* after Mobutu had seized power. The crucial point is that the government of the United States was in a period of transition when Lumumba went absent from the protection of the UN on 27 November, to be taken captive by Mobutu some three days later.[60] However great the CIA's involvement was in the affair, the agency was serving the policy of the outgoing Eisenhower administration, which had been accused by Kennedy during the 1960 election campaign of subverting genuine independence in the Congo. Kennedy was, it is true, informed by Dulles of developments in the Congo whilst a candidate and as president-elect, but these briefings amounted to only general policy overviews. The DCI did not, as far as records show, reveal any operational details to a prospective president whose approach to Congolese problems was very different from Eisenhower's.[61]

Kennedy's projected policy, in brief, anticipated that the United States would align itself with popular feeling in the Congo and stipulated that: (1) the UN presence in the Congo was to be strengthened; (2) efforts to evict the Belgians were to be stepped up; and (3) all of the major Congolese political players were to be encouraged to form a national coalition in the interests of promoting self-determination. The success of the plan was, to a significant extent, dependent on Mobutu ending Lumumba's incarceration, and despite the fact that Kennedy had been uncomfortable with the ex-prime minister's flirtation with the Kremlin, efforts were made by prospective members of the incoming Democratic administration to bring this about.[62] The murder of Lumumba just five days before Kennedy's inauguration impeded the plan that the new president had devised: a plan which in its essence was aimed at countering communism in the third world, and one which, to a greater or lesser extent, had been scuttled by the machinations of the CIA.

Tinkering at the Edges: The Consequences of the Taylor Inquiry Findings

If the outcome of the Congolese crisis signalled that communication between outgoing and incoming administrations regarding intelligence should be improved, and that there was an underlying need for greater executive control over the CIA, then the points were lost on Kennedy. The president's relationship with the agency was very good between January and April 1961. Only after the upheaval of the Bay of Pigs fiasco was Kennedy prompted into ordering General Maxwell Taylor to make a reexamination of the intelligence community generally and the DDP in particular.

Fundamental as the Taylor Committee's inquiry was, however, its overriding recommendations were that the CIA's covert action mission be improved rather than cut back, but that the doctrine of plausible deniability be more stringently adhered to.[63] The amalgamation of secret intelligence gathering and covert operational functions under the umbrella of the CIA had always been a source of friction within the agency and a cause of concern outside of it. Yet rather than looking into the dysfunctional implications of pairing these two disparate missions and recommending improvements, the Taylor Committee merely reiterated the findings of the 1949 Dulles-Jackson-Correa report. It was to be business as usual.

Spies and operators would continue to work together in a single organisation and covert operations would proceed with, if anything, greater vigour than had been the case during Eisenhower's tenure.[64]

At the same time, Kennedy determined that the necessary provisions would be established for his administration to maintain greater control over, and be better informed by, the intelligence community. To this end he reconstituted the PBCFIA as the President's Foreign Intelligence Advisory Board (PFIAB) in May 1961. Whereas Eisenhower consulted infrequently with the PBCFIA, however, Kennedy sought its advice on a more regular basis. To provide more focused authorisation procedures for covert operations, the president split the Special Group into three separate committees. The Special Group (5412) continued to oversee the intelligence community's general covert action effort, while the Special Group (Counterinsurgency), or CI group, directed unconventional warfare in Southeast Asia, and the Special Group (Augmented) – SG(A) – directed and coordinated the clandestine action offensive that Kennedy was to wage against Cuba for the remainder of his presidency.[65]

Much as these changes reflected the president's determination to make the CIA work effectively under his own supervision, they also indicated where his priorities lay. Of all the agency's directorates, it was the DDP that dominated during the Kennedy years, much as it had done in the 1950s. Within the DDP, however, paramilitary operations came into the ascendancy over political action projects and psychological warfare, a reflection of Kennedy's conviction that unconventional warfare was both essential and justified against the backdrop of international tension that characterised his period in power.

Covert operations were, therefore, stepped up anywhere that a tangible communist threat was perceived to exist. In Africa, for example, Kennedy devised policy and strategy on the assumption that the continent's newly emerging nations were susceptible to political encroachments by the Russians. This had led the CIA to establish an African Division – as distinct from the European and Middle East Divisions that had previously shared responsibility for Africa – in 1960, and the number of CIA stations in that continent had seen a 55.5 per cent increase by 1963.[66] What lies behind this statistic is the fact that this period saw Africa become a Cold War battleground on which, for instance, opposing Cuban mercenaries in the respective employ of the United States and the Soviet Union engaged in an open gun battle on a stretch of Lake Tanganyika – in Congolese territorial waters.[67]

The Congo was regarded as one of the "four crisis areas" that the White House faced at the outset of the Kennedy presidency. The other countries mentioned were Cuba, Laos, and Vietnam.[68] Though Kennedy regarded Indochina as being of secondary importance to Cuba, covert action programmes were carried out in Laos and Vietnam, with the aim of reinforcing the general American counterinsurgency effort. Offensive operations against North Vietnam were also conducted from the autumn of 1961 under the command of William Colby, but these were focused primarily on complementing the defensive measures that were being implemented in the south rather than seriously challenging Ho Chi Minh.[69] It has been argued that senior administration and CIA officials deliberately attempted to engage Kennedy's interest in Southeast Asia as a means of distracting the president from his dissatisfaction with the slow progress of his efforts to unseat Castro.[70] Looked at in retrospect, however, the overall scope of the CIA's covert action programme in Vietnam and Laos between 1961 and 1963, escalated in a trend that paralleled the growing American commitment to Indochina.

The DDP's activities in Cuba and Southeast Asia are instructive for what they reveal about Kennedy's management of the agency. What the president did after the shake-up that followed the Bay of Pigs was to split control of the CIA. Responsibility for covert action was concentrated in the hands of Maxwell Taylor, Robert Kennedy, and McGeorge Bundy. Coordination of the Cuban and Southeast Asia programmes was then passed down through a chain of command that saw counterinsurgency specialist Ed Lansdale bypassing DCI, John McCone, and dealing directly with CIA station chiefs and DDP operatives.[71]

Such fundamental change in the agency's command and control provisions may have arisen partly in response to pressure from below that came to light as a result of the CIA's move to a new headquarters at Langley, Virginia in autumn 1961. Concerns were raised in the DDP that the housing of all of the agency's missions in one location was a bad move. Too many people, it was argued, would inevitably come to know more than they needed to know and thereby jeopardise the compartmentalisation that the DDP regarded as crucial for the maintenance of secrecy. The operations directorate therefore argued that it should function as an elite service quite separate from the rest of the agency.[72] Though this proposal was rejected, Kennedy's command structure went some way to allaying DDP fears, because much of the management and coordination of the Cuban and Southeast Asia programmes took place away from Langley, usually in what had formerly been the Map Room of the White House.[73]

The most far-reaching development arising from Kennedy's administrative changes was, however, the reorientation of the DCI's role. Allen Dulles was, of course, sacrificed as a consequence of the Bay of Pigs debacle, along with his DDCI, General Charles P. Cabell, the DDP Richard Bissell, and the DDI Robert Amory.[74] This changing of the guard in the hierarchy of the CIA led to a radical shift in functional priorities within the agency, which began with the appointment of John McCone as Dulles's successor in November 1961.

The Directorship of John McCone

John McCone was not Kennedy's first choice for the CIA directorship. Believing that he needed to appoint someone to the post whom he could trust implicitly and from whom he could "get the right pitch at CIA", the president initially offered the job to his brother. The Attorney General rejected the proposition, however, on grounds that he was a Democrat and was too close to the White House, both of which were regarded by Robert Kennedy as liabilities following the the failure of JMARC. Several other candidates were considered, including Fowler Hamilton, who was soon to become head of AID, but eventually the president plumped for McCone.[75]

Dulles's successor was in many ways a very suitable candidate to fulfil Kennedy's requirements at the CIA. What the agency needed most in the aftermath of the Bay of Pigs venture was a director who could bring its sprawling bureaucracy under control and restore morale. McCone had proven his worth as an administrator in the private sector – at the California Shipbuilding Company – becoming a millionaire in the process. Eisenhower had appointed him chairman of the Atomic Energy Commission (AEC) in 1958, where the would-be DCI had proven adept in bolstering confidence within the AEC's ranks and worked well with the congressional committees that oversaw its activities.[76] This, Robert Kennedy claimed, had led some to charge that McCone was too close to the Legislature. Good relations with Capitol Hill were, however, essential for a prospective DCI if congressional review of the CIA's activities was to remain as cursory as had been the case during Dulles's time.[77] An additional advantage in selecting McCone was the point that his affiliations lay with the Republicans, and his appointment as DCI therefore helped Kennedy to remove the furore that followed JMARC from the domain of partisan politics.[78]

If Kennedy assumed that McCone's appointment would foster greater co-operation across the United States intelligence community as a whole, then the president's optimism was misplaced.[79] This hoped-for objective was fulfilled once – during the Cuban missile crisis – but more generally, interagency relations were as difficult between 1961 and 1963 as they had been during the 1950s.[80] The new DCI, nevertheless, proved to be a very effective administrator of the CIA itself, as is evident from the machinations that led to the establishment of the Deputy Directorate for Science and Technology (DDS&T) in August 1963.

Arguments for the provision of a fourth CIA directorate took root as a consequence of John Kennedy's threat to "splinter the CIA into a thousand pieces and scatter it to the winds" in the aftermath of the Bay of Pigs fiasco.[81] The agency's leadership correctly gauged that the real target of the president's anger was not the CIA generally, but the Directorate for Plans. McCone therefore proposed the transfer of three of the DDP's technically oriented divisions to the DDS&T: an adept piece of management that diminished the DDP's mission and brought it under more rigid control without reducing the overall size of the CIA itself. The creation of the DDS&T signalled more, however, than McCone's ability to protect his own bureaucratic fiefdom. It accelerated the agency's drift towards specialisation in the field of technological intelligence and served as an outlet for interchange between the CIA and the wider scientific and industrial communities: a very necessary requirement if the agency was to remain at the cutting edge of technological research.[82]

In relation to the degree of attention that McCone allocated to each of the directorates under his charge, the *Church Report* stated that the DDP commanded up to 90 per cent of the DCI's time.[83] Given that Robert Kennedy, Maxwell Taylor, and McGeorge Bundy were managing covert operations in Cuba and Southeast Asia, this claim would seem to have overstated the case, and it certainly did not reflect McCone's professional inclinations. As Ray Cline, who succeeded Amory as DDI, pointed out, McCone was "the only DCI who ever took the role of providing substantive intelligence analysis and estimates to the president as his first priority".[84] One clear advantage of raising the profile of the long neglected DDI in this way was that it helped to build bridges with the White House. Innovations such as the *President's Intelligence Check List*, "a no-holds-barred publication" that carried the most sensitive information to be gleaned from the CIA's operational reports, were well-received by Kennedy and so helped to enhance the agency's standing after the precipitous decline that followed JMARC. [85]

The CIA's performance in the field of intelligence production during this period has, however, been a source of controversy, especially as it relates to the Cuban missile crisis. In the aftermath of Khrushchev's removal of Soviet missiles from Cuba, Kennedy is reported to have been disenchanted with the CIA on grounds that it failed, even in its estimates of September 1962, to give adequate warning of the oncoming conflict.[86] This has led some commentators to conclude that the agency performed in a "less than inspiring manner" during the crisis.[87] On the other side of the argument, intelligence officials who were close to events have characterised the missile crisis as "the CIA's finest hour".[88] While drawing perhaps predictable conclusions, these first-hand accounts also shed considerable light on the events and the problems associated with intelligence collection and analysis: a mission which Marchetti and Marks describe as "a guessing game, albeit one that is grounded in fact, logic and experience".[89]

It has been suggested that in presenting its assessment of the worsening situation in Cuba, the CIA failed to take proper account of Soviet strategic doctrine, which laid emphasis on the build-up of economic capacity rather than military power. In the interests of achieving this aim, the argument goes on to say, Khrushchev sought to maintain a minimum deterrent in dealing with the United States. He therefore resorted to military brinkmanship, installing missiles in Cuba in the hope that such a move would enhance the effectiveness of the relatively small Soviet nuclear arsenal.[90]

While this argument carries considerable weight, the real source of the CIA's predictive failure lay in the assumptions on which it based its judgements. Agency logic proceeded from the premise that before emplacing offensive missile systems in Cuba, the Soviet leadership would correctly assess the impact that such a move would have in the United States and veto the plan. Contrary to CIA expectations, Khrushchev did not behave logically, and the agency was perceived by some to have failed yet again. Oleg Kalugin, a KGB officer who was familiar with the circumstances surrounding the Russian decision to site the missiles, supports this line of argument. Kalugin affirms that the KGB regarded Khrushchev as having "acted recklessly, badly underestimating Kennedy's resolve and the severity of the U.S. reaction to the presence of the missiles".[91]

The missile crisis illustrates the inherent limitations of intelligence, which essentially arise from the fact that specific events cannot be predicted with accuracy or confidence. Khrushchev's decision to install the weapons was not knowable until the venture was under way.[92] At the same time, there were some in the CIA, not least of all McCone himself, who suspected the worst. The DCI speculated that Russian military designs in Cuba were aimed at redressing the strategic balance between the superpowers, which was weighted heavily in favour of the United States – especially after the successful testing of the Starfish missile system in July 1962.

Though McCone's suspicions were based on intuition rather than hard fact, he used them as justification to intensify U-2 reconnaissance flights over Cuba, which proved vital in alerting Kennedy to the real nature of Soviet intent in time for the president to act. The U-2 programme was actually turned over to the Air Force during the missile crisis – on 14 October 1962 – but the CIA continued to play a crucial part in the intelligence-gathering effort through satellite systems that reinforced and verified U-2 photographic evidence.[93] The agency was, furthermore, able to draw from Oleg Penkovsky, who revealed that the Russians did not yet have the technological capacity to launch an Intercontinental Ballistic Missile (ICBM) attack against the United States from within Soviet territory: information which strengthened Kennedy's hand immeasurably.[94]

McCone, then, played a decisive part in the resolution of the missile crisis. Yet the affair did not enhance his reputation, for in the aftermath of Khrushchev's climb-down the DCI lost little time in reminding colleagues that he had been right in his judgement of Russian intentions. This was tactless and it irritated officials such as McGeorge Bundy, who complained "I'm so tired of listening to McCone say he was right I never want to hear it again". More serious repercussions for McCone arose from the fact that John Kennedy also resented the DCI's boasting and the relationship between the president and his chief intelligence officer declined considerably after October 1962.[95]

Conclusion

The years 1961 to 1963 marked a turbulent period for the CIA. From optimistic beginnings, agency fortunes plummeted to their nadir through the spectacular failure at the Bay of Pigs, then rose again slowly in the wake of an unprecedented reorganisation, not only of the CIA itself, but of the entire American intelligence apparatus. Though Kennedy threatened to abolish the agency immediately after JMARC, the need for the United States to engage in covert operations and the capacity of the CIA to perform such activities was never seriously questioned. Following the Taylor Report, the Kennedy brothers, especially the Attorney

General, took an interest in covert action that verged on the obsessive and reflected the general interventionist thrust of American foreign and defence policy during this whole period.[96] Nowhere was this more pronounced than in Cuba, the Caribbean and the wider Western Hemisphere.

8

A BANQUET OF CONSEQUENCES: COVERT ACTION IN CUBA AND THE CARIBBEAN 1960–1963

Few short treatises on the undeclared war that John Kennedy waged against revolutionary Cuba between 1961 and 1963 could have greater resonance or be more eloquently-put than an observation made by Robert Louis Stevenson during the previous century in which he opined that sooner or later "we sit down to a banquet of consequences". Much has been made of the strategic and tactical drawbacks of the Bay of Pigs invasion and the subsequent effort to destabilise Cuba with the launch of Operation MONGOOSE, not to mention the questionable ethics of the various attempts made by the CIA to assassinate Fidel Castro. The real flaw in Washington's drive to unseat the Maximum Leader, as Castro came to be known, however, lay in the deeply-held yet ill-conceived assumption that because Castro led a leftist regime that resisted implementing democratic change and adopted Marxist-Leninism, it necessarily followed that widespread discontent existed within Cuba and could be triggered into rebellion through the deployment of covert action. This was not the case and in reality Kennedy had only two choices in confronting Castro, which were either to live with the fact that a communist state lay less than a hundred miles from the Florida coast or to authorise overt military intervention to eradicate the threat.[1]

The consequences of the president's failure to fully recognise these realities and to opt instead to use covert action as a third way of combating Castro were far-reaching. Most significantly, Kennedy's decision not to launch an outright military invasion of Cuba at the point at which the Bay of Pigs went awry led Khrushchev to scent weakness and subsequently test American resolve whenever opportunities presented themselves. What followed was essentially a superpower sparring match that made a close connection between Berlin and Cuba and brought the Cold War to its most dangerous phase with the Cuban missile crisis.[2]

Kennedy, furthermore, bore the consequences of the failure of both Truman and Eisenhower to implement adequate oversight provisions for the management of covert action. The outcome was that the DDP had developed a propensity to overestimate its abilities and achievements, overlook its failures, underestimate its enemies, and habitually preclude its own espionage and counterintelligence experts from gaining access to operational details. At least some of these unwelcome traits were evident in the latter stages of Eisenhower's tenure, most visibly so during Operation HAIK, but under Kennedy, who had none of his predecessor's experience of managing the CIA's covert action mission, they took on hubristic proportions. The result was the Bay of Pigs fiasco.[3]

Though the failure of JMARC led to the introduction of measures designed to monitor the DDP's activities more closely, Kennedy continued to place his faith in the organisation's capacity to unseat Castro. Indeed, covert action remained an essential element of a wider American effort aimed at countering communism and the causes of communism in the Western Hemisphere generally. As had been the case in Western Europe during the late forties and early fifties, economic initiatives, notably Eisenhower's Social Progress Trust Fund and Kennedy's much more ambitious Alliance for Progress, were central to this policy.[4] In its drive to complement these larger American objectives, the CIA mounted preventive operations in the Dominican Republic, Ecuador, and British Guiana between 1960 and 1964 as well as a major defensive programme in Venezuela from 1962 to 1964. For Kennedy, however, the principal challenge came from revolutionary Cuba. Indeed, the American president remained unremitting in his determination to unseat Castro by any means short of invasion until, in November 1963, Lee Harvey Oswald succeeded in doing to Kennedy what the CIA had consistently failed to do to Castro over the past three years.

The Cuban Revolution

On 1 January 1959, Fulgencio Batista y Zaldívar, an archetypal *caudillo* who had dominated Cuban politics for twenty years and ruled directly since 1952, was swept from power by Fidel Castro's 26th of July Movement (M-26-7). These events marked the culmination of a six year campaign which began in 1953, when Castro and his brother Raúl mounted a failed rebellion and were sentenced to fifteen years imprisonment. Pardoned under a general amnesty after eleven months of incarceration, the Castro brothers left for exile in Mexico in 1955. They returned to Cuba in December 1956, however, with Argentinean doctor-turned-revolutionary Ernesto 'Ché' Guevara and 81 followers to launch a second campaign to dislodge the Batista regime. Over the following two years the insurgency gathered ever-greater momentum, and the repressive methods that Batista employed to counter it led only to a steady haemorrhaging in his support. By December 1958, the Cuban dictator's power base had been eroded to the extent that the only option that lay open to him was to flee to the Dominican Republic. The Cuban revolution had thus succeeded and Castro was greeted by cheering crowds as he entered Havana.[5]

Though Castro has long declared himself to have been a Marxist-Leninist from the outset of his career, a close scrutiny of the evidence suggests that his claim amounts to a retrospective vindication of the course that his regime subsequently followed.[6] He did not come to power advocating communism and his relationship with the Cuban Communist Party – Partido Socialista Popular (PSP) – was decidedly cool prior to the success of the revolution. Taking its lead from a cautious and largely disinterested Russian leadership which, to quote a leading authority on Soviet-Latin American affairs, adhered to the concept of "geographical fatalism", the PSP dismissed Castro's insurrectionist efforts as acts of reckless adventurism.[7]

Certainly, there was a definite lack of unanimity in Washington regarding Castro's ideological leanings for almost a year after his accession to power. In essence, the Eisenhower administration pursued a wait-and-see policy, with Christian A. Herter, who had recently succeeded the dying Foster Dulles as Secretary of State, and the newly-appointed Ambassador to Havana, Philip W. Bonsal, dominating the debate about policy direction in the early months of 1959. These officials looked on the future prospects for Cuban-American relations with a reserved optimism that was based on the belief that the Cuban revolution could be guided, as the Bolivian revolution had been, in a direction that was compatible with the interests of the United States.[8]

The balance in administration thinking moved towards the adoption of a harder line following Castro's visit to Washington in April 1959. At this point the Cuban leader was regarded as a volatile neutralist who, because he chose not to request American aid, would be difficult to control. For the next ten months the story was one of Castro moving sharply to the left and becoming increasingly outspoken in his use of anti-American rhetoric. Two events stood as markers in this trend. In September 1959 he addressed the United Nations in New York, projecting a considerably more radical image than had been on display in April and arguing the case for equidistance between the superpowers in the Cold War. By February 1960 he had moved resolutely towards the Soviet camp, hosting a trade fair that was headed by the Russian Vice Premier, Anastas Mikoyan, and which served as the precursor for the two countries signing a commercial agreement.[9]

What should be stressed, however, is that Castro ruled on his own terms, and though by late 1959 he had decided to follow a Marxist course, he did not regard himself as, or intend on becoming, a Soviet puppet. Rather than fitting into the Soviet mould, Castro's wider international ambitions corresponded to the Nasser model. The Cuban ruler saw his appeal as transcending national boundaries and he aspired to establish himself as the leader of a nonaligned Latin American revolutionary bloc that would counterbalance the power of the United States in the Western Hemisphere.[10]

The pursuit of such designs was partly attributable to defensive motives. Like Arbenz, Castro implemented far-reaching agrarian reform, which included the expropriation of domestic and foreign-owned plantations. As a consequence, the Maximum Leader anticipated that the type of action that had been taken against the Guatemalan government in 1954 would be attempted again in Cuba.[11] Havana therefore sought to incite further revolutions in Latin America, the success of which, it was reasoned, would provide Cuba with regional allies and in turn deter the United States from attempting to remove the Casro regime. When the hoped-for revolutions failed to materialise, however, the survival of the new Cuba came to depend on Castro's ability to secure the military protection of the Soviet Union.[12] A shared Marxist-Leninist ideology, Castro calculated, increased the obligation on Moscow to come to Cuba's aid, especially in light of the fact that the Sino-Soviet split was intensifying pressure on the Kremlin to demonstrate its socialist credentials.[13]

The Eisenhower administration's fears of communist penetration in Cuba and of Castro's alignment with the Soviet Union escalated in parallel with this left-ward trend. By October 1959, Washington was adopting an increasingly in-tolerant line. Similarly to the Voroshilov visit to Indonesia, the Mikoyan mission to Cuba merely confirmed the United States in its determination to unseat a difficult third world leader who, in Eisenhower's estimation, was beginning to "look like a madman".[14]

Opening Moves

On 13 January 1960, the 5412 Committee gave conditional approval to Allen Dulles's proposal that the CIA begin "contingency planning" for a covert operation to bring about the downfall of the Cuban government. The CIA established a special task force within J.C. King's Western Hemisphere Division to devise a programme aimed at meeting with the administration's wishes (see appendix 7). Headed by Jake Esterline, who was transferred from his duties as CIA station chief in Caracas, the new grouping operated under the acronym of WH/4 (Western Hemisphere Division, Branch 4) and on 17 March 1960, Dulles, Bissell and King presented its findings to Eisenhower.[15] "A Program of Covert Action Against the Castro Regime" would depend on the creation and development of: (1) a responsible, unified, and appealing Cuban opposition based outside of the island; (2) a mass communications network to ensure the implementation of a powerful propaganda offensive; (3) a covert intelligence and action organisation inside of Cuba; and (4) an adequate paramilitary force based outside of Cuba. Though he expressed reservations about the potential for leakage and breach of security, Eisenhower gave his authorisation for Esterline to proceed with the plan under the overall direction of Bissell.[16]

The strategy to be deployed against Castro was a close approximation of PBSUCCESS. The CIA was to use all means at its disposal and its efforts were to be complemented by a wider campaign involving the State and Defense Departments and the USIA. The overall aim was to secure inter-American support for Washington's efforts to isolate Havana diplomatically and economically, and prepare the way for overt OAS intervention against the Castro regime.[17] There was, however, a further and closely interconnected dimension to the agency's Cuba programme, namely Operation EMOTH, the campaign to overthrow the Dominican Republic's brutal, rightist dictator, Rafael Leonadis Trujillo Molina.[18]

The Dominican Dimension

Eisenhower and later Kennedy had good reasons for seeking Trujillo's ouster. The principal exporter of counterrevolution in the Americas, he targeted the region's burgeoning democracies and thereby undermined United States policy. Within his own borders, Trujillo's corrupt and arbitrary rule was so pronounced that he planted the seeds, albeit inadvertently, for a Cuban-style revolution, which in itself was enough to justify the use of preventive covert action against him. Finally, hatred of Trujillo easily outweighed distrust of Castro in Latin America as a whole and Eisenhower therefore calculated that if he invoked the Betancourt Doctrine and acted against totalitarian regimes of all political hues then he would enhance the prospects of securing hemispheric support for his anti-Castro policies.[19]

Operation EMOTH was, then, conceived and designed to serve as an adjunct to the CIA's Cuba project and, at least until the summer of 1960, the two programmes advanced in parallel. Recommendations that preparations be made to take preventive action in the Dominican Republic were first broached at an NSC meeting on 14 January 1960. This was just one day after Eisenhower approved contingency covert action planning to begin against Cuba, and a similar time period of approximately three months elapsed for more specific proposals to come to light in both cases. A State Department paper that focused on the policies to be pursued in the event of the "flight, assassination, death or overthrow of Trujillo" was, for instance, authorised by Eisenhower in April 1960, within four weeks of his approval of the WH/4 programme.[20] More explicit parallels emerged the following month, when Eisenhower stated that his exasperation with Castro and Trujillo had become so pronounced that he wished to see them both "sawed off".[21]

Debate still surrounds the circumstances of Trujillo's murder by Dominican dissidents on 30 May 1961. That the Church Committee could not establish definitely whether CIA involvement of any kind had figured in the assassination is evidence only of the agency's skill at "erecting screens of detachment" to distance itself and its political masters from potentially damaging repercussions.[22] The extent to which the incoming Kennedy White House was informed about Operation EMOTH is also a subject of conjecture. Robert Kennedy argued that the new administration was not aware of the exact details of what was afoot.[23] In response, Scott D. Brekenbridge, a CIA officer who was familiar with the Dominican operation, maintains that "the highest levels of government in two administrations" encouraged and supported the coup against Trujillo and understood that "the objective could be achieved only by killing [the Dominican dictator]". Breckenbridge goes on to say that he reviewed a cable file containing "detailed reporting from the field on the plans of the dissidents", which was subsequently passed on to the Kennedy White House.[24]

These claims are supported by a February 1961 memorandum in which McGeorge Bundy informed President Kennedy that the State Department regarded the increased diplomatic isolation of Cuba and the Dominican Republic as being imperative "before any drastic action is taken", the implication being against both leaders.[25] For EMOTH to have achieved its intended effect, however, the anti-Trujillo opposition would have needed to act against its intended victim in close conjunction with a successful coup against Castro. A satisfactory outcome to the Dominican campaign was thus not possible once the Bay of Pigs invasion had failed.

Much as assassination was central to Operation EMOTH, it was also attempted against Castro. The effort to kill the Maximum Leader was envisaged as a potential quick fix for solving the Cuban problem. Though it ran concurrently with the CIA's paramilitary operation against the revolutionary government in Havana, the agency's campaign to murder Castro employed different operatives and assets, not to mention strategies and tactics, and it therefore needs to be examined as a separate entity.

Dabbling in a Deadly Art: Assassination and the CIA's Mafia Connection

Assassination is the "most elemental form of paramilitary action", and before deploying it the prospective perpetrator must determine whether or not recourse to such action can be exploited effectively for political ends.[26] This requirement was seen as being fulfilled when the assassination of one or more of Cuba's leaders was first discussed, albeit circumlocutiously, by the 5412 Committee on 14 March 1960. The death of Castro and his colleagues would, the Committee argued, create a vacuum for the Cuban Communist Party to exploit and thereby establish a pretext for the United States and its OAS partners, under the provisions of the Caracas Declaration, "to move in on Cuba in force".[27] Again, in the latter months of 1960, when the CIA opted to sponsor the amphibious invasion of Cuba which came to fruition with the ill-fated Bay of Pigs operation, the assassination of the Maximum Leader was envisaged as a 'second track' to the wider plan: to leave Cuba leaderless while the invasion was taking place, thus optimising the chances of success.[28]

For assassination to succeed, however, other, more practical requirements also need to be adhered to. Above all else, the assassins themselves must be subject to vigorous security controls, not least of all to limit the possibilities of disclosure. In this respect, the CIA's plans to kill Castro were severely flawed, primarily because the agency subcontracted this delicate mission out to America's most experienced killers – the Cosa Nostra.[29]

The CIA-Mafia connection can be traced back as far as 1943 when the OSS secured the syndicate's agreement to engage in clandestine action in Sicily in return for the parole of mob chieftain "Lucky" Luciano. There is, as well, some speculation that the Cosa Nostra played a role in the agency's campaign to defeat the Communist-Socialist alliance in the Italian elections of 1948.[30] No evidence exists, however, to support the case that the link was maintained until 1960.

Exactly who initiated the CIA-Mafia assassination campaign against Castro is also a matter of some doubt and controversy. Bissell refutes claims that the idea originated with him, maintaining that he first heard of the plan to use the Mafia from Sheffield Edwards, the director of the CIA's Office of Security, who had additional responsibility for some of the MKULTRA projects. Edwards and his deputy subsequently became case officers for agency relations with the syndicate and Bissell authorised them to continue with the arrangement.[31] The CIA made direct contact with the Mafia in September 1960 through Robert Maheu, a one-time FBI officer who worked freelance for the agency. He approached John Rosselli, Salvatore 'Sam' Giancana, and Santos Trafficante with the offer of a contract to kill Castro for $150,000. All three were leading underground figures who had ample reason for wanting the Cuban leader dead. On coming to power he had terminated Havana's mob-controlled gambling and vice rackets. Maheu's offer was therefore readily accepted.

If the CIA had bargained on the Mafia resorting to a stereotypical gangland killing of Castro, then the agency was mistaken. A successful attempt on the life of the Cuban leader was, as the mob well understood, dependent on more subtle tactics. Giancana and his cohorts therefore proposed that a number of anti-Castro Cubans be recruited to penetrate the would-be victim's entourage and kill him by poisoning when the opportunity presented itself. The CIA consequently provided the Mafia with pills containing botulinum toxin that could be dissolved in water and these were used in two unsuccessful attempts on Castro's life in early 1961. More fantastic schemes followed, involving cigars treated with deadly toxins and a diving suit that had been coated with death-inducing bacterial powder, none of which succeeded.[32]

Quite aside from the fact that these activities beggar belief, they raise a very fundamental question about the quality of the CIA hierarchy's judgement. Since the agency supplied the Mafia with the poisons and other resources it requested and had extensive contacts with the Cuban émigré community in Miami, from which potential assassins could readily be drawn, why was it necessary to involve the mob at all? The syndicate, in essence, merely devised a strategy, and the CIA was well capable of doing the same without any outside assistance. Indeed, the DDP drew up its own plans for the assassination of Raúl Castro in early 1960. Authorisation to proceed with the venture was cabled to the Havana station only to be withdrawn within hours of the initial approval. This took place in July 1960, some two months before Edwards and Maheu established the Mafia link.[33]

Further debate surrounds exactly who gave authority for the campaign to kill Castro to proceed. Though it is quite possible that Eisenhower did not know of the bizarre tactical details of the CIA's assassination plots, there is a strong likelihood that, as was the case with the action that was simultaneously being planned and executed against Lumumba, the president was aware of and condoned the strategy.

Such moves were not, after all, new to the Eisenhower administration, given that it had been well disposed to consider use of the golden bullet against Arbenz and Sukarno.

For his part, Kennedy does not appear to have authorised the CIA to continue with, or even to have been aware of, the assassination plots that were sanctioned during the final months of Eisenhower's tenure.[34] The new president was not in any way averse, however, to the use of such extreme methods to advance his policy objectives and nor were a number of his key lieutenants. McGeorge Bundy and Walt Rostow, for example, urged Bissell on separate occasions to establish a team to engage in what was euphemistically referred to as "executive action", and assassination was to serve as a major component of Operation MONGOOSE.[35] During March and April of 1961, however, the CIA's assassination campaign had failed to bear fruit and the focus of the anti-Castro programme moved to the largest and most overt of all the agency's clandestine operations.

From Guerrilla Infiltration to Amphibious Invasion: CIA Paramilitary Preparations under Eisenhower

From the time that the CIA was first authorised to develop a plan for the removal of Castro, American policymakers failed to set clear enough operational parameters to limit the agency's activities. Although the basic policy paper of the 17 March 1960 focused its attention on the development of a guerrilla infiltration programme, the CIA devised the document in such a way as to leave enough scope for the project to be expanded into a larger venture. Provision had, for instance, been made for "an adequate paramilitary force outside of Cuba", and a limited air arm under CIA control, which could easily be expanded "if and when the situation [required it]".[36] This was very ambiguous language, for Castro was concurrently strengthening his internal security provisions. As such, determining what was and what was not "an adequate paramilitary force" was bound to come under constant review. Furthermore, by excluding the DDI from any involvement in the Cuba programme, the DDP was able to monopolise the progress reports that reached the president and was therefore in an optimum position to shape the evolution of the venture according to its own designs.[37]

Of the major components that comprised the Cuba project, only the propaganda programme progressed according to plan. Having procured a fifty-kilowatt medium-wave radio transmitter from the Voice of America, the DDP established its 'propaganda shop' on Swan Island, a slip of land in the Caribbean located between Cuba and Central America. David Atlee Phillips, a veteran of PBSUCCESS who was brought in to manage the psychological warfare offensive, calculated that the Cuban population would need to be exposed to six months of anti-Castro propaganda to pave the way for a paramilitary campaign, whatever its scale, and this was readily achieved. Radio Swan began broadcasting on 17 May 1960, thirty days after Bissell had appointed Phillips and exactly on schedule.

Consistent with Washington's desire to be even-handed, the new station attacked Castro and Trujillo in equal measure.[38]

Expediting the political action element of the operation proved to be a far more fractious and ultimately unproductive affair. From the beginning of the Cuban venture, Eisenhower had insisted that the creation of "a popular, genuine government in exile" was essential to provide legitimacy to any subsequent military moves against Havana.[39] The problem was that this was unachievable because the five-group coalition that the CIA selected from the heavily factionalised Cuban exile community in Florida and assembled under the aegis of Frente Revolucionario Democràtico (FRD) proved to be ridden with internecine rivalry.[40]

Compounding the problem further was the selection of E. Howard Hunt to control political action at ground level. Another veteran of PBSUCCESS and an arch-conservative, Hunt proved highly reluctant to recruit anyone of a liberal or leftward persuasion to Frente – a serious flaw given that a left-of-centre political complexion was viewed by Washington as appropriate for its surrogate Cuban opposition. Not only this, but Hunt's assistant, Gerry Droller, entertained no such biases and thus found himself in frequent disagreement with his boss.[41] The unified opposition-in exile that Eisenhower saw as imperative therefore never materialised, which caused the Cuba programme to become an increasingly American-led affair, and in turn opened the way for the metamorphosis of the venture from a guerrilla infiltration programme into a full-scale amphibious invasion.[42]

For its part, the paramilitary component of the Cuba programme was hampered by a still more fundamental problem. The premise on which it was originally based proved to be entirely unworkable, which left the CIA with only two alternatives: either expand the concept beyond recognition or abandon it altogether.

The Cuba project was first approved on the understanding that its core paramilitary component was aimed at creating a guerrilla organisation based on the OSS World War II resistance model. In accordance with these plans, a group of between thirty and one hundred trainees was coached in sabotage and communications techniques during the late-spring and early summer of 1960 at a secure compound outside of Fort Gulick in the Panama Canal Zone. The immediate objective was to infiltrate the would-be guerrillas back into their homeland where they would engage in insurrection and establish one or more resistance strongholds. The ground would thereby be prepared for a more general uprising, which, it was hoped, would be galvanised further through the black propaganda being beamed into Cuba via Radio Swan.[43]

The unfeasibility of the original guerrilla concept quickly became apparent, however. Of the few infiltration missions that were mounted, the insurgents were captured within forty-eight hours of entering Cuba. There was, as well, a growing belief on the part of leading CIA officials that even if the guerrilla strategy succeeded, it would fall short of achieving the minimum critical mass necessary to produce a sufficiently strong psychological effect to precipitate a widespread revolt.[44]

The DDP consequently opted to expand its paramilitary cadres into an infantry force of several hundred men, to be based at Camp Trax in Guatemala and supported by a small tactical air force stationed thirty miles away at Retalhuleu. Although Bissell initiated this decision without consulting with Eisenhower or the 5412 Committee, the president recognised that "changes in the current thinking" warranted changes in WH/4's plans and therefore authorised the transformation of the Cuba operation, on 29 November 1960, from a guerrilla infiltration programme to an amphibious invasion.[45]

This move carried associated risks. Prime among these was the fact that the mushrooming of what was now known as the Cuban Expeditionary Force (CEF) from four hundred to two or possibly three thousand men severely diminished the prospects of maintaining secrecy: an objective that was compromised further by Bissell's willingness to allow the Guatemalan president, Miguel Ydígoras Fuentes, to use the CEF to help suppress an uprising against his regime in mid-November 1960. Thus, by the time that Eisenhower sanctioned the amphibious invasion plan, its existence was known of throughout Latin America and had even leaked on to the pages of the *Miami Herald*. The president was, however, unperturbed. The final decision would be Kennedy's, but Eisenhower's inclination at the time was to press ahead.[46]

Kennedy's Cuban Inheritance: Misconceptions and Hidden Agendas

In relation to the Cuba programme, Kennedy's inheritance was a very difficult one. Once Eisenhower had approved the amphibious invasion plan, the project began to extend far beyond its original proportions and the early months of 1961 saw senior CIA officials, who were apparently ignorant of the plan's shortcomings, grow increasingly optimistic about its prospects. During this period the CEF multiplied to more than three-times its original size, and Special Forces trainers were dispatched to Camp Trax to instruct the brigade in the techniques that would be required for the invasion.[47]

Even if Kennedy had been afforded a breathing space in order to review the plan and determine whether or not to press on, as Esterline advised, JMARC had gathered considerable momentum by January 1961.[48] To have postponed the operation would have called for enormous determination on Kennedy's part, backed up with a knowledge of the logistics and pitfalls of covert action that he simply did not have at this stage. Allen Dulles argued very persuasively, moreover, that cancelling the venture would create its own difficulties, namely a "disposal problem": the danger that demobilised CEF mercenaries, on being transferred from Guatemala to the United States, would speak openly of what they had been involved in and so embarrass the American government.[49] It was under such pressures that the new president advanced hesitantly towards the Bay of Pigs fiasco.

Kennedy was briefed once on the CIA's Cuba plans during the interregnum but was preoccupied with other issues and found little time to scrutinise JMARC before becoming president.[50] He was, nevertheless, an enthusiastic advocate of Washington's right to both depose Castro and use covert action to bring this about. The frequently cited argument that the president was not especially culpable for the Bay of Pigs debacle, because he was misled by his most trusted advisors, who backed the operation with virtual unanimity, is a myth. The chairman of the Senate Foreign Relations Committee, J. William Fulbright was the most vociferous opponent of the CIA's plans, but Chester Bowles, Dean Rusk, Lyndon Johnson and Arthur Schlesinger all expressed similar doubts, and Dean Acheson told Kennedy bluntly that it was not necessary to call in Price Waterhouse "to discover that 1,500 Cubans weren't as good as 25,000 Cubans".[51]

Kennedy knew of these objections but chose to ignore them for several reasons.[52] He had, after all, fought the 1960 election campaign on an anti-Castro platform, charging Eisenhower with complacency for having allowed Havana to fall under communist control. If, after only three months of taking office, the new president had gone back on his election rhetoric and cancelled the Bay of Pigs operation, he would have attracted Republican accusations of hypocrisy and weakness.[53] The CIA's reputation for removing 'communist stooges' had, furthermore, grown enormously over the Eisenhower years. Thus, when Dulles assured Kennedy that the Cuban operation had a greater chance of success than the Guatemala campaign had done in 1954, the inexperienced president was not inclined to argue.[54] At the same time, Kennedy did raise searching questions with the CIA hierarchy over the strategy and tactics it proposed to use.

The agency's amphibious invasion concept was committed formally to paper for the first time on 4 January 1961. It envisaged the CEF as seizing and holding a small lodgement on Cuban soil, which was to include an airfield and access to the sea. Air support was seen as crucial, firstly to attack Castro's military in preparation for the invasion, and secondly to provide cover and tactical support for the CEF once it landed. The primary objective of the invasion force was to "survive and maintain its integrity on Cuban soil". No attempt was to be made to break out of the lodgement unless and until a general uprising against Castro or overt military intervention by the United States occurred. The CIA, nevertheless, projected that the CEF landings would precipitate a general uprising "by thousands of Cubans". In the event that the venture did not run according to plan, the agency assumed that the lodgement would serve as the site for the establishment of a provisional government, which would be recognised by Washington along with "other American states", and given military assistance to bring about the prompt overthrow of the Castro government".[55] Nowhere in this document was there any mention of the CEF becoming guerrillas should the invasion fail. The notion was battened on to the plan by Bissell at a progress meeting on 8 February as part of the effort to persuade the president to go ahead with the project.[56]

From the time of Kennedy's first presidential briefing on the Cuba programme – on 28 January 1961 – through to his authorisation of Operation JMARC in early April of that year, he remained very sceptical about the venture. The root of the problem was that the strategic objectives that the president wished to achieve in executing the plan simply could not be reconciled. Above all other factors, Kennedy insisted that the operation be a 'quiet' affair, with the emphasis being placed on plausible deniability. This was unrealistic anyhow, given the number of press leaks that had taken place. More significantly, the very essence of the invasion plan, when taken at face value, depended on it being conspicuous or 'noisy' enough to attract sufficient attention and support to incite an uprising.

In attempting to square the circle, Kennedy rejected the most feasible invasion option – the so-called Trinidad plan.[57] A coastal city in southern Cuba, Trinidad was reputed to be a hotbed of opposition to Castro. The agency therefore proposed to centre its invasion here, as the most likely location for precipitating a rebellion. Trinidad was, furthermore, contiguous with the Escambray Mountains, to where the CEF could, according to agency calculations, retreat to become guerrillas if the landings failed. In vetoing the Trinidad plan, the president was presented with the stark choice of either abandoning the operation altogether or sanctioning an alternative initiative. It was under such pressures that Kennedy opted for an ill-considered compromise and authorised the Zapata plan.[58]

Two factors stand out in relation to the selection of eastern Zapata and the Bay of Pigs as the location for an amphibious invasion. The first was the unsuitability of the terrain. The area was predominantly swampland, and reefs hampered the approach to the Bay of Pigs. The region was only thinly populated, which in a sense was to the CEF's advantage since it enhanced the prospects of a quiet landing. At the same time, the focusing of the invasion on a sparsely populated area limited the potential of an uprising to take place and in view of the fact that the new landing site was more than forty miles from the Escambray, the CIA's much vaunted guerrilla option was completely unfeasible. Logistically, Zapata boasted a poorly maintained airstrip that was just large enough to accommodate the exile air force. This was, however, more than offset by the fact that the region lacked Trinidad's docks, which meant that most of the CEF's supplies would have to come across open beaches.[59]

The Zapata plan's second overarching drawback was the speed at which it was approved. It was devised by WH/4 between 11 and 14 March, reviewed by the JCS the following day, and authorised by Kennedy on 16 March. The president set two conditions in sanctioning the plan. He reserved the right, as Eisenhower had done, to cancel the operation up to twenty-four hours prior to the landing, and he stipulated that the invasion take place at night-time rather than at dawn, as the CIA-JCS plan had projected.[60] This decision displayed a complete lack of logistical understanding on Kennedy's part. The United States had in fact never mounted an amphibious invasion at night. The president's inexperience again shone through when he asked Bissell whether air strikes were necessary. Kennedy, to quote the

DDP, "wouldn't take yes for an answer".[61] Conspicuous as the president's shortcomings were, however, they were more than matched by the flawed judgement of the CIA officers who were involved in JMARC.

There was, for example, a cruel twist of irony in the CIA's assumption that the PBSUCCESS model could be applied to Cuba. The Maximum Leader had in fact been forewarned of the potential for the United States to mount a covert operation to depose him precisely because of Arbenz's ouster. As a result, Castro neutralised opposition to his regime in Cuba and prepared for CIA action without fear of internal dissent.[62] Equally detrimental to the agency's planning was its tendency to celebrate 'victories' such as TPAJAX and PBSUCCESS and ignore defeats such as HAIK. This bred a sense of omnipotence that permeated the DDP and led the WH/4 mission to assume it would inevitably succeed: that Cubans, like Guatemalans, were intrinsically apathetic and when faced with an American-backed invasion they would put their political affiliations to one side and join the 'winner'.[63]

Duplicity also figured in the CIA's conduct of the Cuban operation, as is evident from the agency's failure to consult with or advise Kennedy on its phase 2 contingencies – to be implemented after the CEF had captured and held the beachhead. Bissell has justified this lack of communication by maintaining that the making of definite provisions for phase 2 was very difficult until the outcome of phase 1 was known.[64] While this argument certainly has some merit, it does not fully explain the CIA's unwillingness to discuss its plans with the president. Indeed, Dulles himself admitted that throughout the Cuban operation, the agency was aware of the inherent drawbacks in its planning but was vague when dealing with Kennedy. In essence, the CIA hierarchy consciously avoided raising questions such as how JMARC could be kept quiet and disavowable yet still arouse internal dissent, and how the whole campaign could achieve its objectives without the support of American combat forces. As such, the agency prevented Kennedy from addressing the operation's most searching issues which, had they been examined in detail, might have persuaded him to abort the operation.[65]

A major element of the CIA's plan was, for example, the projection that the invasion would light the touchpaper for a widespread revolt. There was, however, "no intelligence support covering the internal political situation inside Cuba", and therefore little or no evidence to uphold this proposition.[66] What information the CIA hierarchy did have at hand suggested that the prospects of JMARC succeeding were very slim, because the agency's incoming National Intelligence Estimates were reporting that internal opposition was generally ineffective and that Castro enjoyed enormous popular support.[67] The exclusion of the DDI from the Cuban programme, however, ensured that these details were withheld from Kennedy.

Equally misleading was the CIA's contention that the CEF could adapt to become guerrillas if the invasion failed. Even if the agency had ignored the fact that its earlier efforts to mount a guerrilla campaign had proved fruitless, the Zapata region was more than forty miles from the Escambray mountains. Dulles and

Bissell, nevertheless, sold the guerrilla backdrop option to Kennedy, not because it was tactically feasible but because it could be presented as a fail-safe device. It, in effect, reassured the president that the risks involved in sanctioning JMARC were less than was actually the case: that in the event of the invasion going awry, the operation could still succeed, though to a more limited degree.[68] Deceptive and impractical though it was, the introduction of this safety-net option served CIA designs well because it opened the way for the achievement of a hidden agenda that the agency had long harboured for dealing with the Maximum Leader.

Official records relating to Cuba suggest that both Eisenhower and Kennedy were unyielding in their determination not to permit JMARC to spark any form of overt intervention by United States against Castro.[69] Despite this, the CIA recruited pilots and planes from the Air National Guard to supplement the exile brigade's air force, and used American frogmen teams to mark out the landing beaches once the operation was under way.[70] Much as these moves were made in defiance of the official American policy, they were also indicative of the CIA mindset: a logic that assumed that whatever strictures held true prior to the CEF invasion, the White House would do whatever was necessary, including committing United States troops, to prevent the operation from failing.[71]

The CIA's game-plan was therefore aimed firstly at persuading Kennedy to approve JMARC, which it did by giving optimistic forecasts on the potential for success and assuring him repeatedly that the guerrilla option would serve as an indemnity. It was assumed that, in opting for this course, the president would also approve the full quota of airstrikes outlined in the plan. CIA calculations do not, however, appear to have envisaged the exile air force as enabling fifteen hundred men to break out of the lodgement and advance on Havana against the full might of the Cuban Army. Indeed, even in the weeks leading up to the Bay of Pigs operation, JCS projections anticipated that, in the absence of a popular uprising or substantial CEF reinforcements, Castro's forces could reduce the beachhead regardless of whether or not the brigade's plane's had gained control of the air.[72]

Rather, airpower was viewed by the CIA as being crucial to JMARC because it would enable the CEF to hold the lodgement for a number of days. In the likely event that an uprising failed to materialise during this time, Dulles and Bissell would be in an optimum position to inform the president that: (1) the presence or absence of hard evidence of American involvement in the operation had little bearing on widespread domestic and international perceptions that the United States was the CEF's sponsor; (2) the brigade was ill-equipped to do anything other than hold its ground for a limited period; and (3) the guerrilla option was, under the circumstances, unfeasible. The agency leadership could subsequently invoke its hidden agenda, arguing that, other than allowing the operation to fail, the president had only one choice, which was to intervene openly in support of the CEF.[73]

For the CIA, then, the second phase of JMARC meant only one thing, overt intervention by the United States military against Cuba and the airpower element of the Bay of Pigs campaign was designed to act as the essential trigger to bring this about.[74] In the case of Cuba, the covert action contingencies devised by the CIA did not, therefore, serve American foreign and defence policy, rather the agency attempted to commit Kennedy to a course of action that he was determined to avoid. Culpability for failing to ensure that the president was comprehensively advised was not, however, the CIA's alone. The Joint Chiefs of Staff also bore some responsibility in this respect.

The Joint Chiefs' Role

The first measure that Kennedy implemented following his initial presidential briefing on the Cuba programme was to order the JCS to make a full assessment of the CIA plan. In response, the Pentagon appointed a working group, which evaluated the "CIA Paramilitary Plan, Cuba". The Joint Chiefs approved the group's findings, forwarding them to Defense Secretary Robert McNamara on 3 February and the report was presented for discussion at a full-scale presidential meeting five days later.[75]

The most striking aspect of these proceedings was that the two documents that comprised the Joint Chiefs' findings, the full report and the shorter executive synopsis that was meant to summarise the longer paper, contradicted one another. Deeply critical of the CIA's plans and of its unsubstantiated assumption of an uprising, the full report held out little hope of the CEF succeeding "against moderate, determined resistance". The executive summary, on the other hand, put a different complexion on the JCS evaluation, concluding that "the timely execution of this plan has a fair chance of ultimate success".[76]

What "a fair chance of ultimate success" actually meant is open to speculation. The crucial point is that it was Bissell and not the chairman Joint Chiefs, General Lyman Lemnitzer, who presented the JCS findings at the 8 February meeting. In doing so, the DDP cited the executive summary, emphasising the optimistic note on which it concluded. For their part, McNamara and the Joint Chiefs remained silent throughout the meeting, despite the fact that the CIA had given a skewed interpretation of the Pentagon's analysis.[77]

Bissell suggests that the reluctance of the Defense Department representatives to give full voice to their concerns about the Cuba plan resulted from an unwritten rule in the Washington bureaucracy, whereby whichever agency that was responsible for guiding any given project through government "had the action" and therefore retained primacy over less involved agencies. In the case of the Cuba programme, the CIA "had the action", and once the JCS had fulfilled its remit and reviewed the operation's military aspects, then the Pentagon held back from making its criticisms of JMARC too pronounced because responsibility for the venture rested with the CIA.[78]

True as these points might be, they do not alter the fact that the JCS hedged their bets. The full report made the Joint Chiefs' own position clear to the few individuals who read it, but it also served as an insurance policy in the event of the invasion ending in disaster and an inquiry being launched to determine the extent to which the Defense Department was culpable. The shorter executive summary, in ending on a positive note, gave the CIA enough rope to hang itself but not the JCS, because this document also contained the reservation that "the combat worth of the assault forces is based on second and third-hand reports". This was the only significant concern that McNamara and the Joint Chiefs appear to have raised at the 8 February meeting. A three man team of Army, Navy, and Air Force officers was therefore sent to Guatemala between 24 and 27 February to evaluate the CEF first-hand.[79]

On submitting their report on the combat-worthiness of the exile brigade on 11 March, the Joint Chiefs again took measures to insulate themselves against the potential of a future backlash. While the assessment of the troops was positive, the JCS expressed the reservation that although surprise was essential to the mission's success, the odds against achieving it were 85–15.[80] The Pentagon thus seems to have been more concerned about protecting its own back than advising the president, and McNamara, perhaps because he was new to his job, was a willing participant in the proceedings, deferring to the Joint Chiefs rather than providing them with policy direction. There is, moreover, some evidence to suggest that the JCS were aware of the CIA's hidden agenda. While the brigade was fighting for the beachhead at the Bay of Pigs on 18 April, Admiral Arleigh Burke, the Navy Chief of Staff and the most active of all the American military leaders in Operation JMARC, dispatched two battalions of marines to the ships cruising off Cuba. This was a preparatory move made to ensure that the military was ready to act in the event of Kennedy authorising overt intervention to salvage the botched invasion.[81] Moreover, it was not without precedent. Burke had taken similar action during Operation HAIK, when he sent an amphibious force that included marines and logistical backup to patrol just outside of Indonesian territorial waters and make ready for full-scale American military action against Sukarno.[82]

*   *   *

On 4 April 1961, Kennedy conducted a final session on the Bay of Pigs with his top advisors. After a succinct briefing by Bissell on the supposed merits of the venture, the president asked each official for an assessment of the plan and an opinion on whether or not it should be approved. What stands out most about this gathering is that while several, perhaps even the majority, of those present either had reservations about JMARC or opposed it outright, all except Fulbright gave their blessing to the operation. Dean Rusk, Thomas Mann, and Adolf Berle, all of whom had hitherto opposed the project, voted to proceed, and Arthur Schlesinger, to his lasting regret, remained silent.[83] It seems incredible that Lemnitzer, knowing full well the logistical and strategic inadequacies of the plan, should have sat passively while Bissell once again assured Kennedy and all of those assembled of the viability of the operation. Clearly an advocate of the theory which says that if a point is repeated often enough then it becomes true, the DDP, according to

Fulbright's recollection, stated "if anything unexpected happens then they (the CEF) could *easily* (author's own emphasis) escape to the Escambray Mountains. So it (the plan) couldn't fail".[84] This was manifestly untrue, as Paul Nitze, who also attended the meeting, knew. He had been persuaded earlier by Edward Lansdale that JMARC was ineptly organised, based on a number of false assumptions, and doomed to failure.[85] Yet Nitze also voted to give the green light to the Bay of Pigs operation.

The most feasible explanation for why so many usually strong-willed individuals balked from voicing their doubts is that they already knew what Kennedy's intentions were.[86] He had, after all, made his position vis-à-vis revolutionary Cuba abundantly clear throughout the 1960 election campaign and during his early weeks as president. The Attorney General was, furthermore, widely rumoured to have resorted to heavy-handed tactics prior to the meeting, to intimidate doubters such as Bowles into supporting the plan. For the president and his brother, then, group loyalty took precedence over advice that did not conform to the Kennedy line.[87] Those who were asked to comment on JMARC were therefore too inhibited to spell out their own views and in the process call the underlying assumptions of the president into question – especially so early in the administration. Even Fulbright admitted to feeling intimidated at the meeting and his security of political tenure was not dependent on Kennedy's goodwill, as was the case with the administration officials who were present.[88] The president was not really looking for advice on 4 April 1961. Rather he was asking for confirmation that he was wearing a full set of new clothes when in reality he was stark naked.

The Bay of Pigs Invasion

As the CEF set sail for Cuba between 11 and 13 April from Puerto Cabezas on the eastern coast of Nicaragua, a fundamental divergence of priorities arose between the CIA and Kennedy that ensured the operation had already run into serious difficulties. The agency leadership assumed that the president recognised the importance of airpower to the campaign and that he would authorise enough sorties to incapacitate Castro's Air Force and neutralise his microwave radio links, thereby optimising the CEF's prospects of holding the beachhead.[89] For Kennedy, plausible deniability was paramount, but it was compromised from as early as 15 April, when CIA efforts to disguise the first round of CEF air sorties as the work of Cuban Air Force defectors was exposed as a scam. Exploited by Havana's UN ambassador, who charged that the United States was behind the raids, this embarrassing incident presented Kennedy with the dilemma of how to continue with JMARC while simultaneously avoiding any further exposures. It was under such pressures that he made two conflicting decisions, on 16 April: giving his final authorisation for the invasion to proceed, but cancelling all further air strikes.[90]

Exactly why the president became convinced that the bombing raids, which had featured so prominently in the CIA's plans, were not necessary remains a matter of considerable debate. Peter Wyden suggests that Kennedy was swayed by the advice he received from Rusk, whose views on unconventional warfare were shaped by his wartime military experience. He maintained that in a guerrilla campaign of the kind that was planned against Cuba, air cover was not necessary.[91] The point was that JMARC was not strictly a guerrilla operation, it was an invasion, which demonstrates that a fundamental misunderstanding about the nature of the venture existed at the highest levels of government.

Still more far-reaching considerations, however, informed the president's decision to back-pedal on the issue of airpower. Among all of the concerns that preoccupied the White House during the Bay of Pigs campaign, anticipating Moscow's possible responses to the enterprise was paramount, and these calculations proved imperative in the decision to cancel the second batch of bombing raids. As Kennedy explained to Eisenhower in the aftermath of JMARC, continuing with the air strikes would have unmasked Washington's role in the invasion and this in turn would have presented Khrushchev with an excuse to move on West Berlin. Instigating such a chain of events was, for Kennedy, simply not worth the risk.[92] Though the president's concerns were exaggerated as a result of his erroneous conception of Cuba as a Soviet satellite that the Kremlin was committed to protect, Khrushchev acted in such a way as to confirm Kennedy's fears. On 18 April the Russian leader cabled Washington with a message stating "it is hardly possible to handle matters in such a way as to settle the situation and put out the fire in one area while kindling a new conflagration in another area".[93]

If the cancellation of the second wave of bombing missions had a key influence on the outcome of the Bay of Pigs operation, so too did Allen Dulles's decision to travel to Puerto Rico on 15 April as part of the effort to limit suspicions of there being any American involvement in JMARC.[94] This meant that the option of putting the CIA's arguments across to Kennedy after he had postponed the second batch of bombing missions was left to DDCI General Charles Cabell and Bissell, both of whom declined the offer on grounds that they had been presented with a *fait accompli*.[95]

McGeorge Bundy later maintained that he had a strong feeling that Kennedy would have reversed his decision if the military had told him that the operation would fail without air support.[96] Whether Dulles's arguments would have carried as much weight as Bundy believed the Pentagon's would is a matter of pure speculation. What can be said with near certainty is that Kennedy would have been under greater pressure to at least listen to the CIA's arguments if the DCI had been present to put them forward. Dulles, after all, enjoyed greater professional stature than his senior subordinates and, as a well-connected Republican, he also had considerable political clout, which Kennedy could not ignore.

*   *   *

Beginning on 17 April 1961, the CEF invasion of Cuba had long been doomed to failure by the Kennedy administration's lack of foresight, and inept planning on the part of the CIA. The presence of reefs on the approach to the main landing site ensured that, while the men reached the landing area much of their equipment did not. The CEF transport ships were stranded off shore and, without air support, they soon proved easy targets for the Cuban Air Force. Consequently, by Tuesday 18 April, Castro's expectant and therefore well-prepared military forces were isolating and driving back the insurgency. [97]

That evening Kennedy held a White House reception, after which he called a meeting of his top advisors to discuss the Bay of Pigs crisis. If ever there was an optimum moment for the CIA to invoke its hidden agenda then it was at this gathering. Yet once again Dulles was missing, having left the reception early. The onus was consequently on Bissell to attempt to rescue the situation, but he requested only that Kennedy authorise the use of jets from the Aircraft Carrier *Essex*, which was cruising off the Cuban coast, to assist the brigade. Still determined, quite unrealistically, to conceal American involvement, the president agreed only to a futile compromise. Six unmarked jets from the *Essex* would be permitted to fly over the landing perimeter to protect CEF ammunition supply flights from Nicaragua. This would have been too little too late if the jets had arrived on time. As it was, they arrived late and made no difference to the outcome of Operation JMARC, which ended on the afternoon of Wednesday 19 April with the surrender of the CEF.[98]

Central to the JMARC debate is the issue of whether the defeat of the CEF arose from incompetent management and a deliberate effort to mislead Kennedy on the part of the CIA, or from the failure of the president and the wider Executive to take full cognisance of the operation and its possible ramifications, and either abandon it or ensure that it achieved its objectives.[99] For sure, a considerable portion of the blame lies with Dulles and especially Bissell. If the DDP thought that the Trinidad plan had any chance of success, then he knew that the Zapata plan did not, if for no other reason than that Esterline and Jack Hawkins, the operation's senior paramilitary specialist, had told him so.[100] Yet Bissell agreed to the change in location for the CEF invasion and continued to advise Kennedy that the operation was feasible.

As much as the charge of duplicity can be levelled at Bissell, however, Kennedy allowed himself to be misled and indeed he reproached himself during the period following the Bay of Pigs, asking how he could have been so stupid. Piero Gleijeses perhaps came closest to answering this question when he maintained that JMARC was approved "because the CIA and the White House assumed that they were speaking the same language when, in fact, they were speaking in utterly different tongues".[101] Lack of communication aside, the most crucial drawback in JMARC was that its success hinged on the removal of Castro without damaging the political prestige of the United States: objectives that were irreconcilable once rumours about the operation became widespread and plausible deniability was severely compromised. Kennedy was, nevertheless, enthusiastic about the central aim of JMARC and his determination to dislodge

Castro did not diminish after the Bay of Pigs, regardless of the various inquiries that followed in its wake.

Aftermath

Three major investigations were launched in the aftermath of Operation JMARC. Kennedy initiated a governmentwide presidential commission, headed by Maxwell Taylor; the CIA's Inspector General, Lyman Kirkpatrick, conducted an internal investigation at the behest of Dulles; and Bissell organised an in-house inquiry at the DDP, which was drafted by his deputy, Tracy Barnes.[102] Of the three reports, Kirkpatrick's proved to be the most damning and, as such, was consigned to the agency vaults as a hatchet job, having earned its author the opprobrium of his colleagues.[103] What stands out most with regard to the investigations of the DDP and the Taylor Commission is that prominent amongst those who were selected to conduct these inquiries were individuals who had been directly involved in the Bay of Pigs project. The DDP investigation was headed by Barnes, who as Assistant Deputy Director of Plans (ADDP) was second only to Bissell in the planning of JMARC, while Allen Dulles and Admiral Arleigh Burke featured prominently on Taylor Commission.[104] Given such appointments, the most that Kennedy could have realistically expected from Taylor was an effective damage-limitation exercise, and this is exactly what emerged when his commission reported in June 1961. Although critical of the unwieldly dimensions of the Bay of Pigs operation, Taylor reaffirmed the need for the United States to adopt surreptitious methods to advance its foreign policy aims in the climate of the Cold War, and his recommendations were accepted by Kennedy. [105]

Washington's options for dealing with Castro were, nevertheless, constrained in the period immediately following JMARC, and for the next seven months the president's Cuba policy was aimed at: (1) placing greater emphasis on the Alliance for Progress in order to improve Washington's tarnished relations with its southern neighbours; (2) alerting the Latin American nations to the dangerous and expansive nature of the Cuban revolution; and (3) persuading the OAS to work with the United States to bring about the complete economic and diplomatic isolation of Havana.[106]

The only direct initiative in Cuban-American relations to materialise during this period was made at diplomatic level by Ché Guevara in a private meeting with key Kennedy aide Richard Goodwin, following a session of the Punta del Este Conference in Montevideo, Uruguay on 17 August 1961. Here, Guevara stressed that though Cuba was now "out of the U.S. sphere of influence", the Castro regime would like to establish "at least an interim modus vivendi" that envisaged the United States accepting the legitimacy of the Castro government and guaranteeing not to invade Cuba. In return, Havana would agree not to enter into a political alliance with the "East" (assumed to mean the Soviet Union) and to refrain from exporting the Cuban revolution beyond its own borders.[107]

The problem with this initiative was that its core requirement – American acceptance of Castro's rule – ran entirely contrary to Kennedy's Cuba policy, and would doubtless have caused consternation throughout the Western Hemisphere and in Congress should it have been accepted. An additional disincentive sprang from the concurrent Berlin crisis, the culmination of which was widely perceived as a victory for the United States. To Kennedy, who held to a monolithic view of the communist world, prevailing over Khrushchev in Berlin meant greater pressure on Cuba, a welcome development that counterbalanced the loss of prestige suffered by Washington as a result of JMARC. It was not, therefore, in the American president's interests to allay Castro's fears by pledging not to invade Cuba – especially when increasing volumes of Soviet aid were arriving on the island. Kennedy instead ordered a redoubling of the covert action effort against Cuba, under the auspices of Operation MONGOOSE.

Operation Mongoose:
Lansdale's Destabilisation Strategy

Operation MONGOOSE was sanctioned on 30 November 1961 with the objective of marshalling all available assets to depose Castro.[108] Reflecting the Kennedy brothers' fascination with counterinsurgency doctrine, the venture has been described aptly as a "prototype destabilisation or bleeding programme", aimed at: (1) disrupting the entire fabric of Cuban society and causing widespread discontent towards the governing regime; (2) preventing the Cuban revolution from spreading beyond its own borders; and (3) sparking off a major counterrevolutionary guerrilla insurrection which would attract growing popular support and ultimately lead to the ouster of Castro's government.[109]

Conceived and organised by the newly created Special Group (Augmented), MONGOOSE was a joint CIA-Pentagon enterprise. Headed by special warfare guru Edward G. Lansdale, the programme prioritised the recruitment of military personnel with administrative and counterinsurgency expertise in the hope of preventing the type of organisational failures that the Kennedys and Maxwell Taylor believed to be responsible for the Bay of Pigs fiasco.[110]

For its part, CIA input in MONGOOSE was enormous. Operating under the aegis of Task Force W, the agency component was charged with infiltrating agents into Cuba and sabotaging economic and military targets on the island. These activities were placed under the overall control of William Harvey, who was based at Langley and reported to Lansdale and the SG(A). Theodore Shackley's Miami station (code-named JMWAVE) served as the centre of operations for MONGOOSE. From this base, over four hundred CIA officers controlled more than two thousand contract agents, drawing on an annual budget of over $50 million. A further dimension of Operation MONGOOSE was the role played by Robert Kennedy, who essentially functioned as the project's director. Pressurising all who were involved in the venture, he proved willing to bypass bureaucratic norms and appeal directly to CIA officers at operational level if he deemed it necessary to get results.[111]

Despite the Kennedys' assertion that MONGOOSE was their top priority and that no resources be spared in its pursuit, the programme failed to make any tangible advances. In retrospect, a major cause of the problem centred on their choice of personnel, the most notable being the head of operations. Lansdale's reputation was earned through his successes in containing and, at best, destroying communist-inspired insurrections against western-aligned governments in Manila and Saigon. He, in essence, specialised in *defensive* covert action. The demands of combating Castro, however, called for expertise in the sphere of *offensive* covert action, since the aim was to remove an existing communist regime. Lansdale's methods consequently proved unsuitable for meeting the challenge, just as they had been between 1954 and 1956 when he was called on to conduct what turned out to be an ineffective clandestine action offensive against the newly-established North Vietnamese state.[112]

The Air Force general drew up a precisely-timed, thirty-two task plan which envisaged MONGOOSE as beginning with an intelligence-gathering stage, progressing through four additional phases – action, buildup, readiness, and resistance – and culminating in a full-scale revolt and march on Havana in "the first two weeks of October 1962".[113] Overly-rigid and wholly unrealistic, this strategy was flawed at its most basic level. It placed too much faith in the MONGOOSE planners' capacity to develop an effective underground in Cuba, and it underestimated Castro's ability to suppress dissent and eliminate resistance – much as the CIA's plans of the summer and autumn of 1960 had done.[114]

As with HAIK and JMARC, the enormous scale of MONGOOSE jeopardised the maintenance of secrecy and the programme was also plagued by a chain of discontent that permeated every tier of management. The Kennedys were impetuous in their demands for action and apparently oblivious to the fact that the United States simply did not have enough assets in Cuba to achieve success with MONGOOSE. Meanwhile, the military planners who were attached to the enterprise were pedantic to the point of absurdity in their requests for detailed reports from Harvey, who in turn was resentful of the Kennedys and extremely suspicious of Lansdale.[115]

While MONGOOSE failed to make any positive impact, it did have the negative effects of justifying Castro's moves to tighten his grip on power and helping to provide the impetus for Khrushchev to pour military aid into Cuba. It was against this backdrop that Bissell, in one of his last acts as DDP, activated ZR/RIFLE Project. A standby assassination capability, ZR/RIFLE had been placed under the direction of Harvey at its inception and was therefore easily incorporated into Operation MONGOOSE. The head of Task Force W duly took over the CIA's contacts with the Mafia from Sheffield Edwards and set a new murder campaign in motion.[116]

he agency's renewed partnership with Giancana and his associates proved to be as fruitless as had been the case in 1960. The crucial question, however, centres on whether or not President Kennedy knew of these CIA plans. In this respect, there is strong though not conclusive evidence to support the case that he did.[117] Certainly, a number of key figures within the administration, notably McNamara and Lansdale, knew of the plot to kill Castro, were in favour of such a course, and committed the idea to paper – to the dismay and anger of Harvey.[118]

Whatever Kennedy's involvement in the assassination plots against Castro actually was, it had become clear to the SG(A) by August 1962 that nothing short of direct American military intervention would bring about a change of regime in Cuba. Such an outcome was, moreover, regarded by American planners as being made easier if Castro was dead before the landings took place, as was the case in the run-up to the Bay of Pigs operation. Unlike the calculations that applied during JMARC, however, a full-scale invasion of Cuba was now under serious consideration, and subject to constant review from August 1962 right through to the culmination of Cuban missile crisis.[119]

This modification of policy brought with it a change in how covert action was to be deployed. Though Operation MONGOOSE was essentially designed to create the necessary pretext for an invasion of Cuba, the graduated concept enshrined in Lansdale's programme proved excruciatingly slow, and by August 1962 was still lodged firmly in stage one. In light of these drawbacks, John Kennedy ordered the programme's planners to disregard Lansdale's timed phases and speed up the whole enterprise. From this juncture, MONGOOSE was to complement wider military action, rather than serve as the focus of Washington's anti-Castro effort.[120]

The difficulty with this redesign of priorities was in the president's continuing failure to comprehend that Castro's control over Cuba placed enormous constraints on any type of covert activity – especially when he was expecting it. A frustrated Robert Kennedy was therefore still demanding more zealous execution of MONGOOSE some ten days before U-2 overflights verified the existence of Soviet missile sites in Cuba on 14 October 1962.[121] Indeed, the Attorney General continued to berate the agencies involved in MONGOOSE for failing to carry it out with sufficient aggression during the missile crisis itself, but again the initiatives enacted by the project's planners in response failed to deliver any success:[122] a thankful outcome given that the risk of a single incident triggering war by miscalculation was never higher. As a result, Lansdale found himself and his project increasingly marginalised as the crisis continued and on 30 October, two days after the crisis ended, the NSC closed down Operation MONGOOSE and abolished the SG(A).

This did not, however, draw Kennedy's campaign against revolutionary Cuba to a close. As part of the deal struck by the Soviet and American leaders to conclude the missile crisis, Kennedy gave his "assurances against an invasion [of Cuba]" on the condition that the removal of the Russian missiles took place under UN observation and supervision. Castro refused to permit any on-site inspections, which in effect freed Kennedy from his pledge not to invade Cuba.[123]

Conclusion: The Undeclared War Against Cuba: In-Built Flaws and Ongoing Struggles

The most conspicuous flaw in the covert operations launched against the Castro regime between 1960 and 1962 was the assumption that the PBSUCCESS model, and afterwards the counterinsurgency techniques pioneered by Lansdale, could be deployed in revolutionary Cuba. Conditions in Cuba were markedly different from those that had applied in Guatemala or the Philippines. Castro had a firm grip on power even before the botched Bay of Pigs invasion. He subsequently strengthened his bonds with Moscow and assumed such comprehensive control over his country that many in Washington regarded Cuba as "the sixteenth Soviet republic".[124] The task that confronted the Kennedy administration and the CIA was not, then, one of preventing Marxism taking hold in Cuba. Rather it was one of removing a leftist dictatorship that moved decisively to adopt communism and align itself with the Soviet Union within three years of coming to power.

The true precedent for Cuba, as Bissell later pointed out, was Albania.[125] Offensive covert action had, however, proved futile in the case of BGFIEND, as it had against the Sino-Soviet bloc generally, and it would not have sufficed in Cuba. The overthrow of Castro would have required overt military action. The fact that the CIA included a hidden agenda in the JMARC operation amounted to an implicit recognition of such realities, and indeed the MONGOOSE planners were explicit in pointing to the need for direct American military intervention to sweep Castro from power.

Operation MONGOOSE has since been referred to as "the Kennedy Vendetta", but this most ambitious of covert action programmes was driven by more than just an acute desire for revenge.[126] Cuba was a model for leftists throughout Latin America to emulate and an increasingly well-equipped base for the expansion of communism in the Western Hemisphere.[127] In response, Kennedy sought to, not only quarantine Cuba and overthrow the Maximum Leader, but also immunize Latin America against communism and take preventive action wherever it was deemed necessary.

United States' intervention in Ecuador during 1962 and 1963 provides a case in point. Here, the CIA played a major role in ensuring that Ecuador did not succumb to the appeal of Castroism. The agency first helped to overthrow Jose Velasco Ibarra's regime, replacing it with a government led by Carlos Julio Arosemera, whose ideas, it was believed, were more compatible with United States policy. When it was discovered that this was not the case, Arosemera was also ousted from power.[128]

The specific methods deployed by the agency in these interventions are unclear. What is certain is that Robert Kennedy regarded labour unions as useful instruments for the furtherance of covert action in Ecuador and, more generally, the CIA appears to have applied the European model of the late 1940s to Latin America during the early 1960s.[129] The Alliance for Progress was envisaged as serving as the economic instrument of containment much as the ERP had done, and the CIA worked in conjunction with the host governments, the political and economic elites, and the church to deploy an extensive range of covert operations when the need arose. More particularly, the agency drew on the skills of veteran OSS operative Serafino Romualdi, who appears to have functioned in Latin America much as Irving Brown had done in Europe, organising clandestine action programmes in conjunction with local labour officials and centre-right politicians in a strategy that proved to be especially effective in British Guiana between 1961 and 1964.[130]

The Kennedy administration's intervention in British Guiana warrants specific attention, for it is instructive of the complexities that arose when the issues of decolonisation and communism in the Western Hemisphere overlapped. Although it remained a British colony until 1966, British Guiana's key indigenous political players had pressed consistently for independence since the early 1950s. By the dawn of the following decade the socialist People's Progressive Party (PPP) emerged as the dominant political force and its leader, Cheddi Jagan, was elected prime minister during August 1961 in a first-past-the-post contest that replicated the system favoured by the mother country. Provisions were put in place by London for a transition to independence within four years of the 1961 poll and during this time Jagan was to control domestic affairs, while a British governor was to oversee foreign policy.[131]

If Harold Macmillan's government in London was relaxed about the emergence of an independent British Guiana, then the Kennedy administration was far less enamoured. Despite assurances from the British that Jagan would probably advocate neutralism and seek to sign up to the Alliance for Progress, the preponderant view in Washington was that the Guyanese leader's espousal of democracy and free elections was a ruse. Once the British had left, so the argument went, Jagan would move quickly to adopt Marxist-Leninism and align his country with the Soviet Union and Cuba.[132] Much as the domestic implications of this were seen by Kennedy as far-reaching, he also viewed it as carrying wider risks, for it would undermine the United States' international standing and possibly trigger a war in the Caribbean that could escalate into full-scale superpower conflict.[133] The very limited contact that Kennedy had with Jagan, moreover, did nothing to allay the American president's fears. During a visit to Washington in October 1961, the British Guyanese prime minister was not regarded as having been explicit enough in outlining where he stood in respect of the Cold War divide, which subsequently led Kennedy to disregard the views of liberal advisors such as Arthur Schlesinger Jr., and authorize the DDP depose Jagan.[134]

Similarly to most of the DDP's Western Hemisphere projects, covert action in British Guiana was coordinated closely with wider American efforts to dislodge the sitting government. Initial planning began in May 1961 – before the August elections – and operational responsibility was placed under the control of the Cuba Task Force. The basic thrust of the campaign against Jagan was to bring him down by degrees through the instigation of political and industrial action, while simultaneously promoting his principal rival, Forbes Burnham, as 'Washington's man'. The problem for Kennedy was the political realities of British Guiana: votes were cast along racial lines and East Indians accounted for nearly half of the population. Jagan, as an East Indian, therefore stood to benefit in a first-past-the-post election.[135]

The job of the DDP was thus to ensure that Burnham, the leading Afro-Guyanese candidate, who attracted the support of about a third of the population, and Peter D'Aguiar, a pro-business conservative politician, won sufficient votes to raise doubts about the credibility of Jagan's mandate and so press for another poll under a different electoral system, namely proportional representation.[136] With these ends in mind, the agency mounted a propaganda campaign aimed at bolstering Burnham and D'Aguiar through the use of anticommunist literature and films, but it achieved only limited success in a campaign that saw Jagan prevail as much the best candidate in August 1961.[137]

Following the election, Kennedy sought to reverse the outcome as speedily as possible by curtailing trade between the United States and British Guiana, and authorising two CIA-orchestrated general strikes. Carried out in February 1962 and April 1963, these ventures hinged on the use of similar tactics to those deployed in Ecuador at around the same time: ones that had their precedent in the Italian campaign of 1947 to 1948. Pivotal to the agency's strategy was its use of the very close links it enjoyed with the American labour unions. Key among these was the American Federation of State, County, and Municipal Employees, which along with non-union, CIA-funded conduits, notably the Gotham Foundation, filtered money to Richard Ishmael's Trade Union Council and other conservative British Guyanese organizations. Sustaining the strikers with vital funding, the DDP also provided Ishmael with the resources and manpower to establish a newspaper and a radio station to communicate anti-Jagan propaganda.[138]

Much as these measures generated an air of instability and chaos, they were not enough to unseat Jagan.[139] As such, the achievement of Washington's aims became increasingly dependent on Kennedy persuading Macmillan to replace British Guiana's first-past-the-post electoral system with one based on proportional representation, and delay granting the colony's independence for long enough to ensure an American-friendly Forbes Burnham government took control. This required a gargantuan feat of statesmanship on Kennedy's part, but he achieved it by stressing that the existing provisions would result in Jagan winning any electoral contest in the near future and transforming a newly-independent British Guiana into "the second Communist state in the Western Hemisphere".[140] Extremely sceptical as the Macmillan government might have been, it was also sensitive, if not sympathetic, to the president's standpoint and reluctantly complied with his wishes.

Another clear-cut example of labour unions being deployed to advance CIA objectives during this period was in Venezuela. Here, a spiralling campaign of Cuban-backed insurrection, which began in 1961 and gathered momentum over the next two years, was threatening to bring down Rómulo Betancourt's government in advance of presidential elections scheduled for December 1963.[141] The Betancourt regime was a model that the United States hoped the rest of Latin America would emulate. For the Maximum Leader, then, a successful insurgency against the Caracas government would be of great symbolic significance. It would demonstrate that Venezuelans had chosen communism in preference to an American-sponsored democratic government, while simultaneously undermining United States containment policy in the entire Western Hemisphere.[142]

This was, of course, a high-risk strategy. Kennedy had stated openly in December 1962 that Havana's export of revolution precluded the United States from pledging not to invade Cuba.[143] Castro's resolve was, however, bolstered as a result of a five week-long, high profile visit he made to the Soviet Union in the spring of 1963. The tour served to heal the rift in Russo-Cuban relations that followed the missile crisis and led the Maximum Leader to believe that the Kremlin would defend Cuba should the United States attempt to invade the island.[144] Certainly, Washington regarded the trip was a major setback. The unprecedented welcomes that Castro received at every stage of the visit signalled that Cuba was once again an extension of Soviet power and "a beacon for the future advance of socialism" in Latin America.[145] It was this inter-communist rapprochement, coupled with the worsening situation in Venezuela that led the Kennedy administration to rethink its anti-Castro strategy.

The early months of 1963 found the CIA implementing a series of defensive clandestine action measures to counter Venezuela's leftist guerrillas. Utilising the methods that were proving effective in Ecuador and Latin America generally, the agency drew on labour union support, namely the Confederation of Venezuelan Workers (CTV), which established workers' brigades to prevent communist guerrillas from sabotaging the country's oil reserves.[146] The insurgency continued unabated, however, and it was partly as a consequence of these developments that the CIA was authorised, on 19 June 1963, to renew its offensive against the Castro regime. The latest programme was placed under the control of Desmond Fitzgerald, the former head of the agency's Far East Division, and it deployed similar destabilisation techniques to those that had featured in Operation MONGOOSE, which once again proved futile.[147] Where the CIA did see itself as having a greater chance of success than had previously been the case was in its use of assassination.

If the agency wanted for anything in its attempts to murder Castro then it was an adequate 'delivery system': specifically, an assassin who could get close enough to the Cuban leader to kill him. A constant impediment to the DDP's plans between 1960 and late 1962, this problem seemed devoid of solutions until September 1963, when Rolando Cubela Secades, a one-time Castro supporter and confidante who had become disillusioned with the Maximum Leader, offered to assassinate him. Code-named AMLASH, Cubela was first recruited by the CIA in 1961 and was a tried and tested assassin, having killed Batista's military intelligence chief in 1959. On the negative side of the ledger, he was suspected by the agency's counterintelligence experts of being a 'dangle': a Cuban double agent charged with penetrating the DDP's assassination plots, and in fact these suspicions gained credence in the wake of John Kennedy's own murder.[148]

Regardless of the doubts that the CIA entertained about Cubela, he was an agent-in-place, and on 29 October 1963 he met with Fitzgerald and engaged in a "policy discussion", the specifics of which remain cloudy. Fitzgerald is known, however, to have urged Cubela to persuade other Cuban Army officers to instigate a coup, and AMLASH is on record as stating that a successful coup would have to be preceded by the assassination of Castro. Cubela then asked what "technical support" the CIA could provide to bring about such an outcome. At no point did Fitzgerald give a firm undertaking that the agency was prepared to press ahead with the plan, but he nevertheless did not rule it out.[149]

What seems to have proved decisive in influencing Fitgerald and Richard Helms, who had succeeded Bissell as DDP in late 1961, to go ahead with the AMLASH plot was the discovery of a three-ton arms cache on a Venezuelan beach in November 1963.[150] Questions must be raised as to the authenticity of this find, given that the CIA had itself planted an arms cache on a beach in Guatemala in 1954 in the hope of manufacturing a pretext for the overthrow of Arbenz. Nevertheless, Kennedy regarded the find as providing proof of Cuban involvement in the insurgency against Betancourt and asked Helms to prepare "more complete information" which he, Kennedy, would examine on his return from Dallas and determine what steps to take in response.[151] The evidence suggests, however, that someone in the DDP hierarchy pre-empted the president's decision, because Fitzgerald gave the go-ahead for AMLASH to proceed and the necessary resources were made available to Cubela to enable him to kill Castro, either at long range or at closer quarters, if the opportunity presented itself.

Exactly who authorised this enterprise is unclear. The strictures of plausible deniability dictate that, should the president or the Attorney General have approved the venture, there would be no record of the decision. Whatever the truth might be, the most pertinent point is that the incessant pressure that Robert Kennedy was putting on the DDP to take imaginative and bold action against Castro was authorisation in itself. As it was, the AMLASH plot was brought to an abrupt halt as the direct outcome of John Kennedy's assassination.[152] A campaign that two administrations had pursued vigorously since early 1960 and which had seriously undermined the prestige of the CIA thus ended with Washington having failed to unseat Castro and with Cuban-American relations at a nadir that still persists to this day.

CONCLUSION:
MARCHING AS TO WAR

There was a certain irony in the early evolution of the CIA. Though its covert action mission was designed primarily to serve as a substitute for overt military action and so preserve the peace, it was the onset of war that had the most far-reaching effects on the agency's capacity to conduct clandestine operations. The outbreak of hostilities in Korea was *the* primary catalyst for the unprecedented growth of the OPC/DDP's budget and manpower in the early 1950s.[1] This expansion of resources, along with Bedell Smith's reorganisation of the CIA and Allen Dulles's decision to specialise in specific types of covert action, provided the foundation for the so-called golden era of operations that spanned Eisenhower's presidential tenure. The Vietnam War had more negative and indeed profound consequences, largely as a result of domestic disaffection towards the conflict rather than the CIA's own activities. Most significantly, Vietnam broke up the bipartisan consensus in the sphere of American foreign and defence policy. This had been in place since Truman's time and it had enabled the OPC and later the DDP to conduct their activities largely unimpaired under the sympathetic gaze of the various congressional oversight subcommittees to which the CIA answered.

Entrapment in the quagmire of Southeast Asia caused the American public to seriously question, for the first time, the foreign policy objectives of its government and the actions of the institutions that served it. The Vietnam War, then, ended an era of optimism and confidence that began in 1945 and so defines the limits of the early Cold War era. Washington's entanglement in Vietnam warrants brief investigation, however, not least of all because it demonstrates some of the recurring trends and pitfalls that had confronted the CIA from the time it began conducting covert action.

American involvement in Indochina began in 1950 when the Truman administration adopted NSC 68 and brought Southeast Asia under the containment umbrella. The commitment increased incrementally over the following fifteen years. Eisenhower provided economic aid and air support to the French in their struggle against the Vietminh, but after the fall of Dien Bien Phu and the Geneva Accords of 1954, Washington refocused its efforts. American policy was henceforth geared towards promoting a noncommunist government with strong nationalist, anti-imperialist credentials in Saigon.[2] To complement these moves an effective programme of defensive covert action that centred on the utilisation of nation-building and counterinsurgency techniques was introduced under the direction of Ed Lansdale.[3]

The drawback with this approach was in the Eisenhower administration's decision to follow the recommendations of the CIA and Lansdale, and promote Ngo Dinh Diem as South Vietnamese premier. The task of finding leaders who could command popular support and at the same time fall into line with American policy objectives posed repeated difficulties for the agency. Rather than choosing the best man for the job, the CIA often found itself limited to picking the only available candidate or the best of a bad bunch. The selections of Zahedi, Castillo Armas, and Mobutu spring immediately to mind in citing this problem and the same considerations applied to the choice of Diem.

Following the partition of Vietnam in 1954, the country's Emperor, Bao Dai, acceded to American pressure and appointed Diem as prime minister of South Vietnam. From this point the United States began to bolster the new regime extensively but, for Washington, maintaining Diem was something of a balancing act.[4] On the one hand, he was a fervent nationalist who could be relied upon to counter the spread of communism with vigour. On the other hand, he was a corrupt and repressive ruler, whose consistent refusal to comply with American wishes and implement meaningful democratic reforms was, by the early 1960s, leading his country's political moderates and Buddhists to make common cause with the Vietcong in what was fast becoming a civil war. By 1963, leading State Department officials, notably Averell Harriman and Roger Hilsman, had concluded that the war could not be won with Diem and his brother Ngo Dinh Nhu at the helm.[5] These arguments found favour with Kennedy, who had by then identified Vietnam as the key place to make a stand against communism.[6] Thus, on 24 August 1963 the State Department dispatched a cable to the American Ambassador in Saigon, Henry Cabot Lodge, advising him to assist the South Vietnamese military in a coup that was carried out on 1 November 1963 and resulted in the ouster and murder of Diem and Nhu.[7]

Similarly to the Bay of Pigs invasion and Operation MONGOOSE, both of which served only to strengthen Soviet determination to support Castro, the overthrow of Diem is instructive in demonstrating how covert action could backfire and result in unwelcome consequences for American policy that were not envisaged at the time of authorisation. Indeed, the CIA and the Pentagon had opposed the coup, forecasting that it would make the already unstable situation in South Vietnam a good deal worse. Not for the first time in the agency's history, Washington ignored its predictions. CIA operatives were, nevertheless, ordered to assist in a covert operation that McCone had told the Kennedy brothers would be detrimental to American interests.[8]

Just as the DCI had warned, Diem's removal led to a rapid turnover of successor governments in Saigon and power in South Vietnam was increasingly dispersed. This placed growing responsibility on local leaders, who, despite American counterinsurgency measures, were susceptible to the threats and manoeuvres of the Vietcong in a way that central government was not. South Vietnam was, as a result, further destabilised, which led to the dispatch of more American troops and the commitment that Washington had long sought to limit was thereby heightened.[9]

As with the Korean War, the escalation of hostilities in Vietnam into a full-scale war brought about a change in the DDP's mission. For Washington, successful prosecution of the Vietnam War depended primarily on a three-pronged strategy aimed at: (1) sealing off the South Vietnamese borders; (2) isolating the war zone; and (3) implementing a pacification programme directed at diminishing the strength of the insurgency. The implication of such an approach was that American planners viewed Indochina as a single strategic entity, for the Ho Chi Minh Trail, the supply route through which Hanoi infiltrated manpower and resources into the South, cut through Laos and Cambodia.[10] The option of taking overt action in either of these countries was precluded, however, since both were pledged to remain neutral under the terms of the Geneva Accords of 1954 and the 1962 Geneva Conference on Laos. Consequently, the DDP served two overarching but closely interconnected purposes during the war: supporting the military effort in Vietnam itself and enabling the United States to circumvent the constraints on its freedom to act in Indochina as a whole.

To this end the agency worked closely with the Green Berets, recruiting, training, financing, and directing the Laotian hill tribes (the Hmong), and the Montagnard tribes of the central highlands of Vietnam in what were, at least until 1970, the most effective of all the CIA's defensive and diversionary wartime paramilitary operations.[11] Covert action failed in Indochina, however, when it was deployed for offensive purposes, for much the same reasons as had applied in other 'denied areas'. To begin with, Ho Chi Minh maintained a similarly tight centralised control of his country to that which had been in place in Eastern Europe and the Soviet Republics in the late 1940s and early 1950s. Many of the offensive operations mounted against North Vietnam were, moreover, infiltrated and consequently compromised by enemy agents, just as had been the case with Operation BGFIEND and numerous other ventures that were targeted on the Soviet bloc and Communist China. There was also the point that in Vietnam both sets of indigenous combatants shared the same racial and ethnic mix, and spoke the same language. This factor enabled Ho Chi Minh to penetrate the South Vietnamese action teams that were being infiltrated into the North in the same way that Castro penetrated the émigré groups in Miami, thereby instigating measures that stifled the DDP's plans.[12]

*   *   *

This picture of defensive covert action complementing and advancing American policy objectives to a greater degree than its offensive counterpart had been the case throughout the Cold War. It is, however, a picture that is in need of some clarification. At the most basic level, defensive operations presented fewer obstacles for the CIA than offensive projects did, primarily because the governments of the host countries in Western Europe, Japan and the Philippines, where defensive programmes proved to be most soundly-based and enduring, were as determined to contain communism as was the United States. 'Friendly', pluralist societies such as these provided fertile ground for the CIA's establishment of front organisations, a propensity that increased enormously with the advent of the OPC and its access to counterpart funds. Such resources were instrumental in enabling the United States to provide the material support and manpower for the deployment of the 'third option' on a global scale behind the cover of the CIA's 'private' enterprises, notably its airlines and banks, during subsequent years.

Added to this was the fact that Washington's determination to hold communism at bay was always clear and unequivocal, and successive administrations afforded first the SPG then the OPC/DDP considerable latitude in the drive to ensure that this policy was effective. This held true over the long haul that the Cold War became, and also during short-term crises such as the Italian election campaign of 1948. An early defining moment for the CIA's covert action mission, the SPG's Italian operation bore fruit in part because Angleton had maintained a network of contacts dating back to the wartime period and thus provided the means through which secret American funds were distributed to Italy's centrist political parties. This initiative was not decisive in itself. Rather, it was one of a number of western measures, which, along with the example of the Czech coup, tipped the balance firmly in favour of the Christian Democrats.

De Gasperi's victory, along with the defeat of a communist-led general strike in France the year before, set the pattern whereby the agency supported noncommunist political parties and organisations in Western Europe and Japan for a further forty years. A key plank in Washington's containment policy, clandestine funding also had a downside, however. The injection of CIA aid became a stabilising element in the host countries and once the commitment was made then it had to be sustained in order to ensure that the political equilibrium was maintained.[13] Agency termination of political subsidies would, furthermore, have carried the risk of former beneficiaries exposing the connection, which would have reflected badly on the CIA and damaged the reputation of the United States. What does, nevertheless, emerge from the operations that have been examined is that defensive covert action fulfilled the primary objective for which it was designed: to contain, or more precisely to assist in the drive to neutralize the communist threat in those countries that were lodged firmly in the western camp.

The pursuit of coercive containment and the conduct of offensive operations in the strictly regimented totalitarian states of Eastern Europe and the Far East presented the CIA with a wholly more complex challenge than that which applied outside of the communist world. The agency proved to be more than a match for this task with its propaganda effort in the denied areas. From the time of their inception through to the end of the Cold War, Radio Free Europe and Radio Liberty made crucial contributions to the drive to keep the spirit of freedom alive in Eastern Europe.[14] Of course, communist rule in the Soviet Union and its satellites collapsed primarily because of the inherent political and economic weaknesses of the system itself. The agency was, however, relentless in its campaign to keep the 'captive peoples' focused on these weaknesses, and to create and maintain the perception that a vastly more palatable alternative existed in the West. Indeed, the evidence of the Hungarian uprising suggests that RFE was, if anything, too successful in fuelling the thirst for freedom in the 'captive nations' during the station's early years.[15] Success evaded the OPC/DDP, however, in its deployment of paramilitary and political action behind the Iron and Bamboo Curtains from 1948 through to 1956, and such failure begs an explanation.

The covert offensives mounted by the CIA during Truman's tenure were, it should be stressed, designed to serve different policy requirements from those authorised by Eisenhower against the communist bloc. The Soviet Union was under the dictatorship of Stalin for the entirety of Truman's presidency and communism was on the march during this period, with the establishment of the PRC and the onset of war in Korea. In contrast, Eisenhower was, for all but the first two months of his tenure, faced by a less hard-line Soviet leadership and from July 1953 until the end of his presidency operated under peacetime conditions, which were underscored by the fact that both superpowers were now in possession of thermonuclear weaponry. For the CIA, however, the same core problem reared its head during both the Truman and Eisenhower periods: a lack of clarity at the highest levels of government as to what political action and paramilitary operations against the communist bloc were designed to achieve placed constraints on, and blurred the objectives of, the agency's operations directorate.[16]

If, for instance, the campaigns mounted by the OPC/DDP in Eastern Europe and the USSR between 1949 and the mid 1950s had fulfilled their optimum potential and led to the elimination of the ruling regimes in Tirana, Prague and Warsaw, and brought about the beginnings of the fragmentation of the Soviet Union itself, then the United States would have faced a dilemma. CIA action would have caused a fundamental departure in American policy from containment to rollback, albeit surreptitiously.

Such an outcome might have been to Washington's advantage in the case of Albania. Hoxha's country was not, after all, part of Moscow's defence buffer zone, and its detachment from Russian control, while a symbolic defeat for the Kremlin, would not have posed a direct threat to the security of the Soviet Union and would not, at least in American calculations, have provoked the Russians into risking a direct confrontation with the United States.[17] Otherwise, potentially successful CIA-initiated rollback in the denied areas carried enormous risks and considerable ramifications for American prestige. Washington would, in essence, have been confronted with the problem of determining whether or not to provide overt American support to ensure that the uprisings triggered by the agency were given the chance to succeed. These issues in fact came into sharp focus during the Hungarian uprising – the one instance in which rollback appeared feasible – and Eisenhower judged the risks of overt intervention to be too great. Nagy and his countrymen were thus abandoned to their fate and the limits of what was achievable through offensive covert action were defined in the starkest of terms.

In overall analysis, then, the CIA offensives that spanned the Truman and Eisenhower years were, with the exception of BGFIEND, aimed at a gradual weakening, rather than an abrupt rolling back, of the communist hold on the denied areas. Coercive containment of this kind was, furthermore, predicated on the need to strike the right balance: to recruit and deploy a wide range of assets in preparation for the worst case scenario of Korea, or any subsequent Cold War flashpoint, escalating into a general war involving both superpowers, but to ensure that these preparations themselves did not trigger such a war.

Offensive covert warfare, however, delivered few tangible rewards: much was spent and little was gained, partly because the OPC/DDP was naïve in the objectives it set for itself, but more particularly because successive administrations were uncertain about what they wanted to achieve and CIA offensives thus had little in the way of wider policy objectives with which to mesh. Put simply, to have rolled back communism in the Soviet bloc would have required Washington to implement complementary overt measures, such as the breaking off of diplomatic relations with, or the enforcing of secondary trade boycotts against, the targeted countries.[18] Neither Truman nor Eisenhower was prepared to contemplate making such moves, which restricted the extent to which coercive containment could be effective.

There were also problems on a tactical level. CIA political and paramilitary offensives proved to be ill-conceived and/or poorly executed, as BGFIEND, the boat landings in the Baltic States, and the WiN deception in Poland demonstrated. Equally pertinent is the point that many of these projects were dependent on the OPC/DDP working in close cooperation with MI6, and to a lesser extent with the Gehlen organisation, in what are known as interdependent intelligence alliances. Such arrangements pose fundamental difficulties, in that the penetration of one of the partner services by an adversary opens the way for the penetration of both or, in the cases where more than two agencies are working together, all of the participants.[19] The OPC/DDP's mission was in fact severely impaired by this very problem, as the uncovering of Heinz Felfe, Guy Burgess, Donald Maclean, and most notably Kim Philby demonstrated.[20]

Where the agency scored more satisfactory results was in Iran and Guatemala. These were, however, fundamentally different enterprises from those mounted by the CIA against the communist bloc. Operations TPAJAX and PBSUCCESS were, to begin with, preventive as distinct from offensive ventures, that reflected the expansion of the Cold War to the third world. The removal of Musaddiq was at heart aimed at displacing a leader who the Eisenhower administration regarded as being vulnerable to a Tudeh takeover. In the case of Arbenz's ouster, Washington was seeking partly to prevent communism from creeping into the Western Hemisphere through the back door. That both of the targeted leaders had been democratically elected was of no consequence to Eisenhower. Equally significant was the strategic dimension. In sanctioning Operation TPAJAX, the American president saw himself as striking a blow against what was depicted as communist infiltration of the higher reaches of the Iranian government at a time when the Kremlin was too embroiled in the Berlin riots and the leadership struggle that followed in the wake of Stalin's death, to react with anything other than predictable anti-American rhetoric. For its part, PBSUCCESS was as much an experiment for the Eisenhower administration as Operation BGFIEND had been for Wisner and his colleagues at the OPC. The objective in Guatemala was, in effect, to test the viability of covert action within the context of the wider asymmetry of the New Look, and against the background of concurrent international and domestic difficulties that Eisenhower faced.

The Iran and Guatemala campaigns signalled the high-water mark for the CIA's operations directorate. These ventures were, however, only successes in the short-term. Musaddiq's downfall strangled Iranian democracy in its infancy and opened the way for the authoritarian rule of the shah and the even more repressive Islamic Republic. Guatemala suffered under equally unrepresentative government and decades of civil war that continued into the 1990s. TPAJAX, PBSUCCESS and the earlier, less 'visible' interventions in Syria and Egypt, furthermore, alerted real and potential future targets of the CIA to the dangers of American covert action, thus enabling Nasser and Sukarno to thwart the respective OMEGA and HAIK operations, and Castro to repel the CEF at the Bay of Pigs.

The Indonesian venture and the JMARC campaign had much in common. Both were unwieldly and too large to be kept secret. Both proceeded from the misconception that indigenous opposition backed up with American power would be enough to cause the army to rebel and mount a coup d'état, or, in the case of Indonesia, create the conditions for a separatist regime to take control in Sumatra if the primary objective of overthrowing Sukarno failed. Neither enterprise took sufficient account of how firmly in control the head of state actually was.

Operation HAIK was, however, the CIA's first major debacle since Allen Dulles decided to specialise and concentrate the DDP's efforts on the third world. Smaller-scale Middle Eastern forays not withstanding, there were no real precedents from which to learn, though it should be stressed that Wisner did warn the Dulles brothers that the prospect of the American hand being exposed in the Indonesian campaign was unacceptably high.[21] In the case of Operation JMARC, the CIA and military officers involved had forewarning of the potential for the enterprise to misfire as a consequence of the Indonesian experience. Their failure to take account of these lessons arose as a result of the misplaced assumptions mentioned above and the mistaken belief that Kennedy would do what was necessary in order to prevail, just as Eisenhower had done during the Guatemala campaign.

The most unqualified and public failure in the CIA's history, the CEF's defeat at the Bay of Pigs instigated an escalation of the conflict between Cuba and the United States, which in turn brought about the authorisation of Operation MONGOOSE and the intensification of the agency's assassination plots against Castro. That any record exists of CIA involvement in such a sensitive area as assassination is testimony to the openness of American society. What is less certain is whether such activity was effective as an instrument of policy.

Leaving aside the fact that DDP plans to murder Stalin in 1952 and Arbenz in 1954 were vetoed, there is definite evidence that the agency devised plots to kill five heads of state during the period under study – Lumumba, Trujillo, Diem, the Iraqi dictator Colonel Abdul-Rauf al-Qassim, and Castro. Of these foreign leaders, four were slain by indigenous opponents, some of whom were associated with the agency. There was no proof of direct CIA involvement in any of the killings, but this was entirely consistent with the agency's modus operandi. Plausible deniability demanded no less than that covert action, whatever its nature, looked as if it was the outcome of home-grown developments. In terms of immediate objectives, then, the CIA or more accurately the proxy groups that it used, achieved an 80 per cent success rate with these assassination plots.[22]

On the other hand, only the Lumumba slaying can be deemed to have produced anything approaching the desired effect over the longer term, in that it eased the way for Mobutu, the man deemed to be the least bad of the contenders to take control of the Congo, to rise to prominence in 1961 and seize power four years later. The Trujillo murder, though it was intended to signal American antipathy towards dictatorship of all political hues in the Caribbean and also prevent a repeat of the Cuban revolution in the Dominican Republic, resulted in more of the same corrupt *caudillo* rule. Qassim was, to use Andrew Tully's words, "a dangerous, capricious militarist" who deposed King Faisal's pro-western government in 1958, enlisted communist support, repudiated the Baghdad Pact, and laid claim to Kuwait in 1961. He was thus deemed, justifiably, to represent "a long-range threat to the peace of the Middle East".[23] His ousting from power and subsequent exe-cution by firing squad did nothing to bring enduring stability to Iraq, however, as the rise and fall of Saddam Hussein, and the direct American military involvement in the country that brought the latter event about, has clearly shown. Finally, Diem's killing served only to escalate the conflict in Vietnam and lumber the United States with the problem of finding a viable exit strategy from that country: a similar dilemma to that which would apply in Iraq thirty years later.

Of all the assassination programmes that the CIA is known to have engaged in, the plots against Castro have gained the greatest notoriety. In its attempts to kill the Cuban leader, the agency resorted to the most bizarre of tactics, including the recruitment of Mafia chieftains over whom little control could be exercised. When the plans to murder Castro were first sanctioned, the CIA did have some conception of how such an act would complement wider American policy. The assassination would be timed to occur prior to or in conjunction with the CEF invasion, decapitating the Cuban revolution in its hour of greatest need, and thereby optimising the prospects of a military coup and/or a general uprising.[24] Similar reasoning applied during Operation MONGOOSE, but the real problems with the post-JMARC anti-Castro programmes were that, as with the Albanian venture, Washington took insufficient account of the obstacles that confronted the agency in the target country and, most importantly, the policy guidelines were unclear. CIA covert action may have been the most appropriate vehicle for meeting the Cuban challenge to Betancourt's rule in Venezuela. In respect of long-term relations between Washington and Havana, however, there was no real policy to serve other than to comply as best as possible with the Kennedy brothers' impractical and impetuous calls for the CIA to "get rid of Castro" – the implication being by any means.

In citing the anti-Castro campaigns alongside earlier preventive operations, account needs to be taken of the fact that Cuba was a special case. The objective was not to prevent communism from taking hold, but to remove a Marxist-Leninist regime that was already in power. Covert action, whether it took the form of the PBSUCCESS model or Lansdale's counterinsurgency techniques, was no more able to fulfil this task than it had been in Eastern Europe.

Leaving Cuba aside, preventive covert action defies cut and dried conclusions. Certainly, it secured some tangible shorter-term gains, but they were too often accompanied by negative longer-term repercussions, as developments in Iran and Guatemala following the respective coups of 1953 and 1954 made plain. There was, moreover, an additional associated pitfall, in that while the CIA could remove, or assist in the removal of, leaders whose rule was deemed to be detrimental to American interests, the agency could not always guarantee that the successors it favoured would, on securing their positions, continue to do Washington's bidding. Such was the case in Egypt. The DDP assisted the Free Officers in their ouster of King Farouk, only to discover that Nasser's medium-term policies were at complete odds with those of the United States.[25] Again in British Guiana, the agency helped to depose Cheddi Jagan, only to see its preferred candidate, Forbes Burnham, adopt authoritarian governance, repudiate the United States and align his country with Cuba within ten years of his accession to power.[26]

Not all of the covert operations that the CIA conducted between 1947 and 1963 fit comfortably within the defensive-offensive-preventive delineation. Wartime operations, such as the Montagnard campaign in the central highlands of Vietnam, and the Hmong's efforts in the Laotian panhandle involved a good deal of overlap between defensive and offensive modes of action. An additional factor that presents itself as being worthy of mention in referring to these particular operations is that they generally meshed well with wider American war aims, regardless of the fact that those aims themselves did not meet with ultimate success. In this sense, the wartime campaigns mounted in Indochina by the CIA in partnership with the Defense Department are illustrative of the fact that effective coordination between policy and operations did not always guarantee a positive outcome.

*   *   *

Equally worthy of brief consideration is the impact that covert operations had in influencing wider perceptions of the United States. The CIA interventions that dotted the globe during the fifties and sixties, continued into the 1970s, and gathered renewed impetus under the stewardship of the Reagan administration in the 1980s led many in the developing world, and indeed further afield, to view the United States and the CIA in a decidedly negative and reactionary light. This is rather ironic, given that, for the first twenty years of its existence, the agency was regarded by a preponderance of the political cognoscenti in the United States as being an essentially liberal organization, the leftward leanings of which were pronounced enough to merit the albeit unsuccessful attentions of Joseph McCarthy. What begs explanation, then, is why the portrayal of a meddlesome, bullying America, served by an overly-zealous, unprincipled CIA has come to hold such currency, and the key to addressing this lies in the guiding ethos that informed the agency and its political masters throughout the Cold War.

For the CIA and the successive administrations that it served few means were seen as being beyond the pale in their all-encompassing battle with the Soviet Union and its allies. The United States, of course, preferred to work with centrist parties and actors in its drive to combat communism and promote democracy and free market economics worldwide. As has already been pointed out, this proved to be a feasible and successfully-executed option in the developed countries of Western Europe, where democratic traditions were relatively strong. However, the choices confronting the United States and the CIA were starker in the third world, where colonial or, in the case of the Americas, *caudillo* rule was deeply rooted. For sure, Washington preferred to promote and work with democrats such as Venezuela's Rómulo Betancourt, but the fact was that individuals and parties that fitted into this category were thin on the ground in the developing world. In the absence of the best possible option, then, the White House and the CIA did what they saw as the next best thing: they worked with whatever anticommunist forces were available in any given theatre and deferred any misgivings that might have arisen regarding these sometimes questionable cohorts until after the immediate threat had been neutralized or the Cold War was over.

The consequence of such reasoning was that the agency's history became littered with examples of its having made common cause with a many and varied range of highly dubious allies. Beginning with the aid and succour provided by the OPC to former Nazis, the trend continued for the duration of the Cold War. Agency expertise was, for instance, instrumental in the creation of the National Intelligence and Security Organisation (SAVAK) in the shah's Iran and its Saudi Arabian counterpart, the General Intelligence Directorate (GID), both of which gained notoriety for their routine use of torture and abuses of human rights.[27] Equally damaging to the CIA's long-term reputation was its levering of Mobutu into power in the Congo and Haji Muhammad Suharto in Indonesia, each of whom led corrupt authoritarian regimes that did much to serve their own interests and little or nothing to enhance those of their people.[28] South American military dictatorships also benefited from agency support, as the ouster of Salvador Allende's democratically elected Marxist regime in Chile during 1973 and the subsequent seventeen years of hard-line rule imposed by General Augusto Pinochet amply demonstrated.[29] More significant still in causing the CIA to collaborate with reactionary forces was the coming of Ronald Reagan to the presidency and the advent of the doctrine to which he gave his name. With its very loose definition of what constituted a 'freedom fighter', the Reagan Doctrine called on the CIA to support, not only genuine drives to secure democracy, as was the case with the Polish Solidarity Movement, but also to assist the rightist Nicaraguan Contras and the Mujahideen forces in Afghanistan, neither of which qualified in any way, shape or form as democrats.[30]

The sum total of the CIA's long time resort to such expedients was that it became tainted by association, and so too did the country that it served. Moreover, Faustian bargains of this kind too often resulted in 'blowback', namely unforeseen and negative consequences for American interests. The Iran-Contra affair springs most obviously to mind in making this point.[31] Much worse was the outcome of the funding and support that the Reagan administration in general and the CIA in particular provided for the Mujahideen. In accelerating the withdrawal of Soviet forces from Afghanistan, American supply of Stinger anti-aircraft missiles and other weaponry also helped to create the political vacuum that followed Moscow's retreat in 1989.[32] As such, the CIA's covert support for the Mujahideen paved the way indirectly for the Taliban to seize control in Afghanistan and transform the country into a safe haven for Al Qaeda to train and plan for the September 11 attacks on the Twin Towers and the Pentagon. Given that the consideration which loomed largest in the Truman administration's decision to establish the CIA in the first place was a determination to ensure Pearl Harbor was never repeated, this was the ultimate in paradoxical twists.

In respect of the performance of the agency's operations directorate from the Italian campaign through to the programmes mounted in Cuba and Indochina, however, the results were mixed. While there were instances of over-enthusiasm leading operatives to go beyond what was required of them, the CIA did not in general behave as a rogue elephant, as has sometimes been alleged.[33] DCI's from Hillenkoetter through to McCone sought to ensure that the strategies adopted by the agency were compatible with American policy, even in those instances where policymakers themselves were unclear about what they wanted to achieve.

There is, of course, an inherent problem in gauging the merits and demerits of CIA's performance on an operation-by-operation basis, in that the real successes have by definition remained secret, while the failures have entered the public domain either immediately after the event or belatedly. Perhaps the true measure of CIA covert action was in its cumulative effects. The agency launched a huge number of projects of varying nature, magnitude and impact during its first fifteen years.[34] Taken together, these enterprises provided Washington with a means of circumventing the constraints that postwar advances in international law and Soviet acquisition of atomic and thermonuclear weaponry placed on America's capacity to act overtly. This was a vital imperative and, in conducting it, the CIA's operations directorate played a significant role in shaping the course of the early Cold War and serving notice on the Soviet Union and any other potential adversary that the United States was always willing and often able to counter real and perceived challenges to American interests anywhere and everywhere that they threatened.

Appendix 1 Italian election results for 1946 and 1948
(from Norman Kogan, *A Political History of Italy: The Postwar Years*, p. 40)

Election results, 1946

Parties	1946 Popular vote (in percentages)
Uomo Qualunque	5.3
Monarchist	2.8
Liberal	6.8
Christian Democrat	35.2
Republican	4.4
Socialist	20.7
Communist	19.0
Others	5.8
Total	*100*

Election results, 1948

Parties	1948 Popular vote (in percentages)
Uomo Qualunque	2.0
Monarchist	2.8
Liberal	3.8
Christian Democrat	48.5
South Tyrol Populist	0.5
Republican	2.5
Social Democrat	7.1
Socialist/Communist	31.0
Others	1.8
Total	*100*

Appendix 2 CIA Organisation Chart, 1948 to 1950 (from Montague, *Smith-DCI*, p. 112)

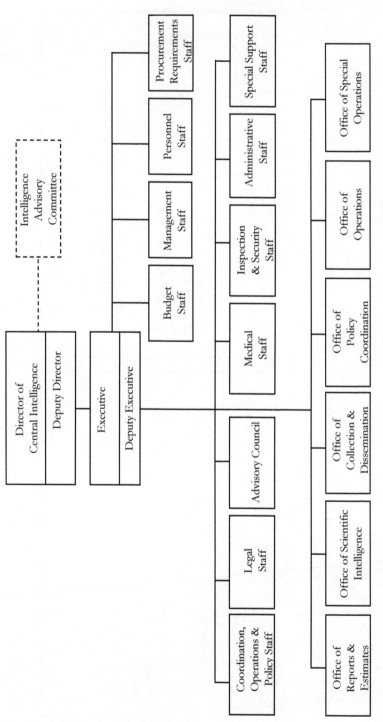

Prior to the establishment of the OPC, CIA covert action was the responsibility of the SPG which was housed in the OSO

Appendix 3 ADPC Wisner, breakdown of OPC's mission
(from *FRUS: Intelligence Community, 1945–50:* 730–731)

Function Group I – Psychological Warfare

Program A – Press
Program B – Radio
Program C – Miscellaneous (direct mail, poison pen, rumors)

Functional Group II – Political Warfare

Program A – Support for Resistance (underground)
Program B – Support for DPs and Refugees
Program C – Support for anti-Communists in Free Countries
Program D – Encouragement of Defection

Functional Group III – Economic Warfare

Program A – Commodity operations (clandestine preclusive buying, market manipulation, and black market operation)
Program B – Fiscal operations (currency speculation, counterfeiting, etc.)

Functional Group IV – Preventive Direct Action

Program A – Support for Guerrillas
Program B – Sabotage, Countersabotage, and Demolition
Program C – Evacuation
Program D – Stay-behind

Functional Group V – Miscellaneous

Program A – Front Organisations
Program B – War Plans
Program C – Administration
Program D – Miscellaneous

Appendix 4 CIA Organisation Chart, 1952 to 1961
(from Montague, *Smith-DCI*, p. 113)

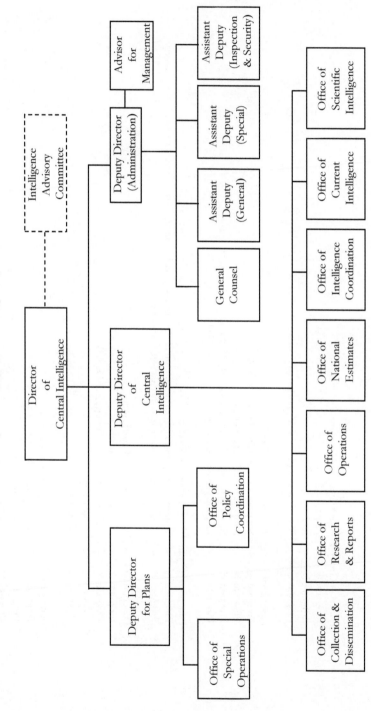

* The Office of Operations (OO) was originally envisaged as being integrated into the DDP but was brought under the jurisdiction of the DDI in March 1952 (see Montague, *Smith-DCI*, pp. 185–189)

Appendix 5 PBSUCCESS Organisation Chart (adapted from the command structure included in Cullather, *PBSUCCESS*, p. 105)

Allen Dulles
DCI

Frank Wisner
DDP

J.C. King
Chief of WH Division

Richard Bissell
Special Deputy

C. Tracy Barnes
Psychological/Political
Advisor

Jake Esterline
War Room,
Washington

Al Haney
LINCOLN Station

Hans Tofte
Chief of Psychological/
Political ops.

Several of the names are classified in the
original chart, but the identities of most of
these individuals are discernible by cross-checking
with the major studies of PBSUCCESS

John Peurifoy
U.S. Ambassador
Guatemala

E. Howard Hunt
Chief of Propaganda

William 'Rip' Robertson
Paramilitary ops.
& Training

Western Hemisphere Division

[DELETED]

David A. Phillips
Radio Propaganda
SHERWOOD

'Tranger,' Chief of Station, Guat.
Succeeded
by John Doherty Apr. 1954

[DELETED]

Appendix 6 CIA Organisation Chart, 1964 (from Ranelagh, *The Agency*, p. 720)

Appendix 7 JMARC Organisation Chart

Adapted from the command structures included in the Paramilitary Study Group Report,
Taylor Report, Annex 1 & Annex 5, box 61A, NSF, JFKL.

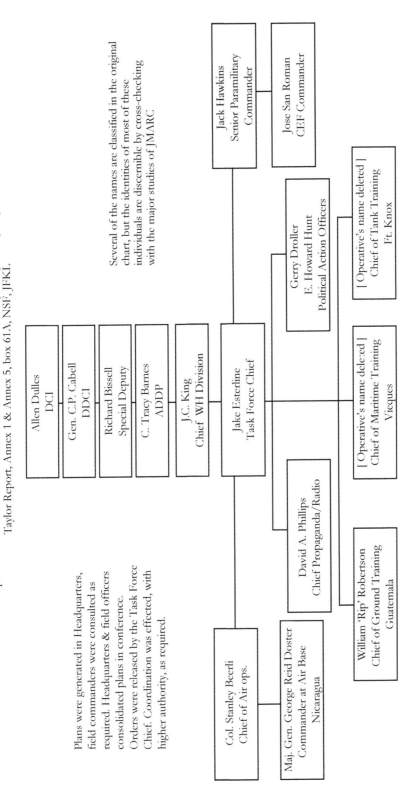

Several of the names are classified in the original chart, but the identities of most of these individuals are discernible by cross-checking with the major studies of JMARC.

Plans were generated in Headquarters, field commanders were consulted as required. Headquarters & field officers consolidated plans in conference. Orders were released by the Task Force Chief. Coordination was effected, with higher authority, as required.

Allen Dulles
DCI

Gen. C.P. Cabell
DDCI

Richard Bissell
Special Deputy

C. Tracy Barnes
ADDP

J.C. King
Chief WH Division

Jake Esterline
Task Force Chief

Jack Hawkins
Senior Paramilitary Commander

Jose San Roman
CEF Commander

Gerry Droller
E. Howard Hunt
Political Action Officers

[Operative's name deleted]
Chief of Tank Training
Ft. Knox

[Operative's name deleted]
Chief of Maritime Training
Vieques

David A. Phillips
Chief Propaganda/Radio

William 'Rip' Robertson
Chief of Ground Training
Guatemala

Col. Stanley Beerli
Chief of Air ops.

Maj. Gen. George Reid Doster
Commander at Air Base
Nicaragua

Notes

Introduction

1. Policy Planning Staff Memorandum, 4 May 1948, *Foreign Relations of the United States, 1945–1950: Emergence of the Intelligence Establishment* (Washington D.C., 1996), 671 – hereafter cited as FRUS.

2. Roy Godson, *Dirty Tricks or Trump Cards: U.S. Covert Action and Counterintelligence* (Washington and London, 1995), pp. 2–3; *Foreign and Military Intelligence – Book 1.* Final Report of the Select Committee to Study Governmental Operations with Respect to Intelligence Activities. United States Senate together with Additional, Supplemental, and Separate Views. *Senate Report*, 94th Congress, 2 session, Report No. 94–755, April 26 (legislative day April 14), 1976 (Washington D.C., 1976), p. 141 (hereafter cited as Church Report).

3. Loch K, Johnson, *America's Secret Power: The CIA in a Democratic Society* (New York, 1989), pp. 22–27.

4. Office of Special Operations Directive No.18/5 (Interim), *FRUS: Intelligence Establishment, 1945–50*: 653, 724–725.

5. Michael J. Warner (ed.), *CIA Cold War Records: The CIA Under Harry Truman* (Washington D.C., 1994), pp. 235–243.

6. Ludwell Lee Montague (with an introduction by Bruce D. Berkowitz and Allan E. Goodman), *General Walter Bedell Smith as Director of Central Intelligence, October 1950–February 1953* (University Park, Pennsylvania, 1992), p. 208; *Church Report*, Bk.1, p. 51.

7. *Church Report*, Bk.1, pp. 107–108.

8. PPS Memo, 4 May 1948, *FRUS: Intelligence Establishment, 1945–50*: 669.

9. Johnson, *America's Secret Power*, p. 17.

10. Sherman Kent quoted in H. Bradford Westerfield (ed.), *Inside the CIA's Private World: Declassified Articles from the Agency's Internal Journal, 1952–1992* (Washington D.C., 1995), xiii.

11. *ibid.*

12. Godson, *Dirty Tricks or Trump Cards*, pp. 36–37.

13   Merle Miller, *Plain Speaking: Conversations with Harry S. Truman: An Oral Biography of Harry
     S. Truman* (London, 1974), pp. 391–392. The proposition that Truman established the
     CIA to collect and evaluate intelligence and that this vision "was subverted from the
     start", is repeated in Tim Weiner's *Legacy of Ashes: The History of the CIA* (New York,
     2007), quote on p. 3. There is, however, a strong body of evidence which makes plain
     that the president was both aware and supportive of what was being done by the
     agency's operations directorate during his tenure. For an overview of this material and a
     rebuttal of the core claim of Weiner's book, that the CIA's sixty-year record is one of
     near unremitting failure, see Nicholas Dujmovic, "Review of *Legacy of Ashes: The History
     of the CIA*", www.cia.gov/library/center-for-the-study-of-intelligence/csi-publications/
     csi studies/studies/vol51no3/legacy-of-ashes-the-history-of-cia.html.

14   NSC 68, "United States Objectives and Programs for National Security", 14 April 1950,
     FRUS 1950, Vol.1: 235–292.

15   Harry Rositzke, "America's Secret Operations: A Perspective", *Foreign Affairs* 53 (1974–
     1975): 334–351, at 335–336; John Prados, *Presidents' Secret Wars: CIA and Pentagon Covert
     Operations from World War II Through the Persian Gulf* (first published Chicago, 1986,
     revised and updated edition, 1996), pp. 30–61; Burton Hersh, *The Old Boys: The American
     Elite and the Origins of the CIA* (New York, 1992), pp. 171–282.

16   Nicholas Cullather, *Operation PBSUCCESS: The United States and Guatemala, 1952–
     1954*, CIA in-house history declassified 1997 and available for consultation at Modern
     Military Branch of the National Archives, Washington D.C. (hereafter cited as NA),
     pp. 17–20. For the published version of the agency's account see Nick Cullather,
     Secret History: The CIA's Declassified Account of Its Operations in Guatemala, 1952–1954
     (Palo Alto, 1999).

17   The most significant primary source on the Iran coup is the CIA's internal history of
     TPAJAX, which was leaked to the *New York Times* in 2000, see Donald N. Wilber,
     Clandestine Service History: Overthrow of Premier Mossadeq of Iran, November 1952-August 1953,
     CS Historical Paper No.208, written March 1954, published October 1969. Also
     indispensable to the study of the coup are Kermit Roosevelt's *Countercoup: The Struggle for
     the Control of Iran* (New York, 1979) and Mark Gasiorowski, "The 1953 Coup D'État in
     Iran", *International Journal of Middle East Studies*, 19(1987): 261–286.

18   Stephen E. Ambrose, *Ike's Spies: Eisenhower and the Espionage Establishment* (New York,
     1981).

19   John Lewis Gaddis, *Strategies of Containment: A Critical Appraisal of American National
     Security Policy* (New York, 1982), pp. 147–153.

20   *Church Report*, Bk.1, p. 109.

21   Wayne G. Jackson, *Allen Welsh Dulles as Director of Central Intelligence, 26 February 1953- 29
     November 1961*, Volume 3, declassified 1994 and available at the Modern Military
     Branch, NA.

22   Quote from Rhodri Jeffreys-Jones, *The CIA and American Democracy* (New Haven and
     London, 1989), p. 82.

23   For an analysis of the rogue elephant charges see *ibid*, p. 208, pp. 214–215.

24 Trevor Barnes, "The Secret Cold War: The CIA and American Foreign Policy in Europe 1946–1956", (part 1), *Historical Journal* 24 (1981): 399–415; Ian Sayer and Douglas Botting, *America's Secret Army: the Untold Story of the Counterintelligence Corps* (New York and Toronto, 1989); Timothy J. Naftali, "ARTIFICE: James Jesus Angleton and X-2 Operations in Italy", in George C. Chalou (ed.), *The Secrets War: The Office of Strategic Services in World War II* (Washington D.C., 1992), pp. 218–245.

25 Memo from DCI Hillenkoetter to Chief of Naval Operations, Denfield, 18 June 1948, *FRUS: Intelligence Community 1945–50*: 715; Memo from Commander Robert Jay Williams to Chief of SPG (Cassady), 23 July 1948, *ibid*: 718.

26 Miles Copeland, *The Game of Nations: The Amorality of Power Politics (London, 1969)*, p. 42; Douglas Little, "Cold War and Covert Action: The United States and Syria, 1945–1958", *The Middle East Journal*, Vol.44, No.1 (1990): 51–57; Douglas Little, "Mission Impossible: The CIA and the Cult of Covert Acton in the Middle East", *Diplomatic History* 28 (November 2004): 663–684, at 670–672; Miles Copeland, *The Game Player: Confessions of the CIA's Original Political Operative* (London, 1989), pp. 158–171.

27 *Church Report*, Bk.1, p. 23; Montague, *Smith-DCI*, p. 208; Richard Crockatt, *The Fifty Years War: The United States and the Soviet Union in World Politics* (London and New York, 1995), pp. 94–95.

28 Fred I. Greenstein, *The Hidden Hand Presidency: Eisenhower as Leader* (New York, 1982), pp. 57–99, pp.155–227.

29 This enterprise became known publicly by its Pentagon code-name of Operation ZAPATA, but as is pointed out in Evan Thomas, *The Very Best Men: Four Who Dared: The Early Years of the CIA* (New York, London, Torornto, Sydney, Tokyo, and Singapore, 1995), p. 241, and Cullather, *Operation PBSUCCESS*, p. 84, its agency cryptograph was JMARC. It is suggested in the introduction to a volume of subsequently declassified documents on the Bay of Pigs that the CIA code-named the operation JMATE, while the Pentagon labelled it BUMPY ROAD, see Peter Kornbluh (ed.), *Bay of Pigs Declassified: The Secret CIA Report on the Invasion of Cuba* (New York, 1998), p. 11. For the purposes of this study, however, the enterprise will be referred to as JMARC.

30 NSC 20/4, "U.S. Objectives with Respect to the USSR to Counter Soviet Threats to U.S. Security", NSC Meetings Folder, Number 27, 23 November 1948, NSC Meetings 14–27, Box 204, President's Secretary's File (hereafter cited as PSF), Harry S. Truman Library, Independence, Missouri (hereafter cited as HSTL).

31 Prime among these works were Philip Agee, *Inside the Company: CIA Diary* (Harmondsworth, 1975); and Victor Marchetti and John D. Marks, *The CIA and the Cult of Intelligence* (New York, 1975).

32 David Wise and Thomas B. Ross, *The Invisible Government* (London, 1964); for details of the *Ramparts* articles see John Ranelagh, *The Agency: The Rise and Decline of the CIA* (London, 1986), p. 471.

33 *Church Report*, Bks.1–5; United States of America, House of Representatives, Select Committee on Intelligence, *CIA: The Pike Report*, with an introduction by Philip Agee (New York, 1977).

34 The key outlets for the agency's more recently declassified material are the records released and/or reproduced through: the Central Intelligence Agency, Freedom of Information Electronic Reading Room (hereafter cited as www.foia.cia.gov); and the Central Intelligence Agency, Center for the Study of Intelligence (CSI). For its part, the State Department has published two volumes that focus on intelligence. The first of these is *FRUS: Intelligence Community 1945–50*. The follow-on volume, United States Department of State, *Foreign Relations of the United States: The Intelligence Community, 1950–1955*, edited by Douglas Keane and Michael Warner, general editor Edward C. Keefer (Washington D.C., 2007), documents the institutional growth of the CIA and the intelligence community as a whole during Bedell Smith's directorshi p. State has also made a good deal of material available online, notably some of the documents relating to the 1954 Guatemala coup, see Foreign Relations, 1952–1954, Guatemala, www.state.gov/r/ho/frus/ike/guat.

Chapter 1

1 Dean Acheson, *Present at the Creation: My Years at the State Department* (New York, 1969), preface, xix.

2 Harry S. Truman, *Memoirs Volume 1: Year of Decisions*, Garden City (New York, 1955), pp. 19–28.

3 Francis L. Loewenheim, Harold D. Langley, and Manfred Jonas (eds.), *Roosevelt and Churchill: Their Secret Wartime Correspondence* (New York, 1975), p. 705.

4 Harriman to Hull, 13 March 1944, *FRUS 1944*, Vol. 4: 981.

5 Robert F. Ferrell (ed.), *Off the Record: The Private Papers of Harry S. Truman* (New York, 1980), p. 16.

6 Walter Isaacson and Evan Thomas, *The Wise Men: Six Friends and the World They Made* (New York, 1986), pp. 257–258; Truman, *Year of Decisions*, p. 99.

7 Robert Messer, *The End of an Alliance: James F. Byrnes, Roosevelt, Truman, and the Origins of the Cold War* (Chapel Hill, 1982), pp. 75–76.

8 Henry Stimson and McGeorge Bundy, *On Active Service in Peace and War* (New York, 1947), pp. 617–637.

9 Byrnes-Stalin meeting, 23 December 1945, *FRUS 1945*, Vol. 2: 752–756.

10 John Lewis Gaddis, *The United States and the Origins of the Cold War, 1941–1947* (New York, 1972), pp. 282–285.

11 Walter Millis (ed.), *The Forrestal Diaries* (New York, 1951), pp. 134–135.

12 Acheson, *Present at the Creation*, p. 51; "American Relations with the Soviet Union: A Report to the President by the Special Counsel to the President", 24 September 1946, in Thomas H. Etzold and John Lewis Gaddis, *Containment: Documents on American Policy and Strategy, 1945–1950* (New York, 1978), pp. 64–71.

13 George F. Kennan, *Memoirs, 1925–1950* (New York, 1967), pp. 292–293; The Long Telegram, 22 February 1946, *FRUS 1946*, Vol.6: 696–709.

14 Bruce R. Kuniholm, *The Origins of the Cold War in the Near East: Great Power Conflict and Diplomacy in Iran, Turkey, and Greece* (Princeton, 1980), pp. 358–359.

15 Clark Clifford, Oral History 276, Vol.1, pp. 169–171, HSTL.

16 Address on foreign economic policy delivered at the Baylor University, 6 Mar. 1947, *Public Papers of the Presidents of the United States. Harry S. Truman. Containing the Public Messages, Speeches and Statements of the President,* 1947, 167–172 (Washington, D.C., 1963) – hereafter cited as *Truman Public Papers;* Gabriel Kolko and Joyce Kolko, *The Limits of Power: The World and United States Foreign Policy, 1945–1954* (New York, 1972), pp. 11–29, pp. 359–361.

17 Gaddis, *Strategies of Containment,* pp. 57–63; Robert H. Ferrell (ed.), *The American Secretaries of State and Their Diplomacy: Volume XV, George C. Marshall* (New York, 1966), p. 109, pp. 129–135. Marshall succeeded Byrnes as Secretary of State in January 1947.

18 Special Message to the Congress on Greece and Turkey: The Truman Doctrine, *Truman Public Papers,* 1947, 176–180; Acheson, *Present at the Creation,* pp. 218–219; Joseph M. Jones, *Fifteen Weeks* (New York, 1955), pp. 133–134; Millis (ed.), *Forrestal Diaries,* pp. 266–267.

19 Millis (ed.), *Forrestal Diaries,* p. 350.

20 Gaddis, *Strategies of Containment,* p. 23; Edward A.Kolodziej, *The Uncommon Defence and Congress* (Colombus, Ohio, 1966), pp. 35–39.

21 Gregory Mitrovich, *Undermining the Kremlin: America's Strategy to Subvert the Soviet Bloc, 1947–1956* (New York, 2000), pp. 11–12; "Capabilities and Intentions of the USSR for Overrunning Northern and Western Europe in 1947, 1948, and 1949", 28 February 1947, Plans and Operations, in Melvyn Leffler, "American Conception of National Security", *American Historical Review* 89 (April 1984): 346–381, at 360.

22 Leffler, "American Conception of National Security", 350–352; Kolodziej, *Uncommon Defense,* pp. 59–60; Melvyn P. Leffler, *A Preponderance of Power: National Security, the Truman Administration, and the Cold War* (Palo Alto, California, 1992), pp. 224–225, p. 149.

23 Leffler, *Preponderance of Power,* p. 149.

24 Special Message to the Congress on Greece and Turkey: The Truman Doctrine, *Truman Public Papers,* 1947, 176–180; George M. Elsey, OH 128, Vol.2, pp. 353–358, pp. 369–372.

25 Robert Divine, "The Cold War and the Election of 1948", *Journal of American History,* 59 (June 1972): 90–110, at 92; Harry S. Truman, *Memoirs. Volume II: Years of Trial and Hope* (New York, 1956), pp. 194–196.

26 Special Message to Congress on the Threat to the Freedom of Europe, 17 Mar 1948, *Truman Public Papers,* 1948, 183–186; Truman, *Years of Trial and Hope,* pp. 194–196.

27 Divine, "1948 Election", 97–109.

28 *Church Report,* Bk.1, p. 99.

29 Psychological and Political Warfare Introduction, *FRUS: Intelligence Community, 1945–50*: 617–619.

30 Anne Karalekas, *History of the Central Intelligence Agency* (Laguna Hills, California, 1977), pp. 27–28 – Karalekas's history first appeared in the "Supplementary Detailed Staff Reports on Foreign and Military Intelligence", in Book 4 of the *Church Report;*

Psychological and Political Warfare Introduction, *FRUS: Intelligence Community, 1945–50*: 620–621.

31 Quote from Thomas Powers, "The Truth About the CIA", *New York Review of Books*, Vol.XL, No.9 (May 1993): 49–55, at 49.

32 *Church Report*, Bk.1, p. 99.

33 Executive Order 9621, Termination of the Office of Strategic Services and Disposition of its Functions, 20 Sept. 1945, *FRUS: Intelligence Community 1945–50*: 44–45; *Church Report*, Bk.1, p. 99; Arthur B. Darling, *The Central Intelligence Agency: An Instrument of Government to 1950* (University Park, Pennsylvania and London, 1990), pp. 20–38.

34 Darling, *The Central Intelligence Agency*, pp. 20–38; Conversation between Adm. Sidney W. Souers and Messrs. William Hillman and David M. Noyes, 15 Dec. 1954, Kansas City, Missouri, "CIA Founding and Dispute", (5 of 5), Student Research File (B File), Papers of Harry S. Truman, HSTL.

35 Walter Trohan, "New Deal Plans Super Spy System", *Chicago Daily Tribune*, 9 Feb. 1945, HSTL; Thomas F. Troy, *Donovan and the CIA: A History of the Establishment of the Central Intelligence Agency* (Frederick, Md., 1981), p. 455.

36 Truman to Byrnes, 20 Sept. 1945, *FRUS: Intelligence Community 1945–50*: 46–47; Anna Kasten Nelson, "President Truman and the Evolution of the National Security Council", *Journal of American History*, 72 (1985): 360–378, at 361–362; Darling, *Central Intelligence Agency*, pp. 56–60.

37 Quote from Harry Rositze, "America's Secret Operations", 335.

38 William Colby and Peter Forbath, *Honourable Men: My Life in the CIA* (London, 1978), p. 68.

39 Souers's Tenure as DCI, Introduction, *FRUS: Intelligence Community, 1945–50*: 316–318; *Church Report*, Bk.1, p. 101.

40 Montague, *Smith-DCI*, pp. 27–28; Charles R. Christensen, "An Assessment of Hoyt S. Vandenberg's Accomplishments as Director of Central Intelligence", *Intelligence and National Security*, Vol. 11, No.4 (1996): 754–764.

41 Karalekas, *History of the CIA*, pp. 13–14; Thomas Powers, *The Man Who Kept the Secrets: Richard Helms and the CIA* (New York, 1981), p. 27.

42 John Magruder, Memo. for Maj. Gen. S. Leroy Irwin, "Assets of the SSU for Peace-time Intelligence Procurement", 15 Jan. 1946, in Warner, *CIA Cold War Records*, pp. 21–28.

43 Memo. from the Lovett Cte. to Secr. of War Patterson, 3 Nov. 1945, *FRUS: Intelligence Community, 1945–50*: 98–105, quote at 104.

44 National Intelligence Directive No.5, 8 July 1946, *ibid*: 391–392; Termination of SSU Operations, SSU General Order No.16, 19 October 1946, *ibid*: 304–305.

45 Warner, *CIA Cold War Records*, xvi.

46 Hersh, *The Old Boys*, p. 178; *Church Report*, Bk.1, p. 102; quote from Darling, *Central Intelligence Agency*, p. 95.

47 Robin W. Winks, *Cloak and Gown: Scholars in the Secret War, 1939–1961* (New York, 1987), pp. 340–341.

48 Darling, *Central Intelligence Agency*, p. 94; *Church Report*, Bk.1, p. 144.
49 Sayer and Botting, *The CIC*, p. 317.
50 John Magruder, Memo. for Maj. Gen. S. Leroy Irwin, "Assets of SSU for Peace-time Intelligence Procurement", 15 Jan. 1946, in Warner, *CIA Cold War Records*, pp. 21–24, quote on p. 24.
51 Darling, *Central Intelligence Agency*, pp. 250–256; Karalekas, *History of the CIA*, p. 26.
52 Souers to Truman, "Planning for Psychological Warfare", Progress Report, 7 June 1946, Intelligence File, PSF, HSTL; Memo., Vandenberg to Truman, 25 February 1947, in Barnes, "The Secret Cold War", 405.
53 Eduard Mark, "The War Scare of 1946 and Its Consequences", *Diplomatic History*, Vol.21, No.3 (Summer 1997): 383–41, at 398. Mark has also produced evidence of earlier covert American intervention against communist forces in Romania, see Eduard Mark, "The OSS in Romania, 1944–1945: An Intelligence Operation of the Early Cold War", *Intelligence and National Security*, Vol.9, No.2 (1994): 320–344.
54 Mark, "The War Scare of 1946", 388–400.
55 *ibid*, 399, 406; Weiner, *Legacy of Ashes*, p. 18.
56 Weiner, *Legacy of Ashes*, pp. 18–19.
57 Mark, "The War Scare of 1946", 399
58 *ibid*, 395, 401.
59 "Testimony on the National Security Act 1947", Vandenberg to the Secretaries of the Armed Services Committee, 29 April 1947, in Barnes, "The Secret Cold War", 405.
60 "National Security Act of 1947", *Hearing before the Committee on Expenditures in the Executive Departments*, 80 Cong., 1 sess. (27 June 1947), in *Church Report*, Bk.1, pp. 143–144; William M. Leary, *The CIA: History and Documents* (Birmingham, Alabama, 1984), pp. 27–30.
61 Clark Clifford to Church Cte., *Church Report*, Bk.1, p. 144; Colby and Forbath, *Honourable Men*, p. 68.
62 William R. Corson, *Armies of Ignorance: The Rise of the American Intelligence Empire* (New York, 1977), pp. 295–298.
63 Karalekas, *History of the CIA*, p. 27; Colby and Forbath, *Honourable Men*, p. 69.
64 Troy, *Donovan and the CIA*, p. 8.
65 Peter Clemens, "Operation Cardinal: The OSS in Manchuria, August 1945", *Intelligence and National Security*, Vol. 13, No.4 (1998): 71–106.
66 Colby and Forbath, *Honourable Men*, p. 69.
67 Karalekas, *History of the CIA*, pp. 13–14, p. 102; *Church Report*, Bk.1, p. 21.
68 Rhodri Jeffreys-Jones, "Why Was the CIA Established in 1947?" *Intelligence and National Security*, Vol. 12, No.1 (1997): 21–40; David Barrett, *The CIA and Congress: The Untold Story* (Lawrence, Kansas, 2005).
69 Saltonstall quoted in *Church Report*, Bk.1, pp. 149–150; Barrett, *The CIA and Congress*.
70 Richard Helms address to conference entitled *The Origin and Development of the CIA in the Administration of Harry S. Truman*, 18 March 1994, p. 50, HSTL.
71 *Church Report*, Bk.1, pp. 149–150; Karalekas, *History of the CIA*, p. 29.

72 Jeffreys-Jones, *CIA and American Democracy*, p. 49.

73 Danny D. Jansen and Rhodri Jeffreys-Jones, "The Missouri Gang and the CIA", in Rhodri Jeffreys-Jones and Andrew Lownie (eds.), *North American Spies* (Edinburgh, 1991), pp. 122–142, at p. 130.

74 Richard Harris Smith, *OSS: The Secret History of America's First Central Intelligence Agency* (New York, 1972), p. 365.

75 Millis, *Forrestal Diaries*, pp. 289–292; Darling, *Central Intelligence Agency*, p. 264.

76 Darling, *Central Intelligence Agency*, pp. 250–256; Karalekas, *History of the CIA*, p. 27.

77 Karalekas, *History of the CIA*, pp. 27–28; Memo of Discussion at 2nd Meeting of the NSC, 14 Nov. 1947, *FRUS: Intelligence Community, 1945–50*: 637–638.

78 *Church Report*, Bk.1, p. 144; Report by the National Security Council on Coordination of Foreign Information Measures, *FRUS: Intelligence Community 1945–50*: 640–642.

79 Darling, *Central Intelligence Agency*, p. 248–250.

80 Corson, *Armies of Ignorance*, pp. 296–297.

Chapter 2

1   CIA Review of the World Situation as it Relates to the Security of the U.S., 12 Feb. 1948, Central Intelligence Reports, folder 1948–1950 (1of 2), box 251, Intelligence File, PSF, Truman Papers, HSTL.

2   Harry Truman to Elizabeth Wallace Truman, 30 Sept. 1947, in Robert H. Ferrell (ed.), *Dear Bess: The Letters from Harry to Bess Truman, 1910–1959* (New York, 1983), pp. 550–551.

3   "The American Paper", (Memo. for the Pentagon Talks of 1947), *FRUS 1947*, Vol.5: 575; NSC 1/2, *FRUS 1948*, Vol.3: 765–769; Jeffreys-Jones, *CIA and American Democracy*, p. 50.

4   Mary McAuliffe address to conference entitled "The Origins and Development of the CIA in the Administration of Harry S Truman", 17 March 1994, p. 7, HSTL.

5   John Lamberton Harper, *America and the Reconstruction of Italy, 1945–1948* (Cambridge, 1986), p. 4.

6   David Hine, *Governing Italy: The Politics of Bargained Pluralism* (Oxford, 1993), pp. 16–24.

7   Harper, *America and the Reconstruction of Italy*, p. 20, pp. 3–4.

8   James E. Miller, *The United States and Italy, 1940–1950: The Politics of Diplomacy and Stabilization* (Chapel Hill and London, 1986), pp. 154–159.

9   James E. Miller, "Taking Off the Gloves: The United States and the Italian Elections of 1948", *Diplomatic History* 6(Winter 1983): 35–55, at 37.

10 Harper, *America and the Reconstruction of Italy*, pp. 88–91, pp. 122–139.

11 Donald L.M. Blackmer, "Continuity and Change in Postwar Italian Communism", in Donald Blackmer and Sidney Tarrow (ed.), *Communism in Italy and France* (New York, 1977), pp. 37–38.

12 Alfonso Passigli, *Patterns of Political Participation in Italy* (New Haven, 1970), p. 110.

13 Ivan M. Lombardo, OH 423, pp. 9–10, HSTL; Ronald L. Filippelli, *American Labor and Postwar Italy: A Study in Cold War Politics* (Palo Alto, California, 1989), pp. 70–71, p. 80.

14 Palmiro Togliatti, *On Gramsci and Other Writings* – edited by Donald Sassoon (London, 1979), pp. 31–32.

15 Joan Barth Urban, *Moscow and the Italian Communist Party: From Togliatti to Berlinguer* (London, 1986), pp. 19–22.

16 Lombardo, OH 423, pp. 10–11, HSTL (Lombardo was a key member of the Italian delegation at the peace treaty negotiations); Secr. of State to Acting Secr. of State, 9 Dec. 1946, *FRUS 1947* Vol.3: 837–843; De Gasperi to Truman, 8 Jan. 1947, *ibid*: 851–852. In January 1947 Saragat founded the Italian Socialist Labour Party (hereafter referred to as the Social Democrats or PSLI). As mentioned in the text, it was at this juncture the Italian Socialist Party of Proletarian Unity (PSIUP) changed its name to the Italian Socialist Party (PSI).

17 Kennan Telegram to US Embassy in Rome, 25 April 1947, *ibid*: 846–847.

18 Marshall's radio announcement, U.S. Department of State, *Department of State Bulletin 1947*, Vol.19 (11 May 1947): 919–924 (hereafter cited as DSB); Lombardo, OH 423, pp. 11–12, HSTL.

19 Central Intelligence Group, ORE 1/1, "Revised Soviet Tactics in International Affairs", 6 January 1947, www.foia cia.gov; Blackmer, "Continuity and Change", pp. 40–45.

20 Urban, *Moscow and the Italian Communist Party*, p. 221.

21 George Elsey, OH 128, Vol.2, pp. 363–364, HSTL.

22 PPS/13, "Resume on the World Situation", 6 Nov. 1947, *FRUS 1947* Vol.1: 771; Harper, *America and the Reconstruction of Italy*, p. 149.

23 Harper, *America and the Reconstruction of Italy*, p. 111.

24 Minutes of the Fifteenth Meeting of the National Advisory Council on International Monetary and Financial Problems, *FRUS 1946*, Vol.5: 894–897.

25 Miller, *US and Italy*, pp. 227–238.

26 PPS/13, "Resume of the World Situation", 6 Nov. 1947, FRUS 1947, Vol.1: 770–777; Memo. from Hillenkoetter to Truman, "Significance of the Establishment of the Communist Information Bureau", 10 October 1947, Memos. for the President and the DCI, 1947 folder (2of 2), box 254, PSF, Truman Papers, HSTL.

27 NSC 1/1, "Concern of the United States for the Safeguarding of the Territorial Integrity and Internal Security of Italy", 14 November 1947, *FRUS 1948*, Vol.3: 724–726.

28 *ibid*; NSC 1/3, "The Position of the United States with Respect to Italy", *FRUS 1948* Vol.3: 775–777.

29 Miller, *US and Italy*, p. 192; Harper, *America and the Reconstruction of Italy*, pp. 151–152.

30 Acting Secr. of State to Secr. of the Army, *FRUS 1948*, Vol.3: 729.

31 Miller, *US and Italy*, pp. 241–242.

32 F. Mark Wyatt interview for CNN Interactive, www.gwu.edu/nsarchiv/coldwar/episode 3/wyatt 2html; Miller, *US and Italy*, pp. 236–237.

33 Miller, *US and Italy*, p. 237, p. 244.

34 Dunn to Marshall, 21 Jan. 1948, *FRUS 1948* Vol.3: 819–822.

35 Dunn to Marshall, 7 Feb. 1948, *ibid*, 827–830.

36 Lombardo, OH 423, pp. 53–54, HSTL.

37 Special Message to the Congress on the Threat to the Freedom of Europe, 17 Mar. 1948, *Truman Public Papers*, 1948, pp. 183–186.

38 CIA, ORE 6–48, "Consequences of Communist Accession to Power by Legal Means", 5 March 1948, www.foia.cia.gov; NSC 1/2, *FRUS 1948*, Vol.3: 765–769.

39 NSC 1/3, *ibid*: 775–777.

40 Department of State to the Embassy of the Soviet Union, 20 March 1948, *FRUS 1948*, Vol.3: 517–518; Secretary of State to Austin, 12 March 1948, *FRUS 1948*, Vol.1: 173.

41 CIA, ORE 23–48, "The Current Situation in the Free Territory of Trieste", 15 April 1948, www.foia.cia.gov; "CIA Review of the World Situation", 12 Feb. 1948, Central Intelligence Reports folder 1948 (1of 2), box 25, Intelligence File, PSF, Truman Papers, HSTL.

42 Miller, Taking "Off the Gloves", 35–55; *DSB*, 21 (28 March 1948): 424.

43 Lombardo, OH 423, pp. 55–56, HSTL.

44 Stephano Luconi, "Anticommunism, Americanization, and Ethnic Identity: Italian Americans and the 1948 Parliamentary Elections in Italy", *Historian* Vol. 62, No.2 (Winter 2000): 285–302.

45 *ibid*.

46 Lombardo, OH 423, pp. 55–56, HSTL; William Blum, *CIA: A Forgotten History: US Global Interventions Since World War II* (London), pp. 25–26, quote on p. 26.

47 CIA, "The Current Situation in Italy", 19 April 1948, United States Declassified Documents Reference System (hereafter cited as DDRS), CDROM Id.: 1975040100041, Fiche No. 1975–54A.

48 See appendix 1, table 2 for details of the 1948 election result.

49 NSC 4/A, 17 Dec. 1947, in Warner, *CIA Cold War Records*, pp. 173–176.

50 Angleton's appointment as head of SSU Italy, entry 108A, RG 226, box 268, NA; Winks, *Cloak and Gown*, pp. 383–386.

51 Tom Mangold, *Cold Warrior, James Jesus Angleton: The CIA's Master Spy Hunter* (New York, 1991), pp. 63–70.

52 Winks, *Cloak and Gown*, p. 372, p. 352.

53 Mangold, *Cold Warrior*, p. 20.

54 Max Corvo, *The OSS in Italy 1942–1945: A Personal Memoir* (New York, Westport Connecticut, and London, 1990), pp. 276–277; Smith, *OSS*, p. 116, p. 98; Naftali, "ARTIFICE", p. 224.

55 Naftali, "ARTIFICE", pp. 224–230.

56 *ibid*, pp. 220–227.

57 Winks, *Cloak and Gown*, p. 372, p. 380.

58 Anthony Cave Brown, *Treason in the Blood: H. St. John Philby, Kim Philby, and the Spy Case of the Century* (London, 1995), pp. 353–356.

59 Michael Goldsmith, "High Duce Aide Found in Hiding", *Washington Post*, 19 Jan. 1947, HSTL.

60 Federico Romero, *The United States and the European Trade Union Movement, 1944–1951* – translated by Harvey Fergusson II (Chapel Hill and London, 1992), pp. 13–14; Filippelli, *American Labor and Postwar Italy*, p. 36.

61 Romero, *US and the European Trade Union Movement*, pp. 14–15.

62 Filippelli, *American Labor and Postwar Italy*, p. 38–40, p. 65.

63 Romero, *US and the European Trade Union Movement*, pp. 50–51.

64 Mangold, *Cold Warrior*, pp. 16–17; Hersh, *The Old Boys*, p. 239; quote from Sayer and Botting, *The CIC*, p. 318.

65 William Clayton to Henry White, *FRUS 1946* Vol.5: 894–897.

66 Filippelli, *American Labor and Postwar Italy*, pp. 71–73.

67 Winks, *Cloak and Gown*, pp. 328–330.

68 Wyatt, CNN interview, www.gwu.edu/nsarchiv/coldwar/episode 3/wyatt 2html.

69 *ibid.*.

70 Winks, *Cloak and Gown*, pp. 328–330.

71 *ibid*, p. 373; Peter Wright with Paul Greengrass, *Spy Catcher: The Candid Autobiography of a Senior Intelligence Officer* (Richmond, Victoria, 1987), p. 104.

72 Memo. for the President, the Secretary of State, and the Secretary of Defense, "Clandestine Air Transport Operations in Europe", 12 Apr. 1948 NSC-CIA Memos., 1948–1950 folder, box 3, CIA File, Records of the NSC, Truman Papers, HSTL.

73 Hersh, *The Old Boys*, p. 293.

74 Office of Special Operations Directive No.18/5, 29 March 1948, *FRUS: Intelligence Community, 1945–50*: 655–661; Darling, *Central Intelligence Agency*, pp. 262–265.

75 Winks, *Cloak and Gown*, pp. 383–384; Deborah Larson, address to conference entitled "The Origins and Development of the CIA in the Administration of Harry S. Truman", 17 Mar. 1994, p. 23, HSTL.

76 *Church Report*, Bk.1, p. 107.

77 Corson, *Armies of Ignorance*, pp. 298–299.

78 *ibid.*

79 American Ambassador to Secretary of State, "For Bohlen from Page" (Top Secret), 12 March 1948, 865.00/3–1248, Diplomatic Branch, RG 59, NA; Director of European Affairs to Undersecretary of State, 3 March 1948, 865.00/3–348, RG 59, NA.

80 Wyatt, CNN interview, www.gwu.edu/nsarchiv/coldwar/episode 3/wyatt 2html.

81 Sallie Pisani, *The CIA and the Marshall Plan* (Kansas, 1991), pp. 41–50.

82 *ibid*; Simpson, *Blowback*, pp. 89–90; Peter Grose, *Gentleman Spy: The Life of Allen Dulles* (Boston and New York, 1994), pp. 284–285.

83 American Ambassador to Secretary of State, 30 January 1948, 865.00/1–30488, RG 59, NA.

84 American Ambassador to Secretary of State, 7 February 1948, *FRUS 1948*, Vol.3: 827–830.

85 Corson, *Armies of Ignorance*, pp. 299–300.

86 *ibid*, p. 298; Pendergast quote in Robert H, Ferrell, *Harry S. Truman: A Life* (Columbia, Missouri, 1994), p. 92; Christopher Andrew, *For the President's Eyes Only: Secret Intelligence and the American Presidency from Washington to Bush* (London, 1995), p. 172.

87 Colby and Forbath, *Honourable Men*, p. 116.

88 Corson, *Armies of Ignorance*, p. 298.

89 Powers, *Man Who Kept the Secrets*, p. 30.

90 Colby and Forbath, *Honourable Men*, p. 118.

91 Corson, *Armies of Ignorance*, p. 298.

92 Powers, *Man Who Kept the Secrets*, p. 30; Leffler, *Preponderance of Power*, p. 237.

93 Colby and Forbath, *Honourable Men*, p. 116.

94 Wyatt, CNN interview, www.gwu.edu/nsarchiv/coldwar/episode 3/wyatt 2html; Dunn to Dept. of State, *FRUS 1948*, Vol.3: 868–870.

95 Blum, *CIA: A Forgotten History*, p. 25.

96 Corson, *Armies of Ignorance*, p. 298.

97 *FRUS 1948*, Vol.3: 868–870.

98 E. Timothy Smith, *The United States, Italy, and NATO, 1947–1952* (New York, 1991), p. 35.

99 Blum, *CIA: A Forgotten History*, p. 27.

100 Lombardo, OH 423, p. 56, HSTL.

101 Andrew, *For the President's Eyes Only*, p. 172; Miles Copeland quoted in Jeffreys-Jones, *CIA and American Democracy*, p. 52.

102 Barrett McBurn, "Tough Welding Job Facing De Gasperi", *Washington Post*, 18 April 1948.

103 Wyatt, CNN interview, www.gwu.edu/nsarchiv/coldwar/episode 3/wyatt 2html.

104 Blum, *CIA: A Forgotten History*, p. 30.

105 Corson, *Armies of Ignorance*, p. 300.

106 Douglas Porch, *The French Secret Services: From the Dreyfus Affair to the Gulf War* (New York, 1995), pp. 282–285; Milovan Djilas, *Conversations with Stalin* (New York, 1962), pp. 181–182, quote on p. 182.

107 Hugh Tovar, B., "Strengths and Weaknesses in Past Covert Action", in Roy Godson, (ed.), *Elements in Intelligence* (Washington D.C., 1981), pp. 71–89, at 73.

108 CIA, "The Current Situation in the Mediterranean and the Near East", 17 Oct. 1947, Intelligence folder 1947 (2of 2), box 254, PSF, Truman Papers, HSTL.

109 Jeffreys-Jones, *CIA and American Democracy*, p. 50.

110 George McGhee, Memo. for McGeorge Bundy, "Counter-Guerrilla Campaigns in Greece, Malaya, and the Philippines", 21 Nov. 1961, Rostow 10/61–11/61 folder, box 326, Meetings and Memoranda, National Security Files (hereafter cited as NSF), John F. Kennedy Library, Boston, Mass., (hereafter cited as JFKL).

111 John Magruder, Memo. for Maj. Gen. S. Leroy Irwin, "Assets of the SSU for Peacetime Intelligence Procurement", 15 Jan. 1946, in Warner, *CIA Cold War Records*, p. 23.

112 McGhee to Bundy, "Counter-Guerrilla Campaigns", NSF, JFKL.

113 PPS/23, "Review of Current Trends in U.S. Foreign Policy", 24 Feb. 1948, *FRUS 1948*, Vol.1 (part 2): 509–529.
114 McGhee to Bundy, "Counter-Guerrilla Campaigns", NSF, JFKL.
115 Jeffreys-Jones, *CIA and American Democracy*, p. 50.
116 CIA General Order No.10, 27 August 1948, *FRUS: Intelligence Community 1945–50*: 724.

Chapter 3

1   NSC 10/2, *FRUS: Intelligence Community,1945–50*: 713–715.
2   *Church Report*, Bk.1, p. 107.
3   *ibid*; the congressional oversight committees that were responsible for the CIA were fully cognisant of the huge growth of the agency's covert action budget that took place between 1948 and 1953 and were supportive of this expansion, see Barrett, *The CIA and Congress*.
4   Rositzke, "America's Secret Operations", 335–336.
5   Robert Lee Wolff, *The Balkans in Our Time* (Cambridge, Mass., 1956), p. 289.
6   Harry Rositzke, *The CIA's Secret Operations: Espionage, Counterespionage, and Covert Action* (New York, 1977), p. 173.
7   Truman quoted in John Ranelagh, *The Agency: The Rise and Decline of the CIA* (London, 1986), p. 118.
8   Dept. of State, Office of Intelligence Research (hereafter cited as OIR) No.4998, "Soviet Internal Situation", 1 July 1949, folder 10, box 256, PSF, Truman Papers, HSTL.
9   CIA, "The Strategic Value to the USSR of the Conquest of Western Europe and the Near East (to Cairo) Prior to 1950", 30 July 1948, folder 10, box 256, PSF, Truman Papers, HSTL.
10   Ambassador to the Soviet Union, Smith, to the PPS, *FRUS 1948*, Vol.2: 1195–1197
11   "Report Prepared by PPS Concerning Western Union and Related Problems", *FRUS 1948*, Vol.3: 61–64; Truman to Congress, 25 July 1949, Truman Papers, White House Central Files, Official File, in Dennis Merrill (ed.), *Documentary History of the Truman Presidency*, Volume 17 (Washington D.C., 1997): 99–103; Timothy P. Ireland, *Creating the Entangling Alliance: The Origins of the North Atlantic Treaty Organisation* (Westport, Conn., 1981); Crockatt, *The Fifty Years War*, pp. 81–82.
12   Ireland, *Creating the Entangling Alliance*; Crockatt, *The Fifty Years War*, p. 82.
13   John Lewis Gaddis, *We Now Know: Rethinking Cold War History* (New York, 1997), p. 50.
14   NSC 68, *FRUS 1950* Vol.1: 243–245, 237–240.
15   Memorandum by the National Security Resources Board, "Comments on the NSC 68 Programs", 29 May 1950, *FRUS 1950* Vol. 1: 316–321.
16   President's Economic Report 1950, *Truman Public Papers*, 1950, 18–30.
17   Gaddis, *Strategies of Containment*, pp. 88–125.
18   Iwan W. Morgan, *Eisenhower versus "the Spenders": The Eisenhower Administration, the Democrats, and the Budget, 1953–60* (New York, 1990), p. 50.
19   Leffler, *Preponderance of Power*, pp. 446–463.

20 Notes on Meeting in JCS Conference Room, Pentagon, 1 Dec. 1950, Papers of Dean Acheson, in Merrill, *Truman Presidency Documents*, Vol.19: 104–111; Crockatt, The Fifty Years War, pp. 104–107; William W. Stueck, *The Korean War: An International History* (Princeton, 1995), pp. 338–353.

21 Richard M. Fried, *Nightmare in Red: The McCarthy Era in Perspective* (New York, 1990).

22 Crockatt, *The Fifty Years War*, pp. 94–95; NSC 68, *FRUS 1950*, Vol.1: 252–253.

23 The SPG devised plans, under the code-name of Project Ultimate, to penetrate the Iron Curtain using high-level balloons, see Memo from DCI Hillenkoetter to Chief of Naval Operations, Denfield, 18 June 1948, *FRUS: Intelligence Community 1945–50*: 715; Memo from Commander Robert Jay Williams to Chief of SPG (Cassady), 23 July 1948, *ibid*: 718. For the OPC's continuation of SPG's Project Umpire plan to broadcast radio propaganda into Eastern Europe and the Soviet Union see Memo. from Assistant Director of Policy Coordination (Wisner) to DCI Hillenkoetter, 29 October 1948, *ibid*: 731.

24 National Security Council Directive on Office of Special Projects, NSC 10/2, 18 June 1948, *FRUS: Intelligence Community, 1945–50*: 713–715.

25 Darling, *Central Intelligence Agency*, pp. 263–268.

26 *ibid.*

27 Jeffreys-Jones, *CIA and American Democracy*, p. 53.

28 Stephen J. Spingarn, Lt. Colonel, MI Reserve, "A Basic Program for the Revitalization of the National Defense Establishment Organization (and its Lower Echelons) Relating to Overseas Counter Intelligence in Time of War and for the Correction of Serious Defiencies in this Organization as Demonstrated by World War II", C.I. Program and Resolution, Addenum of 16 April 1948, (1of 3), box 1, Spingarn Papers, HSTL.

29 Thomas, *The Very Best Men*, p. 29.

30 Wolff, *The Balkans in Our Time*, p. 289; Mark, "The War Scare of 1946", 383–41; Dennis Deletant, "The Securitate and the Police State in Romania, 1948–64", *Intelligence and National Security*, Vol. 8, No.4 (1993): 1–25.

31 Hersh, *The Old Boys*, p. 224.

32 NSC 10/2, *FRUS: Intelligence Community, 1945–50*: 713–715.

33 NSC 20/4, "U.S. Objectives with Respect to the USSR to Counter Soviet Threats to U.S. Security", NSC Meetings Folder, Number 27, 23 November 1948, PSF-NSC Meetings 14–27, Box 204, HSTL.

34 Hersh, *The Old Boys*, pp. 194–216.

35 Darling, *Central Intelligence Agency*, pp. 262–273; quotes from NSC 10/2, *FRUS: Intelligence Community*: 713, 714.

36 Pisani, *The CIA and the Marshall Plan*, pp. 41–50.

37 *ibid*, p. 64.

38 *ibid*, pp. 47–50.

39 W. Scott Lucas, *Freedom's War: The US Crusade Against the Soviet Union, 1945–56* (Manchester, 1999), pp. 108–109.

40 *Church Report*, Bk.1, p. 107.

41   Richard M. Bissell, Jr., with Jonathan Lewis and Frances T. Pudlo, *Reflections of a Cold War: From Yalta to the Bay of Pigs* (New Haven and London, 1996), p. 68.

42   Finance Division to Executive, OPC [Wisner], "CIA Responsibility and Accountability for ECA Counterpart Funds Expended by OPC", 17 October 1949, in Warner, *CIA Cold War Records*, pp. 321–322.

43   Bissell, *Reflections of a Cold Warrior*, pp. 68–69.

44   Thomas, *The Very Best Men*, pp. 40–41; quote by Kermit Roosevelt in Pisani, *The CIA and the Marshall Plan*, p. 75.

45   Frank G. Wisner, Memo for the DCI, "OPC Projects", 29 October 1949, *FRUS: Intelligence Community, 1945–50*: 730–731; Warner, *CIA Cold War Records*, pp. 241–242.

46   For a very good in-house overview of the CIA's analysis of the Russian economy from the early 1950s onwards, see James Noren, "CIA's Analysis of the Soviet Economy", in Gerald K. Haines, and Robert E. Leggett, *Watching the Bear: Essays on the CIA's Analysis of the Soviet Union*, Center for the Study of Intelligence, www.cia.gov/csi/books. The most instructive secondary source on the subject is Egil Forland, *Cold Economic Warfare: The Creation and Prime of CoCom, 1948–1954* (Oslo, 1991).

47   Project TROY file, General Records of the Department of State, Records of the S/P 1947–1953, Box 33, RG 59, NA; the stress that the OPC placed on "the use of foreign agents and indigenous personnel" for its projects is outlined in Charles V. Hulick, Memo. for the Record "Policy Guidance", 19 April 1950, in Warner, *CIA Cold War Records*, pp. 323–324.

48   Wisner, "OPC Projects", 29 October 1949, *FRUS: Intelligence Community*: 730–731.

49   Pisani, *The CIA and the Marshall Plan*, p. 68, pp. 72–73; quote from NSC 10/2, *FRUS Intelligence Community, 1945–50*: 714.

50   This policy first came into effect with the Commerce Department's introduction of two new export licencing regulations, on 31 Dec. 1947 and 15 Jan. 1948, under remaining wartime export control laws. It was later extended with the passage of the Export Control Act of 28 Feb. 1949 – reprinted in Gunnar Adler-Karlsson, with forward by Gunnar Myrdal, *Western Economic Warfare 1947–1967: A Case Study in Foreign Economic Policy* (Stockholm, 1968), pp. 217–219 – and was implemented most rigidly through the Mutual Defense Assistance Control Act (more commonly known as the Battle Act) of 1951. The Eisenhower administration moderated this policy under British pressure but left the essentials in place, see Robert Spaulding Jr., "A Graduate and Moderate Relaxation: Eisenhower and the Revision of the American Export Control Policy, 1953–1955", *Diplomatic History*, Vol.17, No.2 (Spring 1993): 223–250.

51   PSB D-45, 29 July 1953, "Report to the Psychological Strategy Board", p. 7, box 6, PSB Working Files, 1951–1953, RG 59, NA; Adler-Karlsson, pp. 1–28.

52   Adler-Karlsson, *Western Economic Warfare*, pp. 6–7, p. 192.

53   David E. Murphy, Segei A. Kondrashev, and George Bailey, *Battleground Berlin: CIA vs. KGB in the Cold War* (New Haven and London, 1997), pp. 11–12.

54   *ibid*, pp. 12–14.

55   Quote from Forrestal meeting with Bernard Baruch, 15 July 1947, in Millis (ed.) *Forrestal Diaries*, pp. 383–384; Adler-Karlsson, *Western Economic Warfare*, pp. 2–7.

56   Wisner to DCI, "OPC Projects", *FRUS: Intelligence Community, 1945–50*: 730.

57   PSB D-31, 5 Aug. 1952, "A Strategic Concept for a National Psychological Program with Reference to Cold War Operations under NSC 10/5", box 5, PSB Working Files, 1951–1953, RG 59, NA; NSC 174, "United States Policy Toward the Soviet Satellites in Eastern Europe", 11 December 1953, DDRS, CDROM Id.: 1999010100429, Fiche No. 1999-42.

58   The wider OPC/DDP enterprise, of which the counterfeiting measures were part was code-named Operation Marshmallow, see Lucas, *Freedom's War*, p. 151, p. 162, note 154.

59   Bissell, *Reflections of a Cold Warrior*, pp. 208–209.

60   Lawrence Houston interview in Ranelagh, *The Agency*, pp. 217–218.

61   Quote from Lawrence Houston in Pisani, *The CIA and the Marshall Plan*, p. 144.

62   William M. Leary, *Perilous Missions: Civil Air Transport and CIA Operations in Asia* (Birmingham, Alabama, 1984).

63   For detailed and perceptive analyses of MI6 see Stephen Dorril, *MI6: Fifty Years of Special Operations* (London, 2000) and Richard J. Aldrich, *Hidden Hand: Britain, America and Cold War Secret Intelligence* (London, 2001).

64   *War Report of the OSS (Office of Strategic Services)*, Prepared by History Project, Strategic Service Unit, Office of the Assistant Secretary of War, War Department, Washington D.C., 5 September 1947, new introduction by Kermit Roosevelt (New York, 1976), pp. 193–205.

65   Nicholas Bethell, *The Great Betrayal: The Untold Story of Kim Philby's Biggest Coup* (New York, 1984), pp. 33–39.

66   Winks, *Cloak and Gown*, pp. 398–402; Christopher M. Woodhouse, *Something Ventured* (London, 1982), pp. 110–135.

67   Kim Philby, *My Silent War* (London, 1969), p. 142; Winks, *Cloak and Gown*, pp. 396–397.

68   Dorril, *MI6*, pp. 268–299.

69   Prados, *Presidents' Secret Wars*, p. 41.

70   The CIA's in-house history of the American government's relationship with Reinhard Gehlen and his organisation was declassified in 2002, see Kevin C. Ruffner (ed.), *Forging an Intelligence Partnership: The CIA and the Origins of the BND, 1945–49* (Center for the Study of Intelligence, Washington D.C., 1999). It is available at the National Security Archive, George Washington University website at www.gwu.edu/~nsarchiv/ NSAEBB/NSAEDD146.

71   Prados, *Presidents' Secret Wars*, pp. 41–42.

72   PPS/22, "Utilization of Refugees from the Soviet Union in U.S. National Interest", 5 February 1948, in Anna Kasten Nelson, (ed.) *The State Department Policy Planning Staff Papers, 1947–1949* (New York, 1983), pp. 88–90. Preparatory measures for fighting behind Soviet lines were not restricted to the Eastern bloc. The CIA and MI6 are said to have worked in concert with the military arm of NATO – the Supreme Headquarters Allied Powers Europe (SHAPE) – to establish stay-behind networks throughout most

of Western Europe. The existence of such provisions had been rumoured for years prior to Italian Prime Minister Giulio Andreotti's 1990 disclosure of the existence of the GLADIO network, which he alleged had been established in Italy in 1956. Many, though not all, of GLADIO's sister organisations were similarly named after the Roman double-edged sword – the French network, for instance, operated under the tag of GLAIVE but its British counterpart was named 'stay-behind'. The operating procedures of these organisations are said to have varied quite significantly, though all allegedly coordinated their efforts through two NATO-linked instrumentalities – the Allied Clandestine Committee (ACC) and the Clandestine Planning Committee (CPC), see Ganser Daniele, *NATO's Secret Armies: Operation Gladio and Terrorism in Western Europe* (London and New York, 2004).

73 Hersh, *The Old Boys*, pp. 224–229; Christopher Simpson, *Blowback: America's Recruitment of Nazis and Its Effects on the Cold War* (New York, 1988), pp. 96–106.

74 John Loftus, *The Belarus Secret* (New York, 1982); Simpson, *Blowback*, pp. 18–21.

75 Thomas, *The Very Best Men*, p. 32.

76 *ibid*, p 35.

77 Central Intelligence Agency Act of 1949, 20 June 1949, in Warner, *CIA Cold War Records*, pp. 287–294 (immigration clause on p. 292).

78 Simpson, *Blowback*, pp. 112–115.

79 [Gustav Hilger], "Observations on the Communist 'Peace Offensive'", 21 Jan. 1949, in Warner, *CIA Cold War Records*, pp. 243–246; Hersh, *The Old Boys*, p. 251, pp. 277–278; Simpson, *Blowback*, pp. 252–262; Wilson D. Miscamble, *George F. Kennan and the Making of American Foreign Policy* (Princeton, 1992), pp. 183–184; Nicholas Poppe, *Reminiscences*, edited by Henry Schwartz (Washington D.C., 1983).

80 Ruffner, *Forging an Intelligence Partnership*, Vol. 1, parts 2 and 3, Vol. 2, part 4, document 57, www.gwu.edu/~nsarchiv.

81 *ibid*, Vol. 1 part 1; Reinhard Gehlen, *The Service* (New York, 1972), pp. 106–143; Mary Ellen Reese, *General Reinhard Gehlen: The CIA Connection* (Fairfax, Va, 1990), pp. 47–48, pp. 106–108; Hersh, *The Old Boys*, p. 268; Prados, *Presidents' Secret Wars*, pp. 40–41.

82 Sarah-Jane Cork, *US Covert Operations and Cold War Strategy: Truman, Secret Warfare and the CIA, 1945–53* (New York, 2007); Ranelagh, *The Agency*, pp. 149–228; Prados, *Presidents' Secret Wars*, pp. 30–90; Hersh, *The Old Boys*, pp. 240–311; Thomas, *The Very Best Men*, pp. 32–86.

83 Christopher Andrew and Oleg Gordievsky, *KGB: The Inside Story of Its Foreign Operations from Lenin to Gorbachev* (London, 1990).

84 Robert Service, *A History of Twentieth Century Russia* (London, 1997), pp. 297–300.

85 Prados, *Presidents' Secret Wars*, p. 39.

86 *ibid*, pp. 41–44, pp. 53–57.

87 Cave Brown, *Treason in the Blood*, pp. 391–438; Ruffner, *Forging an Intelligence Partnership* www.gwu.edu/~nsarchiv; Markus Wolf, with Ann McElvoy, *Man Without a Face: The Autobiography of Communism's Greatest Spymaster* (London, 1997), p. 51.

88 Prados, *Presidents' Secret Wars*, p. 58.

89 Powers, *Man Who Kept the Secrets*, p. 41.

90 Rositzke, *The CIA's Secret Operations*, p. 171; Andrew and Gordievsky, *KGB*, p. 320.

91 CIA, Intelligence Memo. No.250, "Potentialities for Anti-Soviet Underground Resistance in the Event of War in 1950", 5 April 1950, www.foia.cia.gov; Prados, *Presidents' Secret Wars*, p. 43.

92 Murphy, Kondrashev, and Bailey, *Battleground Berlin*, pp. 113–115; Mitrovich, *Undermining the Kremlin*, pp. 78–79.

93 Murphy, Kondrashev, and Bailey, *Battleground Berlin*, pp. 123–126, pp. 106–107.

94 Prados, *Presidents' Secret Wars*, pp. 55–56; Peter Grose, *Operation Rollback: America's Secret War Behind the Iron Curtain* (New York, 2000), pp. 184–185.

95 George R. Urban, *Radio Free Europe and the Pursuit of Democracy: My War Within the Cold War* (New Haven and London, 1997); Sig Mickelson, *America's Other Voice: The Story of Radio Free Europe and Radio Liberty* (New York, 1983); Cord Meyer, *Facing Reality: From World Federation to the CIA* (New York, 1980), pp. 110–112.

96 Michael Warner "The Origins of the Congress of Cultural Freedom, 1949–50", *Studies in Intelligence* Volume 38, Number 5 (1995 Edition), www.cia.gov/csi/studies/95 unclass/ Warner.html.

97 Frances Stonor Saunders, *Who Paid the Piper? The CIA and the Cultural Cold War* (London, 1999), pp. 58–60; Lucas, *Freedom's War*, pp. 107–109, p. 130.

98 Lucas, *Freedom's War*, pp. 109–111; Warner, "Congress of Cultural Freedom"; Saunders, *Who Paid the Piper*, pp. 381–384; for a detailed and interesting recounting of the animated production of *Animal Farm* and the OPC's role as the 'sponsoring agency' for the film, see Daniel J. Leab, *Orwell Subverted: the CIA and the filming of Animal Farm* (Pennsylvania State University, 2007).

99 Lucas, *Freedom's War*, pp. 93–104, p. 109; Pisani, *The CIA and the Marshall Plan*, pp. 47–53; Saunders, *Who Paid the Piper*, pp. 125–127.

100 Saunders, *Who Paid the Piper*; Hugh Wilford, *The Mighty Wurlitzer: How the CIA Played America* (Cambridge, Mass., 2007).

101 Saunders, *Who Paid the Piper*, pp. 195–215; Wilford, *The Mighty Wurlitzer*, pp. 210–212.

102 Wisner, Memorandum for Deputy Assistant Director for Policy Coordination, "Reported Crisis in the American Committee for Cultural Freedom", 7 April 1952, in Warner, *CIA Cold War Records*, pp. 455–456.

103 Saunders, *Who Paid the Piper*, p. 204.

104 Peregrine Worsthrone, "How Western Culture was Saved by the CIA", *Literary Review* http://www.users.dircon.co.uk/litrev/reviews/1999/07/Worsthorne_on_Saunders.

105 Warner, "Congress of Cultural Freedom".

106 *Church Report,* Bk.1, p. 23.

107 Karalekas, *History of the CIA*, pp. 35–36.

108 Michael E. Haas, *In the Devil's Shadow: UN Special Operations During the Korean War* (Annapolis, 2000), pp. 11–13, p. 35.

109 *ibid*, pp. 14–77.

110 *ibid*, pp. 172–206.

111 Montague, *Smith-DCI*, p. 208.

112 Copeland, *Game Player*, p. 124; Grose, *Gentleman Spy*, p. 322.

113 Karalekas, *History of the CIA*, p. 36.

114 Edward G. Lansdale, *In the Midst of Wars: An American's Mission to Southeast Asia* (New York, 1972), pp. 49–88; Douglas Blaufarb, *The Counterinsurgency Era: U.S. Doctrine and Performance, 1950 to the Present* (New York, 1977), pp. 20–32, 38; H.W. Brands, *Bound to Empire: The United States and the Philippines* (New York and Oxford, 1992), pp. 227–265; Michael McClintock, *Instruments of Statecraft: U.S. Guerrilla Warfare, Counterinsurgency, and Counterterrorism, 1940–1990* (New York, 1992), pp. 106–114.

115 Brands, *Bound to Empire*, pp. 39–59.

116 CIA, "The Current Situation in the Philippines", 30 March 1949, Central Intelligence Agency Reports, folder 1948–1950, (2 of 2), box 251, Intelligence File, PSF, Truman Papers, HSTL.

117 Council Meeting of the Southeast Asia Collective Defense Treaty, 23–25 Feb. 1955, "The Philippine Experience in the Combatting of Communist Subversion", MP (C) (55) D-3/1/Final text, www.icdc.com/~paulwolf/colombia/counterinsurgency.

118 Thomas, *The Very Best Men*, pp. 50–59, quote on p. 56; James Lilley, *China Hands: Nine Decades of Adventure, Espionage, and Diplomacy in Asia* (New York, 2004), pp. 78–83.

119 Frank Holober, *Raiders of the China Coast: CIA Covert Operations during the Korean War* (Annapolis, 1999).

120 *ibid*, pp. 171–194.

121 Major D. H. Berger, USMC, "The Use of Covert Military Activity as a Policy Tool: An Analysis of Operations Conducted by the United States Central Intelligence Agency, 1949–1951", www.globalsecurity.org/intell/library/reports/1995/BDH.htm.

122 William M. Leary "Robert Fulton's Skyhook and Operation Cold Feet: A Good Pick Me-Up", *Studies in Intelligence* Vol. 38, No. 5 (1995), www.cia.gov/csi/studies/95.

123 Lilley, *China Hands*, pp. 78–83.

124 The institutional growth of the CIA and the intelligence community as a whole during Smith's directorship is documented in *FRUS: Intelligence Community, 1950–1955*; Montague, *Smith-DCI*, xvii.

125 Report From the Intelligence Survey Group to the National Security Council, "The Central Intelligence Organization and the National Organization for Intelligence", 1 Jan. 1949, *FRUS: Intelligence Community, 1945–50*: 903–911; National Security Council, NSC 50, 1 July 1949, in Warner, *CIA Cold War Records*, pp. 295–314.

126 Montague, *Smith-DCI*, pp. 55–56, pp. 6–7.

127 Jeffreys-Jones, *CIA and American Democracy*, pp. 65–75.

128 Copeland, *Game Player*, p. 124; Smith quoted in Jeffreys-Jones, *CIA and American Democracy*, p. 66.

129 Montague, *Smith-DCI*, p. 204.

130 Karalekas, *History of the CIA*, p. 37; Memo. from DCI Smith to the Executive Secretary of the NSC (Lay), "Draft of NSC Directive on Covert Operations and Clandestine Activities", 8 Jan. 1951, *FRUS: Intelligence Community, 1950–55*: 69–71.

131 Mitrovich, *Undermining the Kremlin*, pp. 59–61; W. Scott Lucas, "Campaigns of Truth: The Psychological Strategy Board and American Ideology, 1951–1953", *International History Review* (May 1996): 279–302, at 288.

132 Lucas, "Campaigns of Truth", 288–289, quote on 289.

133 *ibid*, 289–302; Mitrovich, *Undermining the Kremlin*, pp. 61–64, p. 125.

134 Karalekas, *History of the CIA*, p. 35.

135 *Church Report*, Bk.1, p. 107; Grose, *Gentleman Spy*, p. 327.

136 Montague, *Smith-DCI*, pp. 232–234.

137 *Church Report*, Bk.1, pp. 103–108; Montague, *Smith-DCI*, pp. 232–234.

138 *Church Report*, Bk.1, pp. 107–108; Grose, *Gentleman Spy*, p. 323.

139 Minutes of a Meeting of the Intelligence Advisory Committee, 20 October 1950, *FRUS: Intelligence Community, 1950–55*: 48; Montague, *Smith-DCI*, pp. 217–227.

140 Karalekas, *History of the CIA*, p. 38; for a first-hand account of Helms's CIA career see Richard Helms, *A Look Over My Shoulder* (New York, 2003); Colby and Forbath, *Honourable Men*, p. 100; Copeland, *Game Player*, pp. 137–138.

Chapter 4

1   The code-name BGFIEND is revealed in Thomas, *The Very Best Men*, p. 38; quote from Anthony Verrier, *Through the Looking Glass: British Foreign Policy in an Age of Illusions* (London, 1983), p. 76; Rositzke, *The CIA's Secret Operations*, p. 173.

2   Quote from Winks, *Cloak and Gown*, p. 399.

3   Of the primary works dealing with the Albania operation Philby, *My Silent War*, is illuminating if only because it gives an inside view of the working relationship between MI6 and the CIA, and of how these organisations regarded their *Albanian* charges. It needs to be treated with caution, however, given Philby's interest in justifying his motives and the possibility that he may have been using the book as a vehicle to spread disinformation and sow discord both within and between the British and American intelligence services. David Smiley, *Albanian Assignment* (London, 1984), pp. 159–164, provides an alternative first-hand insight into the British contribution to the venture. Smiley was a veteran of the SOE who trained Albanian émigrés during the early stages of the campaign. Michael Burke, *Outrageous Good Fortune* (Boston, 1984), pp. 139–169, looks at the enterprise from an American perspective. Like Smiley, Burke had wartime experience in the field of paramilitary action, in his case with the OSS. An early recruit to the OPC, he was given responsibility for organising offensive operations against the Soviet bloc generally, and was one of those charged with training Albanian volunteers for BGFIEND. The fullest secondary treatment of the Albanian campaign is Bethell, *The Great Betrayal*, which lays much of the blame for the failure of the operation at Philby's door, as does Bruce Page, David Leitch, and Phillip Knightley, *Philby: The Spy Who Betrayed a Generation* (London, 1977), pp. 217–221. Ranelagh deals with the enterprise briefly in *The Agency*, p. 150, pp. 156–157, as does Christopher Andrew in *Secret Service: The Making of the British Intelligence Community* (London, 1985), pp. 492–493, and several other works provide good accounts of the essentials of the operation. These

include Verrier, *Through the Looking Glass*, pp. 71–77, Prados, *Presidents' Secret Wars*, pp. 45–51, Anton Logoreci, *The Albanians: Europe's forgotten survivors* (London, 1977), pp. 105–110, and Winks, *Cloak and Gown*, pp. 394–401, which gives an excellent analysis of the American side of the operation. These studies tend towards the view that Philby's treachery was only one element in a plan that was destined to fail anyway, a standpoint that is given further weight as a result of information and insights which emerged later with the publication of Hersh, *The Old Boys*, pp. 261–266, pp. 269–274, pp. 319–323, Thomas, *The Very Best Men*, pp. 38–40, p. 68–71, p. 85, Michael Dravis, "Storming Fortress Albania: American Covert Operations in Microcosm, 1949–1954", *Intelligence and National Security*, Vol. 7, No.4 (1992): 425–442, and Aldrich, *The Hidden Hand*, pp. 160–166.

4 CIA, Intelligence Memo. 218, "Strengths and Weaknesses of the Hoxha Regime in Albania", 12 Sept. 1949, Intelligence Memos. 1949 folder, box 250, Central Intelligence File, PSF, Truman Papers, HSTL.

5 CIA, Special Evaluation No.24, "Prospects for Soviet/Satellite Support for the 'Free' Greek Government", Special Evaluations folder, box 250, CIA File, NSC Records, Truman Papers, HSTL; Department of State Policy Paper on Albania, 21 Sept. 1949, *FRUS 1949*, Vol. 5: 320–322.

6 CIA, Memo. 218, "Strengths and Weaknesses of the Hoxha Regime".

7 *ibid*, CIA, ORE 71–49, "Current Situation in Albania", 15 Dec. 1949, ORE 1949 folder, box 257, Intelligence File, PSF, Truman Papers, HSTL.

8 CIA, Memo. 218, "Strengths and Weaknesses of the Hoxha Regime".

9 Memo. of Conversation by Deputy Director, Office of European Affairs (Thompson) 28 June 1949, *FRUS 1949*, Vol.5: 305–307, quote on 306.

10 *ibid*, quote on 305–306.

11 Hillenkoetter Memo., 25 Oct. 1949, Intelligence Memos. 1949 folder, box 250, Central Intelligence File, PSF, Truman Papers, HSTL.

12 CIA, ORE 71–49, "Current Situation in Albania".

13 CIA, "Satellite Relations with the USSR and the West", 7 Nov. 1949, www.foia.cia.gov.

14 Policy Paper Prepared by Acting Chief of Division of Southeast European Affairs (Campbell), 12 Sept. 1949, *FRUS 1949*, Vol.5: 311–313, quote on 313.

15 John C. Campbell, OH 284, pp. 206–207, HSTL.

16 *ibid*, p. 206.

17 Hersh, *The Old Boys*, pp. 182–183, quote on p. 182.

18 CIA, Intelligence Memo. 232, "Significance of Recent Intensified Soviet Action Against Tito", 5 Oct. 1949, Intelligence Memos. 1949 folder, box 250, PSF, HSTL; CIA, Memo. 218, "Strengths and Weaknesses of the Hoxha Regime"; CIA, ORE 44–49, "Estimate of Yugoslav Regime's Ability to Resist Soviet Pressure", ORE 1948–1949 folder, Intelligence File, PSF, Truman Papers, HSTL.

19 CIA, ORE 71–49, "Current Situation in Albania".

20 Stefanaq Pollo and Arben Puto, *The History of Albania from Its Origins to the Present Day* (London, 1981), p. 265, cited in Winks, *Cloak and Gown*, p. 545.

21 Frank Lindsay, *Beacons in the Night: With the OSS and Tito's Partisans in Wartime Yugoslavia* (Palo Alto, Calif., 1994), p. 334.

22 Department of State Policy Paper on Albania, 21 Sept. 1949, *FRUS 1949*, Vol. 5: 320–322; CIA, Intelligence Memo. 218, "Strengths and Weaknesses of the Hoxha Regime".

23 The Yugoslavs seized the province of Kosovo at the end of World War II and had ambitions to take additional areas of northern Albania, see Logoreci, *The Albanians*, pp. 84–103. The Greeks had laid claim to the Albanian region of northern Epirus. Washington wished to see existing frontiers in the Balkans respected, favouring moves to consider the Greek claim through "an appropriate international body at a later time", Department of State Policy Paper on Albania, 21 Sept. 1949, *FRUS 1949*, Vol. 5: 320–322, quote on 322. For a further appraisal of how Washington saw wider regional factors as impacting on Albania, see CIA, "Current Situation in Albania With Particular Reference to Greek, Yugoslav and Italian Interests", DDRS, CDROM Id.: 1990090102404, Fiche No. 1990–164.

24 Bethell, *The Great Betrayal*, pp. 35–39; the British code-name for the Albanian campaign was Operation Valuable, see Prados, *Presidents' Secret Wars*, p. 46

25 Cave Brown, *Treason in the Blood*, p. 421; Prados, *Presidents' Secret Wars*, p. 46; Philby, *My Silent War*, p. 143.

26 Thomas, *The Very Best Men*, p. 40; Hersh, *The Old Boys*, p. 264.

27 OIR Report No.5112, "Albanian Political Exiles", 28 Nov. 1949, RG 59, NA; CIA, ORE 71–49, "Current Situation in Albania"; Winks, *Cloak and Gown*, p. 397; Simpson, *Blowback*, p. 123. The Free Albania Committee was made up of 40 per cent Balli Kombëtar, 40 per cent monarchist Legaliteti, and 20 per cent smaller anticommunist factions, see Prados, *Presidents' Secret Wars*, p. 50.

28 Dorril, *MI6*, pp. 381–383.

29 *ibid*, p. 377.

30 Winks, *Cloak and Gown*, p. 397; Bethell, *The Great Betrayal*, pp. 55–56; Smiley, *Albanian Assignment*, pp. 159–164; Prados, *Presidents' Secret Wars*, pp. 46–47.

31 Winks, *Cloak and Gown*, p. 397.

32 Thomas, *The Very Best Men*, p. 38; CIA, Intelligence Memo. 218, "Strengths and Weaknesses of the Hoxha Regime".

33 Dorril, *MI6*, pp. 359–361.

34 *ibid*, pp. 364–365.

35 Memo. of Conversation by the Deputy Director, Office of European Affairs (Thompson), 28 June 1949, *FRUS 1949*, Vol.5: 305–307; Memo. of Conversation, by Chief, Division of Greek, Turkish, and Iranian Affairs (Jernegan), 16 Aug 1949, *ibid*, 308–309.

36 Hersh, *The Old Boys*, pp. 263–264, p. 271; Nicholas C. Pano, "Albania", in Joseph Held (ed.), *The Columbia History of Eastern Europe in the Twentieth Century* (New York, 1992), pp. 18–33.

37 Bethell, *The Great Betrayal*, pp. 87–91; Winks, *Cloak and Gown*, pp. 397–398.

38 CIA, ORE 71–49, "Current Situation in Albania"; Thomas, *The Very Best Men*, p. 39; Winks, *Cloak and Gown*, p. 397.

39 Thomas, *The Very Best Men*, pp. 38–39; Bethell, *The Great Betrayal*, pp. 90–91; Winks, *Cloak and Gown*, p. 397; Hersh, *The Old Boys*, pp. 263–264.

40 Winks, *Cloak and Gown*, pp. 397–398.

41 Bethell, *The Great Betrayal*, pp. 83–90.

42 Winks, *Cloak and Gown*, p. 398.

43 Thomas, *The Very Best Men*, p. 39.

44 Tim Weiner maintains that organisation and planning for the Albania project was on something of a downward spiral from the outset: that the planning became "more frantic" and the training "more slipshod" with each mission, see *Legacy of Ashes*, p. 45. This depiction runs contrary to other treatments of BGFIEND, which maintain that security was tightened and training improved following the Karaburun mission, see Burke, *Outrageous Good Fortune*, pp. 139–169; Hersh, *The Old Boys*, p. 271; Thomas, *The Very Best Men*, p. 68; Winks, *Cloak and Gown*, p. 398.

45 Hersh, *The Old Boys*, p. 270.

46 CIA, ORE 71–49, "Current Situation in Albania"; quote from Logoreci, *The Albanians*, p. 72; Simpson, *Blowback*, pp. 123–124.

47 Prados, *Presidents' Secret Wars* p. 48; Hersh, *The Old Boys*, p. 265.

48 Simpson, *Blowback*, pp. 123–124; Hersh, *The Old Boys*, p. 270.

49 Thomas, *The Very Best Men*, pp. 68–70; Winks, *Cloak and Gown*, pp. 398–399.

50 Dorril, *MI6*, pp. 392–394.

51 Hersh, *The Old Boys*, p. 270; Thomas, *The Very Best Men*, p. 84; Bethell, *The Great Betrayal*, pp. 140–143.

52 Dorril, *MI6*, p. 394.

53 *ibid*, pp. 394–395; a CIA report indicated that Moscow was attempting to increase the efficiency of its "puppet forces" in the Balkans. The agency warned "the initiation of any kind of armed aggression in this area by Soviet puppet troops would present the basic issues of the Korean incident all over again, forcing the US either to abandon some of its commitments or disperse its military strength". The removal of Albania as a threat would impair Moscow's position in, and plans for, the region, which gave added impetus to Washington's moves to seek the ouster of Hoxha, see CIA, Review of the World Situation, 19 July 1950, CIG 1946, 1948–50 folder (2 of 2), Intelligence File, box 256, PSF, Truman Papers, HSTL; Thomas, *The Very Best Men*, pp. 68–70; Winks, *Cloak and Gown*, pp. 398–399.

54 Philby, *My Silent War*, pp. 194–199; Bethell, *The Great Betrayal*..

55 Winks, *Cloak and Gown*, pp. 398–399.

56 *ibid*..

57 Philby, *My Silent War*, pp. 194–199.

58 Winks, *Cloak and Gown*, pp. 399–400; Thomas, *The Very Best Men*, pp. 68–71; Ulmer quoted in Hersh, *The Old Boys*, p. 273.

59 Verne Newton, *The Cambridge Spies: The Untold Story of Maclean, Philby, and Burgess in America* (New York, 1991), pp. 249–250, pp. 306–341; Cave Brown, *Treason in the Blood*, pp. 420–436.

60 Interview with Gratian Yatsevich in Hersh, *The Old Boys*, p. 322.

61 Logoreci, *The Albanians*, p. 107.

62 Chapman Pincher, *Too Secret Too Long* (New York, 1984), p. 300. Logoreci numbers those killed, executed, or imprisoned as a result of the operation as running into several hundred, see Logoreci, *The Albanians*, p. 109.

63 NSC 174, "United States Policy Toward the Soviet Satellites in Eastern Europe", 11 December 1953, DDRS, CDROM Id.: 1999010100429, Fiche No. 1999–42.

64 British input had, in fact, been cut back steadily from the time of the first Albania operation. Indeed, British Foreign Secretary, Ernest Bevin had spelt out his doubts as early as September 1949, see Acheson-Bevin-Schuman meetings, September 1949, General File, PSF, HSTL; Hersh, *The Old Boys*, p. 321.

65 PSB D-45, 29 July 1953, "Report to the Psychological Strategy Board", p. 7, box 6, PSB Working Files, 1951–1953, RG 59, NA.

66 Hersh, *The Old Boys*, pp. 321–323; Prados, *Presidents' Secret Wars*, pp. 50–51.

67 Andrew, *Secret Service*, p. 493; Winks, *Cloak and Gown*, pp. 398–399.

68 Interview with Joseph Bryan in Hersh, *The Old Boys*, p. 272.

69 Nicholas Bethell, *Spies and Other Secrets: Memoirs from the Second Cold War* (London, 1994), p. 302.

70 The study of Philby and his impact on the Cold War is extensive, beginning with Hugh Trevor-Roper's *The Philby Affair: Espionage, Treason and the Secret Services* (London, 1968), and E.H. Cookridge's *The Third Man: The Truth About "Kim" Philby, Double Agent* (London, 1968), both of which were published the year before Philby's own memoirs. The following decade saw, among other works on the subject, the release of Andrew Boyle's *The Climate of Treason; Five Who Spied for Russia* (London, 1979) reopen the debate on Philby and the Cambridge spies. A succession of books followed in the 1980s, including Andrew Sinclair's *The Red and the Blue: Intelligence, Treason, and the Universities* (London, 1986), in which it is maintained that the CIA alerted MI5 to the existence of Soviet moles in British Intelligence. Further light has been cast on the Cambridge spies and the Philby case with the publication of Andrew's and Gordievsky's *KGB*, Yuri Modin's *My Five Cambridge Friends* (New York, 1994), and Genrikh Borovik's *The Philby Files: The Secret Life of Masterspy Kim Philby* (New York, 1994). For a useful analysis of CIA counterintelligence chief William Harvey's suspicions concerning Philby see Newton, *The Cambridge Spies*, pp. 306–341. By far the most comprehensive work to appear on Philby, however, is Cave Brown's *Treason in the Blood*.

71 Cave Brown, *Treason in the Blood*, p. 219–223, pp. 363–366.

72 *ibid*, p. 365.

73 Winks, *Cloak and Gown*, p. 401.

74 Cave Brown, *Treason in the Blood*, pp. 421–422.

75 *ibid*, p. 422.

76 Hersh, *The Old Boys*, p. 271.

77 Cave Brown, *Treason in the Blood*, p. 401; Corson, *Armies of Ignorance*, pp. 327–328.

78 Cave Brown, *Treason in the Blood*, pp. 401–402, Sibert quoted on p. 401.

79 The first phase of Trojan projected SAC bombers as striking Moscow, Leningrad and 18 other maximum priority cities with 133 atomic bombs. The second phase was to consist of 70 cities and 292 atomic bombs. The bombers were to be dispatched from bases in the United Kingdom, Okinawa, Cairo-Suez and the United States itself, see *ibid*, p. 403.

80 *ibid.*

81 For detail on VENONA see Robert L. Benson and Michael Warner, *Venona – Soviet Espionage and American Response* (Washington D.C., 1996); Nigel West, *Venona: The Greatest Secret of the Cold War* (London, 1999); John E. Haynes and Harvey Klehr, *Decoding Soviet Espionage in America* (New Haven, Conn., 2000); Christopher Andrew, *For the President's Eyes Only: Secret Intelligence and the American Presidency from Washington to Bush* (London, 1995), pp. 178–179, p. 195. Philby was party to VENONA until J. Edgar Hoover stopped British access, see Cave Brown, *Treason in the Blood*, p. 410.

82 Bethell, *Spies and Other Secrets*, p. 302.

83 Miranda Vickers and James Pettifer, *Albania: From Anarchy to a Balkan Identity* (New York, 1997), p. 256.

84 Frank Lindsay quoted in Thomas, *The Very Best Men*, p. 72.

85 *ibid*, p. 85; Ranelagh, *The Agency*, pp. 204–205.

86 Ranelagh, *The Agency*, pp. 204–206; Thomas, *The Very Best Men*, p. 211.

87 The MKULTRA programme first came to light as the result of a congressional inquiry, see Joint Hearing before the Select Committee on Human Resources, United States Senate, 95th Congress, First Session, *Project MKUltra: The CIA's Program of Research in Behavioral Modification* (Washington D.C., 3 August 1977). This provided a key source for subsequent investigations of the programme. The best study of MKULTRA is John Marks, *The Search for the Manchurian Candidate: The Story of the CIA's Secret Efforts to Control Human Behavior* (London, 1979). The most comprehensive source is 'CIA Behavior Experiments Collection' (John Marks Donation), boxes 1–11, National Security Archive, Gelman Library, The George Washington University, Washington D.C.

88 *Church Report*, Bk.4, pp. 128–130; Simpson, *Blowback*, p. 153; Thomas, *The Very Best Men*, p. 85.

89 Nicholas M. Horrock, "C.I.A. Documents Tell of 1954 Project to Create Involuntary Assassins", *New York Times*, 9 Feb. 1978; for sources relating to Artichoke, see CIA Behavior Experiments, Project Artichoke, box 5, documents 38–461, National Security Archive.

90 *Alleged Assassination Plots Involving Foreign Leaders: An Interim Report of the Select Committee to Study Governmental Operations with respect to Intelligence Activities,* [Church Committee]. U.S. Senate 94 Cong., 1 Sess., Report No. 94–465 (Nov. 20, 1975).

91 Richard Helms quote in Hersh, *The Old Boys*, p. 274.

92 Thomas Braden quoted in *ibid*, p. 296.

Chapter 5

1   *Church Report*, Bk.1, pp. 109–110.

2   Unnamed CIA official quoted in Johnson, *America's Secret Power*, p. 67.

3   Grose, *Gentleman Spy*, pp. 335–337, pp. 435–437.

4   NSC 5811, 24 May 1958, Records of the NSC, Policy Papers, Box 47, RG 273, N.A.

5   For the best *book* on CIA intervention in Tibet see Kenneth Conboy and James Morrison, *The CIA's Secret War in Tibet* (Kansas, 2002). The Tibetan campaign also featured in an *Everyman* TV Documentary entitled *The Shadow Circus: The CIA in Tibet*. Most of the operatives involved in the Tibetan venture took part in this programme.

6   These ventures are commonly categorised along with the offensive operations directed against the communist bloc, see Godson, *Dirty Tricks or Trump Cards*, pp. 36–37; Tovar, "Strengths and Weaknesses in Past Covert Action", pp. 71–89; Johnson, *America's Secret Power*, pp. 101–102, pp. 251–260. Only in the case of Cuba, however, is such an approach correct, because the enterprises that were launched in the other countries and regions mentioned were not aimed at dislodging communist governments that were already in power, but at preventing communists from gaining control in the target countries.

7   H. W. Brands, "Eisenhower and the Problem of Loose Ends", in Günter Bischof and Stephen Ambrose (eds.), *Eisenhower: A Centenary Assessment* (Baton Rouge and London, 1995), p. 126.

8   Robert McMahon, "Eisenhower and Third World Nationalism: A Critique of the Revisionists", *Political Science Quarterly* 101 (1986): 453–473.

9   Dwight D. Eisenhower, *The White House Years: Mandate for Change, 1953–1956* (New York, 1963), pp. 13–22; Charles C. Alexander, *Holding the Line: The Eisenhower Era 1952–1961* (Bloomington, 1975), pp. 7–9.

10 *FRUS 1952–54*, Vol.8: 1130, note 2.

11 Eisenhower to Chiang Kai-shek, 5 May 1953, in Louis Galambos and Daun Van Ee (eds.), *The Papers of Dwight David Eisenhower: The Presidency: The Middle Way*, Volume XVI (Baltimore, 1996), pp. 208–211; Gaddis, *We Now Know*, pp. 107–109.

12 Sherman Adams, *Firsthand Report: The Story of the Eisenhower Administration* (New York, 1961), pp. 48–49; Gaddis, *We Now Know*, pp. 108.

13 Editors' introduction in Bischof and Ambrose (eds.), *Eisenhower: A Centenary Assessment*, p. 9.

14 S.J. Ball, *The Cold War: An International History, 1947–1991* (London and New York, 1998), pp. 66–68.

15 Greenstein, *Hidden Hand Presidency*, pp. 57–99, pp. 155–227.

16 Eisenhower, *Mandate for Change*, p. 279.

17 Galambos and Van Ee (eds.), *Eisenhower Papers: Presidency*, Vol.XV, p. 952, note 6; H. W. Brands, *Inside the Cold War: Loy Henderson and the Rise of the American Empire 1918–1961* (New York and Oxford, 1991), pp. 298–299.

18 Frederick W. Marks III, *Power and Peace: The Diplomacy of John Foster Dulles* (Westport, Conn, and London, 1990), pp. 59–62; Günter Bischof, "Eisenhower, the Summit, and the Austrian Peace Treaty, 1953–1955", in Bischof and Ambrose (eds.), *Eisenhower: A Centenary Assessment*, p. 145.

19 Eisenhower to Nikolai A. Bulganin, 27 July 1955, Galambos and Van Ee (eds.), *Eisenhower Papers: Presidency*, Vol. XVI, pp. 1794–1795.

20 Morgan, *Eisenhower versus "the Spenders"*, pp. 51–53.

21 Alexander, *Holding the Line*, pp. 68–69; Robert A. Divine, *Eisenhower and the Cold War* (New York and Oxford, 1981), pp. 37–39; H.W. Brands, "Eisenhower and the Problem of Loose Ends", in Bischof and Ambrose (eds.), *Eisenhower: A Centenary Assessment*, p. 131.

22 Robert A. Wampler, "Eisenhower, NATO, and Nuclear Weapons: the Strategy and Political Economy of Alliance Security", in Bischof and Ambrose (eds.), *Eisenhower: A Centenary Assessment*, pp. 162–190.

23 John Foster Dulles to CFR, 12 Jan. 1954, *DSB* (25 Jan. 1954): 107.

24 Gaddis, *Strategies of Containment*, pp. 147–149, quote from p. 147.

25 *ibid*, pp. 147–153.

26 The signatories of the Manila Pact, which established SEATO, were the US, the UK, France, Australia, New Zealand, the Philippines, Thailand, and Pakistan, but a special protocol to the treaty extended coverage to Indochina. The US was an associate, though not a fully-fledged member of the Baghdad Pact, which was made up of the UK, Iran, Iraq, Pakistan, and Turkey.

27 Wampler, "Eisenhower, NATO, and Nuclear Weapons", pp. 162–190; Eisenhower himself regarded many of the Gaither Report's recommendations as alarmist, see Dwight D. Eisenhower, *The White House Years: Waging Peace, 1956–1961* (London, 1966), pp. 220–223.

28 Eisenhower, *Waging Peace*, pp. 295–302.

29 *ibid*, pp. 487–489; Divine, *Eisenhower and the Cold War*, p. 130.

30 Gaddis, *Strategies of Containment*, p. 143; Gordon H. Chang, "Eisenhower and Mao's China", in Bischof and Ambrose (eds.), *Eisenhower: A Centenary Assessment*, pp. 195–196; Eisenhower, *Waging Peace*, p. 583.

31 Marks, *Power and Peace*, p. 107.

32 Townsend Hoopes, *The Devil and John Foster Dulles* (Boston, 1973), p. 350.

33 Eisenhower to Foster Dulles, 30 June 1952, Galambos and Van Ee (eds.), *Eisenhower Papers: NATO and the Campaign of 1952*, Volume XIII (Baltimore, 1989), pp. 1264–1265, note 1.

34 "An Historic Week", *DSB* (30 May 1955): 871–876.

35 McMahon, "Eisenhower and Third World Nationalism", 456–457.

36 Gaddis, *We Now Know*, pp. 158–160; Crockatt, *The Fifty Years War*, pp. 175–176, quote on p. 175.

37 Memo. of Conversation, Eisenhower and Foster Dulles, 27 Feb. 1956, folder 4, box 4, White House Memoranda Series, Ann Whitman File (hereafter cited as AWF), Dwight D. Eisenhower Library, Abilene, Kansas (hereafter cited as DDEL).

38   *Church Report*, Bk.1, p. 110.

39   *ibid*, p. 109.

40   Allen Dulles's stewardship of the CIA and intelligence community in general from the 1953 to 1955 period is documented in *FRUS: Intelligence Community, 1950–1955*; Karalekas, *History of the CIA*, pp. 43–44; Montague, *Smith-DCI*, pp. 12–14, pp. 88–94, pp. 43–46; Grose, *Gentleman Spy*, p. 301.

41   Montague, *Smith-DCI*, pp. 263–266.

42   Allen W. Dulles, *The Craft of Intelligence* (London, 1963), p. 195.

43   *Church Report*, Bk.1, pp. 109–110.

44   Dulles, *Craft of Intelligence*, p. 225.

45   Mitrovich, *Undermining the Kremlin*, pp. 122–176: Lucas, *Freedom's War*, pp. 235–246.

46   Frank Lindsay interview with Peter Grose, *Gentleman Spy*, p. 356, note 38.

47   Dorril, *MI6*, p. 400.

48   Wisner quoted in Grose, *Operation Rollback*, p. 189.

49   For details of Operation CANCELLATION see Mitrovich, *Undermining the Kremlin*, pp. 81–82.

50   CIA, Office of Current Intelligence, "The Purge of L. P. Beria", OCI 4514, 10 July 1953, www.foia.cia.gov.

51   Murphy, Kondrashev, and Bailey, *Battleground Berlin*; p. 151; Rositzke, "America's Secret Operations", 335–336.

52   For State Department correspondence on the East German riots see *FRUS 1952–54*, Vol.7, part 2: 1584–1645; Eisenhower to Adenauer, 25 June 1953, Galambos and Van Ee (eds.), *Eisenhower Papers: The Presidency*, Vol. XIV, pp. 325–326; Eisenhower to Adenauer, 23 July 1953, *ibid*, pp. 410–413. For the most comprehensive treatment of this widely overlooked Cold War event see Christian F. Ostermann (ed.), *Uprising in East Germany 1953: The Cold War, the German Question and the First Major Upheaval Behind the Iron Curtain* (Washington D.C., 2001).

53   Allen Dulles quoted at 150th Meeting of the NSC, 18 June 1953, *FRUS 1952–54*, Vol. 7: 1587.

54   Lucas, *Freedom's War*, pp. 180–183.

55   CIA, Office of Current Intelligence, "Comment on the Berlin Uprisings", OCI No.449, 17 June 1953, www.foia.cia.gov; Murphy, Kondrashev and Bailey, *Battleground Berlin*, pp. 169–171.

56   Hersh, *The Old Boys*, p. 377; Grose, *Gentleman Spy*, pp. 356–357.

57   Murphy, Kondrashev and Bailey, *Battleground Berlin*, p. 170. Henry Heckscher was transferred from Berlin to Guatemala, where, under the guise of a coffee merchant, he took part in a defector programme focused on 'turning' elements of the Guatemalan military, see ch.6.

58   Lucas, *Freedom's War*, pp. 182–183.

59   NSC 143/2, "A Volunteer Freedom Corps", 20 May 1953, *FRUS 1952–54*, Vol. 7: 218–220. For a comprehensive account of the VFC, see James Jay Carafano, "Mobilising

Europe's Stateless: America's Plan for a Cold War Army", *Journal of Cold War Studies*, Vol.1, No.2 (Spring 1999): 61–85.

60 *ibid*; Grose, *Operation Rollback*, p. 202.

61 Carafano, "Mobilising Europe's Stateless"; NSC 158, "United States Objectives and Actions to Exploit the Unrest in the Satellite States", President's Papers 1953, Box 1, Office of the Assistant for National Security Affairs, Special Assistant Series, Presidential Subseries, White House Office Files (herefater cited as WHO), DDEL.

62 This programme is cited in several major works as one of the most substantial of the CIA's Eastern European paramilitary/political action ventures of the 1953 to 1956 period and is said to have functioned under the cryptograph of Red Sox/Red Cap, see Winks, *Cloak and Gown*, p. 413; Ranelagh, *The Agency*, p. 287; Grose, *Gentleman Spy*, p. 436; Hersh, *The Old Boys*, pp. 364–365. Evan Thomas raised questions about the Red Sox/Red Cap programme, maintaining that John Mapother, a former case officer in the CIA's Vienna station, had revealed that the agency's planning for Eastern Europe was not as it had been presented in other treatments and that Red Sox and Red Cap, were code-names for quite separate operations, see Thomas, *The Very Best Men*, p. 375, note 8. More recent treatments leave the issue in some doubt. Csaba Békés, Malcolm Byrne and János M. Rainer continue to use the Red Sox/Red Cap code name, see *The 1956 Hungarian Revolution: A History in Documents* (Budapest and New York, 2002), p. 381, while Tim Weiner refers to the programme only as Red Cap, see *Legacy of Ashes*, p. 124. For the purposes of this study, which is here dealing with offensive covert action generally rather than scrutinising the specifics of particular operations, the Red Cap cryptograph is used.

63 Hersh, *The Old Boys*, pp. 364–404; Prados, *Presidents' Secret Wars*, pp. 119–127; Ranelagh, *The Agency*, pp. 207–309; Thomas, *The Very Best Men*, pp. 127–152.

64 NSC 5608/1, "U.S. Policy Towards the Soviet Satellites in Eastern Europe", 18 July 1956, *FRUS 1955–57*, Vol. 25: 216–222.

65 Interviews with Robert Amory and Richard Bissell in Hersh, *The Old Boys*, p. 380.

66 CIA, Soviet Staff Study, OCI No.1960/58, "The Ties That Bind: Soviet Intrabloc Relations, February 1956 to December 1956", 6–8, www.foia.cia.gov.

67 The CIA is said by Peter Grose to have "received its first fragmentary reports" of the speech from defector-in-place Pyotr Popov, see *Gentleman Spy*, pp. 419–420; Dulles, *The Craft of Intelligence*, p. 80; Winks, *Cloak and Gown*, pp. 413–414.

68 Ray S. Cline, *Secrets, Spies, and Scholars: Blueprint of the Essential CIA* (Washington, 1976), pp. 162–164.

69 Hersh, *The Old Boys*, pp. 381–382; Prados, *Presidents' Secret Wars*, pp. 122–123; Winks, *Cloak and Gown*, pp. 413–414.

70 Cline, *Secrets, Spies, and Scholars*, p. 164; Grose, *Gentleman Spy*, pp. 425–426.

71 Notes from the 46th Meeting of the Special Committee on Soviet and Related Problems, 13 Nov. 1956, *FRUS 1955–57*, Vol.25: 436–437.

72 Lucas, *Freedom's War*, p. 230.

73 Notes from the 46th Meeting of the Special Committee on Soviet and Related Problems, 13 Nov. 1956, *FRUS 1955–57*, Vol.25: 437.

74 *ibid.*

75 Lucas, *Freedom's War*, p. 259.

76 *ibid*, pp. 257–258.

77 Corson, *Armies of Ignorance*, p. 371; Thomas, *The Very Best Men*, pp. 146–147.

78 Eisenhower, *Waging Peace*, p. 95.

79 W. Scott Lucas (ed.), *Britain and Suez: The lion's last roar* (Manchester and New York, 1996), p. 97.

80 Karalekas, *History of the CIA*, p. 49.

81 Conboy and Morrison, *The CIA's Secret War in Tibet*.; Memo. of a Discussion at the 400th Meeting of the NSC, 26 March 1959, DDRS, CDROM Id.: 1997070102240, Fiche No. 1997–186.

82 Conboy and Morrison, *The CIA's Secret War in Tibet*.

83 Copeland, *The Game Player*, pp. 86–94; Douglas Little, "Cold War and Covert Action: US and Syria", 51–57; Andrew Rathmell "Copeland and Za'im: Re-evaluating the Evidence", *Intelligence and National Security* Vol.11, No.1 (1996): 89–105.

84 Dulles, *Craft of Intelligence*, pp. 215–230.

85 For a concise and illuminating rendering of CIA involvement in the Middle East, see Little, "Mission Impossible".

86 CIA, NIE-73, "Conditions and Trends in the Middle East Affecting US Security", 15 Jan. 1953, www.foia.cia.gov; NIE-76, "Probable Developments in Egypt", 25 Mar. 1953, *ibid*; CIA, Special National Intelligence Estimate (SNIE) 30–3–58, "Arab Nationalism as a Factor in the Middle East Situation", 12 Aug 1958, *ibid*.

87 Miles Copeland, *Game of Nations*, pp. 62–64; Wilbur Crane Eveland, *Ropes of Sand: America's Failure in the Middle East* (London and New York, 1980), p. 98*n*. The CIA continued to play an active role in Egypt after the fall of Farouk, dispatching $3million in aid to Nasser in 1953 and allegedly recruiting ex-SS intelligence officials to train Egypt's security services, see Copeland, *Game Player*, pp. 158–171; Simpson, *Blowback*, pp. 250–252; Hersh, *The Old Boys*, pp. 331–332.

88 Robert R. Bowie, "Eisenhower, Dulles and the Suez Crisis", in William Roger Louis and Roger Owen (eds.), *Suez 1956: the Crisis and Its Consequences* (New York, 1989), pp. 189–214; CIA, SNIE 30–5–55, "Possible Consequences of the Egyptian Arms Deal With the Soviet Bloc", 12 October 1955, www.foia.cia.gov.

89 Eisenhower to Goodpaster, 3 April 1956, *FRUS 1955–57*, Vol.15: 446–448.

90 Little, "Mission Impossible", 670–671.

91 W. Scott Lucas, *Divided We Stand: Britain, the United States and the Suez Crisis* (London, 1991), pp. 109–112; George Allen to Foster Dulles, 17 July 1956, *FRUS 1955–57*, Vol.15: 849–85; Project OMEGA appears to have resulted from the deliberations of the Middle East Policy Planning Group, which subdivided into two separate groupings. The Alpha Group focused on how an Arab-Israeli peace agreement might be achieved, while the Omega Group concentrated on developing plans that would bring stability to the

Arab world and put a brake on the "rapid drift to the left" that was regarded as taking hold in Syria, Egypt and elsewhere in the Middle East, see Eveland, *Ropes of Sand*, pp. 179–182, pp. 190–193, quote on p. 192.

92 CIA, SNIE 30–3–58, "Arab Nationalism as a Factor in the Middle East Situation", 12 Aug 1958, www.foia.cia.gov; Eveland, *Ropes of Sand*, pp. 250–303.

93 Eveland, *Ropes of Sand*, pp. 180–200, pp. 244–268; Anthony Gorst and W. Scott Lucas, "The Other Collusion: Operation Straggle and Anglo-American Intervention in Syria, 1955–56", *Intelligence and National Security*, Vol. 4, No.3 (July 1989): 576–593; SNIE 30–3–58, "Arab Nationalism as a Factor in the Middle East Situation", www.foia.cia.gov.

94 Eveland, *Ropes of Sand*, pp. 244–247.

95 Church Committee, *Alleged Assassination Plots*.

96 Memorandum of 284th Meeting of the NSC, 10 March 1956, NSC Series, AWF, DDEL; Gorst and Lucas, "The Other Collusion", 576–593.

97 Russell to Foster Dulles, 19 July 1956, *FRUS 1955–57*, Vol. 15: 865.

98 Eveland, *Ropes of Sand*, pp. 99–105, quote on p. 101.

99 *Church Report*, Bk.1, pp. 111–112, quote on p. 112.

100 *ibid*, p. 111.

101 Karalekas, *History of the CIA*, p. 56.

102 Dulles, *Craft of Intelligence*, pp. 194–195.

103 Karalekas, *History of the CIA*, p. 61.

104 Grose, *Gentleman Spy*, p. 348.

105 Dulles, *Craft of Intelligence*, p. 55.

106 Karalekas, *History of the CIA*, pp. 56–57.

107 Andrew, *For the President's Eyes Only*, pp. 196–197, pp. 216–217; James Bamford, *Body of Secrets: How America's NSA and Britain's GCHQ Eavesdrop on the World* (London, 2002), pp. 1–63.

108 Bamford, *Body of Secrets*, pp. 32–63; Andrew, *For the President's Eyes Only*, pp. 219–220.

109 Bamford, *Body of Secrets*, pp. 35–37.

110 An account of the U-2 project was written for the CIA History Staff in the 1980s under the title of *The Central Intelligence Agency and Overhead Reconnaissance: The U-2 and OXCART Programs, 1954–1974*. It was declassified in 2005 and is available on-line, see Gregory W. Pedlow and Donald E. Welzenbach, *The CIA and the U-2 Program, 1954–1974* www.odci.gov/csi/books/U2.

111 *ibid*; James R. Killian, *Sputnik, Scientists, and Eisenhower: A Memoir of the First Special Assistant to the President for Science and Technology* (Cambridge, Mass., 1982), pp. 67–84; Eisenhower, *Waging Peace*, pp. 544–547.

112 William E. Burrows, *Deep Black: The Secrets of Space Espionage* (London, 1988), p. 73.

113 Grose, *Gentleman Spy*, pp. 405–406.

114 Bissell, *Reflections of a Cold Warrior*, pp. 95–99, quote on p. 99; for conditions governing expenditures from the Contingency Reserve, see Memo. for the DCI, 7 Jan. 1959, "Historical background of Functioning of the NSC 5412/2 Special Group and Its

Predecessors – with Special reference to Current Proposals of the President's Board of Consultants", box 10, Policy Papers Subseries, NSC Series, AWF, DDEL.

115 Bissell, *Reflections of a Cold Warrior*, p. 97, p. 100, quote on p. 97; Bamford, *Body of Secrets*, p. 35.

116 Eisenhower, *Waging Peace*, p. 546; Grose, *Gentleman Spy*, pp. 470–471.

117 Eisenhower, *Waging Peace*, p. 483; Francis Gary Powers, with Curt Gentry, *Operation Overflight: A Memoir of the U-2 Incident* (Washington D.C., 2002).

118 Andrew, *For the President's Eyes Only*, pp. 217–221, p. 331, p. 335.

119 Bissell, *Reflections of a Cold Warrior*, p. 140.

120 Ranelagh, *The Agency*, pp. 288–296; Murphy, Kondrashev, and Bailey, *Battleground Berlin*, pp. 205–237.

121 Dulles, *Craft of Intelligence*, p. 221.

122 Memo. for the DCI, 7 Jan. 1959, "Historical Background of Functioning of the NSC 5412/2 Special Group and Its Predecessors – with Special reference to Current Proposals of the President's Board of Consultants", box 10, NSC Series, Policy Papers Subseries, AWF, DDEL.

123 Dulles, *Craft of Intelligence*, pp. 185–191; Barrett, *The CIA and Congress*; Karalekas, *History of the CIA*, pp. 52–54.

124 *ibid*, pp. 46–47.

Chapter 6

1   Crucial to the study of the Iran coup is the CIA's internal history of TPAJAX, see Wilber, *Overthrow of Premier Mossadeq of Iran, November 1952-August 1953*. Kermit Roosevelt's *Countercoup*, is an illuminating if at times self-serving account written by the CIA officer who oversaw Musaddiq's downfall, and Christopher Woodhouse's *Something Ventured* (London, 1982), pp. 108–135, gives a first-hand appraisal from the British standpoint. By far the best secondary analysis of Musaddiq's ouster is Gasiorowski, "Coup D'État in Iran".

2   Quote from David Attlee Phillips, *The Night Watch: Twenty-five Years of Peculiar Service* (New York, 1977), p. 51. Of the works that deal solely with the Guatemala coup, Piero Gleijeses, *Shattered Hope: The Guatemalan Revolution and the United States, 1944–1954* (Princeton, 1991), Richard H. Immerman, *The CIA in Guatemala: The Foreign Policy of Intervention* (Austin, 1982), and Stephen Schlesinger and Stephen Kinzer, *Bitter Fruit: The Untold Story of the American Coup in Guatemala* (New York, 1982) are all essential reading. The CIA's own histories of Arbenz's ouster – Cullather, *PBSUCCESS*, and Gerald K. Haines, *CIA and Guatemala Assassination Proposals 1952–1954*, which are available for consultation at DDEL and NA – were declassified in 1997 and are indispensable. For a published version of the agency's account see Cullather, *Secret History: The CIA's Declassified Account of Its Operations in Guatemala, 1952–1954*. An additional and extensive in-house report was declassified in 2003 and is available at the CIA's Freedom of Information Electronic Reading Room, see "Report on Project PBSUCCESS", est. date 16 Nov. 1954, www.foia.cia.gov.

3   Immerman, *The CIA in Guatemala.*

4   Cullather, *PBSUCCESS*, pp. 21–22.

5   Blanche Cook, *The Declassified Eisenhower: A Divided Legacy* (Garden City, New York, 1981), pp. 181–183.

6   Central Intelligence Agency, ORE 65–49, "The Current Situation in Iran", May 1949, pp. 6–8, NSC-ORE folder (2 of 5), box 219, CIA Files, Records of the NSC, Truman Papers, HSTL.

7   *ibid.*

8   Memo. by the Assistant Secretary of State for Near Eastern, South Asian, and African Affairs (Berry) to the Secretary of State, 14 Mar. 1951, *FRUS 1952–54*, Vol.10: 9.

9   James A. Bill, *The Eagle and the Lion: The Tragedy of American-Iranian Relations* (New Haven and London, 1988), pp. 61–66.

10 The Special Assistant to the President (Harriman) to the Department of State, 24 July 1951, *FRUS 1952–54*, Vol.10: 109–113; Acheson, *Present at the Creation*, p. 506.

11 The Secretary of State to the Embassy in Iran, 26 Sept. 1951, *FRUS 1952–54*, Vol.10: 167–169; CIA, ORE 65–49, "The Current Situation in Iran", HSTL.

12 CIA Special Estimate, "The Prospects for the Survival of the Mossadeq Regime in Iran", 14 Oct. 1952, Meetings folder (2of 2), box 219, NSC Files, PSF, Truman Papers, HSTL; Acheson, *Present at the Creation*, pp. 683–685.

13 Eisenhower to Edward E. Hazlett, Jr., 21 June 1951, in Galambos and Van Ee (eds.), *Eisenhower Papers: NATO and the 1952 Campaign*, p. 368; John L. Helgerson, *Getting to Know the President: CIA Briefings of Presidential Candidates, 1952–1992* (Washington D.C., 1996), pp. 32–34; Untitled and undated memo., Eisenhower Presidential Transition, folder 2, box 118, General File, PSF, Truman Papers, HSTL.

14 Eisenhower, *Mandate for Change*, pp. 161–163.

15 Brands, *Inside the Cold War*, pp. 276–277.

16 NSC Minutes, 1 June 1953, folder 3, box 8, NSC Meetings and Minutes Series, AWF, DDEL.

17 Woodhouse, *Something Ventured*, pp. 117–119; Roosevelt, *Countercoup*, p. 6.

18 Dulles to Embassy in Iran, 2 Mar. 1953, *FRUS 1952–54*, Vol.10: 691; *ibid*, 721. Eisenhower's policy regarding Iran at this time was spelt out in NSC 136/1, "Developments in Iran Affecting U.S. Security", 5 March 1953, DDRS, CDROM Id.: 1998090102844, Fiche No. 1998–244.

19 Wilber, *Overthrow of Mossadeq*, Appendix D; Roosevelt, *Countercoup*, pp. 122–124.

20 Divine, *Eisenhower and the Cold War*, pp. 72–74; Anthony Sampson, *The Seven Sisters: The Great Oil Companies and the World They Made* (London, 1975), pp. 110–112; Daniel Yergin, *The Prize: The Epic Quest for Oil, Money, and Power* (New York, 1991), pp. 445–449.

21 Bamberg, *History of BP, Vol.2*, p. 339, p. 344.

22 Bill, *The Eagle and the Lion*, p. 80.

23 *ibid*, p. 81.

24 Yergin, *The Prize*, pp. 450–479; The Ambassador in the U.K. (Clifford) to Department of State, 20 Oct. 1952, *FRUS 1952–54*, Vol.10: 500; Bill, *The Eagle and the Lion*, p. 78;

Memo. of Discussion, 132nd. Meeting of the NSC, 18 Feb. 1953, box 4, Administration Subseries, NSC Series, WHO, DDEL.

25   Eisenhower quoted in Sampson, *Seven Sisters*, p. 129.

26   Eisenhower to Churchill, 8 May 1953, in Boyle (ed.), *Churchill-Eisenhower Correspondence*, p. 53.

27   Bamberg, *History of BP, Vol.2*, pp. 495–511; Ranelagh, *The Agency*, p. 262; once the oil dispute was settled Iranian oil production rocketed, increasing by 387 per cent between 1957 and 1970, see Yergin, *The Prize*, p. 534.

28   Pisani, *CIA and the Marshall Plan*, pp. 122–123; John Sherman notes on OPC involvement in Iran, OPC folder, box 13, Records of the PSB, HSTL.

29   Wise and Ross, *Invisible Government*, p. 108.

30   Roosevelt, *Countercoup*, p. 2, p. 134; Cullather, *PBSUCCESS*, p. 25.

31   Farhad Diba, *Mossadegh: A Political Biography* (Beckenham, Kent, 1986), pp. 99–100.

32   *FRUS 1949* Vol.6: 479, note 1; Blum, *CIA: A Forgotten History*, pp. 61–62; Eisenhower, *Mandate for Change*, p. 159.

33   Bill, *The Eagle and the Lion*, pp. 67–72.

34   Wilber, *Overthrow of Mossadeq*, pp. 3–4, pp. 9–10, pp. 66–67; Roosevelt, *Countercoup*, p. 1–2.

35   Gasiorowski, "Coup D'État in Iran", 268–269.

36   "United States Attitude Towards Formation of 'Free Government' in Iran", 14 Oct. 1948, box 6980a, RG 59, NA; CIA, ORE 65–49, "The Current Situation in Iran", May 1949, pp. 11–13, NSC-ORE folder (2 of 5), box 1, CIA Files, Records of the NSC, Truman Papers, HSTL; Gasiorowski, "Coup D'État in Iran", 283, note 43;

37   Wilber, *Overthrow of Mossadeq*, p. 57, p. 37, pp. 91–92, quote on p. 92.

38   Gasiorowski, "Coup D'État in Iran", 268–269; Roosevelt, *Countercoup*, p. 179.

39   Copeland, *Game Player*, pp. 187–190.

40   Woodhouse, *Something Ventured*, pp. 111–116; Gasiorowski, "Coup D'État in Iran", 265–266; James F. Goode, *The United States and Iran: In the Shadow of Musaddiq* (London, 1997), pp. 70–83.

41   Gasiorowski, "Coup D'État in Iran", 270; Woodhouse, *Something Ventured*, pp. 116–117.

42   Donald N. Wilber, *Adventures in the Middle East: Excursions and Incursions* (Princeton, 1986), pp. 188–189; Dorril, *MI6*, p. 584.

43   Wilber, *Overthrow of Mossadeq*, Appendix B.

44   Schwartzkopf trained the Iranian police between 1942 and 1948. He was a close friend of the shah's and was the father of the American general of the same name who commanded US troops during the first Gulf War of 1991.

45   Roosevelt, *Countercoup*, pp. 145–147, pp. 156–157.

46   Grose, *Gentleman Spy*, p. 367.

47   Prados, *Presidents' Secret Wars*, pp. 96–97.

48   Grose, *Gentleman Spy*, p. 366, p. 363.

49   Wise and Ross, *Invisible Government*, p. 110.

50 Gasiorowski, "Coup D'État in Iran", 273–274; *New York Times*, 19 Aug. 1953; Wilber, *Overthrow of Mossadeq*, p. 47, Appendix E.

51 Gasiorowski, "Coup D'État in Iran", 274; Dulles, *Craft of Intelligence*, p. 216.

52 Roosevelt, *Countercoup*, pp. 186–197.

53 Gasiorowski, "Coup D'État in Iran", 274–275; Bill, *The Eagle and the Lion*, p. 96.

54 Roosevelt, *Countercoup*, pp. 208–210.

55 Immerman, *The CIA in Guatemala*, pp. 44–57.

56 *ibid*, pp. 22–28.

57 Thomas McCann, *An American Company: The Tragedy of United Fruit* (New York, 1976), p. 56.

58 *ibid*, p. 60.

59 Immerman, *The CIA in Guatemala*, pp. 61–67; Gleijeses, *Shattered Hope*, pp. 149–170.

60 Stephen G. Rabe, *Eisenhower and Latin America: The Foreign Policy of Anticommunism* (Chapel Hill and London, 1988), p. 48; Schlesinger and Kinzer, *Bitter Fruit*, p. 55.

61 Schlesinger and Kinzer, *Bitter Fruit*, pp. 48–61, quotes from Arbenz's speech to the Guatemalan Congress, 1 Mar. 1954, p. 61; Gleijeses, *Shattered Hope*, pp. 36–50.

62 Memorandum of a Conversation between Eisenhower and Guatemalan Foreign Minister Guillmero Toriello, 16 Jan. 1954, *FRUS 1952–54*, Vol.4: 1095–1097.

63 Bissell, *Reflections of a Cold Warrior*, pp. 80–81; Gleijeses, *Shattered Hope*, pp. 64–71.

64 Cullather, *PBSUCCESS*, pp. 17–20, quote on p. 20.

65 *ibid*, pp. 21–22.

66 *ibid*, pp. 22–23, quotes on p. 22 and p. 23.

67 Robert H. Ferrell (ed.), *The Diary of James C. Hagerty: Eisenhower in Mid-Course, 1954–55* (Bloomington, Indiana, 1983), p. 15; Meeting of NSC, 6 Apr. 1954, *FRUS 1952–54*, Vol.13, part 1: 1261.

68 William J. Duiker, *U.S. Containment Policy and the Conflict in Indochina* (Palo Alto, California, 1994), pp. 88–152; Eisenhower, *Mandate for Change*, p. 365.

69 146th Meeting of the NSC, folder 6, box 9, NSC Series, AWF, DDEL; Robert H. Ferrell (ed.), *The Eisenhower Diaries* (New York, 1981), p. 190.

70 Ferrell (ed.), *Hagerty Diaries*, pp. 48–49.

71 Cullather, *PBSUCCESS*, p. 49.

72 Bissell, *Reflections of a Cold Warrior*, pp. 83–84; Cullather, *PBSUCCESS*, pp. 37–38.

73 Cullather, *PBSUCCESS*, pp. 50–52, p. 65; Gleijeses, *Shattered Hope*, pp. 248–249.

74 Frederick W. Marks III, "The CIA and Castillo Armas in Guatemala, 1954: New Clues to an Old Puzzle", *Diplomatic History* 14 (Winter 1990): 67–86, at 69.

75 Cullather, *PBSUCCESS*, p. 52, p. 33; quote in Thomas, *The Very Best Men*, p. 115.

76 Cullather, *PBSUCCESS*, p. 52.

77 *ibid*, p. 35.

78 Gleijeses, *Shattered Hope*, pp. 248–249.

79 Memorandum of a telephone conversation by Under Secretary of State Smith with Eisenhower, 27 April 1954, Telephone Calls, Jan-May 1954 folder, box 5, DDE Diary Series, AWF, DDEL.

80 Cullather, *PBSUCCESS*, pp. 64–67.

81 Gaddis, *Strategies of Containment*, pp. 147–149.

82 Eisenhower, *Mandate for Change*, pp. 424–425.

83 Duiker, *U.S Containment in Indochina*, pp. 140–152.

84 For an excellent analysis see Rabe, *Eisenhower and Latin America*, pp. 42–54.

85 "Declaration of Caracas", *DSB* Vol.30 (22 March 1954): 420.

86 Rabe, *Eisenhower and Latin America*, p. 52.

87 Foster Dulles's address to the Tenth Inter-American Conference, *DSB*, Vol.30 (29 March 1954): 466.

88 Gleijeses, *Shattered Hope*, pp. 274–275.

89 Schlesinger and Kinzer, *Bitter Fruit*, pp. 143–144; quote in Eisenhower, *Mandate for Change*, p. 424.

90 Eisenhower, *Mandate for Change*, p. 327.

91 Greenstein, *Hidden Hand Presidency*, p. 76.

92 *ibid*, pp. 57–99, pp. 155–227, p. 329.

93 Cullather, *PBSUCCESS*, pp. 26–30, quote on p. 29.

94 Richard H. Immerman, "Guatemala as Cold War History", *Political Science Quarterly* 95 (1979): 629–653, at 641; Gleijeses, *Shattered Hope*, pp. 289–292.

95 Gleijeses, *Shattered Hope*, pp. 252–254, quote on p. 253.

96 Cullather, *PBSUCCESS*, p. 29, pp. 61–62, quote on p. 29.

97 *ibid*, pp. 26–27, quote on p. 26.

98 Immerman, "Guatemala as Cold War History", 641.

99 Cullather, *PBSUCCESS*, p. 29; Bissell, *Reflections of a Cold Warrior*, p. 78, pp. 83–85; Phillips, *Night Watch*, pp. 34–38; Grose, *Gentleman Spy*, pp. 374–377.

100 Grose, *Gentleman Spy*, p. 377; quote from Bissell, *Reflections of a Cold Warrior*, p. 83.

101 Eisenhower to Bedell Smith, Phone Calls, 27 Apr. 1954, Phone Calls Jan-May 1954, folder 1, box 5, DDE Diary Series, AWF, DDEL.

102 Haines, *CIA and Guatemala Assassination Proposals*.

103 *ibid*, pp. 1–5, pp. 7–8.

104 quotes on *ibid*, p. 5; Cullather, *PBSUCCESS*, p. 48.

105 Cullather, *PBSUCCESS*, p. 48, p. 50, p. 64; Haines, *Guatemala Assassinaiton Proposals*, pp. 4–9; Grose, *Gentleman Spy*, pp. 376; Thomas, *The Very Best Men*, p. 115.

106 Cullather, *PBSUCCESS*, pp. 50–52, p. 65; Gleijeses, *Shattered Hope*, pp. 248–249.

107 Immerman, "Guatemala as Cold War History", 642; Cullather, *PBSUCCESS*, p. 35.

108 Cullather, *PBSUCCESS*, pp. 50–51, quote on p. 27; Thomas, *The Very Best Men*, p. 115–116.

109 Overview of Operation SHERWOOD (1of 3), box 2, Studies and Other Records of the Central Intelligence Agency in Guatemala, 1952–54, Records of the Central Intelligence Agency, RG 263, NA; Phillips, *Night Watch*, pp. 38–48.

110 Cullather, *PBSUCCESS*, p. 40

111 *ibid*, pp. 57–59; Report No. CS-38807, Subject "Arrival of Arms in Puerto Barrios, Guatemala", 15–18 May 1954, www.foia.cia.gov.

112 Cullather, *PBSUCCESS*, pp. 64–67; Phillips, *Night Watch*, p. 48.

113 Cullather, *PBSUCCESS*, p. 69; Thomas, *The Very Best Men*, p. 119.

114 Bissell, *Reflections of a Cold Warrior*, pp. 87–88.

115 Schlesinger and Kinzer, *Bitter Fruit*, p. 170.

116 Eisenhower, *Mandate for Change*, p. 424.

117 Thomas, *The Very Best Men*, p. 121; Phillips, *Night Watch*, p. 46.

118 Cullather, *PBSUCCESS*, pp. 76–77; quote in Bissell, *Reflections of a Cold Warrior*, p. 89.

119 For the CIA's own detailed breakdown of events for the crucial period of 18–30 June, see "Report on Project PBSUCCESS", Stage 5 – Showdown, pp. 1–29, 16 Nov. 1954, www.foia.cia.gov; Cullather, *PBSUCCESS*, pp. 76–78; Phillips, *Night Watch*, pp. 46–48.

120 "Report on Project PBSUCCESS", Stage 6 – Consolidation, 16 Nov. 1954, www.foia.cia.gov.

121 McMahon, "Eisenhower and Third World Nationalism", 466–467.

122 Godson, *Dirty Tricks or Trump Cards*, p. 126.

123 Joseph Burkholder Smith, *Portrait of a Cold Warrior* (New York, 1976), pp. 197–198, pp. 230–231.

124 Jackson, *Dulles-DCI*, Vol.3, pp. 108–113; Kenneth Conby and James Morrison, *Feet to the Fire: CIA Covert Operations in Indonesia, 1957–1958* (Annapolis, 1999).

125 President's Board of Consultants on Foreign Intelligence Summation 1958, in Arthur Schlesinger Jr., *Robert Kennedy and His Times* (Boston 1978), p. 457.

126 Wilfred T. Neil, *Twentieth Century Indonesia* (New York and London, 1973), pp. 1–38, pp. 323–347.

127 The fullest and most scholarly accounts of American intervention in Indonesia are Conboy and Morrison, *Feet to the Fire*, and Audrey R. and George McT. Kahin, *Subversion as Foreign Policy: The Secret Eisenhower and Dulles Debacle in Indonesia* (New York, 1995). For a concise and up-to-date analysis of Operation HAIK see Weiner, *Legacy of Ashes*, pp. 142–153.

128 Gary R. Hess, *The United States Emergence as a Southeast Asian Power, 1940–1950* (New York, 1987), pp. 166–167, pp. 275–309; Marks, *Power and Peace*, p. 75; Memo. for Mr. James Lay Jr., "Progress Report on Indonesia (NSC 5518)", folder 7, box 16, Policy Papers Subseries, NSC Series, WHO, DDEL.

129 NSC 5506, Future of Economic Assistance to Asia, 24 Jan. 1955, *FRUS 1955–57*, Vol.21: 16–22; Thomas J. McCormick, *America's Half-Century: United States Foreign Policy in the Cold War and After* (Baltimore and London, 1995), pp. 114–118.

130 Conboy and Morrison, *Feet to the Fire*, p. 13; Kahin and Kahin, *Subversion as Foreign Policy*, pp. 36–54; United States Minutes of the ANZUS Council Meeting, Department of State, 4 October 1957, *FRUS 1955–57*, Vol.21: 384–386.

131 *FRUS 1955–57*, Vol.10: 540, 584, 630; Memo. of Discussion Between the President's Citizen Advisors on the Mutual Security Program and the Secretary of State, 25 Oct. 1956, *ibid.* 121; Memo. for the NSC, 6 Sept. 1957, "Special Report on Indonesia", folder 2, box 16, Policy Papers Subseries, NSC Series, WHO, DDEL.

132 Steven I. Levine, "Breakthrough to the East: Soviet Asian Policy in the 1950s", in Warren I. Cohen and Akiri Iriye (ed.), *The Great Powers in East Asia: 1953–1960* (New York, 1990) pp. 304–305.

133 Report of the NSC 1290-d Working Group, 15 February 1955, *FRUS 1955–57*, Vol. 10: 7 (Source: Department of State, S/S-NSC [Miscellaneous] Files: Lot 66 D95, Working Group on NSC 1290-d). No drafting information is given on the top-secret source text to this document. Annex A to this report, containing the status of internal security forces of individual countries is not printed.

134 Dept. of State, OIR Report No. 7527, "The Subversive Threat to Indonesia", 13 June 1957, RG 59, NA; Smith, *Portrait of a Cold Warrior*, p. 220, pp. 211–213.

135 Marks, *Power and Peace*, p. 148; Kahin and Kahin, *Subversion as Foreign Policy*, pp. 54–74, pp. 99–142; Conboy and Morrison, *Feet to the Fire*, pp. 18–30.

136 Prados, *Presidents' Secret Wars*, pp. 134–135; Kahin and Kahin, *Subversion as Foreign Policy*, pp. 54–74, pp. 99–106.

137 Ray Cline, *Secrets, Spies, and Scholars: Blueprint of the Essential CIA* (Washington D.C., 1976), p. 205.

138 PBCFIA Summation, in Schlesinger, *Robert Kennedy*, p. 457. The dominant role that the Secretary of State is said by the PBCFIA to have played is backed up in Bissell's testimony, see Richard M. Bissell, OH 382, p. 15, DDEL. It is also supported by an examination of Foster Dulles's phone conversations relating to Indonesia for the period of January to May 1958, see Phone calls 2 Jan.–2 Mar. 1958 folder, and Phone calls 1 Apr.–29 May 1958 folder, box 8, Telephone Series, Papers of John Foster Dulles, DDEL.

139 333rd Meeting of the NSC, 1 August 1957, *FRUS 1955–57*, Vol.17: 400–402.

140 Ad-hoc Interdepartmental Committee on Indonesia, "Special Report on Indonesia", Office of the Special Assistant for National Security Affairs, NSC Series, folder 1, box 16, Policy Papers Subseries, WHO, DDEL; Weiner, *Legacy of Ashes*, p. 147.

141 356th Meeting of the NSC, 20 Feb. 1958, folder 14, box 9, NSC Series, AWF, DDEL; Telephone call from John Foster Dulles to Allen Dulles, 27 Feb. 1958, Tel. Calls 2 Jan.–2 Mar. 1958 folder, box 8, Telephone Series, Papers of John Foster Dulles, DDEL.

142 Memorandum by DCI Dulles, 31 Jan. 1958, *FRUS 1958–60*, Vol.17: 19–24.

143 Editorial Note, *FRUS 1958–60*, Vol.17: 125; Telegram from the Department of State to the Embassy in Indonesia, 13 May 1958, *ibid:* 163–164 Telegram from the Embassy in Indonesia to the Department of State, 15 May 1958, *ibid:* 174.

144 Weiner, *Legacy of Ashes*, pp. 148.

145 Victor Marchetti and John D. Marks, *The CIA and the Cult of Intelligence* (New York, 1974), p. 40; Robert Amory interview in Hersh, *The Old Boys*, p. 416; 356th Meeting of the NSC, 20 Feb. 1958, folder 14, box 9, NSC Series, AWF, DDEL; Smith, *Portrait of a Cold Warrior*, pp. 229–230.

146 Kahin and Kahin, *Subversion as Foreign Policy*, pp. 159–160.

147 Cline, *Secrets, Spies and Scholars*, pp. 181–183.

148 357th Meeting of the NSC, 6 Mar. 1958, folder 15, box 9, NSC Series, AWF, DDEL.

149 Prados, *Presidents' Secret Wars*, pp. 132–139; Aldrich, *Hidden Hand*, pp. 581–589; Top Secret Memorandum from Brigadier General Edward Lansdale to General Maxwell Taylor on Unconventional Warfare Resources in Southeast Asia, published in *The Pentagon Papers*, reprinted in Marchetti and Marks, *Cult of Intelligence*, pp. 137–138; Jackson, *Dulles-DCI*, Vol.3, pp. 108–111.

150 Jackson, *Dulles-DCI*, Vol.3, pp. 111–112; Prados, *Presidents' Secret Wars*, pp. 139–140. Allegations of an American plot to depose Sukarno were given their first public airing in the Soviet-controlled Indian magazine *Blitz* a mere three days after Eisenhower gave the green light to HAIK, see Weiner, *Legacy of Ashes*, p. 147.

151 Dept. of State, OIR No. 7902, "Rebellion in Indonesia", 18 Dec. 1958, RG 59, NA.

152 *ibid*; Conboy and Morrison, *Feet to the Fire*, pp. 99–107; Kahin and Kahin, *Subversion as Foreign Policy*, pp. 172–174; Weiner, *Legacy of Ashes*, pp. 150–151.

153 Foster Dulles to Cabell, 19 May 1958, Tel. Calls 1 Apr.–29 May 1958 folder, box 8, Telephone Series, JFD Papers, DDEL; Conboy and Morrison, *Feet to the Fire*, pp. 132–154, quote on p. 144. For a good outline of the failings of HAIK and the factors that led Washington to abort the operation see Weiner, *Legacy of Ashes*, pp. 149–153.

154 Marchetti and Marks, *Cult of Intelligence*, p. 29, p. 299.

155 Cline, *Secrets, Spies and Scholars*, p. 132.

156 Gleijeses, *Shattered Hope*, p. 369.

Chapter 7

1 Corson, *Armies of Ignorance*, p. 381.

2 *Church Report*, Bk.1, pp. 115–116.

3 As was pointed out in the introduction, this enterprise became known publicly by its Pentagon code-name Operation ZAPATA, but its agency cryptograph was JMARC, which is the code-name used for this study.

4 Prados, *Presidents' Secret Wars*, pp. 209–211.

5 Bissell, *Reflections of a Cold Warrior*, p. 200.

6 Quote from Godson, *Dirty Tricks or Trump Cards*, p. 47.

7 Irving Bernstein, *Promises Kept: John F. Kennedy's New Frontier* (New York and Oxford, 1991), pp. 22–23.

8 Herbert S. Parmet, *JFK: The Presidency of John F. Kennedy* (New York, 1983), p. 60; Thomas C. Reeves, *A Question of Character: A Life of John F. Kennedy* (New York and Toronto, 1991), pp. 189–201; Arthur M. Schlesinger Jr., *A Thousand Days: John F. Kennedy in the White House* (London, 1965), pp. 61–62.

9 Henry Fairlie, *The Kennedy Promise: The Politics of Expectation* (New York, 1973), p. 76; David Burner, *John F. Kennedy and the New Generation* (Washington D.C., 1988), p. 25; Reeves, *Question of Character*, pp. 101–102, pp. 120–121; Schlesinger, *A Thousand Days*, pp. 291–293, pp. 482–483.

10 Dean Rusk, *As I Saw It: A Secretary of State's Memoirs* (London and New York 1991), pp. 342–343.

11   Gaddis, *We Now Know*, p. 184; W.W. Rostow, *The Stages of Economic Growth: A Non-Communist Manifesto* (first published, Cambridge, 1960, third edition, 1990), p. 142, pp. 164–167.

12   Gaddis, *Strategies of Containment*, p. 203.

13   N.S. Khrushchev, "For New Victories of the World Communist Movement", *Kommunist*, Volume 1 (January, 1961): 3–37, in Stephen T. Hosmer and Thomas W. Wolfe (eds.), *Soviet Policy and Practice toward Third World Conflicts* (Toronto, 1983), p. 15.

14   *Public Papers of Presidents of the United States: John F. Kennedy, Containing the Public Messages, Speeches and Statements of the President*, 1961: 19–28 (Washington D.C., 1962–1964) – hereafter cited as *Kennedy Public Papers*.

15   Gaddis, *Strategies of Containment*, pp. 201–205.

16   Robert McNamara, "The Military Role of Nuclear Weapons: Perceptions and Mispercetions", *Foreign Affairs*, 62 (Fall 1983): 59–80, at 63.

17   Gaddis, *Strategies of Containment*, pp. 214–215; Schlesinger, *A Thousand Days*, p. 310.

18   JFK Message to Congress, 28 Mar. 1961, *Kennedy Public Papers*, 1961, 232; Maxwell Taylor, *The Uncertain Trumpet* (New York, 1959); Gaddis, *Strategies of Containment*, pp. 214–215, pp. 226–227; Selected testimony of Robert S. McNamara, "The Secretary of Defense", in *The National Security Council: Jackson Subcommittee Papers on Policy Making at the Presidential Level* – edited by Senator Henry M. Jackson (New York, 1965), pp. 230–231.

19   Martin E. Goldstein, *Arms Control and Military Preparedness from Truman to Bush* (New York, 1993), p. 77; Alain C. Enthoven and K. Wayne Smith. *How Much Is Enough: Shaping the Defense Program, 1961–1969* (New York, 1971), p. 214; Gaddis, *Strategies of Containment*, p. 218–222.

20   JFK State of the Union Address, 14 Jan. 1963, *Kennedy Public Papers*, 1963, 18.

21   Gaddis, *Strategies of Containment*, p. 217, pp. 223–225; Schlesinger, *A Thousand Days*, pp. 497–498; Richard Reeves, *President Kennedy: Profile of Power* (New York, 1993), p. 69.

22   Rabe, *Eisenhower and Latin America*, pp. 149–150; Rusk, *As I Saw It*, pp. 347–348.

23   William J. Lederer and Eugene Burdick, *The Ugly American: A Novel: with a factual epilogue* (London, 1959).

24   Rostow to Sorensen, 16 Mar. 1961, folder 6, box 324, NSF/Meetings and Memos., JFKL.

25   Theodore Sorensen, *The Kennedy Legacy* (London, 1969), p. 186; Reeves, *President Kennedy*, p. 69.

26   Smith, *Cold Warrior*, pp. 53–54.

27   Sergei Khrushchev, *Khrushchev on Khrushchev: An Inside Account of the Man and His Era* – edited and translated by William Taubman (Boston, Toronto, and London, 1990), pp. 26–31; Burner, *A New Generation*, p. 75.

28   Schlesinger, *A Thousand Days*, p. 275.

29   *ibid*, p. 249.

30   Mark J. White, *The Cuban Missile Crisis* (Basingstoke and London, 1996), pp. 30–31.

31   Michael R. Beschloss, *Kennedy v Khrushchev: The Crisis Years, 1960–1963* (London, 1991).

32   Andrew, *For the President's Eyes Only*, p. 268.

33 Laurence Chang and Peter Kornbluh (eds.), *The Cuban Missile Crisis, 1962: A National Security Archive Documents Reader* (Washington D.C., 1992); Ernest R. May and Philip D. Zelikow, *The Kennedy Tapes: Inside the White House During the Cuban Missile Crisis* (Cambridge, Mass, and London, 1997); Mary C. McAuliffe (ed.), *CIA Documents on the Cuban Missile Crisis, 1962* (Washington D.C., 1992).

34 Harry Howe Ransom, "Secret Intelligence in the United States, 1947–1982: The CIA's Search for Legitimacy", in Christopher Andrew and David Dilks, (eds.), *The Missing Dimension: Governments and Intelligence Communities in the Twentieth Century* (Urbana, Illinois, 1991), p. 210.

35 Schlesinger, *A Thousand Days*, p. 113.

36 Ranelagh, *The Agency*, pp. 350–352, quote on p. 351.

37 Sorensen, *Kennedy Legacy*, pp. 247–248; Corson, *Armies of Ignorance*, pp. 381–382; Powers, *Man Who Kept the Secrets*, p. 134; *Church Report*, Bk.1, p. 117.

38 Corson, *Armies of Ignorance*, p. 382.

39 Nigel Hamilton, *JFK: Restless Youth* (London, 1992), pp. 407–409; Andrew, *For the President's Eyes Only*, p. 257.

40 Karalekas, *History of the CIA*, pp. 67–71.

41 Powers, *Man Who Kept the Secrets*, p. 134.

42 Jeffreys-Jones, *CIA and American Democracy*, p. 127.

43 Karalekas, *History of the CIA*, p. 67.

44 *ibid.*

45 Memo. for Ralph A. Duncan, the White House, from L. D. Battle, Executive Secretariat, Department of State, 9 Mar. 1961, "Analytical Chronology of the Congo Crisis", pp. 1–9, NSF/Countries, box 27, JFKL.

46 *ibid*, pp. 9–21; Discussion at the 456th Meeting of the NSC (18 Aug. 1960), 25 Aug. 1960, folder 9, box 13, Policy Paper Subseries, NSC Series, AWF, DDEL.

47 "Analytical Chronology of the Congo Crisis", pp. 22–29.

48 Church Committee, *Alleged Assassination Plots*, pp. 13–16, quote p. 15.

49 The CIA's 'Congo Cables' covering the crucial period from 26 August to 7 October 1960 are available at the agency's Freedom of Information Electronic Reading Room, www.foia.cia.gov.

50 Church Committee, *Alleged Assassination Plots*, pp. 19–22. All of the key operatives involved in the Congo affair are referred to by their pseudonyms in the Church Committee inquiry but their true identities are unmasked in Ranelagh, *The Agency*, pp. 339–344; Grose, *Gentleman Spy*, pp. 501–504; Prados, *Presidents' Secret Wars*, pp. 233–235. Thus, real names rather than aliases are used in this treatment.

51 Church Committee, *Alleged Assassination Plots*, p. 19–24. In November 1962, the CIA's Inspector General, Lyman Kirkpatrick was informed by an unnamed operative – presumably Lawrence Devlin or Justin O'Donnell – that Richard Bissell had instructed him to assume responsibility for the assassination of Lumumba. Poisoning was the preferred method and the operative was told to consult with Sidney Gottlieb to procure the most appropriate means, see *CIA Family Jewels: Full Report*, p. 464 – declassified in

June 2007, and available at www.gwu.edu/~nsarchiv/NSAEBB/NSAEBB222/family_jewels_full.

52 "Analytical Chronology of Congo Crisis", pp. 29–44.

53 Prados, *Presidents' Secret Wars*, p. 235; Church Committee, *Alleged Assassination Plots*, p. 59.

54 The Congo's wealth in raw materials is cited by Richard Bissell as a key reason for action being taken against Lumumba. The country provided 75% of America's cobalt as well as significant supplies of tantalum, bauxite, iron, manganese, zinc, and gold. See Bissell, *Reflections of a Cold Warrior* p. 142.

55 Discussion at the 456th Meeting of the NSC (18 Aug. 1960), 25 Aug. 1960, folder 9, box 13, Policy Paper Subseries, NSC Series, AWF, DDEL; "Analytical Chronology of the Congo Crisis", pp. 50–60.

56 "Analytical Chronology of the Congo Crisis", pp. 50–60.

57 Church Committee, *Alleged Assassination Plots*, pp. 38–39.

58 *ibid*, p. 31.

59 Ambrose argues that a kidnapping took place, see *Eisenhower: The President 1952–1969* (London and Sydney, 1984), p. 588; Ranelagh maintains, rather ambiguously that Lumumba "broke away from UN custody", see *The Agency*, p. 344; Grose sits on the fence stating that "the exact circumstances surrounding [Lumumba's] death have never been clarified", in *Gentleman Spy*, p. 504.

60 "Analytical Chronology of the Congo Crisis", pp. 60–73.

61 Helgerson, *Getting to Know the President*, pp. 52–53.

62 Ranelagh, *The Agency*, p. 244; Burner, *New Generation*, p. 83; Richard D. Mahoney, *JFK: Ordeal in Africa* (New York, 1983) pp. 37–38, pp. 246–247; Zaki Laïdi, *The Superpowers and Africa: The Constraints of a Rivalry, 1960–1990*, translated by Patricia Baudoin, (Chicago and London, 1990) pp. 13–16.

63 *Operation Zapata: The "Ultrasensitive" Report and Testimony of the Board of Enquiry on the Bay of Pigs* – with an introduction by Luis Aguilar (Frederick, Md., 1981); Marchetti and Marks, *CIA and the Cult of Intelligence*, p. 30.

64 Rositzke, "America's Secret Operations", 344; Jeffreys-Jones, *CIA and American Democracy*, pp. 129–130.

65 Corson, *Armies of Ignorance*, p. 386; *Church Report*, Bk.1, p. 114; Schlesinger, *Robert Kennedy*, p. 477; Karalekas, *History of the CIA*, pp. 67–71.

66 *Church Report*, Bk.1, pp. 119–120; Karalekas, *History of the CIA*, pp. 67–71.

67 Powers, "The Truth About the CIA", 49.

68 Memo. from Rostow to Bundy, 30 Jan. 1961, *FRUS 1961–63* Vol.1:19.

69 Duiker, *US Containment in Indochina*, pp. 249–308; Colby and Forbath, *Honourable Men*, pp. 172–179.

70 Corson, *Armies of Ignorance*, p. 399.

71 Ranelagh, *The Agency*, p. 415.

72 Rosizke, "America's Secret Operations", 347.

73 Andrew, *For the President's Eyes Only*, p. 266.

74 Russell Jack Smith, *The Unknown CIA: My Three Decades with the Agency* (New York, 1989), p. 145.
75 Edwin O. Guthman and Jeffrey Shulman, *Robert Kennedy In His Own Words: The Unpublished Recollections of the Kennedy Years* (London, 1988), p. 253.
76 Jeffreys-Jones, *CIA and American Democracy*, p. 133; John McCone, OH, pp. 1–8, JFKL.
77 Guthman and Shulman, *RFK In His Own Words*, p. 254; *Church Report*, Bk.1, p. 116.
78 Jeffreys-Jones, *CIA and American Democracy*, p. 133; Karalekas, *History of the CIA*, pp. 65–66.
79 Karalekas, *History of the CIA*, p. 73.
80 McCone, OH, pp. 10–13, JFKL; Karalekas, *History of the CIA*, p. 72, p. 76; Patrick Mescall, "The Birth of the Defense Intelligence Agency", in Jeffreys-Jones and Lownie, *North American Spies* (Edinburgh, 1991), pp. 158–201.
81 Marchetti and Marks, *CIA and the Cult of Intelligence*, p. 30.
82 *Church Report*, Bk.1, pp. 118–119.
83 Karalekas, *History of the CIA*, p. 66, p. 74.
84 Ray Cline, *The CIA Under Reagan, Bush, and Casey: The Evolution of the Agency from Roosevelt to Reagan* (Washington D.C., 1981), p. 216.
85 *ibid*, pp. 217–218; Smith, *The Unknown CIA*, p. 140, quote on p. 149.
86 Marchetti and Marks, *CIA and the Cult of Intelligence*, p 311; Corson, *Armies of Ignorance*, p. 398.
87 Jeffreys-Jones, *CIA and American Democracy*, p. 119.
88 McCone, OH, pp. 11–14, JFKL; quote from Smith, *The Unknown CIA*, p. 161.
89 Marchetti and Marks, *CIA and the Cult of Intelligence*, p. 312.
90 Jeffreys-Jones, *CIA and American Democracy*, p. 137.
91 Oleg Kalugin, *Spymaster: My 32 Years in Intelligence and Espionage Against the West* (London, 1994), p. 57.
92 Marchetti and Marks, *CIA and the Cult of Intelligence*, p. 311.
93 Reeves, *President Kennedy*, pp. 338–339; McCone, OH, pp. 10–11, JFKL; Marchetti and Marks, *CIA and the Cult of Intelligence*, pp. 308–311.
94 Greville Wynne, *The Man From Odessa* (London, 1981), pp. 201–208.
95 Powers, *Man Who Kept the Secrets*, p. 162.
96 Schlesinger, *Robert Kennedy*, pp. 459–466.

Chapter 8

1 Bissell, *Reflections of a Cold Warrior*, p. 161; plans for an invasion of Cuba were drawn up prior to the discovery of missile sites in Cuba and were modified during the CMC, see Reeves, *President Kennedy*, pp. 366–367; Chang and Kornbluh (eds.), *CMC Documents*, pp. 5–6, pp. 61–62.
2 Beschloss, *Kennedy v. Khrushchev*.
3 There are several excellent treatments on the Bay of Pigs, including Piero Gleijeses, "Ships in the Night: The CIA, the White House and the Bay of Pigs", *Journal of Latin American Studies* 27(1995): 1–42, Peter Wyden, *Bay of Pigs: The Untold Story* (New York, 1979), and Trumbull Higgins, *The Perfect Failure: Kennedy, Eisenhower, and the CIA at the Bay*

of Pigs (New York and London, 1987). The most significant source for the study of JMARC, however, is Kornbluh (ed.), *Bay of Pigs Declassified*, which includes the Inspector General's Survey of the Cuban Operation, Oct. 1961 (hereafter cited as IG Report), pp. 23–99 and "An Analysis of the Cuban Operation by the Deputy Director (Plans), CIA", 18 Jan. 1962 (hereafter cited as Bissell Rebuttal), pp. 133–224.

4   Rusk, *As I Saw It*, pp. 347–348; Rabe, *Eisenhower and Latin America*, p. 149.

5   Louis A. Peréz, Jr., *Cuba: Between Reform and Revolution* (New York, 1988), pp. 290–292, pp. 308–312; Thomas G. Paterson, *Contesting Castro: The United States and the Triumph of the Cuban Revolution* (New York and Oxford, 1994), pp. 18–30.

6   Fidel Castro to the Junta de Liberaración in Miami, from the Sierra Maestra, 14 December 1957, in Mario Llerena, *The Unsuspected Revolution: The Birth and Rise of Castroism* (London, 1978), pp. 257–270; Jorge I Domínguez, *Cuba: Order and Revolution* (Cambridge, Mass., 1978), p. 145; interview with Fidel Castro for documentary entitled *Cuba Libre*, Sky History Channel, 21 November 1998.

7   Nicola Miller, *Soviet Relations with Latin America, 1959–1987* (Cambridge, 1989), pp. 5–6, p. 10.

8   Rabe, *Eisenhower and Latin America*, p. 126; Philip W. Bonsal, *Cuba, Castro, and the United States* (Pittsburgh, 1971), pp. 39–40; Nixon, *Six Crises* (London, 1962), p. 352.

9   Rabe, *Eisenhower and Latin America*, pp. 125–129.

10   Wayne S. Smith, *The Closest of Enemies: A Personal and Diplomatic History of the Castro Years* (New York, 1987), pp. 45–50; Kornbluh (ed.), *Bay of Pigs Declassified*, pp. 6–7.

11   Paterson, *Contesting Castro*, pp. 241–255; Perez, *Cuba*, pp. 332–336; Rabe, *Eisenhower and Latin America*, pp. 124–125.

12   Smith, *The Closest of Enemies*, pp. 45–50.

13   Miller, *Soviet Relations with Latin America*, pp. 79–84.

14   Discussion at the 432nd Meeting of the National Security Council, 14 Jan. 1960, *FRUS 1958–60*, Vol. 6: 742–743; Bissell, *Reflections of a Cold Warrior*, pp. 152–153; Ambrose, *Ike's Spies*, p. 308.

15   "Chief of WH/4 Branch in CIA", p. 1, box 61A, NSF/Countries, JFKL.

16   Andrew J. Goodpaster, Memo. of Conference with the President, 18 Mar. 1960, Intelligence Matters, folder 14, box 15, Alphabetical Subseries, Subject Series, WHO, DDEL; CIA Policy Paper, "A Program of Covert Action Against the Castro Regime", 16 Mar. 1960, folder 3, box 4, International Series, WHO, DDEL. This paper is also available at Annex 1, box 61A, NSF, JFKL, but the document at the Eisenhower Library has fewer deletions. Bissell, *Reflections of a Cold Warrior*, pp. 152–153.

17   *FRUS 1958–60*, Vol.6: 740–746; IG Report, Kornbluh (ed.), *Bay of Pigs Declassified*, pp. 24–31.

18   Higgins, *The Perfect Failure*, p. 153.

19   Memo. for the President, "Possible Action to Prevent Castroist Takeover of the Dominican Republic", with enclosure, "Proposed Plan of 14 Jan. 1960", 14 Apr. 1960, Intelligence Matters folder, box 15, Administrative Subseries, Subject Series, WHO, DDEL.

20 *ibid.*

21 Church Committee, *Alleged Assassination Plots*, pp. 192–193; Memo. of Conference with the President, 13 May 1960, folder 6, box 4, State Department Subseries, Subject Series, WHO, DDEL.

22 Church Committee, *Alleged Assassination Plots*, p. 215; quote from Scott D. Breckenbridge, *CIA and the Cold War: A Memoir* (Westport, Connecticut and London, 1993), p. 117.

23 Schlesinger, *Robert Kennedy*, p. 491.

24 Breckenbridge, *CIA and the Cold War* p. 117.

25 Bundy, "Memo. for the President", 8 Feb. 1961, folder 5, box 115, President's Office Files (hereafter cited as POF), JFKL.

26 Godson, *Dirty Tricks or Trump Cards*, p. 159.

27 Church Committee, *Alleged Assassination Plots*, p. 93.

28 Kornbluh (ed.), *Bay of Pigs Declassified*, pp. 9–10.

29 Church Committee, *Alleged Assassination Plots*, p. 133; Schlesinger, *Robert Kennedy*, p. 481; Andrew, *For the President's Eyes Only*, p. 252.

30 Smith, *OSS*, p. 86; Jeffreys-Jones, *CIA and American Democracy*, p. 51.

31 Bissell, *Reflections of a Cold Warrior*, p. 157.

32 Church Committee, *Alleged Assassination Plots*, pp. 74–77, pp. 93–97.

33 *ibid*, pp. 93–95.

34 Ranelagh, *The Agency*, p. 358.

35 Church Committee, *Alleged Assassination Plots*, pp. 181–187.

36 Taylor Board, *Operation Zapata*, p. 4

37 Robert Amory Jr, OH, p. 122, JFKL.

38 Phillips, *Night Watch*, pp. 85–91; "Brief History of Radio Swan", Annex 2, box 61A, NSF, JFKL.

39 Goodpaster, Memo. of Conference with the President, "A Program of Covert Action Against the Castro Regime", 17 Mar. 1960, folder 14, box 15, Alphabetical Subseries, Subject Series, WHO, DDEL.

40 Chief of WH/4 Branch, CIA, pp. 2–5, box 61A, NSF, JFKL; Bissell, *Reflections of a Cold Warrior*, p. 155; IG Report, Kornbluh (ed.), *Bay of Pigs Declassified*, pp. 28–29.

41 Phillips, *Night Watch*, pp. 91–92; Ranelagh, *The Agency*, p. 362; Prados, *Presidents' Secret Wars*, p. 180.

42 Bissell, *Reflections of a Cold Warrior*, p. 156.

43 *ibid*, p. 154; Ranelagh, *The Agency*, pp. 358–359; First Meeting of General Maxwell Taylor's Board of Inquiry on Cuban Operations Conducted by the CIA", 23 Apr. 1961, box 61A, NSF, JFKL.

44 Bissell, *Reflections of a Cold Warrior*, pp. 154–155; Gleijeses, "Ships in the Night", 11.

45 Prados, *Presidents' Secret Wars*, pp. 182–183; Memo. of Meeting with the President (29 Nov. 1960), 5 Dec. 1960, box 5, Presidential Subseries, Special Assistant Series, WHO, DDEL; Chief of WH/4, pp. 6–7, box 61A, NSF, JFKL.

46 Gleijeses, "Ships in the Night", 12–13; Prados, *Presidents' Secret Wars*, pp. 188–189; Bissell, *Reflections of a Cold Warrior*, p. 158.

47 Wyden, *Bay of Pigs*, pp. 65–92.
48 Interview with Jacob Esterline and Jack Hawkins in Kornbluh (ed.), *Bay of Pigs Declassified*, p. 259.
49 Taylor Board, *Operation Zapata*, p. 110.
50 Helgerson, *Getting to Know the President*, pp. 58–60; Andrew, *For the President's Eyes Only*, p. 260.
51 White, *Cuban Missile Crisis*, pp. 32–34.
52 Mann to Secretary of State, "List of Conclusions", 15 Feb. 1961, enclosed in Bundy, Memo to President, 18 Feb. 1961, NSF/Meetings and Memos., box 35, JFKL.
53 Parmet, *JFK*, pp. 45–49, pp. 157–163.
54 Schlesinger, *A Thousand Days*, p. 242; Taylor Board, *Operation Zapata*, p. 110, p. 147.
55 Memo for Chief, WH/4, 4 Jan. 1961, pp. 1–2, Annex 14, box 61A, NSF, JFKL.
56 Memo. of Discussion on Cuba, 8 Feb. 1961, folder 7, box 35, NSF, JFKL.
57 Bissell Rebuttal, Kornbluh (ed.), *Bay of Pigs Declassified*, p. 157; Taylor Board, *Operation Zapata*, pp. 8–13.
58 Prados, *Presidents' Secret Wars*, p. 191; Bissell, *Reflections of a Cold Warrior*, pp. 161–162.
59 Wyden, *Bay of Pigs*, pp. 101–102; Higgins, *Perfect Failure*, pp. 95–96.
60 Taylor Board, *Operation Zapata*, pp. 13–16.
61 Evaluation of Military Aspects of Alternate Concepts, CIA Para-Military Plan, Cuba, 15 Mar. 1961, Annex 12, box 61A, NSF, JFKL; Prados, *Presidents' Secret Wars*, p. 199; quote in Bissell, *Reflections of a Cold Warrior*, p. 170.
62 Rabe, *Eisenhower and Latin America*, p. 131.
63 Esterline interview in Piero Gleijeses, "Ships in the Night", 41; Bissell, *Reflections of a Cold Warrior*, pp. 88–90; Kornbluh, *Bay of Pigs Declassified*, p. 17.
64 Bissell, *Reflections of a Cold Warrior*, pp. 194–195; Gleijeses, "Ships in the Night", 30–32.
65 Lucien S. Vandenbroucke, "The Confessions of Allen Dulles", *Diplomatic History* 8(Fall 1984): 365–375.
66 IG Report, Kornbluh (ed.), *Bay of Pigs Declassified*, pp. 63–66, quote on p. 66.
67 Paramilitary Study Group Meeting, "Cuban Internal Situation", 18 May 1961, Annex 20(b), box 61A, NSF, JFKL.
68 Taylor Board, *Operation Zapata*, p. 59, pp. 41–42; Gleijeses, "Ships in the Night", 23.
69 Bissell, *Reflections of a Cold Warrior*, p. 161; *FRUS 1958–60*, Vol.6: 1002; *JFK Public Papers*: 258–260; Higgins, *Perfect Failure*, pp. 58–153.
70 Prados, *Presidents' Secret Wars*, pp. 184–185, p. 204.
71 Vandenbroucke, "The 'Confessions' of Allen Dulles", 370–373.
72 Bissell, *Reflections of a Cold Warrior*, p. 188; "Military Evaluation of the CIA Para-Military Plan, Cuba", enclosed in Lemnitzer to Secretary of Defense, 3 Feb. 1961, p. 2, Annex 9, box 61A, NSF, JFKL.
73 Gleijeses, "Ships in the Night", 38–40;
74 *ibid*; Grose, *Gentleman Spy*, pp. 5181–526; IG Report, Annex D, Revised Cuban Operation, 15 Mar. 1961, Kornbluh (ed.), *Bay of Pigs Declassified*, p. 126–127.

75 "Military Evaluation of the CIA Para-Military Plan, Cuba", enclosed in Lemnitzer to Secretary of Defense, 3 Feb. 1961, Annex 9, box 61A, NSF, JFKL.

76 *ibid*

77 Bissell, *Reflections of a Cold Warrior*, pp. 166–167.

78 *ibid*, p. 198.

79 Lyman Lemnitzer to Robert McNamara, Memo. for the Secretary of Defense, 11 March 1961, Annex 10, box 61A, NSF, JFKL.

80 *ibid*; Taylor Board, *Operation Zapata*, pp. 10–12.

81 Grose, *Gentleman Spy*, p. 523; Vandenbroucke, "The 'Confessions' of Allen Dulles", 371.

82 Telegram from Chief of Naval Operations (Burke) to the Commander in Chief, Pacific (Stump), 7 December 1957, *FRUS 1955–57*, Vol. 22: 533.

83 Schlesinger, *A Thousand Days*, pp. 251–256; Reeves, *Question of Character*, pp. 265–266.

84 Randall Bennett Woods, *Fulbright: A Biography* (Cambridge, 1995), pp. 267–268.

85 Paul Nitze, *From Hiroshima to Glasnost: At the Centre of Decision* (New York, 1989), pp. 183–185.

86 The officials present at the 4 April meeting were: Rusk, McNamara, and Dillon, Fulbright, Nitze, Schlesinger, and William Bundy, Assistant Secretary of State for Inter-American Affairs, Thomas Mann – Mann was actually appointed U.S. Ambassador to Mexico between 4 April and the start of Operation JMARC – and the chairman of the Kennedy Task Force on Latin America, Adolf Berle; Dulles and Bissell represented the CIA, and Lemnitzer and General Thomas D. White represented the JCS.

87 Ranelagh, *The Agency*, p. 367; Schlesinger, *A Thousand Days*, p. 362.

88 Neustadt, Richard E. and Ernest R. May, *Thinking in Time: The Uses of History for Decision Makers* (London, 1988), pp. 140–141; Woods, *Fulbright*, pp. 266–268.

89 Prados, *Presidents' Secret Wars*, p. 200; Ranelagh, *The Agency*, pp. 367–368; Bissell, *Reflections of a Cold Warrior*, p. 171.

90 Taylor Board, *Operation Zapata*, pp. 127–130; Prados, *Presidents' Secret Wars*, p. 202; Rusk, *As I Saw It*, pp. 210–212.

91 Wyden, *Bay of Pigs*, p. 200; Rusk, *As I Saw It*, pp. 211–212.

92 Reeves, *President Kennedy*, p. 95, pp. 99–103.

93 Khrushchev quote in White, *Cuban Missile Crisis*, pp. 37–38.

94 Bissell, *Reflections of a Cold Warrior*, p. 196.

95 Allen W. Dulles, OH, pp. 29–30, JFKL; Taylor Board, *Operation Zapata*, pp. 18–21.

96 Grose, *Gentleman Spy*, p. 520.

97 Taylor Board, *Operation Zapata*, pp. 21–25; Wyden, *Bay of Pigs*, pp. 210–289.

98 Wyden, *Bay of Pigs*, pp. 210–289; Taylor Board, *Operation Zapata*, pp. 25–35.

99 Kornbluh (ed.), *Bay of Pigs Declassified*, pp. 23–102, pp. 133–225.

100 Interview with Esterline and Hawkins *ibid*, pp. 262–264.

101 Gleijeses, "Ships in the Night", 1.

102 Taylor Board, *Operation Zapata*. IG Report, Kornbluh (ed.), *Bay of Pigs Declassified*, pp. 23–102; Bissell Rebuttal, *ibid*, pp. 133–225.

103 IG Report, Kornblu (ed.), *Bay of Pigs Declassified*, pp. 23–102; for an earlier, abridged version of Kirkpatrick's findings see Lyman B. Kirkpatrick, "Paramilitary Case Study – The Bay of Pigs", *Naval War College Review* (Nov-Dec 1972): 32–42.

104 Kornblu (ed.), *Bay of Pigs Declassified*, pp. 133–225; Taylor Board, *Operation Zapata*; Bissell, *Reflections of a Cold Warrior*, pp. 152–190.

105 Taylor Board, *Operation Zapata*; Marchetti and Marks, *CIA and the Cult of Intelligence*, p. 30.

106 National Security Action Memorandum 2422, 5 May 1961, folder 1, box 313, NSF/Meetings and Memos, JFKL.

107 Goodwin, Memorandum for the President, "Conversation with Commandante Ernesto Guevara of Cuba", 22 Aug. 1961, folder 12, box 115, POF, JFKL.

108 Chang and Kornbluh (eds.), *CMC Documents*, pp. 40–41.

109 *ibid*, pp. 23–24; McClintock, *Instruments of Statecraft*, pp. 204–208, quote on p. 205; Mark J. White (ed.), *The Kennedys and Cuba: The Declassified Documentary History* (Chicago, 1999), pp. 71–131.

110 Review of Operation Mongoose by Chief of Operations Lansdale, 18 January 1962, in White, *The Kennedys and Cuba*, pp. 80–95; Lansdale, *In the Midst of Wars*, pp. 371–373.

111 Ted Shackley, with Richard Finney, *Spymaster: My Life in the CIA* (Dulles, Virginia, 2005), pp. 50–57; Prados, *Presidents' Secret Wars*, pp. 210–211; Powers, *Man Who Kept the Secrets*, pp. 134–139; Church Committee, *Alleged Assassination Plots*, p. 141; Bissell, *Reflections of a Cold Warrior*, pp. 201–202.

112 Operations Coordinating Board, Report on Indochina, 12 April 1957, DDRS, CDROM Id.: 1999010100595, Fiche No. 1999–51; Powers, *Man Who Kept the Secrets*, pp. 137–139; Jeffreys-Jones, *CIA and American Democracy*, p. 95.

113 Chang and Kornbluh (eds.), *CMC Documents*, pp. 23–24, quote on p. 24.

114 Bissell, *Reflections of a Cold Warrior*, p. 200; CIA, National Intelligence Estimate "The Situation and Prosects in Cuba", 21 March 1962, in White, *The Kennedys and Cuba*, pp. 116–118.

115 Powers, *Man Who Kept the Secrets*, p. 135, p. 138; Prados, *Presidents' Secret Wars*, pp. 211–212; Helms, *A Look Over My Shoulder*, p. 205.

116 Church Committee, *Alleged Assassination Plots*, pp. 181–184, pp. 314–315.

117 Lyndon Johnson is quoted as having said that Kennedy operated "a damned Murder Inc. in the Caribbean" see Ranelagh, *The Agency*, p. 390. Both Helms and Lansdale say that they were told flatly by John and Robert Kennedy to "get rid of Castro", the assumption being by any means, see Church Committee, *Alleged Assassination Plots*, p. 138.

118 Reeves, *President Kennedy*, pp. 335–337.

119 *ibid*, pp. 366–367; Chang and Kornbluh (eds.), *CMC Documents*, pp. 5–6, pp. 61–62.

120 Chang and Kornbluh (eds.), *CMC Documents*, p. 38; NSAM 181, *ibid*, pp. 61–62.

121 Meeting of the SG(A), 4 Oct. 1962, in McAuliffe (ed.), *CIA -CMC*, pp. 111–113; May and Zelikow (eds.), *Kennedy Tapes*, pp. 442–445.

122 Meeting of the SG(A), 4 Oct. 1962, in McAuliffe (ed.), *CIA -CMC*, pp. 111–113.

123 For details of JFK's renewed effort to depose Castro see Memorandum for the Record
   Drafted by Chairman of the JCS Taylor, 28 February 1963 in White, *The Kennedys and
   Cuba*, p. 308.
124 White, *Cuban Missile Crisis*, p. 31.
125 Thomas, *The Very Best Men*, p. 242.
126 Reeves, *Question of Character*, pp. 277–278.
127 White, *Cuban Missile Crisis*, pp. 29–30.
128 Jeffreys-Jones, *CIA and American Democracy*, p. 132; Unsigned memo., Subject,
   "Arosemera Visit", 23–25 July 1962, folder 8, box 68, NSF/Countries, JFKL; CIA, OCI
   No.2291/63 "Military Junta in Ecuador", 15 July 1963, www.foia.cia.gov.
129 Radosh, *American Labor and US Foreign Policy*, pp. 399–405; Agee, *CIA Diary*, pp. 244–
   245.
130 Serafino Romualdi, *Presidents and Peons: Recollections of a Labor Ambassador in Latin America*
   (New York, 1967).
131 The most comprehensive study of British Guiana both before and after independence is
   Chaitram Singh's *Guyana: Politics in a Plantation Society* (New York, 1988). The best
   account of American efforts to depose Jagan is Stephen G. Rabe, *US Intervention in
   British Guiana: A Cold War Story* (Chapel Hill, 2005). For a shorter version of events see,
   Stephen G. Rabe, *The Most Dangerous Area in the World: John F. Kennedy Confronts
   Communist Revolution in Latin America* (London, 1999), pp. 79–98. In terms of primary
   works, Jagan's own account of events, while partial, is essential reading and effectively
   counterbalances the sizeable volume of sources that depict events from an American
   standpoint, see Cheddi Jagan, *The West on Trial* (New York, 1972).
132 Secretary of State Rusk to Embassy in the United Kingdom, 11 August 1961, *FRUS
   1961–63*, Vol 12: 519–520.
133 Memo. of a Conversation between President Kennedy and Prime Minister Macmillan,
   30 June 1963, *ibid*, 607–609.
134 Memo. of a Conversation between President Kennedy and Prime Minister Jagan, *ibid*,
   536–538.
135 National Security Action Memorandum (NSAM) No. 2413-c, 4 May 1961, folder 5, box
   329, NSF/Meetings and Memos, JFKL; Rabe, *The Most Dangerous Area in the World*, pp.
   82–90.
136 Secretary of State Rusk to Embassy in the United Kingdom, 11 August 1961, *FRUS
   1961–63*, Vol 12: 519–520.
137 Jagan, *West on Trial*, pp. 254–255.
138 Romualdi, *Presidents and Peons*, pp. 346–352; Agee, *Inside the Company*, pp. 393–405;
   Smith, *Portrait of a Cold Warrior*, pp. 357–358.
139 Jagan, *West on Trial*, p. 251.
140 Memorandum of a Conversation between President Kennedy and Prime Minister
   Macmillan, 30 June 1963, *FRUS 1961–63*, Vol 12: 607–609.
141 JCS Report, "Terrorist Activities in Venezuela", 18 Feb. 1963, folder 3b, box 192,
   NSF/Countries, JFKL.

142 Memo. for the Special Group (CI) Assistants, NIS 86, Venezuela, Section 57, Subversion, National Intelligence Surveys, 2 Oct. 1963, www.foia.cia.gov.

143 Schlesinger, *Robert Kennedy*, pp. 538–539.

144 Vladimir Semichastny, Alexandr Alexiev, and Oleg Daroussenko (head of the Cuban Section, Central Committee of the CPSU, 1968–1989), interviewed in the Channel 4 T.V. documentary *Messengers from Moscow*, broadcast 12 Mar. 1995.

145 *ibid.* CIA, NIE No.85–63, "Situation and Prospects in Cuba", 14 June 1963, www.foia.cia.gov.

146 "Intensified Terrorist Activity in Venezuela", 10–16 Feb. 1963 (no agency and unsigned), folder 4a, box 192, NSF/Countries, JFKL.

147 Shakley, *Spymaster*, pp. 69–72; Church Committee, *Alleged Assassination Plots*, pp. 171–172.

148 Church Committee, *Alleged Assassination Plots*, p. 86–88; CIA, Current Intelligence Digest, "Pro-Communist Student Group in Colombia Plans Demonstrations Against OAS Meeting in Bogota", 26 August 1960, www.foia.cia.gov; Jon Lee Anderson, *Che Guevara: A Revolutionary Life* (London, 1997), p. 346, p. 355; Breckenbridge, *CIA and the Cold War*, pp. 114–115.

149 Thomas, *The Very Best Men*, pp. 298–306.

150 Helms interview in Beschloss, *Kennedy v. Khrushchev*, p. 666–667; Roswell L. Gilpatrick, Memo for the President, 27 Feb. 1963, "The Anzoategui Affair", folder 5, box 192, NSF/Countries, JFKL.

151 Cullather, *PBSUCCESS*, p. 40; Beschloss, *Kennedy v. Khrushchev*, p. 667

152 Thomas, *The Very Best Men*, pp. 302–306; Church Committee, *Alleged Assassination Plots*, pp. 89–90.

Conclusion

1 *Church Report*, Bk.1, p. 107.

2 Duiker, *U.S. Containment Policy in Indochina*, pp. 88–247.

3 Colby and Forbath, *Honourable Men*, pp. 141–146.

4 *ibid.*

5 Ranelagh, *The Agency*, pp. 427–430; McClintock, *Instruments of Statecraft*, pp. 126–129.

6 Schlesinger, *A Thousand Days*, pp. 337–339.

7 Department of State to Lodge, 24 August 1963, *FRUS 1961–63*, Vol.3: 628–629; Church Committee, *Alleged Assassination Plots*, pp. 217–223.

8 Colby and Forbath, *Honourable Men*, pp. 215–216; Church Committee, *Alleged Assassination Plots*, pp. 217–223.

9 Church Committee, *Alleged Assassination Plots*, p. 217.

10 NSAM-52, folder 10, box 330, NSF/Meetings and Memos, JFKL.

11 Memo. For Mr. B. Chambers, Director, Working Group, Vietnam, "Transmittal of memorandum Concerning Manpower Utilisation in South Vietnam", 13 February 1963, www.foia.cia.gov; Timothy N. Castle, *At War in the Shadow of Vietnam: U.S. Military Aid to the Royal Lao Government, 1955–1975* (New York, 1998); Prados, *Presidents' Secret Wars*,

pp. 239–260, pp. 261–296; Colby and Forbath, *Honourable Men*, pp. 198–199, pp. 245–288; Jane Hamilton-Merritt, *Tragic Mountains: The Hmong, the Americans and the Secret Wars in Laos, 1942–1992* (Bloomington and Indianapolis, 1993), pp. 130–262; Richard H. Shultz, Jr., *The Secret War Against Hanoi: The Untold Story of Spies, Saboteurs, and Covert Warriors in North Vietnam* (New York, 2000).

12 Shultz, *The Secret War Against Hanoi*.

13 Roger Hilsman OH, JFKL.

14 RFE and Radio Liberty were merged in 1976.

15 Meyer, *Facing Reality*; Mickelson, *America's Other Voice*; see State Department correspondence for the crucial period of the Hungarian uprising, *FRUS 1955–57*, Vol.25: 366–432.

16 Cork, *US Covert Operations and Cold War Strategy*; Godson, *Dirty Tricks or Trump Cards*, p. 46.

17 CIA, Intelligence Memo. 218, "Strengths and Weaknesses of the Hoxha Regime in Albania", 12 Sept. 1949, Intelligence Memos. 1949 folder, box 250, Central Intelligence File, PSF, Truman Papers, HSTL.

18 Godson, *Dirty Tricks or Trump Cards*, p. 36, p. 46.

19 *ibid*, pp. 177–180.

20 Cave Brown, *Treason in the Blood*, pp. 391–438; Wolf, *Man Without a Face*, p. 51.

21 Wisner's doubts about Operation HAIK were raised at an NSC meeting in 1957, and are outlined in Thomas, *The Very Best Men*, p. 158.

22 Grose, *Gentleman Spy*, pp. 328–329; Haines, *Guatemala Assassination Proposals*, pp. 1–12; Church Committee, *Alleged Assassination Plots*; Ranelagh, *The Agency*, p. 336, pp. 344–345. The CIA is also alleged to have planted a bomb on an Air India plane on which Communist China's Foreign Minister Zhou En-lai was scheduled to fly to the Bandung Conference in Indonesia in April 1955. The plan to kill Chou was vetoed by Allen Dulles, but not in time to prevent the bomb from being placed on the plane, which blew up in mid-flight, and it was only because of a last-minute decision by Zhou to change his travelling plans that his life was saved, see *Church Report*, Bk. 4, p. 133.

23 Andrew Tully, *CIA: The Inside Story* (New York, 1962), pp. 73–80, quote on p. 87; Ranelagh, *The Agency*, pp. 344–345.

24 Church Committee, *Alleged Assassination Plots*, p. 95; Thomas, *The Very Best Men*, p. 251.

25 Copeland, *Game Player*, pp. 158–171; Simpson, *Blowback*, pp. 250–252; Hersh, *The Old Boys*, pp. 331–332; Andrew, *For the President's Eyes Only*, p. 226; Lucas (ed.), *Britain and Suez*.

26 Rabe, *The Most Dangerous Area in the World*, pp. 79–98.

27 Little, "Mission Impossible", 666, 686.

28 A CIA report that focused on an impending visit by Mobutu to Washington in 1983 described him as enjoying good relations with the US and seeking, through his visit to America, to enhance his status as a "senior African statesman", see Directorate of Intelligence, "President Mobutu's Visit", 28 July 1983, www.foia.cia.gov. Suharto was, likewise, looked on in a favourable light for many years. He was described in an agency

report dated 9 March 1978 as being "stable domestically and moderate in international affairs", and as contrasting favourably with Sukarno, "whose flamboyant leadership and flirtation with radical communist states led to foreign adventures and economic stagnation", *ibid*.

29 Over 16,000 formerly secret CIA and wider American government records documenting the role played by the United States in removing the Allende regime and supporting Pinochet were made public in 2000 and are available as part of the *Chile Documentation Project* at the National Security Archive, www.gwu.edu/~nsarchiv/latin_america/chile.

30 For an excellent analysis of Reagan's use of intelligence see Andrew, *For the President's Eyes Only*, pp. 457–502.

31 Lawrence E. Walsh, *Iran-Contra: The Final Report* (New York, 1994).

32 CIA, Directorate of Intelligence, "Moscow's Afghan Quagmire: No End in Sight After Eight Years", 20 September 1987, www.foia.cia.gov (this paper was presumably prepared by the Office of Soviet Analysis, though no indication of the originator is provided on the document); Andrew, *For the President's Eyes Only*, pp. 493–494, 499–500.

33 Jeffreys-Jones, *CIA and American Democracy*, p. 208, pp. 214–215.

34 Karalekas, *History of the CIA*, p. 67.

BIBLIOGRAPHY

Unpublished Government Records and Documents

Dwight D. Eisenhower Library, Abilene, Kansas.

Dulles, John Foster, Papers 1951–1959.
Eisenhower, Dwight D., Papers as President of the United States, 1953–1961 (Ann Whitman File).
Eisenhower, Dwight D., Post-Presidential Papers, 1961–1969.
White House Office File.

Oral Histories
Bissell, Richard M.

John F. Kennedy Library, Boston, Massachusetts

National Security Files
President's Office Files

Oral Histories
Amory, Robert
Dulles, Allen W.
Hilsman, Roger
McCone, John A.

National Archives and Records Administration, Washington D.C.

Cullather, Nicholas. *Operation PBSUCCESS: The United States and Guatemala 1952–1954* (Washington, 1994), declassified in 1997 and available for consultation at the Modern Military Branch, NA.
Haines, Gerald K. *CIA and Guatemala Assassination Proposals 1952–1954* (Washington, 1995), declassified in 1997 and available for consultation at the Modern Military Branch, NA.
Jackson, Wayne G. *Allen Welsh Dulles as Director of Central Intelligence*, Volume 3

(Washington, 1973), declassified in 1994 and available for consultation at the Modern Military Branch, NA.

General Records of the Department of State, Record Group 59.

Records of the Central Intelligence Agency, Record Group 263.

Records of the Office of Strategic Services, Record Group 226.

Harry S. Truman Library, Independence, Missouri

Post-Presidential File

Records of the Psychological Strategy Board

Spingarn, Stephen J., Papers

Student Research File

Truman, Harry S., Papers as President of the United States, 1945–1953
    President's Secretary's File
    Records of the NSC

Oral Histories

Campbell, John C.

Clifford, Clark, Vol.1

Elsey, George M. Vol.2

Lombardo, Ivan M.

Electronic Sources and Records

Central Intelligence Agency, Center for the Study of Intelligence, http://www.cia.gov/library/center-for-the-study-of-intelligence

Central Intelligence Agency, Freedom of Information Electronic Reading Room, http://www.foia.cia.gov/

National Security Archive, George Washington University, Digital National Security Archive, http://www.gwu.edu/~nsarchiv/

United States Declassified Documents Reference System, *The Declassified Documents Catalogue.*

Published Government Records

Alleged Assassination Plots Involving Foreign Leaders: An Interim Report of the Select Committee to Study Governmental Operations with respect to Intelligence Activities, [Church Committee]. U.S. Senate 94 Cong., 1 Sess., Report No. 94–465 (Nov. 20, 1975).

Central Intelligence Agency in collaboration with the Harry S. Truman Library. *The Origin and Development of the CIA in the Administration of Harry S. Truman: A Conference Report* (Washington D.C., 1994).

Foreign and Military Intelligence - Book 1. Final Report of the Select Committee to Study Governmental Operations with Respect to Intelligence Activities. United States Senate together with Additional, Supplemental, and Separate Views. *Senate Report,* 94th Congress, 2 session, Report No. 94–755, April 26 (legislative day April 14), 1976 (Washington D.C., 1976).

Joint Hearing before the Select Committee on Human Resources, United States Senate, 95th Congress, First Session, *Project MKUltra: The CIA's Program of Research in Behavioral Modification* (Washington D.C., 3 August 1977).

Operation ZAPATA: The "Ultrasensitive" Report and Testimony of the Board of Inquiry on the Bay of Pigs – with an introduction by Luis Aguilar (Frederick, Maryland, 1981).

Public Papers of Presidents of the United States: Dwight D. Eisenhower, 1953–1961, 8 Volumes (Washington D.C., 1960–1961).

Public Papers of Presidents of the United States: John F. Kennedy, 1961–1963, 3 Volumes (Washington D.C., 1962–1964).

Public Papers of the Presidents of the United States: Harry S. Truman, 1945–1953, 8 Volumes (Washington D.C., 1961–1966).

United States Department of State, *Department of State Bulletin, 1947–1954*, (Washington D. C., 1947–1954).

United States Department of State. *Foreign Relations of the United States 1945–1950: Emergence of the Intelligence Establishment* – edited by Glenn W. Fantasie (Washington D.C., 1996).

United States Department of State, *Foreign Relations of the United States: The Intelligence Community, 1950–1955*, edited by Douglas Keane and Michael Warner, general editor Edward C. Keefer (Washington D.C., 2007)

United States Department of State, *Papers Relating to the Foreign Relations of the United States, 1944–1966* (Washington D.C., 1861–).

United States of America, House of Representatives, Select Committee on Intelligence, *CIA: The Pike Report* – with introduction by Philip Agee (London, 1977).

War Report of the OSS (Office of Strategic Services), prepared by History Project, Strategic Services Unit, Office of the Assistant Secretary of War, War Department – with a new introduction by Kermit Roosevelt (New York, 1976).

Warner, Michael J. (ed.), *CIA Cold War Records: The CIA Under Harry Truman* (Washington D.C., 1994).

Published Documents, Papers and Transcripts

Chang, Laurence, and Peter Kornbluh (eds.), *The Cuban Missile Crisis: A National Security Archive Documents Reader* (New York, 1992).

Darling, Arthur B., *The Central Intelligence Agency: An Instrument of Government to 1950* (University Park and London, 1990).

Etzold, Thomas H., and John Lewis Gaddis, *Containment: Documents on American Policy and Strategy, 1945–1950* (New York, 1978).

Galambos, Louis, and Daun Van Ee (eds.), *The Papers of Dwight David Eisenhower: NATO and the Campaign of 1952*, Volumes XII and XIII (Baltimore and London, 1989).

Galambos, Louis, and Daun Van Ee (eds.), *The Papers of Dwight David Eisenhower: The Presidency: The Middle Way*, Volumes XV and XVI (Baltimore and London, 1996).

Helgerson, John L., *Getting to Know the President: CIA Briefings of Presidential Candidates 1952–1992* (Washington D.C., 1996).

Karalekas, Anne, *History of the Central Intelligence Agency: Supplementary Detailed Staff Reports on Foreign and Military Intelligence, Final Report, Senate Select Committee to Study Governmental Operations with Respect to Intelligence Activities*, 94th Congress, 2nd Session, April 23, 1976, S. Report No. 94–755, 4: 1–107 (Laguna Hills, California, 1977).

Kornbluh, Peter (ed.), *Bay of Pigs Declassified: The Secret CIA Report on the Invasion of Cuba* (New York, 1998).

McAuliffe, Mary S. (ed.), *CIA Documents on the Cuban Missile Crisis, 1962* (Washington D.C., 1992).

May, Ernest R. and Philip D. Zelikow (eds.), *The Kennedy Tapes: Inside the White House During the Cuban Missile Crisis* (Cambridge, Mass, and London, 1997).

Merrill, Dennis (ed.), *Documentary History of the Truman Presidency*, Volumes 17 and 19 (Washington D.C., 1997).

Montague, Ludwell Lee, (with an introduction by Bruce D. Berkowitz and Allan E. Goodman), *General Walter Bedell Smith as a Director of Central Intelligence: October 1950–February 1953* (University Park, Pennsylvania, 1992).

Nelson, Anna K. (ed.), *The State Department Policy Planning Staff Papers, 1947–1949* (New York, 1983).

Ostermann, Christian F. (ed.), *Uprising in East Germany 1953: The Cold War, the German Question and the First Major Upheaval Behind the Iron Curtain* (Washington D.C., 2001).

Wilber, Donald N., *Clandestine Service History: Overthrow of Premier Mossadeq of Iran, November 1952–August 1953*, CS Historical Paper No. 208, written March 1954, published October 1969, leaked to the *New York Times* and published on its website in 2000.

INDEX

D'Aguiar, Peter, 180
De Gasperi, Alcide, 25–33, 36, 40–41, 43,
  45, 50, 186
Defense Department, 15, 16, 22, 46, 104,
  137, 169, 170, 192
Democratic Party, 6, 14, 50, 125, 150
Deputy Directorate for Administration
  (DDA), 68
Deputy Directorate for Intelligence (DDI),
  103, 104
  creation of, 68
  HAIK and, 134
  JMARC and, 162, 167
  PBSUCCESS and, 126
Deputy Directorate for Plans (DDP), 2–6,
  87, 94–95, 108, 187–188, 190, 191
  Albania and, 80–81, 85
  Berlin riots and, 96
  creation of, 68, 69
  Cuban and related Western Hemisphere
    operations of, 158–181
  Eastern European operations and, 61,
    95–99
  economic warfare and, 56
  Far East operations and, 64–66
  Guatemala and, 119–120, 125–129
  Hungarian uprising and, 92, 98–99
  Indonesia and, 129–136
  Iran and, 111–118
  John Kennedy and, 138, 143–145,
    148–154
  Middle East operations and, 101–103
  Tibet and, 100–101
  U-2 spy plane and, 105–107
  Vietnam War and, 184–185
Deputy Directorate for Science and
  Technology (DDS&T), 151
Devlin, Lawrence, 146, 147
Diem, Ngo Dinh, 184, 185, 190
Dien Bien Phu, 5, 120, 121, 183
Dodge Plan, 131
Dominican Republic, 156, 160, 190
Donovan, William J., 16, 17, 20, 22, 39
Dosti, Hasan, 78
Droller, Gerry, 163
Dulles, Allen W., 68, 98, 101, 112, 117, 133,
  146
  Berlin riots and, 96
  CFR and, 39, 52, 94
  Cuba and, 158, 164–168, 172–174
  directorship of CIA and, 5, 93–94, 100,
    107–108, 183, 189

Guatemala and, 122, 125–126, 128, 136
  John Kennedy and, 143, 148, 150, 174
Dulles, John Foster, 5, 94, 97, 110, 112,
  120–121
  Eastern European operations and, 97
  Guatemala and, 124, 126
  Indonesia and, 131, 133–135
  New Look policy and, 89–93
  nonalignment and, 92–93
Dulles–Jackson–Corea report, 66, 148
Dunn, James C., 30, 40, 41

East Berlin, 96, 143
East Germany, 5, 55, 96, 97
Eberstadt Report, 16
Economic Cooperation Administration
  (ECA), 53, 55
Economic Stabilisation Fund, 38
Ecuador, 156, 178, 179, 181
Eden, Anthony, 123
Edwards, Sheffield, 84, 161, 176
Egypt, 6, 52, 87, 102, 103, 112, 189, 191
Einaudi, Luigi, 25
Eisenhower, Dwight D., 4, 8, 87–88,
  107–108, 138, 183
  assassination plots and, 146, 159–160,
    161, 162
  Berlin riots and, 96
  CIA and, 87–88, 94–108, 143–144
  Congo and, 145–147
  Cuba and, 157–159, 162–164
  Dominican Republic and, 159–160
  Eastern Europe operations and, 95–99,
    187–188
  Far East operations and, 88, 100–101
  Guatemala and, 4–5, 110, 118–129, 136,
    189
  Hungarian uprising and, 92, 98–99
  Indochina and, 5, 110, 120–121, 123,
    183–184
  Indonesia and, 129–136, 189
  Iran and, 4–5, 109–110, 112–118, 136,
    189
  Middle East operations and, 101–103,
    189
  New Look and, 4–5, 89–93, 139–140
  nonalignment and, 91–93
  NSA and, 104–105
  U-2 spy plane and, 105–106
Eisenhower Doctrine, 102
EMOTH, Operation, 159
ENGROSS, Operation, 61

Lightning Source UK Ltd.
Milton Keynes UK
UKHW020133150721
387196UK00003B/90